ACCOUNTING, THE SOCIAL AND THE POLITICAL: CLASSICS, CONTEMPORARY AND BEYOND

Related titles

Advances in Accounting – Reckers
Published: Vol. 21 0762312033

Studies in Managerial and Financial Accounting – Epstein/Lee
Published: Vol. 14 Performance Measurement and Management Control

Advances in Accounting Behavioural Research – Arnold
Published: Vol 8. 0762312181

Advances in Public Interest Accounting – Lehman
Published: Vol 11. Corporate Governance 076231205X

Research in Governmental and Non-Profit Accounting – Copley
Published: Vol. 11 0762311231

Advances in Management Accounting – Epstein/Lee
Published: Vol. 12 0762311185
Forthcoming: Vol. 13 0762311398

Research in Professional Responsibility and Ethics in Accounting – Jeffrey
Published: Vol. 9 0762311258
Forthcoming: Vol. 10 0762312394

Advances in Accounting Education, Teaching and Curriculum Innovations – Schwartz
Published: Vol. 6 0762311436

Research in Accounting in Emerging Economies – Wallace (desceased)/Briston/Saugaran/Samuels
Published: Vol. 6 0762310766

The Real Life Guide to Accounting Research *Humphrey and Lee*
Published: 0080439721

Studies in the Development of Accounting Thought
Forthcoming: The Life and Writings of Stuart Chase, CPA (1888-1985) 0762312130 Vol. 8 Vangermeersch
Published: Accounting: How to meet the challenges of Relevance and Regulation 0762310782 Flegm Vol. 7

ACCOUNTING, THE SOCIAL AND THE POLITICAL: CLASSICS, CONTEMPORARY AND BEYOND

EDITED BY

Norman B. Macintosh

School of Business, Queen's University, Kingston, Canada

and

Trevor Hopper

Manchester Business School, University of Manchester, UK

2005

ELSEVIER

Amsterdam – Boston – Heidelberg – London – New York – Oxford
Paris – San Diego – San Francisco – Singapore – Sydney – Tokyo

ELSEVIER B.V.
Radarweg 29
P.O. Box 211, 1000 AE
Amsterdam
The Netherlands

ELSEVIER Inc.
525 B Street, Suite 1900
San Diego
CA 92101-4495
USA

ELSEVIER Ltd
The Boulevard
Langford Lane
Kidlington
Oxford OX5 1GB, UK

ELSEVIER Ltd
84 Theobalds Road
London WC1X 8RR
UK

First edition 2005

British Library Cataloguing in Publication Data
A catalogue record is available from the British Library.

ISBN: 0-08-044725-2

⊗ The paper used in this publication meets the requirements of ANSI/NISO Z39.48-1992 (Permanence of Paper).
Printed in The Netherlands.

Preface

The book is partly the outcome of the *International Forum on the Future of Management Accounting, Control and Information System Research* held at Queen's University, Canada, May 2002. Each of the dozen or so participants, all eminent scholars with worldwide reputations in their own right, were asked to select one or two articles they had published [alone or with co-authors] that they ranked as their personal favorites. In addition, in order to flesh out the selection of readings, they also suggested articles of other authors, which they believed have special significance for the field and have made significant contributions in the recent decades to accounting thought. Anonymous reviewers of a preliminary draft also made suggestions which have been taken into consideration in making the final selection of articles. The final choices, of course, are highly idiosyncratic. Nevertheless, the result, we believe, is an excellent and valuable source of readings of exceptional quality.

Acknowledgements

Acknowledgement is due to the School of Business, Queen's University, Kingston, Canada for sponsoring the *International Forum on the Future of Management Accounting, Control and Information System Research*. The financial contribution of The Certified General Accountants of Ontario International Business Research Centre at Queen's University towards word processing work is also gratefully acknowledged. Our thanks also goes to all the management accounting scholars who came to Canada from afar to participate in the Forum and who took time out from their hectic schedules at home researching, writing, editing journals, teaching, etc. They are: Richard Baker, Salvador Carmon, David Cooper, Jesse Dillard, Mahmoud Ezzamel, Sten Jönsson, Elton McGoun, Pekka Pihlanto, Vaughan Radcliffe, Angelo Riccaboni, Alan Richardson and Teri Shearer. Finally, but most importantly, we must thank Linda Freeman, without whose exceptional organizational skills, miraculous word processing ability and communication expertise, this book would never have seen the light of day.

Contributors

Armstrong, Peter, *University of Leicester*
Arnold, Patricia J., *University of Wisconsin, Milwaukee*
Arrington, C. Edward, *The University of North Carolina*
Baker, C. Richard, *Adelphi University*
Burchell, Stuart, *London Graduate School of Business Studies (formerly)*
Busco, Cristiano, *University of Siena*
Carmona, Salvador, *Universidad Carlos III de Madrid*
Chua, Wai Fong, *University of New South Wales, Australia*
Clubb, Colin, *University of Warwick*
Cooper, Christine, *University of Strathclyde*
Cooper, David J., *University of Alberta*
Covaleski, Mark A., *University of Wisconsin, Madison*
Dillard, Jesse F., *Portland State University*
Dirsmith, Mark W., *Pennsylvania State University*
Dugdale, David, *University of Bristol*
Ezzamel, Mahmoud, *University of Cardiff*
Francis, Jere R., *The University of Iowa*
Gutiérrez, Fernando, *Universidad Pablo de Olavide*
Hedberg, Bo, *University of Gothenburg*
Hopper, Trevor, *University of Manchester*
Hopwood, Anthony G., *Saïd Business School, University of Oxford*
Hughes, John, *London Graduate School of Business Studies (formerly)*
Jones, T. Colwyn, *University of the West of England*
Jönsson, Sten, *University of Gothenburg*
Laughlin, Richard C., *Kings College, London*
Lukka, Kari, *Turku School of Economics and Business Administration*
Macintosh, Norman B., *Queen's University*
McGoun, Elton G., *Bucknell University*
Miller, Peter, *London School of Economics*
Mouritsen, Jan, *Copenhagen Business School*
Nahapiet, Janine, *Templeton College, University of Oxford*

O'Leary, Ted, *Manchester University*
Oakes, Leslie S., *University of New Mexico*
Pihlanto, Pekka, *Turku School of Economics and Business Administration*
Quattrone, Paolo, *Saïd Business School, University of Oxford*
Powell, Andrew, *University of Aston (formerly)*
Riccaboni, Angelo, *University of Siena*
Richardson, Alan J., *Schulich School of Business, York University*
Roberts, John, *University of Cambridge*
Samuel, Sajay, *Independent Scholar*
Scapens, Robert W., *University of Manchester*
Shearer, Teri L., *Queen's University*
Sherer, Michael J., *University of Essex*
Taylor, Phil, *University of Stirling*
Thornton, Daniel B., *Queen's University*
Tinker, Anthony M., *Baruch College, CUNY*
Townley, Barbara, *Edinburgh University*
Welker, Michael, *Queen's University*

Contents

Introduction

Accounting today, including its double-entry-bookkeeping technique and its decision-making role, is one of the most universally taught subjects globally. For most of the world, accounting is thought of as something mundane that bookkeepers do as 'keepers of the records and accounts' and 'preparers of income tax returns' for organizations and individuals. Those who are a little closer to what actually goes on, however, see accountants as preparing reports and providing information which gets used by all kinds of decision makers in both the private and the public sectors. But in the last couple of decades many academics have been pushing the boundary of accounting, thinking well beyond even this perspective to focus on its wider role and impact on organizations and society at large.

This book contains thirty-five articles along these lines. It aims to bring this body of thinking to a wider constituency and thus expand the scope of traditional ways of thinking and teaching accounting. One important audience is upper level under-graduate and graduate students in professional accounting programs. The book is also geared at masters and doctoral students since it provides a broad sampling of influential research studies presented in an accessible format.

The articles selected should also be of vital interest to thoughtful, sophisticated professional accountants in industry, commerce and government, especially those who are concerned about the current state of accounting and the profession as the twenty-first century, with its Enron accounting scandals and such, gets under way. The hope here is that the book will help to bridge the gap between busy practitioners and the careful research of accounting scholars.

The articles are presented in abridged form in order to highlight the authors' main messages. This process of trimming down each article is, metaphorically speaking, like boiling sap to bottle only the maple syrup. In doing so, however, every care was exercised to maintain the integrity of the original content and of the author's style. Readers who are especially interested in particular articles can readily look up the unabridged originals, which contain the detailed arguments that bolster the main ideas, as well as the supporting footnotes and bibliographies.

The book is partly the outcome of the 'International Forum on the Future of Management Accounting, Control and Information Systems Research' held at Queen's University, Canada in May 2002. Each participant was asked to select one or two articles they had written, alone or with co-authors, which ranked as one of their personal favorites. In addition, in order to flesh out the readings they were

Accounting, the Social and the Political
N. Macintosh and T. Hopper (Editors)
© 2005 Elsevier Ltd. All rights reserved.

asked to suggest articles of other authors, which they believed have made significant contributions in recent decades to accounting thought.

The readings are organized into three main sections — Classics, Contemporary and Beyond. The *Classics* are those that were seminal in that they represented what at the time were highly original ideas and which have since been the source of inspiration for much follow-up accounting research and theorizing. The *Contemporary* section includes a collection of more recent articles, ones which in their own way make a significant contribution to current ways of thinking about the broader role of accounting in organizations and society. The *Beyond* section contains articles which, while some might see them as 'far out', each could well signal major research and theorizing trails for up-and-coming generations of accounting academics and practitioners. As such, they are harbingers of future accounting thinking. Finally, the *Future Directions* postscript speculates on the future direction and possibilities for research and theory concerning accounting and the social.

Part I

Classics

The articles in this Classics section gestured in important ways towards new directions for accounting research and theory building. As such, they opened up uncharted territories and outlined fresh ways of understanding and thinking about accounting other than the traditional economics-based approach. Each turned out to be a seminal 'pointer reading' that inspired others to follow a similar path.

The Burchell, Clubb, Hopwood, Hughes & Nahapiet (1980) article depicted accounting, not merely as a collection of techniques for managing financial resources but also as a vital power resource occupying an ever more significant role and position in organizations, society and its institutions. It is widely referenced even today. Hedberg & Jönsson's (1978) pioneering paper argued for expanding the boundaries of accounting theory to include information systems which make people think, use their intuition and provide cognitive and interpretive maps, rather than merely rely on them to churn out answers for them. The Tinker (1980) article proved to be another trailblazer introducing the Marxist radical structural political economy as a supplement to the conventional neo-classical marginalist economics perspective, for accounting research and theory building. And the Cooper & Sherer (1984) piece filled in the details of a political economy approach.

Several seminal articles introduced different conceptual frameworks into the field of accounting research. Hopper & Powell (1985) outlined how the Burrell & Morgan (1979) four-paradigm framework (functionalism, interpretivism, radical humanism and radical structuralism) could serve as a valuable way of understanding management accounting systems. Chua (1986) filled out the epistemological and ontological underpinnings of this scheme. Roberts & Scapens (1985) introduced Anthony Giddens' structuration theory as a sensitizing device for analyzing management accounting systems in their historical circumstances revealing how they are vehicles for bringing signification, domination and morality into the daily routines of agents in organizations.

Looking further a field, several articles drew on the works of eminent social–philosophical scholars as ways of viewing accounting in a broad societal sense. Hopwood (1987) & Miller & O'Leary (1987) looked to the work of Michael Foucault to theorize accounting as a disciplinary discursive regime rendering individuals as objects to be measured, disciplined, punished and normalized. Laughlin (1987) showed how developments by the Frankfurt School of Social Philosophy scholars, particularly the ideas of Jürgen Habermas, could make a valuable contribution to seeing accounting as a vital steering mechanism in society.

Along similar lines, Richardson (1987), following Antonio Gramsci's critique, showed how accounting can work as a hegemonic control mechanism — penetrating institutions throughout society. Finally, Arrington & Francis (1989), following Jacques Derrida, demonstrated the relevance of deconstructionist readings to reveal how accounting texts, particularly theoretical ones, cannot guarantee a single coherent meaning, thus revealing the politics of the accounting texts.

Each of these articles, in its own way, proved to be a trailblazer, sowing the seeds for future generations of accounting researchers and theories.

Chapter 1

The Roles of Accounting in Organizations and Society[1]

Stuart Burchell, *London Graduate School of Business Studies (formerly)*
Colin Clubb, *University of Warwick*
Anthony G. Hopwood, *Saïd Business School, University of Oxford*
John Hughes, *London Graduate School of Business Studies (formerly)*
Janine Nahapiet, *Templeton College, University of Oxford*

Accounting has come to occupy an ever more significant position in the functioning of modern industrial societies. Emerging from the management practices of the estate, the trader and the embryonic corporation, it has developed into an influential component of modern organizational and social management. Within the organization, be it in the private or the public sector, accounting developments now are seen as being increasingly associated not only with the management of financial resources but also with the creation of particular patterns of organizational visibility, the articulation of forms of management structure and organizational segmentation and the reinforcement or indeed creation of particular patterns of power and influence. What is accounted for can shape organizational participants' views of what is important, with the categories of dominant economic discourse and organizational functioning that are implicit within the accounting framework, helping to create a particular conception of organizational reality.

At a broader social level, accounting has become no less influential as it has come to function in a multitude of different and ever changing institutional areas. The emergence of the modern state has been particularly important in this respect. The economic calculations provided by enterprise-level accounting systems have come to be used not only as a basis for government taxation, but also as a means for enabling the more general economic management policies of the state to grow in significance and impact. Accounting data are now used in the derivation and implementation of policies for economic stabilization, price and wage control, the regulation of particular industrial and commercial sectors and the planning of national economic resources in conditions of war and peace and prosperity and depression. Indeed, in its continuing search for greater economic and social efficiency the state has been an

---

[1]Reproduced (in an abridged form) from S. Burchell, C. Clubb, A. Hopwood, J. Hughes and J. Nahapiet, 'The Roles of Accounting in Organizations and Society', *Accounting, Organizations and Society*, 1980, vol. 5, no. 1, pp. 5–27, with permission of Elsevier.

Accounting, the Social and the Political
N. Macintosh and T. Hopper (Editors)

active agent both for the continued development of accounting systems in industrial and commercial enterprises and for their introduction into more sectors of society.

Such extensions of the accounting domain have had major implications for the development of both accounting thought and practice. As the theorists of management control now recognize, accounting can no longer be regarded as a mere collection of techniques for the assessment of individual economic magnitudes. Whilst procedures for the derivation of various categories of cost and economic surplus are still important, the growth of the modern business enterprise has resulted in their incorporation into more all embracing forms of organizational practice which can enable the coordinated and centralized control of the functional, divisionalized and now, the matrix and project-oriented organization. Similarly, the increasing demands for financial information made by the capital markets, agencies of the state and organizations within the accounting profession itself have resulted in more extensive and rigorous approaches to financial reporting and disclosure. Accounting problems have seemingly got ever more detailed, precise and interdependent, resulting not only in the need to articulate new practice but also to formally explicate what previously had been implicit in practice.

As a result of such developments, accounting has gained its current organizational and social significance. No longer seen as a mere assembly of calculative routines, it now functions as a cohesive and influential mechanism for economic and social management. But why should this be the case?

Institutionalization, Abstraction and the Search for Rationales

It is possible to identify many tendencies underlying the development of the accounting craft. One could point to particular aspects of the emerging bodies of knowledge and practice or to the changing patterns of influence on them. Alternatively, one could highlight developments in the organizational and social significance, which accounting has had or changes in the organization of accounting itself. For the purpose of the present argument two particular tendencies are identified: the increasing institutionalization of the craft and the growing objectification and abstraction of accounting knowledge.

The institutionalization of accounting has occurred at both the organizational and societal levels. Within both business and governmental organizations, bookkeeping came to take on a new significance and influence as accounting became a more all-embracing form of organizational practice. Implicated in budgeting and standard costing, organizational segmentation and control and planning and resource allocation, the accountant came to be an increasingly respected member of the management cadre. Accounting departments were created, specialist staff recruited, emergent accounting systems formalized, standardized and codified and links with other forms of management practice established. Moreover, accounting itself came to be a more fragmented endeavour with the growing separation of the preparation of the financial accounts from the presentation of internal financial information and the management of corporate liquidity and financial structure.

   Such organizational developments were themselves intertwined with the profes-
sionalization of the accounting craft. Almost from their birth, the professional
institutes provided an interface between the growing agencies of the state and
business enterprises. Indeed with the establishment of professional accounting
institutes, many of the subsequent institutional innovations in the accounting area in
the US and the UK were to arise at the interface between them and the expanding
regulatory agencies of the state. So, initially at least, the Securities and Exchange
Commission in the US made rather limited use of its regulatory powers in the
accounting area, allowing the profession to invest in that chain of institutional
mechanisms for the explication, standardization and codification of financial
accounting practice which would progress through the accounting Principles Board
to the Financial Accounting Standards Board. Not dissimilar developments occurred
later in the UK with the Accounting Standards Steering Committee being created in
response to governmental pressure and the desire of the professional institutes to
preserve their powers of self-regulation. Elsewhere, however, the institutionalization
of accounting was a more direct result of the activities of the state. In pre-war
Germany, for example, legal and institutional mechanisms for the standardization of
enterprise accounting were introduced in the context of the mobilization of the
national economy for war and in France, these innovations were adapted after the
war to provide the information which was required for microeconomic planning by
agencies of the state.
   Certainly, the state came to act on accounting in the name of both accountability
and the furtherance of organizational and social efficiency. Professional institutes
and those agencies concerned with accounting regulation adopted a similar stance,
although they also emphasized the role which accounting could serve in improving
the flow of information useful for the investment decisions of shareholders. And
those practicing accounting within organizations came to point to its relevancy in
improving organizational efficiency and the maintenance of organizational control.
   Such roles were not necessarily mere interpretations of accounting practice. Roles
could emerge at a distance from practice, often shaped by very different institutional
contexts and bodies of thought, and thereafter serve as bases for changing practice.
Providing the imperatives for accounting, their relationship to the practice of
accounting need be only indirect.

The Imperatives of Accounting

We are all familiar with those stated roles of accounting which grace the
introductions to accounting texts, professional pronouncements and the statements
of those concerned with the regulation and development of the craft. Latterday
equivalents of the preambles of old which appealed more directly to heavenly virtue
and authority, they attempt to provide a more secular basis for the accounting
mission. In such contexts, accounting is seen to have an essence, a core of functional
claims and pretentions. It is, or so we are led to believe, essentially concerned with
the provision of 'relevant information for decision making', with the achievement of

a 'rational allocation of resources' and with the maintenance of institutional 'accountability' and 'stewardship'. Such functional attributes are seen as being fundamental to the accounting endeavour. Justifying the existence of the craft, they provide rationales for continued accounting action.

Another rather different set of imperatives for accounting has originated from those scholars who have seen accounting systems as mirrors of the societies or organizations in which they are implicated. At the societal level, this has involved seeing accounting as essentially reflective of the organization of social relationships. Feudal societies are seen to require feudal accounting systems; capitalist societies, capitalist modes of accounting; and the era of the post-industrial society necessitates a new framework for the accounting craft. The translation of such thinking to the organizational level has been more recent, influenced by the emergence of contingency schools of thought in the study of organizational behaviour.

Indeed many of the functional claims that have been made for accounting have emerged at a distance from the practice of accounting. Emanating from professional institutes, bodies concerned with the regulation of the accounting craft, agencies of the state and not least in importance, the academy itself, they very often reflect the pressures on those bodies and their need for a public legitimacy and rationale for action. Formulated in the context of particular institutional needs and actions, the functional claims attempt to provide rather particular interpretations of the accounting mission. In the academy in particular, the public roles that have been articulated have often reflected the influence of other bodies of thought and practice with which accounting as an autonomous body of knowledge has become intertwined. The influences of conventional economic discourse and administrative theory have been particularly important in this respect.

Accounting Systems and Organizational Practice

Recognizing that the present state of knowledge precludes either a comprehensive or an authoritative account of the ways in which accounting information is implicated in the processes of organizational decision making, we base our own analysis on the rather particular understandings of decision making in organizations formulated by Thompson & Tuden (1959). Whilst overly simple, their perspective nevertheless added to the traditional view by characterizing various states of uncertainty and, as a consequence, a range of possible approaches to decision making. By doing so, it provides a basis for discussing at least some of the diverse ways in which interests in accounting can arise out of the processes of organizational decision making.

As can be seen in Figure 1.1, Thompson and Tuden distinguished between uncertainty (or disagreement, for that has the same effects at the organizational level) over the objectives for organizational action and uncertainty over the patterns of causation which determine the consequences of action. When objectives are clear and undisputed, and the consequences of action are presumed to be known, Thompson & Tuden highlighted the potential for decision making by computation. In such circumstances, it is possible to compute whether the consequence of the

		Uncertainty of objectives	
		Low	High
Uncertainty of	Low	Decision by computation	Decision by compromise
cause and effect	High	Decision by judgement	Decision by inspiration

Figure 1.1: Decision making and the location of organizational uncertainty.

action or set of actions being considered will or will not satisfy the objectives that have been laid down and agreed beforehand. As cause and effect relationships become more uncertain however, the potential for computation diminishes. Thompson and Tuden then saw decisions being made in a judgemental manner, with organizational participants subjectively appraising the array of possible consequences in the light of the relatively certain objectives. Just as the introduction of uncertainty into the specification of the consequences of action resulted in a different approach to decision making, so did the acknowledgement of debate or uncertainty over the objectives themselves. With cause and effect relationships presumed to be known, Thompson and Tuden thought that disagreement or uncertainty over the objectives of action would result in a political rather than computational rationale for the decision making process. A range of interests in action are articulated in such circumstances and decision making, as a result, tends to be characterized by bargaining and compromise. When even patterns of causation are uncertain, Thompson and Tuden pointed out that decision making tends to be of an inspirational nature. With so little known beforehand rationales for action were seen as emerging in the course of the decision making process itself.

Using an all too unsatisfactory 'machine' analogy, Figure 1.2 outlines a set of organizational roles, which might help us to appreciate some of the ways in which accounting systems function in practice. Given low uncertainty over both the consequences of action and the objectives for action, we approach the management scientist's definition of certainty, where algorithms, formulae and rules can be derived to solve problems by computation. Alternatively this situation might represent what Simon (1960) has called structured decision making, where the

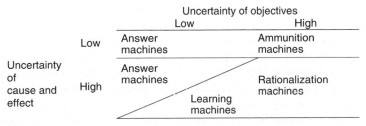

Figure 1.2: Uncertainty, decision making and the roles of accounting practice.

intelligence, design and choice phases are all programmable. In either case, accounting systems can serve as 'answer machines', providing the simple investment appraisal methods, stock control systems and credit control routines which grace many management accounting texts.

With clear objectives but uncertain causation, the situation is more complex. One might expect that this is where organizational participants would need to explore problems, ask questions, explicate presumptions, analyze the analyzable and finally resort to judgement. Rather than providing answers, accounting systems might be expected to provide assistance through decision support systems or inquiry systems. In fact, we do find such 'learning machine' uses of the accounting function: access facilities, *ad hoc* analyses, what-if models and sensitivity analyses are available and used in organizations. However, this is also the area of decision making where we have seen enormous extensions of more traditional approaches to computation practice. For the uncertainty, some would claim, has been seen as a threatening but not inevitable state of the world, need to be masked, if not reduced, by an investment in the advancement of calculative systems. Accordingly, the accountant has devised systems which can themselves absorb rather than convey the surrounding uncertainties. Together with the management scientist, optimizing models and maps of probabilistic and risk analysis have been developed and applied. Often trying to inculcate an aura of relative certainty, the 'answer machine' extensions to the accounting craft often have presumed or imposed particular forms of economic and scientific rationality, which have an equivocal relationship at best to those rationalities which are implicated in the processes of organizational decision making.

Given uncertainty or disagreement over objectives but relative certainty over causation, values, principles, perspectives and interests conflict. Standards for appraisal and criteria for guiding the organizational task are inherently problematic. Here political processes are important in the decision-making process and modes of accounting can arise as 'ammunition machines' by which and through which interested parties seek to promote their own particular positions. Striving to articulate the desirability of particular conceptions of the organizational mission and to selectively channel the distribution of information, parties implicated in organized action can introduce new mechanisms for organizational control and the management of information flows.

Similarly, we suspect that the uncertainties inherent in decision making by inspiration can create the need for accounting systems to serve as organizational 'rationalization machines'. Seeking to legitimize and justify actions that already have been decided upon, in such circumstances an accounting for the past can have a rather particular organizational significance and value.

Admittedly simplistic, our framework of accounting roles is nonetheless suggestive. By pointing to the different ways in which the accounting craft might be used to create particular conceptions of organizational clarity, it enables us to articulate a variety of roles which accounting systems might serve. Our discussion focuses on those extensions of computational practice which seemingly have extended the scope of 'answer machine' approaches, the emergence and use of organizational 'ammunition machines' and the roles which accounting might play in the rationalization of organizational action.

Organizational 'Ammunition Machines'

Rather than creating a basis for dialogue and interchange in situations where objectives are uncertain or in dispute, accounting systems are often used to articulate and promote particular interested positions and values. For the organization is almost invariably characterized by conflicts over both basic orientations and the organizational means which are likely to achieve particular ends. Rather than being cohesive mechanisms for rational action, organizations are constituted as coalitions of interests. They are arenas in which people and groups participate with a diversity of interests with political processes being an endemic feature of organizational life. The mobilization and control of the organization, in the name of any interest, are problematic endeavours.

For once in operation, accounting systems are organizational phenomena. Indeed having their own *modus operandi* they themselves can impose constraints on organizational functioning, often contributing in the process to the effective definition of interests rather than simply expressing those which are pregiven. So, although they might be able to be influenced by particular participants, accounting systems can rarely, if ever, be the exclusive domain of a single interest. Rather they become mechanisms around which interests are negotiated, counter claims articulated and political processes explicated. They may influence the language, categories, form and even timing of debate, but they can rarely exclusively influence its outcomes.

Accounting and the Rationalization of Action

The imperatives of the accounting mission have focused exclusively on roles for accounting which precede decision making. Even accountings for the past have been given a future rationale. However, in organizations, decisions, once made, need to be justified, legitimized and rationalized. There is often a need for a retrospective understanding of the emergence of action, for an expression of a more synoptic organizational rationale or at least one, which is seemingly consistent with formal expressions of organizational aims.

Accounting systems can be and often are implicated in such organizational processes. The widespread use of capital budgeting procedures has resulted in the availability of justification devices for proposals for organizational action which have gained early commitment and support, as well as the simple provision of information for and prior to decision making for those proposals which remain problematic to the end. Similarly, budgets and plans can be built around what is to be.

Hopefully, we have succeeded in demonstrating the divergence between the functional claims that are made on behalf of the accounting craft and the roles which it serves in practice. Whilst accounting can be and is acted upon in the name of its essential imperative, it functions within that complex of political processes which constitute the organization. We have at least pointed to how the pressures to account can arise out of organizational functioning, how accounting can strive to shape conceptions of organizational reality and, in turn, how accountings and accounting systems can reflect as well as shape the pressures of action. Rather than being essential to the accounting mission, the roles which accounting serves in organizations are created, shaped and changed by the pressures of organizational life. They are implicated in action, rather than being prior to it.

The Social Significance of Accounting

A multitude of different social significances have been attached to accounting. For Marx, accounting served as an ideological phenomenon. Perpetrating a form of false consciousness, it provided a means for mystifying rather than revealing the true nature of the social relationships which constitute productive endeavour. Others, whilst adopting a less dogmatic stance, have nonetheless pointed to the mythical, symbolic and ritualistic roles of accounting. In such a context accounting has been seen as implicated in the operationalization of dominant economic and social distinctions, the creation of symbolic boundaries between competing social agents and the provision of a basis on which rationales and missions can be constructed and furthered. Conveying a pattern of economic and social meanings, it has been seen to be at least partially fulfilling demands for the construction of a symbolic order within which social agents can interact.

References

Simon, H.A. (1960). *The new science of management decision*. New York: Harper & Row.

Thompson, J.D., & Tuden, A. (1959). Strategies, structures and processes of organizational decision, in J.D. Thompson *et al.* (eds). *Comparative studies in administration*. Pittsburgh: University of Pittsburgh Press.

Chapter 2

Designing Semi-Confusing Information Systems for Organizations in Changing Environments[1]

Bo Hedberg and Sten Jönsson,   *University of Gothenburg*

Organizations have many stabilizers but quite often lack proper destabilizers. They establish fixed repertoires of behavior programs over time, and many grow too rigid and insensitive to environmental changes. Drifting into changing environments, they react with delayed and improper responses.

Current information — and accounting — systems do more to stabilize organizations than to destabilize them. They filter away conflicts, ambiguities, overlaps, uncertainty, etc. and they suppress many relevant change signals and kill initiatives to act on early warnings.

Organizations in changing environments need information systems which enable them to stay alert and to detect problems, changes and conflicts in time. Accounting information can be used to stimulate organizational curiosity, facilitate dialectical decision processes and increase organizations' ability to cope with variety in their environments. This article formulates some principles for design of information systems that can destabilize organizations with planned confusion — in times when they ought to be confused.

Information — and accounting — systems are sometimes thought of as being neutral with respect to their impacts on organizations' behavior. The argument is that they represent potential resources which can assist and aid decision makers in many different ways, and that their impacts are determined by the way they are used. This is true, in a sense. Formalized information systems and information technologies are not good or bad, *per se*. But, there are information systems which offer less discretion to decision makers than others, and which lead to organizational rigidity; and there are information systems which stimulate organizations to experiment and innovate, and which foster organizational flexibility. Those who design information systems do indeed influence the behavior of organizations, and the behavioral impacts of system designs are increasingly being recognized. It appears that the majority of modern information systems, and particularly computerized ones, have made organizations more rigid rather than more flexible.

---

[1] Reproduced (in an abridged form) from B. Hedberg and S. Jönsson, 'Designing Semi-Confusing Information Systems for Organizations in Changing Environments', *Accounting, Organizations and Society*, 1978, vol. 3, no. 2, pp. 47–64, with permission of Elsevier.

All information systems imply a world view that contains assumptions about what information is relevant, which characteristics of the environment are essential, who the decision makers are, etc. These world views are usually implicit. They grow obsolete, but they do not change immediately as the world changes. Indeed, information systems often tether organizations to yesterday's perceptions.

Traditional accounting systems are good illustrations of this. They reflect a historical situation when the company was considered as identical with the owner-entrepreneur who had been trusted to handle shareholders' and lenders' money and who reported his stewardship to those groups of people. Other resources, such as personnel and know-how, which certainly are important to a company's survival but which historically have lacked the backing of powerful interest groups, were not included in the information systems. These power balances are changing today: powerful trade unions and worker representatives in management have other priorities and demand other reporting. Environmental protection interests require other additions, and changing values in our society as a whole have put pressure on the development of human resources accounting, environmental exchange accounts and social audits. The old accounting world views are clearly obsolete, but changes have been modest so far. Old information systems and their implicit world views are solidly established, and they resist change. Monetary measures are still dominant. Implicit world views in information systems frequently serve as conserving forces and delay organizations' adaptation to changing environments.

There are also indications that modern information systems tend to hamper organizational search and filter away significant amounts of relevant uncertainty, diversity and change signals. It appears that many modern information systems dysfunctionally add to organizations' inertia. Access to more information and more advanced decision aids does not necessarily make decision makers better informed or more able to decide. Examples from our own research can illustrate this point.

Information Systems and Organizational Change

Information systems affect organizational change. A study of 10 Swedish conglomerates of formerly family-owned firms revealed how formalized information systems delayed necessary reorientations. The newly created umbrella organizations employed laissez-faire strategies initially and were satisfied to provide financial support to strategic initiatives taken by the subsidiaries. Information systems were local. The head offices received infrequent aggregated reports for overall control.

Then a recession caused financial problems in many of the rapidly growing subsidiaries. The conglomerates typically reacted with considerable delays and suffered severe losses before old strategies were abandoned and replaced by new ones. The need to redesign and implement adequate corporate information systems delayed strategic reorientations significantly. As a result of these design problems, many of the conglomerates came out of phase with the business cycle and failed to benefit from the consecutive economic upturn. Most of the conglomerates detected environmental changes too late. Before they realized, the need to act and began redesigning their information systems to grasp the new situation, they lost slack and ended up with little room for strategic maneuvering. The information systems delayed the detection of problems, and systems redesign almost paralyzed organizational action during the upturn of the crisis.

Old and inefficient information systems often delay organizations' responses to environmental changes. But new and advanced information systems do not necessarily make organizations function better. The three examples illustrate that very conscious and considerable design efforts are needed, if information systems are to change organizations' behaviors and reduce their inertia. Conventional information systems are often too time consuming to redesign. They leave organizations in chaotic states when needs for reorientations are discovered. New information systems as such do not change decision makers' behaviors. Standard operating procedures must be unlearnt if new potentials are to be utilized. But, even deliberate attempts to design for organizational curiosity and continuous learning may fail due to organizational climate, peer group pressure and difficulties to reframe human minds. Although we know of no completely successful attempts to design information systems so that organizations adapt and respond more readily to changes, our own experiments and mistakes begin to suggest some design principles that could make organizations' life in changing environments somewhat easier.

Matching Cognitive Mappings to the Nature of the Environment

The problems which changing environments pose can hardly be reduced, but it might be possible to assist organizations to detect changes and to deal with environmental complexity. Viable organizations must have a reasonable fit between the complexity and changeability of their environments, and the complexity and flexibility of the cognitive mappings through which they interpret situations and develop actions. Organizations in stable, benevolent environments can benefit from developing highly complex and integrated decision models and mental maps, while organizations in turbulent and rapidly changing environments must keep the complexity of their mental maps at a bare minimum. The former ones are like organizational palaces, which indeed can be built when conditions are controlled and sites are on long-term lease. The latter ones should rather be like organizational tents, and their members should leave unnecessary luggage behind and travel light.

There is a risk that our emphasis on cognitive fit between organizations and their environments leads to static interpretations, and we want to avoid that by all means. Organizations travel in changing environments, so fit is indeed a dynamic concept. The environment can be problematic all along, but there can still be different requirements on the information systems. Organizations that enter into unknown environments need to discover as soon as possible that situations are new and that old experiences must be doubted. They need destabilizers until they wake up. Then, when they have analyzed their new situation and begun to invent responses, it may well be that their information systems should filter out new problem signals and shelter emerging new routines and strategies. We have found such cyclic patterns in organizations' development which appear to call for information systems that not, only are contingent upon the nature of an organization's environment but also upon the state of the organization itself. Organizations change their myths — action theories — over time and in an orderly pattern. Various myth phases call for sheltering and consolidation.

Organizations' Myth Cycles

Thus, our main proposition is that organizations develop over time through wave patterns of myths. The waves constitute cycles with spurts of enthusiasms, largely built on wishful thinking that initiate vigorous action, followed by a decline in the unifying and directing force of the leading idea, or set of ideas. The final decline — which results from the interaction between plans and real outcomes, ends in a crisis. As a consequence of the crisis, the organization often accepts a new strategy without any struggle between proponents for the old and the new strategy.

In order to demonstrate the function of myths in the strategy formulation process it is necessary to discuss some ontological aspects of the strategy concept. First; it is important to stress that strategies are action-oriented. This means that only an agent can have a strategy. It also implies that the holders of strategies usually do something, and when they act repeatedly they create habits and accumulate inertia. Second; a strategy has two parents — the myth which is the decision makers' theory for understanding the world and motivating their actions, and the situation as perceived through the filter that the myth provides. Third; strategy formulation always takes place in the presence of and in opposition to ruling myths and strategies. This means that new strategies must challenge and disprove the usefulness of the established strategies in order to take over and be successful. This is a difficult task, since the established strategies are consolidated through empirical evidence and have been in use for some time, while the arguments for the new strategies must be based on analogues and speculations. Applying a strategy to a situation means implicitly to test the myth on which it is based. The feedback information that results can be used as arguments against the established strategies and the ruling myths. It is thus possible to argue cognitively against established strategies, but it is much more difficult to gather empirical evidence to be used as arguments in support of new strategies.

The main features of our perception of the development and replacement of myths over time are the habit forming and filtering effects of the established strategy that create inertia which in turn results in crises, and the enthusiasm for a solution-in-principle to the crisis situation that overcomes inertia and initiates vigorous action based on a new myth. A wave pattern is the result over time.

We postulate that organizations only can change their mode of behavior towards the environment significantly when ego-attribution dominates. This leads to the conclusion that it is not desirable that an information system is designed and believed to be the provider-of-the-truth. A combination of an experimental attitude and a perception of the information system as a biased measuring instrument seems more appropriate, especially when organizations travel through changing environments.

Designing Information Systems for Organizations in Changing Environments

Strategies are organizations' theories for understanding the world. They consist of sets of hypotheses that should be tested and elaborated. The design of information systems is part of the formulation of a research program. A research program is a plan for the testing and elaboration of a theory. As illustrated in Figure 2.1, the information system (I) generates the evidence (E) from the real system (R), against which the predictions of the theory (T) are evaluated. If the evidence (E) and the theory (T) are judged to be incompatible, the experimenter has to decide whether to trust the evidence and revise or reject the theory, or to distrust the evidence and redesign the measuring instrument (I). If the evidence fits the theory, more elaborate and detailed hypotheses can be tested.

If this research paradigm is applied to the situation of organizations in changing environments, it follows that the strategy of the organization is the theory to be tested. The core of the strategy (theory) is the domain definition of the organization. The domain definition in turn defines the dimensions which the information system should measure. Evaluation of the strategy is possible only if the domain definition of the organization is stated explicitly (and is known to every member of the organization). Elaboration or falsification due to changing environments requires that strategies are stated in falsifiable forms.

The confrontation between theory and evidence envisaged above presupposes that testing the theory is the main concern. In that case, the objective of the information system should be to describe reality in relevant dimensions (descriptive research). Evaluation should be left to the experimenters and the results should be subject to debate.

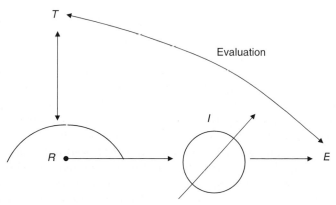

Figure 2.1: A research paradigm.

One problem remains; the risk of testing a theory prematurely, before it is elaborated enough to constitute a basis for evaluation at all. Here the analogy with a research paradigm falters. The theory of science very rarely deals with theory generation. We have to resort to inductive reasoning based on our own research. Strategy formulation as a rule takes place in a hostile environment — as a challenge to the existing strategy. The new strategy therefore, has to build up enough emotional impetus to break through established patterns. This is typically done in crisis situations where a change in environment has been detected, but where it has not been agreed what action is appropriate. This is where the self organizing forces (politics) are given room to generate hypotheses about what are the relevant problems to deal with from now on.

Evaluation of actions and strategies could also be built into organizations and triggered by the information systems. There could be predetermined revision periods, when organizational processes are evaluated and changed. Since formalized information systems and advanced decision models tend to freeze organizations into certain structures and behaviors, one could build in obsolescence, or last-day-of-use signals, at the time of designing, so that overdue usage of decision parameters and design assumptions is counteracted. All computerized models and information systems could, for example, easily have a last-day-of-use subroutine which prohibits further use until decision makers have decided explicitly to extend the lifetime of implicit factors — such as the world view, the selection of information sources, the decision parameters, etc. of the system, or have initiated work towards systems revisions.

Less mechanical triggering would build upon the notion of problem-triggered search and on the related findings about cognitive reactions to noxious stimulation to counterbalance the growth of cognitive complexity and facilitate reframing. One way of making potential problems more visible is to increase the noxity proportion of the decision base, which organizations utilize. This could in many instances be accomplished by simply avoiding to filter away inconsistencies and incompatible information as presently is done. Unfiltering and short-circuiting organizations' communication channels are relatively easy means to make decision environments more trigger rich.

All in all, this points towards design principles which differ considerably from current design ideals, and which turn many systems characteristics previously considered as liabilities into assets. Thus, in addition to striving for order and clarity, consistency and rationality, those who design information systems for organizations in changing environments should also be concerned with installing processes which can counteract and balance these virtues. This is where ambiguity, inconsistency, multiple perspectives and impermanency come in. Semi-confusing information systems require learning mechanisms so that they can help organizations exploit previous experiences and detected causalities, but they need unlearning mechanisms also so that they can do away with obsolete knowledge and behaviors. Dissension can be used to counteract consensus. Dissatisfaction can help maintain long-term contentment. Scarcity can help organizations from being immobilized by affluence. Doubts make plans useful. Inconsistencies can keep organizations together and trade many evolutionary steps for traumatic revolutions. Imperfection can harness rationality so that wisdom results. Hedberg *et al.* (1976) caricatured these central organizational balances with six aphorisms:

1. Cooperation requires minimal consensus,
2. Satisfaction rests upon minimal contentment,
3. Wealth arises from minimal affluence,
4. Goals merit minimal faith,
5. Improvement depends on minimal consistency,
6. Wisdom demands minimal rationality.

The fulcra for each of these six balances may vary from time to time. The wave pattern of myths which we suggested as an important feature of organizations' life, implies that the strength of destabilizing processes should be varied so that organizations in early myth phases receive relatively less change signals and are allowed to build up and consolidate their cognitive structures, while organizations which have developed mature myths and turned from ego-attribution to environment-attribution need relatively more destabilizers, so that predictions are challenged and excess cognitive complexity is counteracted.

This suggests that organizations in changing environments should be able to change their filtering systems, as their strategies and myths change. Maybe they should tune their information systems for different cognitive styles over time and provide for more intuition-feeling in cognitive build-up phases and relatively more sensation-thinking when the major need is to counteract complexification. Or, building on Ornstein's assertions about the different functions of the right and left brain hemispheres (Ornstein 1975), there may be a case for a right-hand side information system that operates in a rather holistic, simultaneous and impressionistic way during the nursing phases of a myth cycle, while later on left-hand side systems, providing information for sequential, linear, analytical information processors, would be needed. Managing may require one dominant mode of decision-making behavior, and planning another (Mintzberg 1975).

Figure 2.2 summarizes these suggested design features with respect to how they could affect organizations, individual decision makers, and the amount of signals that reach an organization.

Epilogue

These general directions and principles for information systems designs, which are suited for organizations in changing environments are certainly easier to state than to operationalize and to implement. Our excuse for weathering them so prematurely is that we believe that they are important and that they are right. As scientific myth builders we find ourselves in a phase where we have to trust our guts, rely on an intuition-feeling mode of reasoning, and put forward a solution-in-principle.

Components	Needs	Design Features
Organization (social system)	Experimental behavior	Evaluative man (Wildavsky 1972; Campbell 1969). Evolution operation (Box & Draper 1969). Optimizing unknown criteria (Starbuck 1974) Self design (Hedberg *et al.* 1976; Landau 1973; Wildavsky 1972)
	Variety in communications	Informal communication networks (Grinyer & Norburn 1975) Role ambiguity (Burns & Stalker 1961) Shortcircuiting levels or groups (Hedberg 1976)
Individuals (decision makers)	Variety in perception	Mixed cognitive styles (Mason & Mitroff 1973; Mintzberg 1975) Mixed learning styles (Kolb 1974; Wolfe 1976) Multidimensional reporting (Haseman & Whinston 1976) Reframing (Watzlawick *et al.* 1974) Dialectics (Mason 1969; Mitroff & Betz 1972)
	Variety in evaluation	Ambiguous objectives (Burns & Stalker 1961; Grinyer & Norburn 1975) Multiple evaluation criteria (Gordon *et al.* 1974)
Change signals	Counteract stability (a) Routinized triggering	Predetermined revision periods (March & Simon 1958) Last-day-of-use for administrative routines (Hedberg 1976) Planned sequences of experiments (Starbuck 1974)

	(b) Contingent triggering	(Mature myth phases)
		MUCH
		↑ *Semi-confusing information systems:*
		      - unfiltering
		      - inconsistency
		      - incompatibility
		      - dialectics
		↓ (Hedberg *et al.* 1976; Hedberg & Jönsson 1977)
		LITTLE
		(Infant myth phases)

Figure 2.2: Summary of suggested design features

Yes, our right-hand brain hemispheres did this sketching. The work for the left-hand side hemispheres remains.

References

Box, G.E.P., & Draper, N.R. (1969). *Evolutionary operation*. New York: Wiley.
Burns, T., & Stalker, G.M. (1961). *The management of innovation*. London: Tavistock.

Campbell, D.T. (1969). Reforms as experiments. *American Psychologist*, 409–429.

Gordon, G., Tanon, D., & Morse, E.V. (1974). *Hospital structure, costs, and innovation*. Working paper: Cornell University.

Grinyer, P.H., & Norburn, D. (1975). An empirical investigation of some aspects of planning for existing markets; perceptions of executives and financial performance. *Journal of the Royal Statistical Society*, series A.

Haseman, W.D., & Whinston, A.B. (1976). Design of a multidimensional accounting system, *The Accounting Review*, 65–79.

Hedberg, B. (1976). Mott ett man v̄rerbart industrisamhölle, in B. Hambraeus & E. Tengstr m̄ (eds). *Vad kan du och jag g r̄a Δt framtiden?* Stockholm, Bonniers, 131–139.

Hedberg, B., Nystrom, P.C., & Starbuck, W.H. (1976). Camping on seesaws: Prescriptions for a self-designing organization. *Administrative Science Quarterly* (March), 41–65.

Hedberg, B., & Jönsson, S. (1977). Strategy formulation as a discontinuous process. *International Studies of Management and Organization*.

Kolb, D.A. (1974). On management and the learning process, in D.A. Kolb, I.M. Rubin & J.M. McIntyre (eds). *Criticism and the growth of knowledge*. Cambridge: University Press.

Landau, M. (1973). On the concept of a self-correcting organization. *Public Administration Review*, 533–542.

March, J.G., & Simon, H.A. (1958). *Organizations*. New York: Wiley.

Mason, R.O. (1969). A dialectical approach to strategic planning. *Management Science*, B403–B414.

Mason, R.O., & Mitroff, I.I. (1973). A program for research on management information systems. *Management Science*, 11–24.

Mintzberg, H. (1975). Planning on the left side and managing on the right. Working paper: Institut Administration des Enterprises, Aix-en-Provence.

Mitroff, I.I., & Betz, F. (1972). Dialectical decision theory, a meta-theory of decision making, *Management Science*, 11–24.

Ornstein, R. (1975). *The psychology of consciousness*. New York: Jonathan Cape.

Starbuck, W.H. (1974). Systems optimization with unknown criteria. *Proceedings of the 1974 International Conference on Systems, Man, and Cybernetics*. New York, de Gruyter, 217–230.

Watzlawick, P., Weakland, J.H., & Fisch, R. (1974). *Change; principles of problem formation and problem resolution*. New York: Norton.

Wildavsky, A. (1972). The self-evaluating organization. *Public Administration Review*, 509–520.

Wolfe, J. (1976). Learning styles rewarded in a complex simulation with implications for business policy and organization behavior research. *Proceedings. 36th Annual National Meeting of the Academy of Management*.

Chapter 3

Towards a Political Economy of Accounting: An Empirical Illustration of the Cambridge Controversies[1]

Anthony M. Tinker, *Baruch College, CUNY*

What does the figure at the bottom of an income statement mean? What interpretations may we put on it? Business firms trade in factor and product markets that form part of a society's economy. As profit is a result of a trading in these markets, may we conclude that profit is indicative not only of the firm's market viability but also its social efficiency in utilizing society's resources? Alternatively, the rate of profit may reflect the social power of capitalists. In this view, the magnitude of expenses in the income statement (including profit) is indicative of social, institutional and monopolistic power rather than social efficiency and productivity.

The two views of what an income statement tells us correspond with two theoretical positions that have dominated the history of economic thought: classical political economy and neo-classical marginalist economics. When applied to the income statement, these two theories offer conflicting explanations as to what income signifies and how it is determined.

Table 3.1 summarizes the theoretical differences between these two viewpoints: it shows that they differ not merely as to what profit means but also as to how the rate of profit is determined. For example, marginal productivity theory adopts an approach that is almost akin to that of engineering: it deals with the manner in which physical resource inputs are transformed into outputs and the role played by profit as an efficiency criterion in this process. Conversely, political economy attributes the division of income (and therefore the rate of profit accruing to capital) to the distribution of power in society and the social–political and institutional structure that mirrors that distribution of power.

The marginalist explanation concentrates on what are called the forces of production. In economic analysis these are brought together in a production function analysis. They include the technological aspects of the input and the output quantities and their transformation coefficients. In contrast, political economy relies

[1]Reproduced (in an abridged form) from Anthony M. Tinker, 'Towards a Political Economy of Accounting: An Empirical Illustration of the Cambridge Controversies', *Accounting, Organizations and Society*, 1980, vol. 5, no. 1, pp. 147–160 with permission of Elsevier.

Accounting, the Social and the Political
N. Macintosh and T. Hopper (Editors)

Table 3.1: Conflicting explanations of profit.

	Neo-Classical Economics (Marginalism)	**Classical Political Economy**
Meaning attributed to profit	Indicator of economic efficiency	The returns to capitalists
Theoretical explanation as to how the rate of profit is determined	Marginal productivity theory focusing on the forces of production	A social and political analysis that focuses on the social relations of production

on the social relations of production: an analysis of the division of power between interest groups in a society and the institutional processes through which interests may be advanced.

The differences between these theoretical alternatives are crystallized by the empirical case study of a UK-based multinational (Delco) that operated in Africa. Delco operated an iron-ore extraction business in Sierra Leone for 46 years. The firm closed down in 1976. The research attempts to link the firm's accounting history with its social and political history. A periodization analysis of the historical data is used to illustrate the link between socio-political and accounting variables. The 46 year history of Delco is divided into three periods: early colonial, late colonial and post-colonial. An income statement is then prepared for each period that summarizes the distribution of the firm's income for that period. The differences between the three income statements (i.e. changes in the distribution of income) are then linked with changes in the social and political conditions underlying the figures.

Table 3.2 contains a sample of sales and expense items from the income statements of Delco. The expenses are shown in monetary terms and as a percentage of sales revenue. Our earlier questions may now be directed to the data in Table 3.2: are the returns to investors, labor and government institutions indicative of their marginal productivity in production? Is there a notion of social justice in this marginalist's explanation in the sense that each factor input gets its 'just' rewards by earning an amount commensurate with the value of what it contributes?

The subdivision of the venture into three main periods (each with its own income statement) suggests an alternative explanation of the distribution of income. Associated with the income statement data for a period is a unique configuration of social and political conditions. We will see how these two are related: the income data is a product of the socio-economic reality and differences between items in the three income statements may be traced to the changes in that reality. In this fashion, we may use political economy to explain and predict accounting numbers.

Table 3.2: Sample of items from three income states of Delco Ltd.

	Early Colonial Period		Late Colonial Period		Post-Colonial Period		Total	
	1930–1947		1948–1967		1968–1975		1930–1975	
	£m	%	£m	%	£m	%	£m	%
Sales proceeds	35	100	267	100	102	100	424	100
Expenses: Taxes	0.8	1.6	1.5	0.6	0.2	0.2	2.5	0.6
(UK government taxes)								
Taxes (Sierra Leone	1.0	1.7	37.9	14.2	1.1	1.0	40.0	9.0
government)								
Wages (white labor)	4.9	8.9	19.7	7.4	6.8	6.6	31.4	7.4
Wages (black labor)	7.6	13.8	15.0	5.6	10.3	10.1	32.9	7.8
Profits	4.7	10.3	31.3	11.7	5.9	5.7	42.9	10.1

Marginalism and Accounting

Very few scholars would deny that marginalist economics has had a tremendous impact on shaping accounting theory. This is not to say that contemporary accounting practice is simply 'applied marginalism', but if 'theory' has played any role in determining practice then marginalist theory has probably contributed more than any other to the practice of accounting. This particular economic theory has provided guidelines for income definition, asset valuation and more recent work in financial standard setting.

The attraction that marginalism holds for accounting theorists may be understood if we reflect on the conceptual structure of marginalism. The power and strength of marginalism stems from its potential in linking 'rational' decision making at various levels: the individual level; the level of the firm and that of an entire economy. While its ability to achieve this conceptual integration has been frequently challenged, marginalism has few rivals today as an organizing frame for accounting thought. Indeed, it might be argued that marginalism has advanced beyond the theoretical domain to penetrate the subconscious of even the most ardent 'practitioner'. Thus, Keynes aptly referred to 'practical men who believe themselves to be exempt from any intellectual influences are usually the slave of some defunct economist' (Keynes 1936: 383).

Marginalist economists such as Fisher (1930), Hicks (1946) and Hirshleifer (1971) have developed concepts of economic value and economic income that are related to the worth of future consumption possibilities. Subject to certain qualifications, cash flow information may be used to assess the present value of these future possibilities. These marginalist ideas already form part of accounting policy: present value calculations are used in valuing leases and assessing such expenses as economic depreciation and certain employee pension items. In these areas, there is no difference between the marginalist concept of value.

Accounting theorists have developed methods that, directly and indirectly, attempt to measure the marginalist's concept of value and income. The Cambridge Controversies are concerned with the validity of the marginalist's concept of value and income. They challenge the conclusion that, for a given market rate of interest, we can conclude that one technique is socially preferable. If we are unable to make this conclusion then marginalism begins to lose some of its advantages as a coherent, integrated schema for accounting policy.

Yet the marginalist explanation is tautological: we begin by asking how the rate of profit is determined and the answer is with reference to the quantity of capital and its marginal revenue product. We then ask how these are determined and the reply is by assuming a division of future income and discounting the returns to capital with the market rate of interest. All that has been said is that the market rate of interest is a function of the market rate of interest (and an assumed income distribution).

It should be stressed that this deficiency refers to marginalism as a theory, not necessarily to capitalism as a system of economic organization. Obviously, market discount rates do exist in reality; what the Cambridge criticisms highlight is the inability of marginalism (*qua* theory) to explain how these market prices are formed and (therefore) how capitalism works.

Leading marginalists have acknowledged the difficulties raised for neo-classical economics by the Cambridge Controversies. Paul Samuelson has stated:

> The discussion shows that the simple tale told by Jevons, Bohm-Bawerk, Wicksell and other neo-classical writers ... cannot be universally valid (1966: 576) ... If all this causes headaches for those nostalgic for the old time parables of neo-classical writings, we must remind ourselves that scholars are not born to live an easy existence. We must respect and appraise the facts of life (1966: 583).

Professor Ferguson has concluded that 'neo-classical economic theory is a matter of faith ... I personally have the faith' (Ferguson 1969).

One of the most interesting consequences of the Cambridge Controversies has been the reinstatement of classical political economy to the center of economic discussion. This has involved a return to the concerns of Ricardo and an acknowledgment that the scope of marginalism, defined in terms of competitive markets (the sphere of exchange), needs to be supplemented with political and social concepts if we are to understand how a capitalist economy works.

An Alternative Framework: Political Economy

Political economy differs from neo-classical (marginalist) thought, in that it recognizes two (not one) dimensions of capital: firstly as (physical) instruments of production and secondly as man's relationship to man in social organization. The first dimension represents the economic forces of production, the second the social relations of production. Figure 3.1 shows how these two concepts of capital are interrelated in shaping social and economic life.

In Figure 3.1 the social relations are represented by various social institutions (e.g. legal, state, educational, religious, law and order, political, government administration). These institutions ensure that rights and obligations (e.g. property rights) can be pursued and enforced: they provide the ground rules for an economic order. Different kinds of society (feudal, slave, capitalist, etc.) are characterized by different kinds of social relations and therefore, different institutional arrangements.

The following analysis of Delco not only attempts to show how the financial benefits from a mining venture were distributed, it also tried to explain how this distribution occurred as a result of institutional and social forces. The study shows how the market was governed by successive institutional forces (including the military, the colonial government and a bureaucratic management function). This amounts to a theoretical explanation (in sociological terms) of the social forces that determine market prices (and therefore accounting data). The Cambridge Controversies have shown theories of workable competition and marginal productivity as inadequate for accounting data. Thus, we rely on theories of

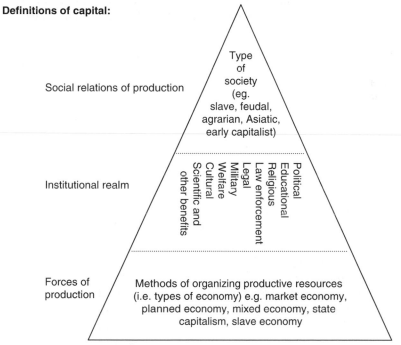

Figure 3.1: The two concepts of capital and their relationship.

imperfect competition and political economy to explain income distribution and profit.

Conventional Financial Appraisal of the Venture

The study of the Scottish owned iron ore company, Delco, spans its 46 year life beginning in the early colonial period, and tracing its expansion through the late colonial period until its collapse in 1976 under a post-colonial state of Sierra Leone.

In order to investigate the Delco Company, a computer simulation model was created that included all the main financial flows involving Delco throughout the period. These monetary flows were then adjusted by an inflation index in an attempt to present all monetary amounts in units of the same purchasing power (thus all calculations are expressed in 1976 pounds sterling equivalents). These inflation-adjusted amounts were then used to compute *ex ante* profitability indices and other measures for assessing the value of the venture. Thus, for the shareholders of Delco, the project produced a 13% inflation-adjusted, internal rate of return (or 16% before inflation). Table 3.3 shows how the total 46 year (inflation-adjusted) sales proceeds were distributed between various parties.

Table 3.3: The distribution of inflation adjusted ore sales proceeds (CIF Prices) 1930–1975.

	£m	%
CIF ore sales proceeds	424.14	100
Capitalist agencies		
Distributed between:		
1. Shippers	169.66	40.00
2. UK suppliers	104.11	24.54
3. Delco owners	42.70	10.07
4. White directors, management and employees	31.40	7.40
5. UK government	0.51	0.59
6. UK leaseholders	0.62	0.15
	351.00	82.75
Sierra Leone constituents		
7. S.L. government	39.87	9.40
8. Black labor: manual staff	26.84	6.33
9. Tribal authorities	6.16	1.45
	73.14	17.25
Total	424.14	100

Table 3.3 presents the project (*ex post*) from a financial viewpoint. For an outlay of £500,000 in 1930 (approximately 3 million in 1976 pounds sterling), the project generated a present value of £18.6 million at a 3% discount rate — after allowing for inflation. In October 1975, Delco (Sierra Leone's second largest export earning industry) went into voluntary liquidation and with it, the several thousand employment opportunities its operates generated. Table 3.3 is not concerned with whether some participants made 'excess profits' from the venture. This would imply that we could say what 'normal profits' were for the situation. What is of interest are the factors that led to the shares taken by participants and the reasons why those shares change over time.

Alternative Analysis of the Venture: A Periodization Analysis

It is at this point that a new way of interpreting accounting data may be introduced. Table 3.4 provides a series of income statements: a periodization

Table 3.4: Periodization table: Distribution of CIF sales proceeds by periods.

	Early Colonial Period		Late Colonial Period	Post-Colonial Periods	
	1930–1976 £m	1930–1947 £m	1948–1956 £m	1957–1967 £m	1968–1975 £m
CIF proceeds	424.14	55.08	94.50	171.81	102.81
European Participants					
Shippers	169.66	22.03	37.80	68.71	41.12
UK suppliers	104.11	12.86	27.50	26.58	37.26
Owners and investors	42.70	5.67	7.79	23.37	5.87
White directors, management and employees	31.40	4.91	3.88	15.79	6.82
UK government	2.51	0.88	0.02	1.44	0.17
UK leaseholders	0.62	0.07	0.20	0.27	0.11
	351.00	46.42	77.19	136.16	91.35
African participants					
S.L. government	39.87	0.96	12.21	25.67	1.08
Black labor: manual	26.84	7.61	5.06	8.14	6.01
Salaries staff	6.16	-	-	1.77	4.30
Tribal authorities	0.27	0.09	0.04	0.07	0.07
	73.14	8.66	17.31	35.65	11.46

analysis. The period covered by each income statement in Table 3.4 represents a particular institutional regime (early colonial, late colonial and post-colonial). Each regime had its own unique configuration of social and political institutions.

From the early colonial to the late colonial period, we see the percentage share of proceeds collected by the British constituents gently declined (from 84 to 79%) and this decline is accompanied by increasing allocations (mainly through taxation) to the Colonial state whose share of the proceeds reaches a peak in the beginning of the post-colonial period (from 1.7 to 14.9%). These figures together with other records of the period, indicate that with the passage from early to late colonial conditions, the British colonial system that made mineral extraction possible in the form of military, ideological and other support was gradually devolved to a growing and an increasingly bureaucratic group in Freetown. The important thing to note is that the basic relations of production characteristic of capital enterprises, i.e. the relationships between the factors of production: capital versus land and labor, remain unaltered. For instance, the returns to the tribal authorities (representing the original owners of the land) and to black wage labor remain perfectly stagnant throughout the entire period. None of the new and swelling government revenues directly or indirectly ever benefited the native workers, people and local authorities in the iron-producing province. However, they did serve to secure the continued co-operation of the state.

In its general outline, this situation prevailed throughout the post-colonial period except for one important additional variable which progressively frustrated the financial position of the company. This concerns the appearance and the rise of a new participant, namely a contingent of black-salaried staff. In response to pressures for indigenization after independence, Delco began to recruit black managerial, clerical and technical supervisory staff, most of whom were not 'productive' in the usual sense. The agreements of 1967 and 1972 formulated this indigenization programme in increasingly stringent terms. By the time of its closure, Delco employed some 218 supervisory salaried staff of whom 164 were Sierra Leoneans earning an average annual salary of £3041. In 1974, this black-salaried contingent received a total income of £422,320, not much below the total wage bill £513,215 of black manual labor numbering 2317. We should interpret the bonanza in black-salaried staff as an attempt by the company to retain the approval and support of influential groups in Sierra Leone. By the mid-1970s, the expanding indigenous pressure coupled with the prospect of diminishing returns from the mine induced the Company to leave. In doing so, it was simply following a strategy for survival in a market context.

We have seen how the 46 year history of Delco's operations in Sierra Leone can be classified into a series of institutional regimes, each with its own income statement. Each regime consists of a configuration of socio-political forces that determine the distribution of the revenue shown in the income statement. Each regime is a development from the previous one in the sense that it is an outgrowth from, and response to, the contradictions and instabilities of the previous era. The final collapse of Delco took place in a new episode in this sequence of institution regimes.

Implications

While accountants are becoming more rigorous in their understanding of the economic realm, a commensurate degree of rigor also is required concerning the political and social realms. Some may find this suggestion rather alien. All too often political and social problems are relegated to common sense status, not deserving systematic scientific investigation. However, political and social conditions predicate any economic analysis, thus the accounting results are only as good as their political and social precepts.

In order to understand the processes of price formation and income distribution within advanced industrial societies, one needs to take into account the second dimension of 'capital', i.e. the state of social relations. Thus, trade unionism, institutionalization of welfare demands and other supply conditions — the 'sociological datum' to which Maurice Dobb refers — need to be reflected in any model for explaining price formation and income distribution. Institutional and social forces are often treated as market 'imperfections' or aberrations. It is the contention here that in the analysis of multinational and monopoly business (conditions of imperfect competition) these 'aberrations' must become central to the analysis.

We have seen from the Delco case how coercive and ideological social forces were taken on different guises in different periods of history. This is not a tale of wealth generation and the 'justice' of marginal productivity measures in net present values and accounting rates of return, but the story of a system that was so unstable that it failed to meet even the minimum viability test: it did not offer weaker parties (i.e. black employees) enough returns to enable them to reproduce an economic role in the longer term.

One important lesson from the Delco case concerns the belief that we may entrust to the free play of market forces the task of working out socio-economic problems. The Cambridge Controversies demonstrate this belief to be fallacious: markets are not 'free' but structured and we have to discern the structure if we are to explain the distribution of income (including the magnitude of profit). With examples from early colonialism, it is relatively easy to agree on the importance of the military (rather than marginal productivity) factors in determining the profit–wage ratio. Similarly, we have little difficulty detecting other such socio-political forces in societies 'unlike' our own. What needs to be done in political economy is to construct a theory for explaining income distribution and market conditions in our industrial societies.

References

Ferguson, E.E. (1969). *The neo-classical theory of production and distribution.* Oxford: Cambridge University Press.
Fisher, L. (1930). *Theory of interest.* London: Macmillan.

Hicks, J.R. (1946). *Value and capital* (2nd Edition). London: Oxford University Press.

Hirshleifer, J. (1971). *Investment, interest and capital.* Englewood Cliffs, NJ: Prentice-Hall.

Keynes, J.M. (1936). *The general theory of employment, interest and money.* London: Macmillan.

Samuelson, P.A. (1966). 'Summing up' in paradoxes in capital theory: A Symposium. *Quarterly Journal of Economics,* 568–583.

Chapter 4

The Value of Corporate Accounting Reports: Arguments for a Political Economy of Accounting[1]

David J. Cooper,   *University of Alberta*
Michael J. Sherer,   *University of Essex*

Traditional Approaches to Valuing Accounting Reports

Existing research on the choice of accounting methods for corporate reports emphasizes private interests. In particular, shareholders' interests predominate in studies of the effects of accounting information on individual users. Attempts at assessing the social value of accounting reports, using the approach of marginal economics to information or the analysis of economic consequences also exhibit, in their execution, a pronounced shareholder orientation. This paper suggests that an alternative approach, the Political Economy of Accounting, may be fruitful. This approach seeks to understand and evaluate the functions of accounting within the context of the economic, social and political environment in which it operates. Research within this framework is identified as having normative, descriptive and critical qualities.

Our position, that the objectives of and for accounting are fundamentally contested, arises out of the recognition that any accounting contains a representation of a specific social and political context. Not only is accounting policy essentially political in that it derives from the political struggle in society as a whole, but also the outcomes of accounting policy are essentially political in that they operate for the benefit of some groups in society and to the detriment of others.

An alternative framework for analysing the role of accounting information, designated as a political economy of accounting, is presented hereafter. A political economy of accounting emphasizes the infrastructure, the fundamental relations between classes in society. It recognizes the institutional environment which supports the existing system of corporate reporting and subjects to

[1]Reprinted (in an abridged form) from D.J. Cooper and M.J. Sherer, 'The Value of Corporate Accounting Reports: Arguments for a Political Economy of Accounting', *Accounting, Organizations and Society*, 1984, vol. 9, no. 3/4, pp. 207–232, with the permission of Elsevier.

Accounting, the Social and the Political
N. Macintosh and T. Hopper (Editors)

critical scrutiny those issues (such as the assumed importance of shareholders and securities markets) that are frequently taken for granted in current accounting research.

Corporate Reports in Capital Allocation

Accounting theory has long been concerned with the interests of individual private shareholders. Whilst many theories have concentrated on aiding shareholders in decisions concerning their income, wealth and even utility, the prescriptions derived from this research include calls for accounting reports to be simplified, accounting policy makers to concentrate on the needs of naïve investors, and the need for education of individual shareholders in accounting and financial matters. A potential consequence of these prescriptions would be to redistribute wealth from one group of 'knowledgeable' shareholders to another group of 'naïve' shareholders. Indeed, it is an implicit value judgement of this type of research that such a redistribution is a beneficial consequence in itself. In effect, shareholders are depicted as individuals operating within an environmental vacuum and this allows the design of corporate accounting reports to be considered as if it were only of private interest.

But the omission of any consideration for the immediate environment, the capital market, in which the shareholder class operates, ignores wider effects which may ensue from such prescriptions. Research into shareholder usage and understanding cannot by itself assess whether the above re-distribution would lead to a more appropriate allocation of resources within the capital market, let alone to a higher level of welfare for all members of society. Understanding individual responses may be of interest in contributing to a general understanding of accounting (elaborating users and their settings), but it is unlikely that individual behaviour translates to aggregate market responses.

Consideration also needs to be given to the important but frequently neglected question of equity, intra and inter, and all the mechanisms for allocating capital in the economy. Capital is allocated by several markets, including the property and labour markets (for human capital) as well as by a number of organizations (e.g. banks) and public institutions, such as nationalized and regulated companies, and national and local governments.

Within this wider set of allocation mechanisms, the choice of an accounting measurement system becomes much more complex. These mechanisms are directly affected by the accounting information produced by listed corporations. Many allocators of capital resources other than the stock market also have an interest in the choice of accounting measures and disclosures. Although in the future it may be shown that what is 'good' for the stock market is also 'good' for these other allocators of capital and hence the economy as a whole, it is a question that is rarely addressed in the accounting literature.

Corporate Reports in a Contracting Context

One of the more recent developments in theories of corporate reporting has been a shift from an emphasis on the use of accounting in predicting variables 'of interest' to a concern with the use of accounting in contractual relationships between corporate stakeholders.

There seem to be at least two problems with this approach. Firstly, it tends to elevate markets to the status of an immutable and ideal benchmark. That is, markets are treated as the standard by which other institutional arrangements are to be judged. Market failures, such as information asymmetry and non-excludability may be recognized but by assuming the perfect adaptability and omniscience of market participants, other institutional possibilities are dismissed. There is no recognition of the social, contrived nature of markets or of their historical specificity. Consequently, this approach almost invariably reinforces the existing market system or recommends reduction in intervention in market operations so that the market can operate according to its own logic. In short, the emphasis on market efficiency which is inherent in this approach relies on the belief (derived from marginal welfare economics), that market efficiency is a necessary condition for social welfare improvements. The problem with this belief is that it is based on extremely dubious assumptions and an untenable instrumentalist philosophical position.

The problem with the contracting approach is common to all traditional approaches based on marginalist economics. A concern with 'users' of corporate accounts (for decision making involving prediction or for stewardship) may be able to address issues of private value but does not seem able to deal with the social value of these reports. By focusing on one subset of participants in society — active market agents — it ignores issues of social welfare which incorporate the well being of all members of society.

Similarly, accounting researchers might also question the normative and descriptive validity of the notion of rational choice assumed by marginal economic theory. That is to say, individuals may not only be unable to behave consistently but they may also wish not to do so. Thus, some of the seemingly innocuous assumptions about rational choice that form the basis of much of the public choice literature (including Arrow's Impossibility theorem) may be contested.

A Political Economy Approach

In the previous sections we have critically reviewed the prevailing approaches adopted in the literature for evaluating the form and content of alternative corporate accounting reports. Our criticisms have been directed towards the partial equilibrium analysis of these approaches and the bias which they exhibit in favour of the shareholder and manager classes in society. The remainder of the paper contains our arguments for an alternative approach which explicitly attempts to counter-balance this bias. In this way, we hope to encourage research which looks at how accounting functions within the broader structural and institutional environment in which it operates. To distinguish this approach from those above, we shall describe it as a Political Economy of Accounting (PEA).

The study of accounting would benefit from an approach that emphasizes institutional features and influences, a trans-disciplinary mode of investigation and the study of processes towards dynamic equilibria. Although there may be many different variants of political economy, most emphasize the inter-relationship between political and economic forces in society. In relation to an assessment of the value of corporate accounting reports, a PEA suggests that any such value is likely to be contested as it is shaped in (and shapes) both the political and economic arenas.

Features of a Political Economy Approach

The PEA we are emphasizing is characterized by three features. The study of accounting should recognize power and conflict in society, and consequently should focus on the effects of accounting reports on the distribution of income, wealth and power in society. The conventional view assumes that power is widely diffused and that society is composed of individuals whose preferences are to predominate in social choices and with no individual able to consistently influence that society (or the accounting function therein). Such a pluralist view seems to ignore a substantial volume of evidence that presents alternative views of society. One alternative view suggests that the mass of people in society are controlled by a well defined elite. A second alternative view is that there is a continuing conflict in society between essentially antagonistic classes.

By bringing power to the forefront of accounting analysis, we suggest that these alternative views of society be taken seriously by accounting researchers. Instead of assuming a basic harmony of interests in society which permits an unproblematic view of the social value of accounting reports, a political economy of accounting would treat value as essentially contested, with accounting reports operating in specific interests (e.g. of elites or classes). The way these reports might operate include mystification and legitimation. They illustrate how the distribution of income for a specific enterprise (a multinational) may be determined by the distribution of power amongst its participants rather than by any economic imperative. The classifications used in corporate accounting reports focus attention away from an account of who benefits from the enterprise. More generally, accounting theories themselves are a product of the society in which they operate and cannot be regarded, except in the most trivial sense, as neutral: they serve specific interests.

A second feature of the PEA is the specific historical and institutional environment of the society in which it operates. Most accounting research treats the economy as if it were made up of price taking units with constant returns to scale, instantaneously moving from one equilibrium to another equilibrium on the Paretian frontier. There is little recognition that the economy is dominated by large corporations, often operating in oligopolistic or monopolistic markets. Disequilibrium is a standard feature of the economy. And the state, far from being the passive actor for social welfare, is actively involved in managing the economy. The role of the state is central to an understanding of accounting policy, for the latter is strongly interrelated with at least one obvious element of state activity, namely taxation. With the increasingly apparent 'fiscal crisis' where governments cannot fund their desired level of spending, the contradictory position of the state in acting on behalf of large firms and commercial interests whilst at the same time attempting to preserve social harmony and its own legitimacy, has become increasingly apparent.

The third element of a PEA of accounting involves the adoption of a more emancipated view of human motivation and the role of accounting in society; that is, a view that acknowledges the potential of people (and accounting) to change and reflect differing interests and concerns. It has been a tenet of conventional economics and accounting that the factors that shape human preferences and motivations cannot be investigated. Consequently, it has not seemed possible (or desirable) to distinguish the cause and nature of 'genuine' needs and those which result from demonstration, ostentation, advertising and other learnt factors. To the extent that people are concerned solely with economic self-interest, this self-interest may be seen as a consequence of the way society is organized rather than an unalterable characteristic of people. A concern for a more emancipated view of human motivation would recognize the possibility, for example, that accounting practices may contribute to alienation at work and to the pursuit of private interest. For instance, ignoring externalities (social costs) when 'accounting' for corporate activities may encourage self-interest at the expense of social interests.

Contrary to an emancipated conception of the role of accounting in society, accounting practice is frequently viewed as a passive function which responds to, rather than changes, the environment in which it operates. In the same way as the medical profession may have a legitimate concern with housing, social conditions and public health (e.g. the quality of sewerage and water supplies) in order to carry out a role of say, improving the health of the community, so the accounting profession may have legitimate concerns in relation to its immediate environment (e.g. the commercial and financial sectors of the economy). Attempts to resolve technical issues without consideration of this environment may result in an imperfect and incomplete resolution due to the acceptance of current institutions and practices. One of the strengths of the Corporate Reports (ASSC 1975) was that it saw the need to change legal definitions of accountability if accounting reports are to have value in improving stewardship and thereby social welfare.

Imperatives of a Political Economy Approach

The characteristics of a PEA approach may be encapsulated in three imperatives.

Be Explicitly Normative Accounting researchers should be explicit about the normative elements of any framework adopted by them. All research is normative in the sense that it contains the researcher's value judgements about how society should be organized.

The suggestion that accounting researchers should be explicit about the normative elements of their research is intended to facilitate coherence in accounting research and to encourage researchers to identify the purposes of their activities. Our suggestion for making such values explicit would serve two broad purposes. Firstly, it would aid the identification and evaluation of individual pieces of research within the context of a particular paradigm or research programme. Secondly, it would facilitate an evaluation of different paradigms and would encourage recognition that political and value choices are inherent in choices about accounting.

Be Descriptive   Accounting is essentially practical, it is executed by and it influences the behaviour of individuals and classes inside and outside organizations. To understand the practice of accounting, or accounting in action, we suggest more attention be given to descriptive studies in accounting research. Such studies would attempt to describe and interpret the behaviour of accounting and accountants in the context of the institutions, social and political structures and cultural values of the society in which they are historically located.

Be Critical   The final exhortation concerns the attitude of the researcher, him or herself. In order to develop and evaluate alternative paradigms and methodologies, the researcher needs to exhibit critical awareness, not only of the extant research but also of the relationship between the supply of accounting research and the demand for it by various interests, including the profession, managers and the funding institutions.

The criterion of critical awareness goes beyond conventional notions of researcher independence; it requires that the researcher considers the kinds of accounting which may be worthwhile outside the context of the existing environment as well as the process which led to and may lead from that context.

Whether critical theory can in practice be applied to accounting research depends on whether researchers can free themselves from the attitudes and orientations which result from their social and educational training and which are reinforced by the beliefs of the accounting profession and the business community. Socialization processes have produced accounting researchers who may exhibit subconscious bias in the definition of the problem set of accounting and the choice of theories to analyse and solve these problems. The criterion of critical awareness involves recognizing the contested nature of the problem set and theories and demystifying the ideological character of those theories.

The exhortation to be critical, then, goes beyond the concerns for independence in the face of increasing professional pressures for 'relevant and useful' accounting research. It also goes beyond concerns to critically assess the claims by corporate managers that changes in accounting reports will have undesirable consequences on the corporate sector and the public interest. It involves a recognition of the contested nature of the accounting problematic and indeed the concept of what is or is not in the public interest.

Suggestions for Research Within a PEA Framework

A Political Economy of Accounting (PEA) is thus a normative, descriptive and critical approach to accounting research. It provides a broader, more holistic, framework for analysing and understanding the value of accounting reports within society as a whole.

Accounting and Social Welfare

Accounting research increasingly argues that all accounting policy decisions, including the choice of the appropriate accounting measurement system, must be made by reference to the contribution each alternative makes to overall social welfare. Aggregate social value might include factors such as national income, literacy, distribution of wealth, morbidity, employment and artistic creativity. Note, however, we are not advocating conventional social accounting or cost benefit analysis where incommensurate dimensions are compressed into the single dimension of money and valued in relation to market prices.

Accounting as Ideology

In situations where there is a conflict about the objectives of social activity, accounting information has an ideological function in that it is used to legitimize particular activities or rationalize past behaviour. Research into this ideological role may take the form of investigating which interests in the economy are bolstered and which interests are undermined by the accounting measurement system currently used in corporate reports.

A PEA approach — by emphasizing the institutional features of society and adopting a conflict model of society — provides a framework for studies which attempt to uncover the influence that narrow sectional interests have in defining accounting problems and indeed the choice of feasible ways of resolving these problems. Thus, the problems in accounting for multinational companies are conventionally interpreted in terms of the problems for the multinationals — in relation, for example, to currency translation. The problems of multinational companies might however be seen from the perspective of host countries. From a host country perspective, problems inviting solutions in which accounting may have a part to play include transfer pricing rules, pricing of technology and control of remittances to home countries. It has been suggested that the largest benefits from the international standardization of accounting practice accrue to multinational corporations and auditing firms. Similarly, the large research effort into inflation accounting in the UK in the late 1960s and early 1970s may have been influenced by factors other than the rate of inflation in the economy. There had been a significant shift in the distribution of income away from profits and dividends to wages and hence the pressure for an inflation accounting standard may be associated with a desire to re-distribute wealth 'back' towards shareholder interests.

Research into the process of identifying accounting problems might also consider how financial sponsorship encourages types of accounting research. The extent to which these funding organizations are themselves independent of the clients of accounting and indeed their understanding of the nature of the public interest deserve the attention of accounting researchers.

Conclusion

It follows that although we accept that it is desirable (within a democratic society) to encourage a variety of scientific research programmes in accounting research, this paper argues that many markets (including markets for research) are not neutral in their activities or in their effects. Therefore, it may be insufficient to rely on the market for accounting research to foster research which is significantly different in approach from the existing paradigm. Rather, in order to develop a political economy of accounting, normative, descriptive and critical research needs to be actively promoted and nurtured.

References

Accounting Standards Steering Committee. (1975). *The Corporate Report* (ICAEW).

Chapter 5

Making Sense of Research into the Organizational and Social Aspects of Management Accounting: A Review of its Underlying Assumptions[1]

Trevor Hopper, *University of Manchester*
Andrew Powell, *University of Aston (formerly)*

Introduction

A central notion behind this paper is that certain fundamental theoretical and philosophical assumptions underline *any* piece of research — there is no such thing as a totally objective or value-free investigation. Given this initial claim it is thought that the underlying assumptions behind any piece of work should be recognized and assessed by researchers to ensure that they are consistent with their personal beliefs. In other words, researchers into the management sciences should consider their own values and beliefs concerning the nature of society and the social sciences.

In order to assist people in this task, previous research into the organizational and social aspects of accounting is reviewed and grouped into various schools of thought within a basic sociological framework devised by Burrell & Morgan (1979).

Classifying Social Theories

The Burrell & Morgan framework is constructed from two independent dimensions based on assumptions regarding the nature of social science and the nature of society respectively. The social science dimension in turn consists of four distinct but related elements: assumptions about ontology, epistemology, human nature and methodology.

Ontology concerns the nature of 'reality'. On the one hand, the social world and its structures can be regarded as having an empirical, concrete existence external to,

[1]Reproduced (in abridged form) from T. Hopper and A. Powell, 'Making Sense of Research Into the Organizational and Social Aspects of Management Accounting: A Review of Its Underlying Assumptions', *Journal of Management Studies*, 1985, vol. 22, no. 5, pp. 429–465, with permission of the *Journal of Management Studies*.

independent of and prior to the cognition of any individual. At the other extreme reality is depicted as existing only as a product of individual consciousness — the external social world consists simply of concepts and labels created by people to help them understand reality and negotiate a shared conception of its nature with others.

Epistemology is concerned with the nature of knowledge — what forms it takes and how it can be obtained and transmitted. One end of a continuum assumes that knowledge can be acquired through observation and built-up piecemeal; at the other extremity, knowledge is attributed with a more subjective and essentially personal nature — the social world can be understood only by first acquiring knowledge of the subject under investigation.

Assumptions about human nature refer to the relationship between human beings and their environment. People's behaviour and experiences can be regarded as being completely determined and constrained by their external environment or, on the other hand, people can be viewed as being potentially autonomous and free-willed, and capable of creating their own environment.

The three sets of assumptions outlined above have direct methodological implications. If the social world is treated as the same as the physical or natural world, then methods from the natural sciences tend to be utilized to locate, explain and predict social regularities and patterns — statistical techniques are often used to test hypotheses and to analyse data collected by standard research instruments, such as questionnaires and surveys. Alternatively, if the subjective experiences of individuals and the creation of a social world is stressed, then methods that allow insight into an individual's inner world are emphasized – for example, participant observation and in-depth interviews.

Although analytically distinct, there are often strong relationships between the positions adopted on each continuum, and so Burrell & Morgan integrate them within an 'objective–subjective' dimension — one end emphasizing the objective nature of reality, knowledge and human behaviour, the other stressing subjective aspects.

The other major dimension defines two alternative and fundamentally different approaches to society: one is concerned with regulation, order and stability and sets out to explain why society tends to hold together; the other focuses on the fundamental divisions of interest, conflicts and unequal distributions of power that provide the potential for 'radical change'.

These two independent dimensions are combined to form four mutually exclusive frames of reference: functionalist, interpretive, radical humanist and radical structuralist (see Figure 5.1). In order to do this, Burrell & Morgan create a dichotomy between 'objective' and 'subjective' approaches, even though the dimension relating to social science assumptions was constructed as a continuum. This article regards this dimension as continuous and divides studies concerning the organizational and social aspects of accounting into three main categories — functional, interpretive and radical — two of which straddle Burrell & Morgan's mutually exclusive frames of reference. The functional literature is further divided

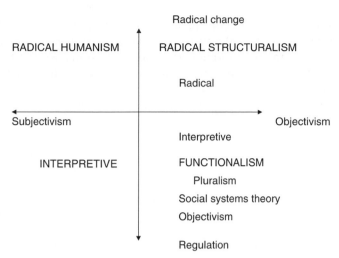

Figure 5.1: Accounting schools and sociological paradigms. (Adapted from Burrell & Morgan 1979: 29, 30)

into three sub-groups — objectivism, social systems theory and pluralism. The location within Burrell & Morgan's framework of each group is indicated in Figure 5.1.

Functional Approaches

Objectivism

Burrell & Morgan locate Classical Management Theories in the most objective region of the functional paradigm. The work espouses a scientific basis to administration, based on beliefs that the organizational world possesses the characteristics of the physical one. Thus, it is claimed, administrative principles can be derived by systematic study of cause and effect relationships. The behaviour of the employee is taken to be passive and determinable by managerial manipulation of situational variables.

Much of conventional management accounting is based on this approach. Standard costing, for example, is inextricably linked with Scientific Management. Neo-classical economics provides a basis for marginal costing and financial management and reinforces notions of control based on assumptions of economic man, and organizations with unitary goals headed by a single decision-maker.

Much of conventional accounting can be placed in the most objective and regulatory region of the functionalist paradigm. Organizations are treated as stable empirical phenomena that have, or should have, unitary goals, normally profit maximization. Human nature is taken to be calculative and instrumentally rational, but essentially passive. Thus, control accounting is depicted as stabilizing and programming behaviour by allocating to positions sub-goals derived from the organizational goals, and monitoring performance by formal feedback. Compliance is reinforced by tying performance to economic reward structures. The ontology is realist: there is assumed to be a real state of economic affairs and organizational relationships which the accounting system seeks to model.

Social Systems Theory

Probably because of the limitations of objectivism with respect to the social nature of man and how extra-organizational factors bear on control, many accounting studies have incorporated more complex models of motivation and organizational design. Much of this work is derivative of organization theory which, in the 1960s and 1970s tended to use social systems theory to view its subject. Open systems, characterized by exchanges with the environment, were particularly influential.

Accounting Dysfunctions   Several early behavioural studies of accounting systems noted that unintended and undesirable consequences often arose when conventional methods were applied. The works point to the limits of bureaucratic control and illustrate how changes may occur in social systems. Unfortunately, such considerations tended not to be appreciated or explored by many of the accounting researchers. The awareness of 'behavioural dysfunctions' merely spurred on their endeavours to refine measurements to rectify such aberrations.

Psychological Theories Dysfunctional consequences can also occur through messages being misinterpreted or interpreted differently. A growing number of accounting researchers have examined the effect of alternative accounting techniques on management decisions by studying the information processing of individuals. Much of this work is now subsumed under the title of Human Information Processing approaches to accounting.

The essential thrust of the work is to determine what factors affect the quality of individual decision making. Output variables include the speed, quality and reliability of judgements, and perceptions of their quality and of the information given.

The work adopts a functional frame of reference, for although people are viewed as imperfect information processors, the processing is assumed to be systematic and capable of revelation by scientific study. Decision making is depicted deterministically as an interaction between objective characteristics of the information set and innate characteristics of the subjects. Ontologically, the world is taken to be prior to individual cognition, the problem is their imperfection in perceiving it. The options for improving accounting decisions lie in either changing the way information is presented, or educating the decision maker in better methods of processing information, or replacing him or her with a model.

Social Psychological Theories   Social psychological approaches to management accounting are essentially complementary to human information processing ones. Both seek to reduce dysfunctional consequences of accounting systems by improving their design. Social psychologists however concentrate on motivation rather than information processing. Typically their research takes a defined budgetary variable like participation and relates it to social psychological factors, such as interpersonal relationships between peers and supervisors. The assumption, which is questionable, is that greater morale or job satisfaction increases output.

Whilst social psychologists recognize that human desires may conflict with those of the organization or other parties to it, in its advocacy of participative methods, it tends to assume that these are reconcilable. Little account is taken of possible inequalities of power between parties to the participative process, or of the fact that in some instances goal differences may be irreconcilable. Thus, the approach is often criticized for a pro-managerial and manipulative bias.

Structural Theories   Neither psychological nor social psychological theories have paid much attention to how structures of organizations might affect the processes under scrutiny. The classic study of comptrollers' departments by Simon *et al.* (1954), focused on organizational issues such as the roles of accountants, and their relationship to structure, training and socialization. Despite the wide citation of this work little investigation of structure ensued in accounting.

The design of accounting control systems is central to Chandler's (1966) thesis on the strategy and structure of industrial enterprises. The work has much of value. Through historical analysis it illustrates how new forms of accounting controls, such as responsibility accounting and capital based measures like R.O.I., were related to developments in capitalism, especially the emergence of large corporations and changes in their management controls. When corporate developments and associated accounting changes are crudely portrayed as inevitable coping responses to new technology, the work is very functional, in that it emphasizes how individuals and organizations are constrained by an external world.

Open Systems Theories   Much of the work discussed so far has adopted a 'closed systems' approach, seeing control as achievable by regulating internal organizational variables, be they psychological, social psychological or structural. An 'open systems' approach on the other hand regards organizations as organisms that process inputs from the environment back as outputs. Its ecological orientation stresses the interdependence between the organization, its internal sub-systems and the environment. Open systems provides a means of viewing and describing subjects of study. An attraction of open systems is its ability to relate different resolution levels of analysis and various disciplines.

Typically, open systems accounting work does not confine itself to economic flows, but extends to political, social and technological ones. Central to this scheme are cybernetic notions of requisite variety, black boxing, modelling and resolution levels. Cybernetics as an epistemology stresses learning and evolution by the avoidance of undesirable end states. In an accounting context, it is significant that the technique, oriented cybernetic applications have tended to have difficulties in incorporating behavioural aspects of the problem. Hedberg & Jönsson (1978) and Hertog (1978) are examples of accounting studies in the epistemological tradition of cybernetics: both examine how accounting systems might be designed to provoke and facilitate organizational learning and, hence, shift actions to less environmentally threatening states. Both criticize accounting systems for being traditionally oriented towards stabilizing organizations rather than provoking change and adaptation.

Whilst a biological analogy of organizations is not inevitable when open systems is used, accounting theorists in this school often assume so, with several consequences. First, organizations and environments tend to be taken as objective, even though experience in defining boundaries and key variables suggest they are subjective creations by the modeller. Secondly, when control systems are described as determined by the variety in the environmental and organizational needs for survival, there is a strong assumption of 'functional imperatives' which can deflect attention from the choices key decision makers make regarding which environments are operated in, and what controls are employed. Thirdly, by stressing the need for integration for the survival of the whole, there is a presumption of a 'functional unity' to organizations, which may divert attention from issues of power and conflict. Consequently, there can be a thin dividing line between when open systems and cybernetics is a method of analysis and when it becomes an ideology for cooperation towards the *status quo*.

Contingency Theories   What is now commonly termed 'contingency theory' seeks to provide a reconciliation and synthesis of the conclusions emerging from a variety of organizational studies. The work of industrial psychologists and the human relations school is combined with open systems theory and that which empirically measures structural characteristics of organizations. Its principal thesis is that different organizational principles are appropriate under different environmental circumstances, and within different parts of the organization. Effective operation of enterprises is seen as dependent upon there being a suitable match between its internal organization (including structures, styles of leadership and decision making), and the nature of the demands placed upon it by its tasks, size, environment and members' wants. Many researchers into management accounting have consciously adopted and encouraged this approach, probably to explain otherwise contradictory observations.

The assumptions behind contingency theory are similar to those underlying an open systems approach – the key relationship between an organization and its environment can be understood in terms of the organization's need to survive, and the fact that there are certain functional imperatives for the various sub-systems. Although the processual nature of organizations is emphasized, much of the research cited has tended to use questionnaires to take snapshots of temporary structural manifestations followed by detailed statistical analysis, rather than observing the processes first hand over time.

Contingency theory has been criticized for paying insufficient attention to the discretion possessed by key decision makers and how values, beliefs and ideologies may influence choices. Contingency theory tends to portray management in a technical role, matching organizational design to the dictates of contingent factors. By emphasizing technological determinism and neglecting how control systems may be a product of social cultures, ideologies and power struggles, attention is deflected from alternatives based on different values.

The social systems and objectivist approaches both stress regulation to achieve order and equilibrium within a unitary and essentially managerial approach to organizational effectiveness. Consequently, they are located towards regulation in the classificatory framework of Figure 5.1. For traditional management accounting within the objectivist approach this may now be widely accepted. It assumes that profit maximization increases the welfare of the participants and society, and that the task of the accounting control system is to programme and monitor behaviour towards such ends.

Systems theorists have tended to take survival as the criteria for organizational effectiveness. However, large organizations tend to have low mortality rates, therefore surrogate measures of factors believed to lead to survival are often taken, such as whether constituent systems have sufficient inducements to prevent the system from breaking down, or whether there are sufficient integrative mechanisms. But by emphasizing the necessity for harmonious and lasting integration of parts to maintain the functional whole, systems theory can lend itself to a pro-managerial definition of problems as explained earlier.

Neither of the above unitary approaches significantly addresses issues of power and conflict. Whilst they may claim to be objective and value free, by failing to examine alternative perspectives, they may in fact be merely reproducing dominant ideologies and reinforcing them by prescribing accounting systems designed upon such lines.

Pluralism

Industrial relations is an area where issues of power, conflict and sectional interests are more overt and where presumptions of unitary organizational goals have been seen as inappropriate. Some writers have advocated pluralism as a more realistic approach to organizational control. Here, organizations are taken to be comprised of sectional groups with divergent and often mutually inconsistent goals. Common purpose exists only insofar as groups are interdependent. Control is achieved by maintaining a network of rules and regulations that permit bargaining between the groups. The aim being to contain rather than eliminate conflict by negotiating courses of action which permit each group maximum freedom consistent with the binding constraints laid down by other groups.

Thus, organizations are seen as loose coalitions; often decisions are taken sequentially to allow different criteria and hence different sectional ends to be met; formal organizational goals may represent little more than the means of securing external legitimacy. A major variable determining outcomes is the relative power of groups, and the concern of researchers is to explain and predict such outcomes rather than prescribe them. Despite not being extensively tapped by accounting researchers, pluralism is potentially a source of fresh ideas and insights into management accounting and it introduces many of the themes that are examined in the subsequent alternative approaches.

First, pluralistic studies shed light on the issue of how accounts and accounting rules are initially created. Rather than assuming that they are the product of objectively rational procedures based on a value free and neutral perspective, as does much of the previous work discussed, pluralism suggests they arrive from sectional interests and are then mediated through political processes.

Accounts may derive from sectional interests and be modified by bargaining and negotiated consensus, but they are also integral to the relative strengths of the parties to such processes, being an important power resource, namely information. The suggestion of pluralism is that managers use, seek and develop accounting to bolster a perspective, i.e. as an 'ammunition machine' rather than treating it as providing answers through a single calculus (Burchell *et al.* 1980). If so, then budgetary control may principally be a means of instituting and promoting bargaining whereby participants can stake out claims, discover alternative claims and meanings to organizational events, enrich their understanding of the organization and secure a degree of consensus. Facilitating such processes by designing accounting systems that permit the creation of several perspectives, and which encourage learning through dialogue and dialectics may be preferable to refining systems that, as is often the case, purport to give a single version of the truth (Ibid.).

Pluralist notions applied to accounting are not limited to bargaining between managerial interests, but can and have been extended to industrial relations and financial reporting. The Corporate Report (Accounting Standards Committee 1975) in its advocacy of financial reporting for a disparate range of sectional interests, sometimes conflicting, has overtones of pluralist ideas.

Lastly, the scepticism of pluralism towards official statements offers insight into the status and significance of accounting data emanating from meetings. Burchell *et al.* (1980) note that accounting data often emerged from political processes and decisions rather than preceding them. The suggestion is, as several writers have argued, that accounting serves to reassure decision makers and to legitimize their actions, rather than reflecting an underlying reality. Gambling (1977) saw accounting as a political process and compared it with witchcraft, in that both provided the 'machinery to accommodate awkward facts in a way which does not undermine fundamental beliefs of the culture' and which does not expose the gaps in that culture's knowledge.

Such ideas overlap and, indeed, often draw from, interpretive ideas on socially created realities. Also, recent pluralistic work often uses interpretive methods. However, pluralism tends to presume purposeful and self-interested behaviour arising from a realist ontology. Bargaining arises due to different, but reconcilable, objective interests rather than individuals seeking to create meaning through social interaction. Whilst socially created accounting is recognized, it tends to be seen as a deliberately manipulative act to seek external legitimation and to mask underlying realities. Thus, much of pluralism is underpinned by a realist ontology. Its ability to absorb within its approach, interpretive ideas and methods, has led the writers to classify it in Figure 5.1 as less objective than the functional approaches discussed previously.

The essential difference between pluralism and other approaches examined so far is its focus on interests, conflict and power. Whilst pluralism is perhaps less committed to normative design than earlier approaches, and more interested in observing and understanding accounting in action, it is unable or unwilling to pass judgement on the relative powers of parties to negotiations or the ends each pursues. As such, pluralism is part of the sociology of regulation within a broad framework of preserving the *status quo*.

Interpretive Theories

An interpretive approach emphasizes the essentially subjective nature of the social world and attempts to understand it primarily from the frame of reference of those being studied; as Laing (1967: 53) pointed out, 'persons are distinguished from things in that persons experience the world whereas things behave in the world'. The focus is on individual meaning and people's perceptions of 'reality' rather than any independent 'reality' that might exist external to them.

If reality is seen solely in terms of individual consciousness (leading in the extreme case to solipsism and the denial that external objects of any sort have an independent reality), the problem becomes one of explaining the common sense belief of a real social world without reifying social phenomena. This hurdle is overcome by acknowledging that although our realization of the world is unique, it is also at least to some extent an experience shared by others. It is suggested that understanding of the conduct of others is obtained through a process of interpretation. People constantly create their social reality in interaction with others. It is the aim of an interpretive approach to analyse such social realities and the ways in which they are socially constructed and negotiated.

The idea is that by using interpretive research methods, to study how accounting meanings are socially generated and sustained, a better understanding of accounting will be obtained. In addition, by permitting research questions to emerge from the research process, rather than being predetermined at its outset, it is hoped that they will be more pertinent to the problems of the subjects.

Interpretive work stresses the constant uncertainty confronting individuals seeking to make sense of the world they inhabit. Through language, they negotiate an understanding shared by others. Thus, it may be that accounting may be regarded as a 'common language' for the discussion and resolution of contentious issues. If so, it might be argued that accounting system designers may have to pay greater attention to the subjective models of clients and the processes whereby they are created.

Boland (1982) utilizes such ideas in an accounting context, arguing that accounting is a ceremony or ritual played out to reinforce the myth that large organizations are subject to external checks upon their societal effectiveness. Such behaviour is seen as a consequence of the accounting profession trying to reconcile conflicting ideological pressures placed upon it. However, the myths spawned and the associated technology have produced a bias against reform. The work is interesting in underlining the social creation of accounting, and how meanings attached to it help maintain the *status quo*, but questions about which ideological pressures are most significant, and whose purposes are served by such myth creation and stabilization are left unexplored. The work of the following radical theorists is critical in that it extends the accounting problematic to such issues.

Radical Theories

In contrast to functional and interpretive approaches, radical theorists view society as being composed of contradictory elements and pervaded by systems of power that lead to inequalities and alienation in all aspects of life; they are concerned with developing an understanding of the social and economic world that also forms a critique of the *status quo*. Moreover, by accepting the dominant ideology and by not questioning the fundamental nature of capitalism, functional and interpretive theorists are seen as helping sustain and legitimize the current social, economic and political order; thus traditional accounting theory is regarded as adopting a managerial frame of reference and as supporting the *status quo*. A theme central to all radical theories is that the nature and organizing principle of a society as a whole is both reflected in and shaped by every aspect of that society. Consequently, no single part of a capitalist society can be fully understood without comprehending capitalism in its entirety.

Burrell & Morgan divide theories of radical change into two sections (radical structuralism and radical humanism). The former focuses on the fundamental conflicts that are both a product of, and reflected in, industrial structures and economic relationships, e.g. surplus value, class relationships, structures of control, whilst the latter emphasizes individual consciousness, alienation through reification, and the way this is dominated by ideological influence, not least through language. The difference between the two approaches is akin to that between the functional and interpretive approaches. In other words, radical structuralism treats the social world as being composed of external objects and relationships independent of any particular person, while radical humanism emphasizes individual perceptions and interpretations. The mutually exclusive division of radical theories by Burrell & Morgan carries the danger that concerns of radical structural analysis are seen as incompatible or irreconcilable with those stressing consciousness, rather than seeing both as dialectical aspects of the same reality. Consequently, the subjective–objective dimension in Figure 5.1 is to be regarded as continuous.

Despite the burgeoning of new-Marxist economic and organizational analysis in the last decade, which often imposes directly on accounting issues, it has received little attention in the accounting literature. Central to Marx's attempts to understand capitalism is his theory of value and the relationships between value, abstract labour and money. Several recent writers, particularly radical economists, have sought to reconsider his conceptions and relate them to modern forms of capitalist calculation. In other words, attempts are being made to link the principles of modern accounting to Marxist work on the fundamental mechanisms of the appropriation of surplus value — the process by which some would suggest that capitalism lays the seeds of its own destruction.

An appreciation of how accounting is related to broader social processes and structures can be derived from studies of the occupation of accountancy and its professional organization. Johnson (1980) has argued that work processes organized as accountancy were not conceived of having some functional significance for society generally, but rather they were viewed as functioning in relation to a specific and determining historical process: the appropriation of surplus value and the accumulation and concentration of capital. Such work reflects developments in an influential critical perspective of professions, which rather than seeing them in terms of an altruistic model stressing specialized skills, knowledge and self regulation through common values and ethics, instead exposes professional autonomy and to sustain monopolies of knowledge which have common roots with the dominant ideology of capitalist society. Thus, professional self regulation and the consequent mystification of knowledge is perceived as being inherently and fundamentally harnessed to the unequal distribution of political power and authority in a class divided society.

Braverman (1974: 302) similarly links accounting to the appropriation of surplus value and class relationships noting that, 'as capitalism becomes more complex and develops into its monopoly stage, the accounting of value becomes more complex'. His historical analysis of the detailed division of labour, Scientific Management and hierarchical centralized organization explicates them as devices for strengthening capitalist control over the means of production through lessening the power of craft labour, rather than as responses to competitive pressures, or adjustments stemming from new technologies. Accounting may be seen as integral to the control of labour processes and constituting a labour process in itself. With regard to the latter, detailed investigation of the labour process within accountancy may be a fruitful area of study.

Burrell & Morgan (1979: 381) depict the central theme of Braverman's work as thus:

> The complexity of the division of labour under capitalism is regarded as requiring an immense amount of social control which lies beyond the capabilities of the public functions of the total society. The internal planning of such corporations becomes in effect, social planning to fill the large gaps in social control left by the state.

Braverman's work is deterministic and objective and thus shares many of the methodological problems of functionalism. Particularly important is the lack of regard paid to individual consciousness: subjection to inequities and degradation does not automatically lead to an understanding of causation and actions to prevent them. As the interpretive writers argue, consciousness is socially created. Many radical theorists would agree, but would add that it is distorted and biased towards the goals of dominant groups, particularly through language. In addition, processes of reification mystify individual under-standing of the world and allow man to be dominated by creations of his own consciousness.

The tension between accounting being presented as objective facts and its socially created sources has been noted in earlier sections. Some accounting studies, picking up such contradictions, have viewed accounting as an ideological phenomenon that serves to mystify social relationships and reinforce unequal power distributions. For example, Merino & Neimark (1982), through such a perspective, challenge the conventional rationale that the disclosure provisions of the 1933 and 1934 United States Securities Acts were an attempt to improve information to investors; instead they argue that the legislation was intended as propaganda to respond to popular criticism of market competition and security market manipulations.

The theme of such studies is that accounting measures alienate through subordinating behaviour to perceived imperatives which are in fact socially created, are malleable and serve specific interests integral to the creation of alienation in the first place. Laughlin (1983), recognizing this, advocates the use of the critical methods of Habermas to provide a better understanding of accounting as a language and to provoke discourses leading to enlightenment.

There is a paucity of explicit accounting research adopting a radical perspective. If it is that most accounting practitioners are mainly interested in preserving the present economic system, then the only relevance a radical approach may have for them may lie in the insights it offers to further reinforce their techniques of control. However, a vital question is whether changes in accounting practice, together with other pressures and agencies for change, can help bring about a more desirable form of society. Radical studies of accounting can assist such a debate through developing four interrelated areas.

First, an understanding of how and whether management accounting is biased towards managerial definitions and the resolution of managerial problems and, if so, how and whether it is related to the alienation of the workforce. Secondly, an awareness of how meanings attributed to accounting language and concepts are developed, and an understanding of the ideological influences on this process and its subsequent effects. Thirdly, a greater understanding of how accounting is related to societal power structures and political processes. Fourthly, an increased historical knowledge of how management accounting controls within organizations have developed in relation to the evolution of modern capitalism — taking into account social, political and economic factors. Such work might form a base for developmental work on accounting systems which are based on alternative values and are not exclusive to managerial interests.

References

Boland, Jr., R.J. (1982). Myth and technology in the American accounting profession. *Journal of Management Studies, 19*(1), 107–127.

Braverman, H. (1974). *Labor and monopoly capital.* New York: Monthly Review Press.

Burchell, S., Clubb, C., Hopwood, A.G., Hughes, J., & Nahapiet, J.C. (1980). The roles of accounting in organizations and society. *Accounting, Organizations and Society, 5*(1), 5–27.

Burrell, G. & Morgan, G. (1979). *Sociological paradigms and organisational analysis.* London: Heinemann.

Chandler, A.D. (1966). *Strategy and structure.* Boston: MIT Press.

Gambling, T. (1977). Magic, accounting and morale. *Accounting, Organizations and Society, 2*(2), 141–152.

Hedberg, B., & Jönsson, S. (1978). Designing semi-confusing information systems for organizations in changing environments. *Accounting, Organization and Society, 7*(3), 284–320.

Hertog, J.F. (1978). The role of information and control systems in the process of organizational renewal: Roadblock or roadbridge. *Accounting, Organizations and Society, 3*(1), 29–45.

Johnson, H.T. (1980). Markets, hierarchies and the history of management accounting. Paper presented to 3rd International Congress of Accounting Historians. London Business School, August 16–18.

Laing, R.D. (1967). *The politics of experience.* New York: Ballantine.

Laughlin, R.C. (1983). The need for and nature of a critical theoretic, methodological approach to the design of enterprise accounting systems. Paper presented to the Accounting Methodology Workshop, E.I.A.S.M., Brussels. December.

Merino, B.D., & Neimark, M.D. (1982). Disclosure regulation and public policy. A Sociohistorical Reappraisal. *Journal of Accounting and Public Policy, 1*(1), 33–57.

Simon, H.A., Guetzkow, H., Kozmetsky, G., & Tyndall, G. (1954). *Centralization vs decentralization in organizing the controller's department.* New York: Controllership Foundation Inc.

Chapter 6

Radical Developments in Accounting Thought[1]

Wai Fong Chua, *University of New South Wales, Australia*

This paper argues that accounting research has been guided by a dominant, not divergent, set of assumptions. There has been one general scientific world-view, one primary disciplinary matrix. And accounting researchers, as a community of scientists, have shared and continue to share a constellation of beliefs, values, and techniques. These beliefs circumscribe definitions of 'worthwhile problems' and 'acceptable scientific evidence'. To the extent that they are continually affirmed by fellow accounting researchers, they are often taken for granted and subconsciously applied.

Recent Classifications of Accounting Perspectives

To perceive commonality amidst theoretical diversity, one has to examine the philosophical (meta-theoretical) assumptions that theories share. Recently, comprehensive dimensions have been proposed. For instance, Cooper (1983) and Hopper & Powell (1985) rely on the sociological work of Burrell & Morgan (1979) and classify accounting literature according to two main sets of assumptions: those about social science and about society. Social science assumptions include assumptions about the ontology of the social world (realism vs nominalism), epistemology (positivism vs anti-positivism), human nature (determinism vs voluntarism), and methodology (nomothetic vs ideographic). The assumption about society characterizes it as either orderly or subject to fundamental conflict. These two sets of assumptions yield four paradigms — functionalist, interpretive, radical humanist, and radical structuralist. Particular accounting theories may then be classified using these four paradigms.

[1]Reproduced (in an abridged form) from Wai Fong Chua, 'Radical Developments in Accounting Thought', *The Accounting Review*, 1986, vol. LXI (October), no. 4, pp. 601–632, with permission of the American Accounting Association.

Accounting, the Social and the Political
N. Macintosh and T. Hopper (Editors)

A Classification of Assumptions

The first set of beliefs pertains to the notion of knowledge. These beliefs may be sub-divided into two related sets of epistemological and methodological assumptions. Epistemological assumptions decide what is to count as acceptable truth by specifying the criteria and process of assessing truth claims. For instance, an epistemological assumption might state that a theory is to be considered true if it is repeatedly not falsified by empirical events. Methodological assumptions indicate the research methods deemed appropriate for gathering valid evidence.

Second, there are assumptions about the 'object' of study. A variety of these exist, but the following concerns about ontology, human purpose, and societal relations have dominated much debate in the social sciences. To begin with, all empirical theories are rooted in an assumption about the very essence of the phenomena under study. Physical and social reality, for instance, may be presumed to exist in an objective plane which is external to an independent knower or scientist. Within this perspective, people may be viewed as identical to physical objects and be studied in the same manner. Alternatively, these beliefs could be criticized for reifying individuals and obscuring the role of human agency. People, it may be argued, cannot be treated as natural scientific objects because they are self-interpretive beings who create the structure around them. Yet other ontological positions which attempt to dialectically relate this reification-voluntarism debate have also been advocated. Whichever position is adopted, the issue of ontology lies prior to and governs subsequent epistemological and methodological assumptions.

Further, there are assumptions about how people relate to one another and to society as a whole. Every social theory makes assumptions about the nature of human society — is it, for example, full of conflict or essentially stable and orderly? Are there irreconcilable tensions between different classes, or are such differences always effectively contained through a pluralistic distribution of resources?

Third, assumptions are made about the relationship between knowledge and the empirical world. What is the purpose of knowledge in the world of practice? How may it be employed to better people's welfare? Is it intended to emancipate people from suppression or to provide technical answers to pre-given goals?

Mainstream Accounting Thought — Assumptions

Beliefs about Physical and Social Reality

Ontologically, mainstream accounting research is dominated by a belief in physical realism — the claim that there is a world of objective reality that exists independently of human beings and that has a determinate nature or essence that is knowable. Realism is closely allied to the distinction often made between the subject and the object. What is 'out there' (object) is presumed to be independent of the knower (subject), and knowledge is achieved when a subject correctly mirrors and 'discovers' this objective reality.

This ontological belief is reflected in accounting research as diverse as the contingency theory of management accounting. All these theories are put forward as attempts to discover a knowable, objective reality. This inference is based on the absence of any expressed doubt that the empirical phenomena that are observed or 'discovered' could be a function of the researchers, their *a priori* assumptions, and their location in a specific, socio-historical context. Thus, a stock market return is discussed as an objective fact that may be classified as normal or abnormal. Similarly, 'competitive' environments, 'sophisticated' management accounting techniques, 'shirking', 'adverse selection', and 'response to feedback' are characterized as representations of an objective, external reality.

Beliefs about Knowledge

This prior assumption leads to a distinction between observations and the theoretical constructs used to represent their empirical reality. There is a world of observation that is separate from that of theory, and the former may be used to attest to the scientific validity of the latter. In philosophy, this belief in empirical testability has been expressed in two main ways: (a) in the positivist's belief that there exists a theory-independent set of observation statements that could be used to confirm or verify the truth of a theory, and (b) in the Popperian argument that because observation statements are theory-dependent and fallible, scientific theories cannot be proved but may be falsified.

Accounting researchers believe in the empirical testability of scientific theories. Unfortunately, they draw on both notions of confirmation and falsifiability with considerable unawareness of the criticisms of both criteria and of the differences between the two.

But, as Christenson (1983) shows, the philosophical position of the proponents of positive accounting is muddled at best — conforming neither to Friedman's instrumentalism nor to Popper's falsification criterion but apparently appealing to the discredited position of the early logical positivists.

This hypothetico-deductive account of scientific explanation has two main consequences. First, it leads to the search for universal laws or principles from which lower-level hypotheses may be deduced. To explain an event is to present it as an instance of a universal law. Second, there is a tight linkage between explanation, prediction, and technical control. If an event is explained only when its occurrence can be deduced from certain premises, it follows that knowing the premises before the event happened would enable a prediction that it would happen. It would also enable steps to be taken to *control* the occurrence of the event. Indeed, the possibility of control and manipulation is a constitutive element of this image of scientific explanation.

Beliefs about the Social World

Mainstream accounting research also makes two important assumptions about the social world. First, it is assumed that human behavior is purposive. Thus, although people may possess only bounded rationality; they are always capable of rational goal-setting, whereby goals are set prior to the choice and implementation of strategic action. Also, human beings are characterized as possessing a single super-ordinate goal: 'utility-maximization'. Within this abstract notion of utility, theories differ as to what may provide utility. Principal-agent theory assumes that an agent will always prefer less work to more, while finance theory assumes that a shareholder/bondholder will desire the maximization of the expected, risk-adjusted return from an investment.

Moreover, although only individuals have goals, collectivities may exhibit purposive behavior that implies consensual goals or common means which are accepted by all members — for example, the maximization of discounted cash flows or the minimization of transaction costs. These assumptions about purposive behavior are necessary because accounting information has long been ascribed a technical rationale for its existence and prosperity: the provision of 'useful' and 'relevant' financial information for the making of economic decisions. And, usefulness presumes some prior need or objective.

Second, given a belief in individual and organizational purpose, there is an implicit assumption of a controllable social order. While conflicts of objectives, for instance, between principals and agents and between functional departments are recognized, they are conceptualized as manageable. Indeed, it is the effective manager's duty to remove or avoid such conflict through the appropriate design of accounting controls, such as budgets, cost standards, cost allocations and divisional performance criteria. Organizational conflict is not seen as reflective of deeper social conflict between classes of people with unequal access to social and economic resources. Constructs such as sustained domination, exploitation, and structural contradictions do not appear in mainstream accounting literature. And conflicting interest groups are classified as possessing different legal rights within a given system of property rights — for example, creditors versus share-holders. They are not categorized using antagonistic dimensions such as class or ownership of wealth. Further, conflict is usually perceived as being 'dysfunctional' in relation to the greater corporate goal (whatever it may be). The accounting researcher then seeks to specify procedures whereby such dysfunctions may be corrected.

Finally, some mainstream researchers imply that organizations and 'free' markets have an inherent tendency to achieve social order. Left to themselves, organizations appear to 'naturally' evolve administrative and accounting systems that minimize transaction costs in changing environmental conditions. Also, the desirable amount of financial disclosure may be determined by the 'free' play of market forces with a minimum of state intervention. People and markets, thus appear to achieve order by themselves.

Mainstream Accounting — Limitations

This supposedly neutral position of mainstream accounting runs into difficulties. This itself is a value position which cannot logically be argued as 'superior' to a position that judges goals in the name of some ideal. Weber (1949) recognized that the very distinction between fact and value is itself a value judgment. Also, it amounts to conservative support, however indirect, of the status quo. By not questioning extant goals, there is a tacit acquiescence with what is. Such support helps to legitimize extant relations of exchange, production and forms of suppression.

A second limitation relates to the assumption of human purpose, rationality, and consensus. When these consensual goals of 'utility-maximization' are examined, they invariably are the goals of the providers of capital. Although accountants and auditors sometimes suggest that they act in 'public interest', it is generally accepted that both managerial and external financial reports are intended to protect the rights of investors and creditors.

A third limitation of the set of dominant beliefs is the lack of awareness of controversies within the philosophy of social science which have questioned realism and the empirical testability of theories. Post-empiricist philosophy has generally agreed that observations are fallible propositions which are theory-dependent, and therefore cannot act as the neutral arbitrator between competing theories. Indeed, the search for a trans-historical, permanent criterion of acceptability is now seen as a futile exercise.

Mainstream accounting research has, nevertheless, attempted to develop useful, generalizable knowledge which can be applied in organizations to predict and control empirical phenomena. It has insisted on certain standards of validity, rigor, and objectivity in the conduct of scientific research. But these once liberating assumptions have ignored new questions being raised in other disciplines, imposed ever more severe restrictions on what is to count as genuine knowledge, and obscured different and rich research insights.

The Interpretive Alternative

This alternative is derived from Germanic philosophical interests which emphasize the role of language, interpretation, and understanding in social science. As Schutz (1962, 1964, 1966, 1967) has been one of the most influential proponents of this alternative, his ideas form the core of the description here.

Beliefs about Physical and Social Reality

Schutz begins with the notion that what is primordially given to social life is an unbroken stream of lived experience. This 'stream or consciousness' has no meaning or discrete identity until human beings turn their attention (self-reflect) on a segment of this flow and ascribe meaning to it. Experience to which meaning has been retrospectively endowed is termed behavior. Social science is generally concerned with a special class of meaningful behavior — actions — which is future-oriented and directed towards the achievement of a determinate goal. Because actions are intrinsically endowed with subjective meaning by the actor and always intentional, actions cannot be understood without reference to their meaning.

Beliefs about Knowledge

Given this view of a subjectively created, emergent social reality, the research questions that are pertinent are: how is a common sense of social order produced and reproduced in everyday life; what are the deeply embedded rules that structure the social world; how do these typifications arise, and how are they sustained and modified; what are the typical motives that explain action? In essence, the interpretive scientist seeks to make sense of human actions by fitting them into a purposeful set of individual aims and a social structure of meanings.

How does one carry on this task of interpretive understanding? Initially, it was mistakenly thought that the observer had to 'jump into the shoes/skins' of the observed. Such a notion has been rightly discarded. However, it remains difficult to specify precise procedures for the conduct of interpretive research, such methods being similar to those of the anthropologist. They emphasize observation, awareness of linguistic cues, and a careful attention to detail. Each item of information has to be interpreted in the light of other items drawn from the language and ideology of the 'tribe' under investigation rather than through *a priori* definitions. Meanings are themselves built on other meanings and social practices. As such, 'thick' case studies conducted in the life-world of actors are preferred to distant large-scale sampling or mathematical modeling of human intention.

Beliefs about the Social World

The main beliefs about people are (a) the ascription of purpose to human action, and (b) the assumption of an orderly, pre-given world of meanings that structures action. However, Schutz argues that purposes always have an element of pastness, for only the already experienced may be endowed with meaning in a backward, reflective balance. Further, purposes are grounded in changing social contexts and are not pre-given.

Theory and Practice

Interpretive knowledge reveals to people what they and others are doing when they act and speak as they do. It does so by highlighting the symbolic structures and taken-for-granted themes which pattern the world in distinct ways. Interpretive science does not seek to control empirical phenomena; it has no technical application. Instead, the aim of the interpretive scientist is to enrich people's understanding of the meanings of their actions, thus increasing the possibility of mutual communication and influence. By showing what people are doing, it makes it possible for us to apprehend a new language and form of life.

Some researchers have attempted to study accounting in action and to investigate its role as a symbolic mediator. The interpretive perspective indicates that, in practice, accounting information may be attributed diverse meanings. Accounting numbers are inadequate representations of things and events as experienced by human beings. Because of this, actors will seek to transcend the formality of the numbers and manipulate their symbolic meaning to suit their particular intentions and this suggests that the ever-expanding demand for accounting information may be because of this intrinsic ambiguity which allows complex trade-offs among interest groups.

Second, not only are accounting meanings constituted by complex interpretive processes and structures, they help constitute an objectified social reality. For example, the traditional responsibility accounting map of the organization helps to consolidate a particular view of hierarchy, authority, and power. Accounting numbers give visibility to particular definitions of 'effectiveness', 'efficiency', and that which is 'desirable' and 'feasible'. In this way, accounting numbers may be used to actively mobilize bias, to define the parameters permissible in organizational debates, and to legitimize particular sectional interests.

Accounting information is particularly useful for legitimization activities because they appear to possess a neutral, technical rationality. Numbers are often perceived as being more precise and 'scientific' than qualitative evidence. Even among actors/players who are aware of the imprecision of these numbers, public debates continue to be organized around such numbers because that is considered the proper arena for discussion.

Third, the interpretive perspective questions the traditional view of accounting information as a means of achieving pre-given goals. Information may be used to accord rationality after the event. Similarly, accounting information may be used to retrospectively rationalize action and to impose a goal as though it always existed.

Finally, the interpretive perspective does not assume that conflict is inevitably 'dysfunctional'. The concept of 'dysfunction' does not arise because no priority is given to particular human goals. Goals and their priority are argued to be constituted through human interaction.

As can be seen, changing the set of philosophical assumptions about knowledge and the empirical world gives us a new purpose for theorizing, different problems to research, and an alternative standard to evaluate the validity of research evidence. There is much to be gained by moving accounting into the life-world of actors.

Interpretive work, however, also possesses weaknesses. There have been three major criticisms of the approach. First, it has been argued that using the extent of actor agreement as the standard for judging the adequacy of an explanation is extremely weak. Second, the perspective lacks an evaluative dimension. Habermas (1978), in particular, argues that the interpretive researcher is unable to evaluate critically the forms of life which he/she observes and is therefore unable to analyze forms of 'false consciousness' and domination that prevent the actors from knowing their true interests. Third, the interpretive researcher begins with an assumption of social order and of conflict which is contained through common interpretive schemes. Given this and the focus on micro-social interaction, there is a tendency to neglect major conflicts of interest between classes in society.

These difficulties have given rise to various attempts to transcend the problems of both mainstream and interpretive perspectives, such as the critical alternative.

The Critical Alternative — Assumptions

Beliefs about Physical and Social Reality

The most distinctive idea that the majority of researchers in this perspective share dates from the work of Plato, Hegel and Marx. It is the belief that every state of existence, be it an individual or a society, possesses historically constituted potentialities that are unfulfilled. People are able to recognize, grasp, and extend the possibilities contained in every being. It is this quality which distinguishes human beings as universal, free beings.

However, human potentiality is restricted by prevailing systems of domination which alienate people from self-realization. These material blockages operate both at the level of consciousness and through material economic and political relations. At one level, ideological constructs may be embedded in our modes of conceptualization, in our categories of common-sense and taken for granted beliefs about acceptable social practices. At another, repression may be effected through rules governing social exchange and the ownership and distribution of wealth.

Another belief concerns the relationship between parts (individuals, groups, organizations) and the whole (society). Critical researchers argue that because any finite thing is both itself and its opposite, things taken as isolated particulars are always incomplete. The particular exists only in and through the totality of relations of which it is a part. Therefore, what a finite thing is and what it is not may only be grasped by understanding the set of relations that surround it. For example, accountants are not isolated particulars. They exist only in the context of groups, classes and institutions. They are what they are by virtue of their relations as sellers of services, employees, professionals, etc. In this manner, the true form of reality lies not with particulars but with the universal that comes to be in and through particulars.

This emphasis on totality leads to a particular view of the object–subject distinction. Social structures are conceptualized as objective practices and conventions which individuals reproduce and transform, but which would not exist unless they did so. Rather, society provides the necessary, material conditions for the creative subject to act. At the same time, intentional action is a necessary condition for social structures. Society is only present in human action, and human action always expresses and uses some or other social form. Neither can, however, be identified with or reduced to the other. Social reality is, thus, both subjectively created and objectively real.

Further, because of the belief in human potentiality, there is an emphasis on studying the historical development of entities that are conceptualized as coming to be. Reality as a whole, as well as each particular part, is understood as developing out of an earlier stage of its existence and evolving into something else. Indeed, every state of existence is apprehended only through movement and change, and the identity of a particular phenomenon can only be uncovered by reconstructing the process whereby the entity transforms itself.

Beliefs about Knowledge

Critical philosophers accept that the standards by which a scientific explanation is judged adequate are temporal, context-bound notions. Truth is very much in the process of being hammered out and is grounded in social and historical practices. There are no theory-independent facts that can conclusively prove or disprove a theory.

Foucault, for example, eschews a transcendent criterion for the establishment of truth. He writes (1977: 131), 'truth is a thing of this world: it is produced only by virtue of multiple forms of constraint. And it induces regular effects of power...'. The scientist cannot emancipate truth from every system of power; he/she can only detach the power of truth from the forms of domination within which it operates at a particular time. By contrast, Habermas (1976) seeks to establish a quasi-transcendental process for rational theory choice, that simultaneously recognizes the historically grounded nature of all norms and yet seeks to transcend it.

Finally, there is greater emphasis on detailed historical explanations (Foucault emphasizes the 'genealogical approach') and 'thick', ethnographic studies of organizational structures and processes which show their societal linkages. The emphasis on long-term historical studies is especially important given the prior belief that the identity of an object/event can only be grasped through an analysis of its history — what it has been, what it is becoming and what it is not. Such historical analysis also serves the critical function of exposing rigidities and apparently ahistorical relations that restrict human potentiality.

Beliefs about the Social World

Critical researchers view individuals as acting within a matrix of intersubjective meanings. Thus, like the interpretive researcher, it is accepted that social scientists need to learn the language of their subject/object. The process of coming to an understanding is also agreed to be context-dependent as social scientists are necessarily immersed in and engaged with their socio-historical contexts. However, critical researchers argue that interpretation *per se* is insufficient. It cannot appreciate that the world is not only symbolically mediated, but is also shaped by material conditions of domination. Language itself may be a medium for repression and social power.

A critique of ideology is considered necessary because fundamental conflicts of interest and divisions are seen to exist in society (indeed, are endemic to contemporary society) and to be institutionalized via cultural and organizational forms. The organization is viewed as a middle-range construct, a microcosm of society that reflects and consolidates alienating relations. Because of this, distinctions between societal and organizational levels of analysis are blurred. One level is seen to support and be supported by the other, and conflicts within organizations create and are created by societal divisions.

Theory and Practice

Theory now has a particular relationship to the world of practice. It is/ought to be concerned with 'the freedom of the human spirit', that is, the bringing to consciousness of restrictive conditions. This involves demonstrating that so-called objective and universal social laws are but products of particular forms of domination and ideology. Through such analysis, it is intended that social change may be initiated, such that injustice and inequities may be corrected. Their moral position is that such domination ought to be exposed and changed. Social theory is therefore seen to possess a critical imperative. Indeed, it is synonymous with social critique.

Accounting research as social critique has several important characteristics. First, accounting is no longer seen as a technically rational, service activity which is divorced from wider societal relationship. Instead, accounting as a discourse with a particular mode of calculative rationality is argued to constitute and be constituted by macro conflict between different classes (for example, capitalist/manager vs worker, the State vs multinational corporations). At the micro-organizational level, the accounting calculus paints a picture of the 'cake' that is available for distribution and reports on how such distributions have been made. At the macro-societal level, these numbers influence taxation policy-making, wage bargaining, and economic restructuring. In all these situations, wealth transfers are involved and the accounting calculus is seen as playing (or potentially playing) a vital role in effecting such transfers.

Second, critique emphasizes the totality of relations (social, economic, political, ideological). As a result, the perspective engenders a new interest in certain macro-structural phenomena that are neglected in mainstream accounting research. An example is the role of accounting information in the regulation of and by the State. The State holds a pivotal position in the complex of human relations and is expanding the use of accounting information. Here, accounting numbers may be called upon to perform tasks for which they are not equipped: the quantification of welfare trade-offs in activities where neither the inputs nor the outputs desired are clearly specified. Hence, accounting/auditing information may only be used symbolically to rationalize or legitimize power relations.

In addition, the greater use of accounting calculation in the public sector could be because the State finds it difficult to manage the demands of organized capital and labor. Such structural conflict could represent macro-economic problems that the State must be seen to manage: inflation, stagflation, long-term unemployment, an ever-increasing state bureaucracy, and limited opportunities to raise State revenue and to reduce expenditure.

Within a critical perspective, the accounting profession is no longer theorized as a neutral group which evolves in response to rational demands for useful information. Instead, it is an aspiring occupational monopoly that seeks to further its own social and economic self-interests through (a) particular professional ideologies (for example, the universal service ethic), and (b) the policing of change-able and ambiguous relations with other professions, corporations, and the government. For instance, to preserve its territorial advantage from the challenge of engineers, investment advisors, and the State, the accounting profession in the US, UK and Australia has had to institute new membership controls and standard-setting bodies. Such reforms, however, often are claimed to be for the 'protection of the public'.

Fourth, the focus on totality also promotes organizational studies that integrate micro- and macro-levels of analysis. This has the effect of avoiding the traditional distinction between management and financial accounting. For instance, exploitative relations or forms of domination at the societal level are seen to be reflected and affected through organizations.

Finally, critical theorists claim that the view of accounting information as social control and as a mediator of conflict has often been obscured (mystified) by powerful, ideological ideas embedded in mainstream accounting thought. Accounting is claimed to be a service activity which is 'neutral as between ends', when in fact the goals of the owners of capital are implicitly given priority. Also, accountants are pictured as professionals who are independent of biases and who offer universal service to the community. Such claims are, however, seen as highly dubious. Due to the difficulty of policing compliance to the professional ideals of independence and competence at the level of the individual practitioner, peer supervision is often only rhetorical rather than real.

In summary, this perspective offers new insights that are worthy of consideration. As the State plays an ever-increasing role in the economic domain, as the use of accounting information expands in the private and public sectors, and as accountants become more involved with policy-making at the macro-level, it may no longer be useful to distinguish the political/social from the economic effects of accounting numbers. Nor may it be helpful to separate the organization from its wider structural relationships. Critique may then offer a way of understanding the role of accounting in these complex contexts.

Conclusion

This paper has sought to move accounting debate beyond the stalemate of 'incommensurable' paradigms which cannot be rationally evaluated. It has argued that mainstream accounting thought is grounded in a set of common assumptions about knowledge and the empirical world which both enlighten and yet enslave. These assumptions offer certain insights but obscure others. By changing them, new insights may be gained which can potentially extend our knowledge of accounting in action within organizational and societal contexts. Two main alternatives were discussed: the interpretive and the critical. It is hoped that the challenges posed by these alternatives will stimulate consideration and debate.

References

Burrell, G., & Morgan, G. (1979). *Sociological paradigms and organizational analysis. Elements of the sociology of corporate life*. London: Heinemann Educational Books Ltd.

Christenson, C. (1983). The methodology of positive accounting. *The Accounting Review*, January, 1–22.

Cooper, D.J. (1983). Tidiness, muddle and things: Commonalities and divergencies in two approaches to management accounting research. *Accounting, Organizations and Society*, 2/3, 269–286.

Foucault, M. (1977). *Discipline and punish: The birth of the prison*. (Translated by A.M. Sheridan). London: Allen Lane.

Habermas, J. (1976). *Legitimation crisis*. (Translated by T. McCarthy). London: Heinemann Educational Books Ltd.

Habermas, J. (1978). *Knowledge and human interest* (2nd Edition). London: Heinemann Educational Books Ltd.

Hopper, T., & Powell, A. (1985). Making sense of research into the organizational and social aspects of management accounting: A review of its underlying assumptions. *Journal of Management Studies*, September, 429–465.

Schutz, A. (1962). *Collected Papers*, Vol. I (Edited and with an introduction by M. Natanson). Dordrecht, The Netherlands: Martinus Nijhoff.

Schutz, A. (1964). *Collected Papers*, Vol. II (Edited by Avrid Broderson). Dordrecht, The Netherlands: Martinus Nijhoff.

Schutz, A. (1966). *Collected Papers*, Vol. III (Edited by I. Schutz). Dordrecht, The Netherlands: Martinus Nijhoff.

Schutz, A. (1967). *The phenomenology of the social world*. (Translated by G. Walsh and F. Lehnert). Evanston, IL: Northwestern University Press.

Weber, M. (1949). *The Methodology of the Social Sciences*. New York: The Free Press.

Chapter 7

Accounting Systems and Systems of Accountability — Understanding Accounting Practices in their Organizational Contexts[1]

John Roberts, *University of Cambridge*

Robert W. Scapens, *University of Manchester*

This paper elaborates a theoretical framework for analyzing the operation of systems of accountability within organizations. It represents an attempt to understand accounting practices in their organizational contexts. Two broad sets of concerns have informed our thinking. First, by concentrating on accounting practice we sought to remedy what we saw as the rather piecemeal and overly technical character of much of the contemporary accounting research. A great deal of accounting research focuses rather narrowly on particular elements of accounting systems — budgeting, investment, inflation accounting, etc., often with an implicit concern to improve the efficiency of these systems.

Our second broad concern was to locate accounting within its 'organizational context'. In general, academic accountants have adopted a rather accounting-centric approach to research. Accounting has been treated as if it were a functionally autonomous sphere of practice, and consequently there has been a corresponding neglect of the relationships between accounting and other functional areas within organizations. There is, we believe, a need for more basic conceptual work on the nature of accounting. The only way to understand accounting practice is through an understanding of the organizational reality which is the context of accounting, and which is the reality that the accounting systems are designed to account for.

The Duality of Structure

Cohen talked of the 'paradox' of social reality whereby '... the properties of the elements of social phenomena obtain many of their characteristics from the

---

[1]Reproduced (in an abridged form) from John Roberts and Robert Scapens, 'Accounting Systems and Systems of Accountability — Understanding Accounting Practices in Their Organisational Contexts', *Accounting, Organizations and Society*, 1985, vol. 10, no, 4, pp 443–456 with permission of Elsevier.

larger phenomena of which they are part, while the larger entities obtain their characteristics mostly from the relations between the parts of which they are composed' (Cohen 1968: 11–12).

Contemporary social theory, according to Giddens, rather than seeking to elucidate this paradox, merely takes up one side to the neglect of the other. Thus Functionalism, Systems Theory and Structuralism regard the individual as produced (determined) by society, whilst Interpretative work presents a view of the individual as the producer of social reality. In Giddens' terminology these different schools of social theory treat the relationship between subject and object, between the individual and society, as a 'dualism'. They all build, albeit in different ways, upon what for Giddens is a false belief in the separability of subject and object. As a consequence of this dualistic assumption most social and also organizational theorists generate theory, which is respectively either over-voluntaristic or over-deterministic. In place of this dualism Giddens proposes a theory of '*the duality of structure*', in which the relationship between subject and object is described in the form of a dialectic. Action and structure, he argues, rather than being antinomies, 'presuppose one another'.

Such a perspective is particularly relevant for the understanding of the organization. There is an emphasis upon life; organization is not something that exists outside time, but instead is produced and reproduced through time. Organizations are not treated as entities that have an existence independent of acting individuals (as it is the case with Functionalism and Systems Theory), nor are they viewed as the given context for action and interaction (as it is typically the case with Interpretative Theory). Instead organizations themselves comprise the *interdependent social practices* of skilled (knowledgeable) subjects. It is the centrality of the notion of practice or practices and in particular, the analysis of the interdependent character of practices with the concepts of 'system' and 'structure' that make Giddens' (1976, 1979) work an attractive framework for understanding the significance of accounting in the production and reproduction of organizational life.

Giddens uses the concept of 'system' in a way which seeks to avoid the dangers of reification and determinism by tying the analysis of systems directly to practices. He uses the term 'systemness' to refer to interdependence of action and argues that systems should be analyzed as institutionalized forms of interdependent social practices. The term 'integration' is used by Giddens to refer to the degree of interdependence of action involved in a system. He draws a distinction between 'social integration' and 'system integration'. 'Social integration' is concerned with systemness at the level of face-to-face interaction and 'system integration' with systemness at the level of relationships between groups and collectivities.

Whilst Giddens uses the term system to refer to the visible pattern or forms of interdependence in society, he uses the concept of 'structure' to explain the continuity and spread (reproduction) of these particular forms of interdependence between individuals and groups *through time*. In explaining his concept of 'structure', Giddens draws a comparison between speech as an element of action and interaction, and 'language' which he argues should be viewed as a 'structure' or 'structural property' of a community of speakers. Whereas, speech is always situated in space and time, language is a 'virtual order' outside of subjects, and outside of space and time. Speech involves the activity of subjects, language does not and, in this sense, is subjectless; although language as a structure is only reproduced through being drawn upon in speech by subjects. Finally, speech is intentionally produced in communication with others, while language is neither an intended product of any one subject nor oriented towards another.

Generalizing from this, Giddens argues that structures can be understood as 'systems of generative rules and resources' which, though existing 'outside time and space', provide the 'binding of time and space in social systems'. Whereas structuralism views action as being determined by such structures, action and structure are in a dialectical relationship; structures are both 'the medium and the outcome' of interaction.

Giddens suggests that structures can themselves be differentiated into structures of Signification (meaning), Legitimation (morality) and Domination (power). The structuring of any particular context of interaction involves people drawing on and thereby reproducing these structures. Accordingly, any interaction can be analyzed in terms of '... three fundamental elements; its constitution as meaningful, its constitution as a moral order, and its constitution as the operation of relations of power' (Giddens 1976: 104).

Accounting Systems and Systems of Accountability

Accountability in its broadest sense simply refers to the giving and demanding of reasons for conduct and, in this broad sense, accountability can be seen as 'a chronic feature of daily conduct' (Giddens 1979: 57). In this paper, our focus is on the intended and actual impact that the use of accounting information has in shaping and maintaining particular patterns of accountability within organizations.

At a general level, following Giddens, systems of accountability in organizations can be seen to provide for the 'binding' of organizational time and space. It is perhaps, obvious that accounting practices create a strict temporal order for organization. Quite literally, accounting structures organizational time by dividing the flow of organizational life into 'accounting' periods and generating regular reports, budgets and appraisals with all their related practices. Accounting involves the binding of organizational space in the very real sense in which one of the most important boundaries of an organization is defined by the boundaries of its system of accountability. To be part of an organization is to be subject to that organization's system of accountability; a customer is not accountable to someone within an organization, in the same way that an employee is accountable. Within these boundaries the physical organization of space in terms of hierarchical, functional and divisional patterns are not just reflected in, but are also reproduced through the operation of systems of accountability. At a more detailed level, again following Giddens, one can analyze the operation of systems of accountability in particular contexts of interaction in terms of individuals drawing upon and thereby reproducing particular structures of Signification (meaning), Legitimation (morality) and Domination (power).

As a language, accounting provides organization members with a set of categories, or 'system of relevances' in terms of which they can make sense of what has happened, anticipate the future, and plan and assess action. Thus, for example, the accounting categories of cost, profit, contribution, return on investment serve as a structure of meanings which are drawn upon by organization members both to order their experiences of one another and in terms of which to orient their actions. These meanings however are neither frozen nor unambiguous. Thus, the precise significance of events interpreted through these categories is open to differential interpretation, to elaboration, to negotiation and to dispute. As such, accounting viewed as a structure of meaning merely conditions rather than determines accounting practices, and through such use the structures of meaning, which are accounting, themselves gradually evolve and change.

Accounting practices, however, involve much more than the production and reproduction of meaning. Systems of accountability also embody a moral order; a complex system of reciprocal rights and obligations. The practice of accounting institutionalizes the notion of accountability; it institutionalizes the rights of some people to hold others to account for their actions. Viewed in this way, the practice of accounting can be seen to involve the communication of a set of values, of ideals of expected behaviour, of what is approved and disapproved. The practice of accounting involves communicating notions of what *should* happen, and it is only on the basis of these notions that sense is made of what has happened. Budgeting is perhaps the most obvious example of how what has happened is constantly evaluated in terms of expectations as to what should have happened.

In any particular context of interaction there will, of course, be a certain contingency. The reciprocal rights and obligations will be open to negotiation and differential interpretation. The way in which rights and obligations are defined will depend, in part, on how past events have been defined — i.e. on the interpretation which is placed on events which have already happened, and how and why they happened. One of the obvious difficulties involved in the practice of accounting is that the complex interdependence of action in organizations often makes it very difficult to determine who is responsible, and therefore who should be held accountable for particular events.

The rights and obligations defined through the practice of accounting are typically supported by a whole series of positive and negative sanctions ranging from disapproval and praise, to the manipulation of financial incentives and career prospects. This leads us to the third structural element of systems of accountability. Accounting practices can be seen to involve the operation of relations of power.

Giddens employs the word power in both a broad and a narrow sense. In its broad sense, he suggests that the analysis of power is inextricably tied to the analysis of action, i.e. the power to do. In discussing power in this sense, he refers to what he calls the 'transformative capacity of human action': i.e. the power of human action to transform the social and material world. Organization constitutes a conscious attempt to enhance the productive power of human action through co-ordination. Viewed in this way, one could view the power relations embodied in systems of accountability as a resource for organization.

These systems carry the information that enables diverse practices to be integrated and co-ordinated. Given the size and complexity of contemporary organizations integration would be impossible without the regular information flows which accounting systems facilitate. By providing a common language and a definition of mutual rights and obligations, accounting allows for organization. Accounting serves as a means of directing and realizing the productive potential of organization. This is perhaps a very appealing view of the role of accounting in organizations; a view that accountants would perhaps adopt or emphasize.

There is, however, another sense in which Giddens uses the word power — namely in the sense of 'power over' — in other words, power as the domination of some individuals by others. In general, accounting researchers have not explicitly recognized the use of accounting as an instrument of domination — i.e. as the means whereby some people seek to control and coerce others. To recognize accounting as a means of domination does not necessarily deny the enabling potential of accounting, as described above. However, it is important to distinguish between the two forms of power relationships and to recognize the tension between them.

The operation of relations of power in the practice of accounting can be seen in the asymmetrical character of systems of accountability. It is the subordinate who must account to the superior; this accountability is not usually reversed. Typically, the superior will have a variety of resources to draw upon in order to induce others to conform with his or her wishes. Rather than negotiate the meaning of events or reciprocal rights and obligations, the superior may seek to use the resources at his or her disposal to impose a definition of what has happened and who is responsible. This is one of the ways in which the practice of accounting, in contemporary organizations at least, becomes less concerned with the integration of diverse activities, and more concerned with the domination of some individuals by others.

Again, however, it is important to recognize that in any particular context of interaction there will be a certain contingency. Whatever the asymmetry of resources available to people, no one will be entirely without resources. Furthermore, those in subordinate positions are frequently adept at using resources to protect or expand their areas of discretion. Thus, for example, it has long been recognized that information in organizations is not neutral, but is itself an important power resource. Since, the superior is often dependent on the subordinate for the provision of the information with which he or she is then assessed, the subordinate has many opportunities to conceal, distort or dress the information which he or she channels through the system. Indeed, the way in which accounting systems are designed often implicitly reflects the superior's recognition of and attempts to circumvent or limit their dependence on subordinates.

Struggles over the control of information, whilst important, do not exhaust the relevance of power in the understanding of accounting practice. Systems of accountability may work as systems of domination through imposing a particular framework of categories upon organization members. Arguments may be won or lost and information concealed or distorted, but the most important victory perhaps lies in influencing the terms within which an argument is conducted. Accounting is significant in organizations, not just as a functional specialism alongside production, marketing, etc., but because it frequently provides the common language through which the activities of engineers, salesmen and so on are integrated and assessed. The real power of accounting perhaps lies in the way in which, as a structure of meaning, it comes to define what shall and shall not count as significant within an organization.

Conclusion

The conventional view of accounting information is that it acts like a mirror or picture, which neutrally and objectively records the 'facts' about what has happened in an organization over a particular period of time. The framework outlined above attempts to go beyond the image or picture created by accounting to explore the conditions and consequences of its production and use. Seemingly, the closer one gets to the production and use of accounting information, the more the apparent solidity or reality of the image crumbles. In its place emerges a sense of the tenuous and recursive nature of the relationship between the image or picture produced in the Accounts, and the flow of organizational events and practices that the Accounts purport to record.

Traditionally accounting research has been oriented either to gathering data about contemporary forms of accounting information, or more practically, through technical and conceptual work, to improving or changing the 'resolution' of the image given in Accounts. There is value in such work as long as the researcher does not fall into the trap of believing that the image can be made into a perfect representation of reality. Although we all as individuals can and must 'objectify' reality, social reality is not itself an object, but rather a flow of interrelated events and practices that is changed by the nature of our own and others' perceptions. An alternative avenue for research, the one that we have proposed, is to explore the conditions and consequences of the production and use of accounting information, and in this way to begin to develop an understanding of the way that accounting information not only reflects, but through different forms of use also shapes and legitimizes organizational social realities.

References

Cohen, P. (1968). *Social theory*. London: Heinemann.
Giddens, A. (1976). *New rules of sociological method*. London: Hutchinson.
Giddens, A. (1979). *Central problems in social theory*. London: Macmillan.

Chapter 8

The Archaeology of Accounting Systems[1]

Anthony G. Hopwood,   *Saïd Business School, University of Oxford*

As a discipline, accounting has invested a great deal in the articulation of abstract bodies of knowledge concerned with what it should be. Ideas exist as to good, indeed, 'best', costing practice, good planning, good modes of management reporting and good approaches to the appraisal of new investment possibilities. Attempts have been made to tease out the abstract characteristics of good co-ordination and direction, and their implications for the reform of accounting practice. Both economic and cognitive conceptions of decision making and its rationality have been related to the accounting concrete. Regimes of thought thereby have been developed which have an existence and dynamic of change that are not dependent on the practice of the accounting craft.

By drawing on bodies of knowledge from such more autonomous discourses as economics, political theory, public administration and psychology or emergent notions of strategic management, as well as by abstracting from the practice and functioning of the craft itself, accounting can be evaluated in terms of what it is not. Specific practices can be appraised on the basis of their conformity to more general notions of management and the manageable. An abstract external body of knowledge can be imposed on them both to assess their adequacy and to reform them so that they can become what they really should be. Accounting is seen as being able to be mobilized and changed in the name of an abstract image of its real potential.

Such a view of accounting development also ignores the duality of the inter-actions between accounting and ideas of its potential. In both historical and organizational terms, the apparatus of organizing has played a profound role in influencing our conceptions of the organization. Ideas about organizational goals, functions and functioning have emerged amidst the development of specific means of organizational action and calculation. Equally, organizational participants have not been defined externally to the practices in which they are engaged. The concepts of management and the manager were actively constructed in a

[1]Reproduced (in an abridged form) from Anthony G. Hopwood, 'The Archaeology of Accounting Systems', *Accounting, Organizations and Society*, 1987, vol. 12, no. 3, pp. 207–234, with permission of Elsevier.

Accounting, the Social and the Political
N. Macintosh and T. Hopper (Editors)

particular way at a particular socio-historical juncture and are inseparable from the practical means of administration and calculation which were, and still are, implicated in their emergence and functioning. There was no *a priori* manager to whom one can appeal as having interests and needs which can mobilize the development of management practices. Equally, there was no primeval concept of accounting which shaped the development of accounting as we now know it. Accounting has emerged in a more positive way than the mere realization of an essence. Indeed, in part, the present imperatives of accounting which can and do guide its development have emerged from the practice of the craft. And, in similar terms, accounting practice needs to be seen as playing a more active role in creating rather than merely enabling organized endeavour. Accounting change is as much a history of organizational construction as organization realization and enablement.

Rather than seeing organizational accounts as a technical reflection of the pregiven economic imperatives facing organizational administration, however, they are now being seen to be more actively constructed in order to create a particular economic visibility within the organization and a powerful means for positively enabling the governance and control of the organization along economic lines. Accounting, when seen in such terms, is not a passive instrument of technical administration, a neutral means for merely revealing the pregiven aspects of organizational function. Instead its origins are seen to reside in the exercising of social power both within and without the organization. It is seen as being implicated in the forging, indeed the active creation, of a particular regime of economic calculation within the organization in order to make real and powerful quite particular conceptions of economic and social ends.

From such a perspective, organizational options, decisions and actions are seen as being positively shaped by the ways in which they intersect with accounting practices. Accounting is seen as having played a very positive role in the creation of a manageable organizational domain. A regime of economic visibility and calculation has positively enabled the creation and operation of an organization which facilitates the exercising of particular social conceptions of power. Economic motives have been made real and influential by their incorporation into legitimate and accepted economic facts. The labour process in the organization has been exposed, ordered and physically and socially distributed. The resultant organizational facts, calculations, schedules and plans have positively enabled the construction of a management regime abstracted and distanced from the operation of the work process itself.

So, although functioning within the organization, accounting is best seen from such a perspective as an artifact residing in the domain of the social rather than the narrowly organizational. It has been implicated in the radical transformation of the organization in the name of the social. Indeed, accounting is considered as one of the important means by which the organization is incorporated into the social domain.

In the context of such an agenda for development, the subsequent discussion has only a modest aim. Using some instances of accounting change, an attempt is made to tease out some of the processes at work at the organizational level. By drawing on some specific illustrations of accounting in action, the aim is to illuminate some of the factors that are implicated in the processes by which organizational accountings become what they are not.

On Putting Accounting where Accounting was not

Josiah Wedgwood was a successful entrepreneur in the early days of the British industrial revolution. A man of scientific and analytical temperament, as well as acute commercial acumen, Wedgwood quickly established himself as the supplier of pottery to the wealthy. His business quickly became a very profitable and rapidly expanding one.

Initially Wedgwood made little use of accounting, particularly for what would now be seen as management purposes. Accounting information did not inform his product and pricing decisions or the selection of his methods of work. Indeed Wedgwood himself admitted that 'he could do little more than guess at costs' and 'further conceded that his attempts at total costing were out by a factor of two' (McKendrick 1973: 49).

That situation was to change however. In 1772, the expansion came to an abrupt end. The pottery industry was caught in a major economic recession. In times of such crisis, business methods often are re-examined. With such an aim in mind, Wedgwood started to turn his attention to the level of his production expenses. And it was in this context that his cost accounts were born.

Wedgwood had the idea that he might better survive the recession if he could lower his prices in order to stimulate demand. Such a view was conditioned, however, by the need to ensure that the price still exceeded the cost. And there the problem arose. For although a concept of cost entered into the discourse of commerce and trade, and could thereby mobilize action, there was no well established apparatus for operationalising the discursive category. Cost remained an idea, not a fact.

It was the facts of costing that Wedgwood set out to discover. The task was not an easy one. No established procedures were available for observing the inner workings of the organization through the accounting eye. The organization could not be readily penetrated. The facts of costing had to be laboriously created rather than merely revealed. Comparing his financial accounts with his emergent costings, he found that the two did not agree.

His subsequent inquiries revealed 'a history of embezzlement, blackmail, chicanery, and what Wedgwood called "extravagance and dissipation"' (McKendrick 1973: 61). His head clerk, Ben, whom he had 'long been uneasy on this account being fully perswaded (*sic*) that matters were not right with...His Case acc^ts being always several months behind, & yet to jump exactly right when he did Balance them' (McKendrick 1973: 61), had had his hand in the till. On further investigation, Wedgwood found that 'the plan of our House in Newport St.', where the clerks resided, 'is rather unfavourable to Virtue & good order in young men', 'that the housekeeper was frolicking with the cashier', 'that the head clerk was ill with "the foul Disease" and had "long been in a course of extravagance and dissipation far beyond anything he has from us (in a lawfull way) wd. Be able to support"' (McKendrick 1973: 61).

Only after such revelations as to the sources of accounting inconsistency did Wedgwood feel confident in his newly fledged facts. Immediate steps were taken to correct the matter. A new clerk was installed and, in order 'to put the necessary business of collecting into a way of *perpetual motion*' (McKendrick 1973: 62, emphasis in original), a routine of weekly accounts implemented.

The birth of Wedgwood's accounts had been difficult and laborious. There had been no easy relationship between the idea of costing and a specific programme of intervention in the organization conducted in the name of that idea. Costs had had to be constructed rather than merely revealed. An organizational economy grounded in a domain of accounting facts had to be forged painstakingly rather than merely exposed.

Once constructed, however, Wedgwood had a powerful instrument for observing the organization in economic terms. His strategic conception of the role which records could play in the management of crisis had resulted in a means by which he could penetrate the inner workings of the organization. A new visibility had been created. The organization had been colonized by economic facts. A calculative means had been found for conceiving the functioning of the organization in different terms. An accounting eye had provided Wedgwood with a new means for intervening in the organization.

As McKendrick (1973: 54) notes, Wedgwood's costing 'had other more permanent repercussions on his business management'. In often unanticipated ways, the organization was changed in the name of the knowledge of it. For 'by his own persistence, by an unfailing attention to detail, by founding, if not creating, the traditions of a foreman class and equipping it with rules and regulations, he transformed a collection of what in 1765 he called "dilatory, drunken, idle, worthless workmen" into what ten years later he allowed to be "a very good sett of hands"' (McKendrick 1961: 46). What is more, Wedgwood's observations could now be conducted indirectly. No longer did he have to rely solely on walking around the pottery constantly on the lookout for 'unhandiness', scolding those individuals who did not follow his instructions (McKendrick 1961: 43–44). Such personal observation and supervision could start to be complemented by the exercising of control at a distance, both in time and space. Wedgwood now had available to him the basis of a more anonymous and continuous means of surveillance.

Accounting, Organizing and the Organization

Turning to an organization which already has a long history of accounting, the aim is to consider in a little more detail some of the processes through which organizational accounts change as they become intertwined with the organization itself.

M was established in the early days of the present century. In the business of industrial component manufacturing, it quickly established itself as an international enterprise with manufacturing and marketing establishments in a wide variety of countries through the Western world. *M* grew rapidly. Those were years of prosperity and expansion with good profits and a high return on assets employed.

But this situation changed after 1960. Although product demand eased slightly, change was most evident on the supply side of the industry. In particular, the entry of Japanese manufacturers into the world market ushered in a decade of fierce competition. During the 1960s, the total value of Japanese output rose by over 350% but their exports increased by almost 1700%. Suddenly *M* was exposed to intense competition and this was greatest at the volume end of the market where, on certain individual products, the Japanese selling price was below *M*'s calculated unit cost.

The perception of an external market threat thereby resulted in a detailed examination of internal manufacturing operations. At that time the batch production methods used by *M* gave a large measure of independence to the separate functions of the manufacturing process. This resulted in a great deal of operational flexibility. Rush orders could be injected easily into the system and the ramifications of machine breakdowns minimized. Such an approach was not suited to more concentrated and, consequently, higher volume production, however. The lack of interoperation handling equipment resulted in long throughput times and high inventories. Moreover batch production of this type put a heavy burden on local production control systems, stores personnel, operators, inspectors and factory supervisors. So very active consideration was given to alternative production methods.

M decided to move, as far as possible, to production organized by means of multi-machine lines. The capital costs of this type of plant were high, but production speeds were increased, throughput time was reduced and, as a consequence, inventory requirements were reduced also. However, those advantages were gained not only at the expense of higher capital investment but also at the loss of considerable operational flexibility. The production systems would have to become more autonomous of the market, the very turbulence of which had been the initial stimulus for change.

Production methods, product policies and production locations were thereby all radically changed in the name of cost. All of these strategic considerations had been infused not only by the language of cost, however, but also by the specific accounting calculations in use at *M*. The reduction of a *measured* notion of cost had been a primary aim. In the deliberations and policy initiatives, cost had operated not only as an influential abstract category entering into the language of strategy but also as a seemingly precise outcome of a specific set of accounting procedures.

In such ways the technical practices of accounting became intertwined with the managerial functioning of *M*. Organizational policies came to be interdependent with the accounting representation of them. For a complex set of accounting rules defined what was and was not to be regarded as costly. Definitions of 'productive' and 'unproductive' cost categories influenced the changes made to specific production locations and eventually, the production of specific products. Rules by which overhead costs were to be allocated to production operations, and by what means, had a significant impact on reported cost levels. Debates over the capacity assumptions on which overhead costs were to be allocated were similarly influential in the highly detailed cost assessments, as were the technical procedures for determining how frequently standard costs were to be updated to take account of inflation and exchange rate fluctuations. Also of great importance were the procedures for accounting for operational change in M.

For although the problems of the company had originated from the perception of a changing environment, M's accounting system operated under assumptions of steady state production. The calculation and reporting of set-up and order costs and operation start costs were such that although the financial ramifications of stable production were made clearly visible, the equally significant implications of production changes were much less visible and the costs of operational flexibility and inflexibility did not enter into the accounting calculations at all.

In all of these ways, not only did the rhetoric of accounting come to play a significant mediating role in the policy deliberations but also the very particular physical, spatial and temporal assumptions and biases incorporated into M's formal accounting systems came to influence the relative preferences assigned to the various production strategies. The accounting system started to be not only reflective of M but also constitutive of its options and policies.

As a result of these changes, consideration also had to be given to the formal organizational structure of M. Previously, the company had been structured around the national manufacturing and marketing units. As relatively self-contained entities, they had constituted useful business responsibility units. Performance was measured on an annual basis in traditional balance sheet and income statement terms. Longer term planning of the enterprise as a whole had been attempted but had proved a difficult and unsatisfactory endeavour. Now, however, M was a more integrated and centralized organization. The relationships between local marketing and manufacturing had been severed. Local sales were no longer dependent on local production. Performance in total was more dependent on central decision making. With this in mind, the whole organization started to be structured along product lines.

In the midst of such organizational changes, it was recognized that the previous rudimentary controls were no longer adequate. Consideration had to be given to a more frequent, more disaggregated reporting system. Budgeting became a more iterative and time consuming process. Even when arrived at, the budget was updated by a regular series of quarterly plans. The centre now needed to be much more closely informed of local developments and revisions in local expectations. Local performance, in turn, was assessed monthly with the previous summary financial information now being replaced by an extremely detailed reporting of financial, marketing, operating and even personnel results. And, in such a newly centralized enterprise, even local performance was now conditioned by centrally mediated and much contested accounting policies for transfer prices and the allocation of costs.

The accounting system and its resultant problems now started to be a complex residue of marketing, production and organizational strategies. Just as accounting had mediated some of the early crucial policy decisions, now accounting was itself subject to the implications of some of its own effects.

Accounting was firmly embedded in the organization rather than being any clearly separable part of it. The organization was not independent of the accountings of it. Although at a point in time the practices of accounting could be identified, their functioning was intertwined with that of the organization in both reflective and constitutive ways. Accounting had provided an operational and influential language of economic motive, its calculations had infused and influenced important policy decisions, and the visibilities it created played an important role in making real particular segmentations of the organizational arena. Accounting not only reflected the organization as it had been but it also played a not insignificant role in positively making the organization as it now is.

Accounting and the Residues of the Organizational Past

Such constitutive roles of accounting provide a major focus for analyzing Q, also a major manufacturing enterprise. Like M, it also had to face extreme market turbulence and change. Increasing competition, changing consumer expectations and a squeezing of profit margins also engendered in Q a sense of organizational crisis.

As an organization, Q is even more information intensive than M. It has invested heavily in formal information and control systems, paying particular attention to those of a financial and accounting nature. The tentacles of these systems penetrate deep into the manufacturing, marketing, distribution and administrative functions of the enterprise. Detailed aspects of the organization are made economically visible on a very regular basis. Standards, budgets and plans play a central role in the co-ordination and integration of a very large, functionally specialized and geographically dispersed organization. Indeed, it is through the formal flows of economic information that many important aspects of Q come to be known, managed and assessed. No pockets of local autonomy are consciously allowed to exist. Not only are all the parts of the vast, dispersed and varied enterprise drawn together by the information systems, which provide the basis for the operational governance of Q, but also the rhythms of the accounting year thereby become very influential components of the organizational construction and management of time. The accounting eye is indeed a significant and omnipresent one.

A market crisis was to make such an information regime increasingly problematic however. With mounting uncertainty, the need for information that was not collected became ever greater. The senior management of Q started to realize that what it had been regarding as a detached and independent source of illumination — information — was in fact a direct reflection and an integral component of its system of administration and governance. What had been controlled — costs, profits, variances and volume — had given rise to an information residue. What had not been controlled, but what was now seen to be in need of control, was unreflected in the organization's battery of information systems. The previously unmanaged — quality, detailed aspects of the functioning of the production process, employee and managerial commitment and motivation, throughput times and operational inventory holdings, technological progress, the detail of customer responsiveness — resided in the domain of the unknown.

In the context of such a perception of crisis, important aspects of the organization of *Q* that had been positively shaped by its regime of information systems started to be regarded as problematic. The batteries of standards, budgets and plans were seen as creating a relatively inflexible and inward looking enterprise. The phrase 'paralysis by analysis' started to enter the organizational vocabulary. It was perceived that emphasis had been placed on the management of the normal rather than the irregular. The management of the abstract had created an organization that found it difficult, if not positively traumatic, to respond to the particular.

The systems of information also were recognized as having played a very crucial role in the creation of conceptions of time in *Q*. Not only was the continual stream of organizational action periodized in a very particular way, but also the regime of routine planning and reporting had resulted in a celebration of the present and the short-term. By extensive processes of budgeting and planning, the future had been brought into the present, seemingly becoming more certain, less contingent, less debatable and, possibly, less readily subject to influence in the process. After an era of emphasizing the immediate in many aspects of its management, *Q* now found it extremely difficult to instill a more proactive conception of an influencable and manageable longer term future.

Although autonomous developments could and did take place in the design and functioning of *Q*'s accounting systems (and which by feeding into the functioning of the organization, could subsequently lose their autonomy), accounting in *Q* had become a phenomenon that could not be regarded as being in any sense separable from the enterprise as a whole.

Past investments, in a finely tuned economic visibility had radically increased the salience of the economies that could be gained from functional specialization, geographical dispersion and a regime of administrative co-ordination. The accounting eye had become a very strategic one. The organization had been mobilized in the name of what was known of it. Economic objectives and strategies for meeting them had been given a very precise meaning. Investments had been made in the context of a very particular economic knowledge. As a result, *Q* was now composed of different machines and different people with different skills located in different places, and subject to a different management regime. What is more, *Q* now needed its accounting systems in order to function as it did. They satisfied needs that they had played a role in creating. The present structuring of the organization presumed the existence of accounting. No longer just discrete technical procedures, the accounting systems were infused into the organization itself.

The creation of accounting residues that, in turn, played a role in creating the organization in which the accountings functioned had been an important part of Q's development. A visibility had become a reality. But that visibility had not always been so centrally implicated in the functioning of Q. It had been born amidst a different reality, serving different purposes than those now required of it. The accounting residues had been laid down in an organization different from that which Q now is.

Important features of the emergent economic visibility had been created in the context of attempts to control the labour process. A conflictful and organized work force had provided one significant base for the rise of a regime of economic calculation and administration in Q. The control of economically orientated effort had been a mobilizing problem. Investments had been made in the specification of work expectations, in the linking of effort to reward and in the measurement and control of actual performance. A regime of detailed economic calculation had been created in order to render visible in a quite particular manner, the functioning of the operational core of the organization. The social control of work had provided an important incentive for Q's investment in an enhanced visibility of the economic.

Now, however, that socially constructed visibility had created an enterprise organizationally dependent on the resultant knowledge. The organization had been reformed in the name of the knowledge of it. A managerial regime based on facts and analysis had arisen. More precise articulations of objectives had been made, and these had been diffused throughout the organization by means of the accounting calculus. New segmentations of work had been initiated in the organization and new bases for administrative expertise forged. What had been initiated in the organization in the name of the social came to function in the name of both the organizational and the social.

On the Consideration of Accounting in Motion

Together the cases illustrate not only that accounting can be conceived as being in motion, but also that such a perspective provides a rich insight into the organizational practice of accounting and its consequences for action. What conventionally have been seen to be the statics of the accounting craft have been seen to be in the process of changing, becoming thereby, what they are not. And such a portrayal has enabled an analysis of some of the ways in which accounting, by intersecting with other organizational processes and practices, influences the patterns of organizational visibility, significance, structure and action.

For all three organizations, accounting had played some role in their transformation. The processes through which their accountings had become what they were not were starting to become, or already were, embedded in the very fabric of their functioning. Particular regimes of accounting facts had been created. An operational significance was given to economic and managerial categories and rhetoric. A seemingly precise and specific calculus had entered into organizational deliberations and debate. Accounting, in being propagated and changed, had become implicated in wider processes of organizational perception, governance and strategic mobilization.

Whilst it is recognized that organizational life involves a continuous dialogue between the possible and the actual, and that thereby conceptions of an accounting potential can play a role in mobilizing accounting change, this is not to attach an obviousness, a priority or an imperative to the rhetorical claims that are associated with the accounting craft or to provide them with any privileged role in enabling accounting to become what it was not. The effects of such claims need to be seen as arising from their interaction with the other circumstances that characterize organizational life rather than an all embracing, powerfully penetrating and unproblematic logic.

Reflecting the need to articulate a wider appreciation of accounting in action and the processes by which it changes, the analysis of the cases has been conducted in terms of a number of analytical themes. Emphasis has been placed on the particular visibilities created by accounting systems and the means by which they, in turn, shifted perceptions of organizational functioning, mediated the recognition of problems and the options available for their resolution, and infused the patterns of language, meaning and significance within the organization. From such a stance, attention was directed to the constitutive as well as the reflective roles of accounting. For although it was recognized that a diverse array of other factors could and did impinge upon the accounting craft, at times causing it to shift its focus of attention and locus of organizational embodiment, equally the analyses were undertaken with an awareness of the more enabling properties of accounting itself.

By moulding the patterns of organizational visibility, by extending the range of influence patterns within the organization, by creating different patterns of interaction and interdependence and by enabling new forms of organizational segmentation to exist, accounting was seen as being able to play a positive role in both shifting the preconditions for organizational change and influencing its outcomes, even including the possibilities for its own transformation. Through such mutual processes of interaction, accounting was conceived as a phenomenon embedded within the organization rather than as something that had a meaningful independent existence. The forms that it took and the influences that it had were not seen as being able to be appreciated outside of the context of the other organizational practices, functions and processes with which it became intertwined. Together they reflected a particular specificity of alignments and although it was sometimes possible to distinguish one organizational phenomenon influencing another, the analysis was conducted in terms of the possibility for, but not the necessity of, such influences since the mobilizing factors were often so numerous, diverse, ambiguous and uncertain, and had such an equivocal *a priori* relationship to the craft of accounting, that change, be it accounting or otherwise, was seen as being something that was created rather than determined. So although not frequently analyzed, the importance of accounting's constitutive roles should not be under-emphasized. They represent one of the significant ways in which accounting becomes embedded in the organization of which it is a part.

It was with such metaphors in mind that the task of analysis was seen to be an archaeological one of carefully and cautiously sorting through the sediments of organizational history, however recent, to reconstruct the ways in which the present emerged from the past. However, as Foucault (1972, 1977) has come to use the terms, the mode of analysis mobilized in the present discussion has features of both a genealogy and an archaeology. An 'archaeology tries to outline particular configurations' (Foucault 1972: 157) in order to reveal 'relations between discursive formations and non-discursive domains (institutional, political events, economic practices and processes)' (162). As in the present analysis, an archaeology strives to isolate the conditions of possibility of social and organizational practices and bodies of knowledge aiming to reconstruct 'a heterogeneous system of relations and effects whose contingent interlocking' (Gordon 1980: 243) constitute the basis on which practice is formed, functions and has its effects. Moreover, it is the active construction of an archaeology that creates a sensitivity to the power creating potential of bodies of knowledge and organizational and social practices that come to create a conception of reality within which they function.

Genealogy, on the other hand, concerns itself with ruptures and transitions whereby words, categories, practices and institutions adopt new meanings and significances as they become intertwined with new purposes and new wills, an equally important theme of the present discussion. With its emphasis on change, it is the genealogical perspective that serves to alert us to the dangers of assuming any underlying coherence, tendency or logic, such as progress, mobilizing patterns of historical and organizational transformation towards some ultimate fulfillment or conclusion. As Foucault (1977: 146) made clear, genealogy 'does not pretend to go back in time to restore an unbroken continuity that operates beyond the dispersion of forgotten things'.

Although the present investigations have been both more focused and constrained than the inquiries undertaken by Foucault, they nevertheless have provided an appreciation of some of the ways in which accounting can both be transformed by and serve as a vehicle for the transformation of the wider organization. Both a fluidity and a specificity have been introduced into our understanding of accounting in action. The significances attached to accounting have been shown in the process of their reformulation. The craft has been seen as becoming embedded in different organizational configurations and serving very different organizational functions in the process of its change. The mobilizing vehicles for these changes have been seen as residing in a very diverse number of organizational processes and practices and, not least, in accounting itself.

References

Foucault, M. (1972). *The archaeology of knowledge*. London: Tavistock.

Foucault, M. (1977). *Language, counter-memory, practice*. Oxford: Basil Blackwell.

Gordon, C. (1980). Afterword, in M. Foucault. *Power/knowledge*. Harvester.

McKendrick, N. (1961). Josiah Wedgwood and factory discipline. *The Historical Journal, 24*, 30–55.

McKendrick, N. (1973). Josiah Wedgwood and cost accounting in the Industrial Revolution. *Journal of Economic History, 33*, 45–67.

Chapter 9

Accounting and the Construction of the Governable Person[1]

Peter Miller,   *London School of Economics*

Ted O'Leary,   *Manchester University*

The concern of this paper is historical. It addresses one familiar event within the literature of the history of accounting — the construction of theories of standard costing and budgeting in the first three decades of the twentieth century. A different interpretation of this event is offered from that commonly found. This is seen to have significant implications for the relevance of historical investigation to the understanding of contemporary accounting practices. Instead of an interpretation of standard costing and budgeting as one stage in the advance in accuracy and refinement of accounting concepts and techniques, it is viewed as an important calculative practice which is part of a much wider modern apparatus of power which emerges conspicuously in the early years of this century.

The concern of this form of power is seen to be the construction of the individual person as a more manageable and efficient entity. This argument is explored through an examination of the connections of standard costing and budgeting with scientific management and industrial psychology. These knowledges are then related to others which, more or less simultaneously, were emerging beyond the confines of the firm to address questions of the efficiency and manageability of the individual.

Accounting has remained remarkably insulated from important theoretical and historical debates which have traversed the social sciences. Accounting history, for example, is a context in which one can begin to substantiate this lack of a problematisation of the roles of accounting. A standard concept which guides accounting history is one that sees accounting as essentially having functional roles in society, albeit ones which can change (American Accounting Association 1970). Little or no suspicion seems to surface that different methodological starting points could be entertained, which could lead to rather different understandings of accounting's history.

---

[1]Reproduced (in an abridged form) from Peter Miller and Ted O'Leary, 'Accounting and the Construction of the Governable Person', *Accounting, Organizations and Society*, 1987, vol. 12, no. 3, pp. 235–265, with permission of Elsevier.

Accounting, the Social and the Political
N. Macintosh and T. Hopper (Editors)

The utility of accounting history, its potential in relation to current theoretical and practical concerns, is that through elucidating the resolution of past incongruities of accounting with its environment, it could facilitate the more effective resolution of such issues in the present. The image to be gained is that accounting can enmesh with its context in ways that are inevitable, given some overwhelming environmental shift, and that may even be socially desirable. We do not find such an interpretation of accounting history to be persuasive.

One way of countering such an approach is to invert the perspective. Accounting would then no longer be viewed as becoming, or as having the capacity to become, an increasingly refined technical apparatus. It would also no longer be viewed as neutral but rather seen, once the veils of current misperception have been drawn back, to clearly reflect and to serve certain economic or political interests. Such an approach has achieved considerable currency when applied to disciplines other than accounting.

We are not persuaded by this line of argument either. Central to it is a notion that there is a more or less direct and unproblematic relation between economic and/or political interests, and the knowledges and techniques which are held to represent such interests. The terms and categories through which such interests are represented are seen to have no effects. Whether it is a thesis centered on a notion of knowledge as a 'servant of power' or knowledge viewed as representing class interests, the difficulties remain. The notion of control in such a view comes to substitute for notions of progress or evolution in standard histories. Whereas, the latter see accounting as progressing in terms of an unproblematic social utility, the former see history as the elaboration of better and subtler forms of control.

It seems to us that there is a very real need to develop an understanding of accounting and its past which is distinct from these two approaches. This is the thrust of our attempt in this paper, undertaken through a discussion of the emergence of standard costing and budgeting within the accounting literature, and the relation between these and a number of other related social and organizational practices. Our concern is with a particular episode in the history of accounting which we see as crucial, and its relevance and implications for understanding contemporary accounting.

If our concern in this paper can be called historical, it entails an understanding of historical processes which is unfamiliar in the accounting literature. It may be useful to refer to one or two landmarks in relation to which the concerns of this paper may be identified.

The interpretation of historical processes we have utilized takes much of its inspiration from the work of Michel Foucault (1973, 1977, 1981). Over a period of some twenty years, Foucault has worked on what can be called a series of histories, or genealogies, of the emergence of the human sciences. His studies have covered medicine, the emergence of psychiatry, and the prison to name just some of the more important. The historical focus for these has generally been on the period around 1800, which he sees as a crucial point in the formation of the modern era.

The notion of genealogy is deceptively simple. It concerns centrally a questioning of our contemporarily received notions by a demonstration of their historical emergence. The point of history in this sense is to make intelligible the way in which we think today by reminding us of its conditions of formation. Whether the terms be efficiency, rationality or motivation, genealogical analysis helps us to appreciate their ephemeral character. But genealogy is not just a matter of de-bunking, a valuable enough enterprise in its own right. It concerns also a particular approach to the tracing of the emergence of our frequently unquestioned contemporary rationales. This is one which does not entail looking for a single point in history which would be the point of origin of our current practices. The emergence of our contemporary beliefs is viewed rather by reference to a complex of dispersed events. Genealogy does not lead us to solid foundations; rather, it fragments and disturbs what we might like to see as the basis of our current ideas and practices.

Applied to accounting it means questioning a search for the origins of accounting in the invention of techniques, whether in recent centuries or in antiquity. Other types of events, such as the political objectives of states, but also historical contingency, particular national conditions and the development of related disciplines, all enter into the explanation. Genealogy opens out into a much less certain field than the standard histories of accounting would lead us to believe.

Perhaps, the most crucial aspect of Foucault's work of relevance to this paper concerns the relationship between knowledge and power. Foucault's arguments on this question are distinctive. He suggests that we can understand the development of modern societies in terms of power, and the shift in its mode of exercise. The broadest shift he refers to is one which he suggests took place around 1800 and is from what he calls sovereign power to disciplinary power.

Foucault's arguments concerning power are closely linked to his investigation of the emergence of the human sciences (Foucault 1970). The shift he identifies from sovereign to disciplinary power is intimately connected with changes in our forms of knowledge. His argument is expressed in the formula 'power/knowledge' and the constitutive interdependence of the two terms of the equation — the operation of the human sciences should be understood in relation to the elaboration of a range of techniques for the supervision, administration and disciplining of populations of human individuals. This is seen to take place in particular institutions and in social relations in a wider sense. Thus, our attempt in this paper is to understand how one important period in accounting's history has been influenced by the above themes.

Standard Costing and Budgeting

Between 1900 and 1930, there appears in the accounting literature an initial delineation of theories of standard costing and budgeting. This is a novel event within accounting. At a purely technical level, the innovation brought about was nothing less than an entire re-casting of the definition of cost accounting. Its primary concern would henceforth no longer be the ascertainment of only the actual costs of production of activities. There would be an expansion of domain to permit a concern for the future as well as for the past.

What interests us here is the way the existing histories construe the development of standard costing. They tend to narrate the emergence of standard costing and budgeting according to two distinct criteria. One of these consists in a careful and detailed exposition of the ideas and techniques in the terms of those who, at the time, had developed or articulated them. A second approach which Solomons (1968), for example, adopts is to construe these novel practices through the lens of progress, to outline the difficult and often error-prone paths whereby costing has progressed to its current level of sophistication. Thus, for example, he points to 'weaknesses' in one of the early outlines of a standard costing, that of Emerson (1919), indicating its failures in analytic power and in clarity of thought relative to writing which follows it in time.

We wish in this paper to place a different interpretation on the emergence of standard costing. We do not view the development of standard costing and budgeting as part of the unfolding of a socially useful theoretical–technical complex, whose underlying logic is one of progress. We wish to locate it rather as an important contribution to a complex of practices which exist in the form of socio-political management whose concern is with individual persons and their efficient functioning.

Standard costing and budgeting provided quite novel theorization and technique which served to render visible the inefficiencies of the individual person within the enterprise. In routinely raising questions of waste and inefficiency in the employment of human, financial and material resources, they supplemented the traditional concerns of accounting with the fidelity or honesty of the person. Cost accounting could now embrace also the individual person and make them accountable by reference to prescribed standards of performance. With this step, accounting significantly extended its domain, enmeshing the person within a web of calculative practices aimed not only at stewardship but efficiency also. We can identify the shift entailed in the emergence of standard costing during the period 1900 and 1930 across a number of central texts of that period.

By 1930, there had been a clear establishment, in texts on both sides of the Atlantic, of several new prominent additions to the vocabulary of costs accounts keeping. These are 'the standard cost', 'the variance analysis', 'the budget' and 'budgetary control'. This is the break up with which we are concerned including its implications. One way of designating the change would be from the 'registration of costs of production' to 'the rendering of all activities capable of suspicion as to their costliness'.

For our concerns in this paper, there is one crucial dimension to this innovation. The principle of standard costs made it possible to attach to every individual within the firm norms and standards of behaviour. Everyone, in relation to all activities which they directly carried out or directed, could be rendered susceptible to a continual process of judgment. This implanting of norms moreover concerned not just norms of physiological behaviour for the worker at the bench, but also the mental activity on the part of the executive.

With this step the possibility of a knowledge of every individual within the enterprise was established. A visibility and an allocation of responsibility could be attached to the individual. The person's activities were at last rendered knowable according to prescribed standards and deviations from the norm. Standard costing and budgeting made possible a pinpointing of responsibilities for preventable inefficiencies at the level of the very individual from whom they derived. The human element in production, and most importantly the individual person, could now be known according to their contribution to the efficiency of the enterprise.

At the level of the enterprise standard costing and budgeting contributed, we suggest, a facilitative technology which enabled a whole range of activities of the person to be rendered visible and accountable. Within the enterprise, one could at last literally make all individuals accountable.

In its purest form, such a type of power consists in the individual attending to his or her own deficiencies. It is a form of power in which the individual becomes an auto-regulated entity, but one for whom the standards according to which they judge their lives have been established for them. Standard costing and budgeting is, we suggest, central to such a process.

The Firm as a Site in the Construction of the Governable Person

The ambiguities of the word efficiency enabled it to operate across a series of dispersed strategies concerned with managing the life of the person. These ranged from broad political platforms to psychological and sociological concerns with individuals who deviated from specified norms in a variety of ways. We argue that the standard costing–budgeting complex can be viewed in terms of such a preoccupation. Standard costing and budgeting, however, were intended to operate within a particular site — that of the firm. Our concern now is to identify the way in which standard costing and budgeting, in conjunction with scientific management and industrial psychology, came to define the firm as a very particular kind of space. It should be one in which efficiency and rationality would prevail.

The creation of a standard costing within the accounting literature, accounting historians have acknowledged, owes a considerable debt to that movement which, originating in the USA, became known as 'scientific management'. According to Solomons (1968: 37), for example, one cannot read R. W. Taylor's paper of 1903 on Shop Management without noticing that it contains many of the essential elements of what would later become standard costing.

Taking scientific management and cost accounting as an interlinked complex, we wish to suggest an explanation as to the kind of project to which it contributed. This was one in which notions of efficiency identified at the level of the individual could come to be expressed in money terms and related to expected standards and norms.

Undoubtedly, the body of thought and practice that became known as scientific management was enmeshed within that American question for national efficiency. According to F. W. Taylor (1913: 5–7), in the introductory pages of his celebrated *Principles of Scientific Management*, the task was to advance national efficiency through remediation of those vast wastes which, going far beyond the poor use and inadequate conservation of natural resources, secreted themselves within the daily actions of everyone. Roosevelt had been prophetic, says Taylor, in regarding the conservation of natural resources as no more than preliminary to such a wider question of the efficiency of the person and, thereby, of the nation.

Prior to its intersection with scientific management, cost accounting's prime defect was that it had: 'Failed most utterly and dismally to achieve what should be the primary purpose of any cost system, namely, to bring promptly to the attention of the management the existence of preventable inefficiencies so that steps could be taken to eliminate these at the earliest possible moment' (Harrison 1930: 8).

In rectifying this deficiency cost accounting would expand its domain. It would supply the engineers and their scientific management with a facilitative technology for expressing their norms and standards in terms of money. The earlier concern of cost accounting with the registration of the movements of workers and materials as they 'attached' themselves to production would be augmented. This expansion would reflect a concept of the worker as almost certainly inefficient, needing to be enmeshed within a routinely applicable calculative apparatus which standard costing would provide.

This alliance of cost accounting with the engineers was important in the construction of norms of efficiency. It provided a way for making the individual worker routinely knowable and accountable in terms of wasted actions. And scientific management was such an individualizing endeavour *par excellence*. It was a matter of ceasing to treat workers only in the anonymous terms of groups, classified by trade or skill. Attention was to be paid instead to the performance of each individual worker. Taylorism would insist that each worker be singled out, to be rewarded or punished on the basis of his or her individual performance.

This is precisely where standard costing again becomes significant. Together with budgeting it would seem to have provided an important escape route, allowing the principles of standardizing and normalizing to move away from the factory floor. At least in principle they could now embrace everyone within the firm. Standard costing, which had already enmeshed the factory worker within a calculus of efficiency would now move on, by means of the budget or profit plan, to do the same for executives.

If Taylorism and scientific management more generally had envisaged the enterprise as machine-line, cost accounting, through the budget and budgetary control, would provide a means for rendering that image operational. Money would, as it were, become the common currency with which to integrate and aggregate the activities of individuals as components. For both brain-work and physical-work, indeed for every accountable person within the firm, standards and deviations therefrom reckoned in money could record the individual's contributions, and also their failure to contribute, to the ends of the machine as a whole. At hand was a calculative apparatus through which deep questions of responsibility could routinely be pressed upon individuals.

What was now being addressed was how the psyche of the worker might be known and managed, so as to serve efficiency on an even grander scale than the promise of the engineers and the cost accountants. The industrial psychologists can be seen as a further group that would invade the firm, generating and applying a knowledge of the individual. With this, the development concerns of the mind as well as of the body would be introduced into the project of enmeshing the individual within the norms of economic performance.

It would establish a laboratory within which to place the person as a subject upon whom experiments could be conducted. This would place it alongside the natural sciences. Its peripatetic laboratory would be the factory, industrial psychologists moving freely from the one to the other with great ease. The early industrial psychologists share with Taylorism an appeal to efficiency as a transcendent purpose. They too, it seems, want their endeavour placed beyond the reach of politics.

Implications and Conclusions

We have noted the alliance of scientific management and costing. From its earliest beginnings, it seems, the scientific management literature had recognized the power of an efficiency measurement grounded in costs and profits. And we have noted the influence of scientific management on the construction of standard costing, which itself merges into budgeting. The resultant calculative apparatus was to entail the possibility for going beyond a routine rendering visible of only the factory-floor worker's efficiency. We have viewed the superimposition of a notion of standardized magnitudes upon the traditional accounting statements of income and financial position as facilitating the normalization (in terms of economic accomplishment) of everyone within the firm. Budgeting, one might say, would serve as an escape-route by which standards could leave the factory floor and enmesh, potentially, everyone in the firm. Without effacing the notion of the person as potential thief, that long-standing stewardship concern of accounting, standard costing and budgeting would render accessible to various expert and authoritative interventions the individual as 'almost certainly inefficient'.

Cost accounting would expand its domain, to enmesh the person in a calculus of expectations. In constructing a notion of the person in this manner we have argued that standard costing and budgeting provided a facilitative technology whereby, in time, various interventions to improve the person's performance would become possible. For the whole project of enmeshing the person within norms of efficiency, once begun, came quickly enough to be seen as a complex, sophisticated endeavour.

In looking at such processes in this manner, we have wanted to suggest a way of viewing accounting as having contributed to a more general project of socio-political management. This is one which operates through a variety of expert knowledges and practices. The efficiency of individuals and their contribution to collective efficiency is central to such processes. But the efficiency of the person in the firm, as we have seen Taylor point out, is not something which can be observed with the naked eye. Indeed, one might say, it cannot exist until what is to be regarded as normal or standard has first been constructed. But once a norm is to hand, and especially when it gains expression within a routinely applicable calculative apparatus like standard costing or budgeting, the person can become a subject for various human sciences. The deviations of the person from a norm, with all of their possible causes and consequences, become available for investigation and for remedial action. And, we would suggest, one distinctive contribution of standard costing, hitherto apparently ignored, is its contribution to a much wider process, whereby the life of the person comes to be viewed in relation to standards and norms of behaviour.

We do not feel that our concerns in this paper can be adequately captured by referring to a general process of rationalization of Western industrial societies (Weber 1978). In talking of projects for social and organizational management, we have wanted to emphasize the actual construction of such projects, and to the terms in which they are constructed. We have sought tentatively to explain how accounting supplies an important contribution to a complex of interventions directed at providing mechanisms for the implication of individuals within the life of the organization and of society.

References

American Accounting Association (1970). Report of the committee on accounting history. *Accounting Review.* Supplement to Vol. XLV.

Emerson, H. (1919). *Efficiency as a basis for operation and wages.* New York: Engineering Magazine Co.

Foucault, M. (1970). *The order of things.* London: Tavistock.

Foucault, M. (1973). *The birth of the clinic.* London: Tavistock.

Foucault, M. (1977). *Discipline and punish.* Harmondsworth. Allen Lane/Penguin.

Foucault, M. (1981). *The history of sexuality,* Vol. 1. Harmondsworth: Penguin.

Harrison, G.C. (1930). *Standard costing.* New York: Ronald Press.

Solomons, D. (1968). The Historical development of costing, in D. Solomons (ed.). *Studies in cost analysis.* London: Sweet and Maxwell.

Taylor, F.W. (1913). *The principles of scientific management.* New York: Harper and Brothers.

Weber, M. (1978). *Economy and society,* G. Roth & C. Wittich (eds). Berkeley: University of California Press.

Chapter 10

Accounting Systems in Organizational Contexts: A Case for Critical Theory[1]

Richard C. Laughlin, *Kings College, London*

Accounting Theory and Practice and the Significance of Critical Theory in such a Context

To view an accounting system as a technical, organizationally independent phenomenon is increasingly being questioned. Although accounting systems undoubtedly have technical aspects, these need to be understood with reference to the context in which they are placed which supplies the important meanings for these more tangible elements.

One particular way in which accounting systems can be understood by reference to their social context is to view them as types of organizational language systems. They are, as language systems, human artifacts which model certain aspects of organizational life whose 'terms' and 'sentences' (the more technical aspects of their design) find meanings in the historical, organizational and societal context in which they are 'uttered'. These meanings may be regarded as variable, if one follows the approach of the later Wittgenstein (1953), to language as suggested by leading figures in the modern theory of language (cf. Austin 1961; Searle 1969). As a result, universal general meanings cannot be assured.

Despite these doubts two points are clear about their nature. Firstly, meanings need to be discovered and defined by human actors, and this is to be achieved through that distinctly human attribute, namely language. Secondly, there is every possibility that these meanings go beyond the present organizational context. In this sense, the meanings may transcend the organization. Two most obvious areas of transcendence are apparent: firstly in terms of history, and secondly in relation to the social or societal context. The real meanings behind the more technical aspects of accounting systems design may be found in contextual variables in previous generations, or equally in social or societal variables due to the close interconnections between organizations and society.

---

[1]Reproduced (in an abridged form) from Richard C. Laughlin, 'Accounting Systems in Organisational Contexts: A Case for Critical Theory', *Accounting, Organizations and Society*, 1987, vol. 12, no. 5, pp 479–502 with permission of Elsevier.

Accounting, the Social and the Political
N. Macintosh and T. Hopper (Editors)

Critical Theory

Critical theory refers principally to the work of members of the Institute of Social Research founded in Frankfurt in 1923. The most prominent figures in this tradition are Max Horkheimer, Theodor Adorno, Herbert Marcuse and Jürgen Habermas. Critical theory is a diverse and, to a certain extent, disparate set of ideas.

The primary concern of all critical theorists was, and still is, with a historically grounded social theory of the way societies and the institutions which make them up, have emerged and can be understood. Interpretation is never for its own sake but forms a part of the important understanding which can allow some desired 'transformation' of societies and their institutions so that a 'true, free and just life' can be assured. This practical and critical concern with the change and development of societies and institutions indicates the role and significance of theory for these writers: theory becomes the vehicle for a historically grounded interpretation and transformation to occur.

Critical theory is a vehicle through which understanding about reality can be achieved and transformation of concrete institutions occur. Understanding is always to be related to the concerns with desired transformation. It is 'critical' in the sense that it holds the view that the present is not satisfactory, that reality could be better than it is, and that the methodological aspects of critical theory can create this improvement which marks out this thinking as essentially 'critical'.

Historical analysis, to a critical theorist, supplies not only the insights into the past but also the methodological tools for change in the future. Points of progress in the past and the mechanisms which have permitted their emergence form the methodological apparatus for change in the future. This view rests upon a prior belief as to what constitutes progress or regression for society. Historical analysis is not some value free activity, but is undertaken with a particular purpose in mind: to analyse points of progress, to discern the mechanisms leading to their emergence, and to allow these to be used again to encourage societal development to a truer, freer and more just life for all.

Critical theory, however, cannot claim the status of a well established and validated approach to the understanding of society and the transformation of its institutions; it is, on the contrary, based on assumptions which are subject to debate and question. The primary assumptions are: firstly, that society has the potential within itself to be what it is not; secondly, that conscious human action is capable of moulding the social world to be something different and 'better'; and thirdly, that this can be promoted by utilizing the aids and props which critical theory can supply. The (second) humanistic assumption rests on a particular position concerning the ability of conscious human action to change the social world. It thus takes a particular position on an issue which has dominated and divided philosophical discussion for centuries. In this respect, critical theory is open to attack by those who opt for a view either of determinism or those who remain justifiably agnostic at this stage in our understanding.

The Relevance of Critical Theory for Accounting Research

Three key characteristics of critical theory can be identified with a view to illuminate the technical and social aspects of accounting systems.

Firstly, critical theory proposes dynamically linking theory to practice. Theory, to a critical theorist, must always have some sort of effect on practical 'real world' phenomena.

Secondly, critical theory sees critique, change and development as vitally necessary components of the practically based research endeavour. This unabashed concern for critique of the *status quo* and the need for transformation to achieve a 'better' life could inject a fundamental ethical dimension into accounting research.

Thirdly, critical theory views social organizations in a historical and societal context. The concern is to identify the often hidden meanings which reside in these contexts. Critical theory has always been addressed as going beyond the tangible to the unseen and unclear contextual elements to discover the 'real' meanings and factors which produce change. To the extent that accounting systems find their meaning in the underlying social factors, with change in the former being dependent on changes in the latter, then critical theory may well supply a methodological framework for addressing these issues.

For these reasons, it is argued that critical theory may also supply a useful vehicle for understanding and changing accounting systems in organizational contexts.

Alternative Methodological Approaches in Critical Theory and their Relevance in Accounting

Each of the four key individual representatives of critical theory (Horkheimer, Adorno, Marcuse and Habermas) has taken different perspectives on the nature of historical development.

Different Perspectives on Critical Theory

Max Horkheimer held different interpretations during his life about historical development. His overarching view about the human race and society was that things were not as they should be but the desire and ability to change to achieve emancipation was 'immanent' to humanity.

The most complex and difficult of the critical theorists to summarize is Theodor Adorno. His principal concern was with issues of philosophy and the nature of truth. However, like all critical theorists his views about truth, theory and methodology came from an analysis of history. Historical reality was far from optimal according to Adorno (1966). He maintained that reality constantly did not match up to some pre-defined (although unspecified) set of concepts which Adorno applied to it.

Arguing from a different stance, Herbert Marcuse viewed history as a constant repression of human individuals whose immanent potential to achieve a better world for themselves and their society was almost extinguished (cf. Marcuse 1955, 1964).

Repression for Marcuse was not a matter of physical violence but was a domination of creative human potential by the logic of western industrial life and its consumerist logic. Marcuse propounded a critical methodology which was intended to expose this repression and, in the process, generate the momentum for the necessary change which would ensue. Critical theory was to contribute to the enlightenment required before the repression of life in the affluent west could be ended.

From a seemingly less radical perspective Habermas focussed on the role of language in societal developmental processes. He maintained that despite the many repressive points in the history of western society there is much that registers real progress. Habermas' theory of social evolution maintains that society has progresses due to the expanding and developing language skills of societal members. This realization gives rise to what Habermas calls his 'logic of development' or methodological approach in our terminology, which centres on different language processes which when operative would, according to Habermas, generate even greater progression.

The four critical theorists each provide a different methodological approach, whether this be applied to a society, an organization or an accounting system. It is argued, however, that Habermas' model has the greatest potential both as a methodological approach for understanding and changing accounting systems design and for investigating social phenomena more widely.

There are three reasons for making this claim. Firstly Habermas' methodological approach focuses on language and communication as the element which is vital in allowing understanding to occur and nonviolent change to happen. As such, the approach is built upon a very basic rational skill which marks out our uniqueness as human beings. It can be argued that accounting systems, which can be seen as the technical elements of a type of organizational language system, need to be understood and changed through language, if we are to discover and alter the social meanings which adhere to them.

Secondly, Habermas' methodology, unlike the other critical theorists' approaches, does not presume some prior ideal state for the phenomena before an investigation can ensue — the ideal is discovered through the process rather than being part of the defined attributes of the approach formulated at the outset. Thus, using Habermas' thinking in an accounting context we need not start with an ideal design with which we compare the actual as we would have to using, say, negative dialectics. Rather, we discuss the nature of the accounting system and through this structured and defined discourse discover the improvements which are necessary.

Thirdly, and finally, Habermas specifies clearly the nature and type of the processes which are necessary to generate understanding and change in the phenomena under investigation. Unlike the other critical theorists, Habermas extensively discusses the requisite details surrounding the required language processes, whereas most of the other approaches remain in embryonic generalities. For all these reasons, Habermas' methodological approach seems to offer more promise than the other three as an approach for understanding and changing accounting systems design.

Some Preparatory Insights into Habermas' Approach and its Relevance to Accounting in Organizational Contexts

Habermas' methodological approach is derived by reference to what he calls a 'life-world', 'Systems' and 'language decentration' (Habermas 1974, 1981a, 1981b). The life-world is, to Habermas, a type of cultural space which gives meaning and nature to societal life. Whilst separate and distinct from the more tangible (technical) visible 'systems' it is the social reality which gives these systems meaning and attempts to guide their behaviour through 'steering mechanisms'. Systems are the 'self-regulating action contexts which co-ordinate actions around specific mechanisms or media, such as money or power' (Thompson 1983: 285). They are, in this sense, distinct elements whilst at the same time intended to be the tangible expression of the cultural life-world. Language decentration traces the way individuals develop their language skills which, to Habermas, enables the differentiation of the life-world and systems and the development of both.

His theory is intended to cover the way Western societies have developed over the centuries. The three main stages of social evolution ('mythical', 'religious-metaphysical', 'modern'), according to Habermas, can be traced to increasing levels of differentiation of and in the life-world and systems in societies. These changes, in turn, are traceable to the expansion of language capacities, where individuals progressively move from a position of 'primitive egocentrism' towards a language capacity 'for coping with the external world, the social world and the world of inner subjectivity' (Giddens 1982: 323) in a differentiated but integrated manner. It is this ability to articulate the differences and interrelationships of the technical (the external world), the cultural (the social world) and the individuality (the world of inner subjectivity), which have allowed our differentiated cultural systems and tangible institutions to arise.

Yet our inability to differentiate and retain the social and technical spheres as separate has led, according to Habermas, to a process of 'inner colonization' of the social life-world by the technical system. The technical sphere overpowers the social, far exceeding its boundaries. To avoid this situation, either the life-world can defend itself against further inner colonization or it can re-establish its superiority while still maintaining its differentiated nature from the systems. Habermas sees the concern for defence being the current situation. Yet he would maintain that long term development can only occur with the re-emergence of the significance of the cultural life-world and movements in this which are seen to happen through the adoption and use of a particular methodological approach which, not surprisingly, is language based.

This methodology attempts to expose the distinct nature of the technical and social spheres (systems and life-world). This is to be achieved through the language processes which, according to Habermas, created their differentiated but integrated nature in the first place. The approach relies on the use of language processes which can heighten the ability of human beings to articulate the nature of and interconnections between the three 'worlds' of reality (the 'external', the 'social' and 'inner subjectivity'), which will be vital if we are to understand and change any phenomena we need to investigate.

The actual details of these language processes are extremely complex and somewhat scattered through Habermas' writing, although the clearest overall picture of them is contained in the new introduction to *Theory and Practice* (1974: 1–40). In this work, Habermas articulates three key stages in this language process ('formulation of critical theorems', 'processes of enlightenment' and 'selection of strategies' stages) each of which have different natures, purposes and intentions. However, all have an overriding concern with exposing the integrated social and technical aspects of any phenomena and changing the balance and nature of the two. This is primarily to be led through changes in the social, as we will see in the following section when we apply this logic in an accounting context.

Habermas' thinking addresses an issue central to the debate between those who see accounting systems as nothing more than technical phenomena and those who view them as having important social roots. Whilst Habermas does not focus specifically on accounting phenomena, his more general concerns with the domination of the technical over the social and the need for an exposure of both and of their interrelationships has considerable relevance to accounting. Habermas would quite understand why it is that some accounting theorists only see accounting as a set of techniques for constructing profit and loss accounts, balance sheet, budgets, etc. and their desire to encourage the use of these technical developments in all organizations to improve efficiency. This, to Habermas, is an expected and understandable outcome where the technical is overriding and divorced from the social. However, he would be equally adamant of the need for change in this unbalanced situation.

In an accounting context, this implies that accounting discourses have been limited to talking about alternative measurement approaches, to concepts such as cost, profit, etc. and more or less efficient systems of evaluation (as in capital budgeting), thereby restricting our understanding about accounting system design. This also restricts the possibilities for practical change and may well explain why so many of our textbook models of efficient systems remain unused in practice. Our surprise at this lack of usage is because we have not yet realized the significance of culture in determining the acceptability of any technical system. To change this situation we need to change the linguistic processes and the vocabulary we use for our descriptive understanding about the nature of accounting systems and for the processes necessary to achieve real changes in these systems in practice.

Habermas' Methodological Approach for Understanding and Changing Accounting in Organizational Contexts

The approach forms a process of discovery, from a critical perspective, into the fundamental nature of any accounting system leading to changes in both the technical nature of this system as well as the context which gives it meaning.

From a point of ignorance, about even the technical aspects of any particular organization's accounting system the approach enables both the researchers and those actively involved in the organization (the researched) to critically clarify these technical elements (e.g. the specific nature of the external reporting system and of the internal accounting control process) along with exposing the social roots (e.g. the cultural factors and historical reasons behind these factors or the technological roots, such as compliance to the laws and standards of the accounting regulatory bodies for external report design and the cultural reasons for this compliance). It then takes both groups into actively seeking changes in either, or both, of these technical elements and the social roots in the context of a model of 'progress' (to be defined in the discourse) for both the organization and the society of which it is a part.

The approach forms a process of discovery, from a critical perspective, into the fundamental nature of any accounting system leading to changes in both the technical nature of this system as well as the context which gives it meaning. From a point of ignorance about even the technical aspects of any particular organization's accounting system, the approach enables both the researchers and those actively involved in the organization (the researched) to critically clarify these technical elements (e.g. the specific nature of the external reporting system and of the internal accounting control process) along with exposing the social roots (e.g. the cultural factors and the historical reasons behind these factors or the technological roots, such as compliance to the laws and standards of the accounting regulatory bodies for external report design and the cultural reasons for this compliance). It then takes both groups into actively seeking changes in either, or both, these technical elements and the social roots in the context of a model of 'progress' (to be defined in the discourse) for both the organization and the society of which it is part.

The Quasi-Ignorance and Critical Theorems Stages

The process of enquiry starts with the researchers at the 'quasi-ignorance' stage. This is here the researchers, having initially secured access, are faced with virtual ignorance at the outset about most of the variables of importance. To move from the 'quasi-ignorance' stage researchers, adopting and accepting the discursive processes, attempt, through reflective and iterative processes, to produce critical theorems about the accounting system. These critical theorems start with an exposure of the more obvious tangible elements of the accounting system (e.g. this accounting system has a budget system and financial statements with these characteristics are produced through this process, approved by these people etc.) and then, through iterative processes, critically explores the hidden roots which lie behind these technical elements such as through technological or more technical factors and from life-world and steering mechanisms which, in turn, have their own historical and structural underlying reasons for their nature.

The Processes of Enlightenment Stage

At the 'enlightenment' stage, the intention is that both researchers and researched come together to critically assess the accuracy or inaccuracy of the agreed conclusions from the 'critical theorems' stage. The aim of this 'enlightenment' stage is the same as that for the 'critical theorems' stage (i.e. to arrive at an explanatory consensus with all their historical, structural, technological roots laid bare). At a basic level, therefore, the processes of these two stages are exactly the same, although there are two basic differences.

The first difference concerns the introduction of other, uniquely important, discursive partners — the inaptly named 'researched' as we have called them — and the problems created through introducing these individuals into the discourse. Both the commitment of these individuals and their ability to operationalize, even understand, the various discursive processes may be limited. It is for this reason that a prior 'therapeutic discourse' (Habermas 1974: 34) between the researchers and the researched is necessary so as to enable the researched to adopt and use the discursive processes.

The second difference between the 'critical theorems' and 'enlightenment' stages concerns the fact that the researchers put before the researched their view as to the technical elements and social roots of the particular accounting system under investigation. There is, therefore, a recognized and acknowledged asymmetry at the outset of this 'enlightenment' stage in terms of both insights into the phenomena of interest as well as a greater ability to use and adopt the critical discursive processes. Habermas recognized this initial asymmetry, but maintained that the prior 'therapeutic discourses' followed by the demands for an equal opportunity for offering insights (speech acts) should enable the researched not simply to react to the researcher's thoughts but to actually create new explanatory theories.

The Selection of Strategies Stage

There appear to be three mutually exclusive strategies for accounting change. Firstly, there is the need to change the cultural or social roots (the life-world and steering mechanism) with subsequent changes in the technical accounting system elements. Implicit in this strategy is the view that the changes in the more obvious and tangible elements of the accounting system need to follow rather than lead changes in the cultural life-world elements.

A second general strategy for change is with regard to the actual technical systems where these elements have already overshot 'acceptable practice' from the cultural life-world which is intended to guide their nature. This strategy would try to bring the technical elements in line with their cultural roots.

In accounting terms this might, for instance, involve abandoning a computerization plan or refusing to produce accounts based on the procedures advanced by the standard setting bodies due to these technical advances being out of line with cultural expectations and desires.

Thirdly, and finally, change could ensure with regard to the life-world to bring it in line with the overshot systems elements. This would be the case if there is 'positive' inner colonization occurring, i.e. the systems are purposefully and rightly overshooting the present state of the organizational life-world. Obviously, this situation means that the, primarily, technological roots (often societal steering mechanisms) are 'right' from a societal or other perspective and thus the organizational life-world should change. A typical accounting example of this behaviour would be a cultural adaptation rather than resistance, to governmental or standard setters' pronouncements.

A Concluding Comment

We have tried to show how Habermas' methodological approach can be applied to understanding and changing accounting systems and the organizational contexts which give them meaning. Before reflecting more generally about the value of this approach for these concerns, it is important to address and reiterate one further point.

This concerns the possible constraints upon knowing and acting but which have not been drawn out in the above discussion. This discussion gives the impression of a certain surety about the movement between the stages and the precision of the conclusions forthcoming. The reality is that a vast range of constraints may prevent the steady movement between stages and reduce the insights gained and actions forthcoming (particularly at the 'selection of strategies' stage). As we shall indicate in the following section, these need to be more fully understood in order to reduce them through clearly defined strategies. Neither Habermas nor other critical theorists have specified to date the mechanisms by which this may be achieved.

An Evaluation of Habermas' Model as a General Methodological Approach for Understanding and Changing Accounting Systems

Firstly, its overarching concern is to go beyond the tangible and behind the more obvious possible explanatory linkages. Accounting systems are technical phenomena, yet their nature is moulded by social factors. The latter are particularly significant in so far as they contribute to both the understanding and change of technical elements. The approach suggested by Habermas takes these relationships as a starting point and goes further than other methodological approaches in insisting on a constant iterative critique of all postulated insights into these interrelationships.

This focus on the social roots often has to probe into highly sensitive matters which may well be rather uncomfortable to expose (e.g. issues about the foundation reasons for the existence of the organization). This rigour, even though potentially disturbing, may well take us into real levels of understanding and lasting change in our accounting domain, which are sadly lacking at the moment.

Secondly, it sets the nature of understanding exclusively in the context of lasting and meaningful change and development. As we have already indicated, theories are not valued for their own sake; their meaning, significance and the very nature are moulded by their ability to facilitate change. It seems appropriate that the academics of the accounting profession should be involved not only with accounting practice *per se* but in a proactive, critical and developmental expression of this concern. However, it is only right and necessary that these proactive concerns should also not be imposed but should be formulated in conjunction with practitioners themselves in the pursuit of meaningful change.

Thirdly, the approach, based on a developmental process of discovery rather than a reality assumed to be static, needed to be accessed through structured techniques. Habermas starts from the premise that reality needs to be accessed through imaginative human actors using discursive processes which may not be reproducible in quite the way traditional scientists would demand. In this sense Habermas is quite close to Feyerabend (cf. 1975) allowing and encouraging free thinking human beings to discover a much looser concept of knowledge. Yet Habermas would maintain the need for some structural conditions around the discursive process to determine, both by those in the discourse as well as those outside, whether the resulting conclusions are 'justified' and 'grounded'. Accounting systems in particular organizations cannot be assumed to be universal phenomena like gravity or friction. Equally, it cannot be assumed that they will not possess these qualities. We need a methodology that keeps open the opportunity for both but also allows us to judge, in some sense, the 'validity' of the insights forthcoming. It can be argued that the Habermasian approach satisfies these demands.

References

Adorno, T.W. (1966/1973). *Negative Dialektic*. Frankfrst: Suhrkamp; *Negative Dialectics* (Trans. E.B. Ashton). New York: Seabury Press.

Austin, J.L. (1961). A plea for excuses. Reprinted in J.L. Austin, *Philosophical Papers*. Oxford: Clarendon Press.

Feyerabend, P. (1975). *Against method*. London: New Left Books.

Giddens, A. (1982). Reason without revolution? Habermas' theorie des kommunikativen handelns, *Praxis International*, 2, 318–338.

Habermas, J. (1974). *Theory and practice* (Trans. J. Viertel). London: Heinemann.

Habermas, J. (1981a). *Theorie des kommunikativen handelns band II: Zur kritik der funktionalistischen vernunft*. Frankfurt: Suhrkamp.

Habermas, J. (1981b). *Theorie des kommunikativen handelns band I: Handlungsratinalitat und gesellshaftliche rationalisieurung*. Frankfurt: Suhrkamp. *The Theory of communicative action Vol. 1: Reason and rationalisation of society* (Trans. T. McCarthy). London: Heinemann (1984).

Marcuse, H. (1955). *Eros and civilisation: A philosophical inquiry into freud.* Boston: Beacon Press.

Marcuse. H. (1964). *One dimensional man.* Boston: Beacon Press.

Searle, J.R. (1969). *Speech acts: An essay in the philosophy of language.* London: Cambridge University Press.

Thompson, J.B. (1983). Rationality and social rationalization: An assessment of Habermas's theory of communicative action. *Sociology, 17,* 278–294.

Wittgenstein, L. (1953). *Philosophical investigations.* Oxford: Basil Blackwell.

Chapter 11

Accounting as a Legitimating Institution[1]

Alan J. Richardson,   *Schulich School of Business, York University*

Recently, there have been suggestions that accounting may be usefully studied as a legitimating institution. The common focus of these is the ability of accounting, as a set of beliefs and techniques, to link actions and values, i.e. to make those actions legitimate. Implicit in this is that accountants are the medium through which the legitimating role of accounting knowledge is enacted. Although others may use accounting information, this information gains its credibility, and hence its potential for motivation and control, in part through its association with independent professionals.

This perspective is consistent with work on the sociology of the professions which regards the professions as occupational groups which have gained a social mandate to define what is right and wrong within a specific sphere of activity. This function requires a combination of technical skill and authority, and emphasizes the political nature of all professional activity.

The concept of legitimation has a long and rich history within sociological and political theory. It was not, however, developed within a single theoretical tradition, rather, there are three major perspectives — structural-functionalist, social constructionist and hegemonic — on the concept of legitimation, each offering different insights and suggesting different research issues.

The Nature of Legitimation

The process of legitimation, in general terms, may be seen as an attempt to establish a semiotic relation between action and values. The structuralist-functionalist perspective presumes that both values and actions are defined by the functions which must be performed for a social system to survive. The relationship between values and actions is presumed to be unique and the evaluation of this link is a technical function.

The social constructionist perspective regards values as emerging from interaction among members of a society. These values are tied to emergent and institutionalized

---

[1]Reproduced (in an abridged form) from A. Richardson, 'Accounting as Legitimating Institution', *Accounting, Organizations and Society*, 1987, vol. 12, no. 4, pp. 341–355 with permission of Elsevier.

actions through a process of discourse directed by certain experts in legitimation (e.g. priests, elders, professionals).

The hegemonic perspective, finally, regards values as an aspect of elite ideologies which are tied to actions which sustain and further the interests of these elites. The link between values and actions in this case is 'false' (with reference to some ideal state), but is accepted by those affected.

The process of legitimation concerns the moral evaluation of action. The legitimation of action is necessary for that action to occur where: an actor is seen to have a choice in the actions he or she may take; the resource requirements or consequences of action for others are non-trivial; other actors' participation cannot be coerced; and their consent is necessary for the actor to undertake his or her planned action or avoid penalties for past actions. The legitimation of action requires the acceptance of an actor's claim that his or her action is congruent with the values of those with whom he or she must interact.

Accounting may be seen as a legitimating institution to the extent that it mediates the mapping between action and values. In particular, accounting fills this role by structuring relations among actors and acting as the medium through which organizational control is exercised; serving as a sanctioning basis for action; and/ or, defining or constraining the perception of action in a given situation. Three dominant perspectives on organization and the conduct of this role are outlined in Table 11.1 and reviewed next.

The Structural-Functionalist Perspective

A Theoretical Overview

The structural-functionalist perspective in sociology includes the work of Comte, Durkheim, Pareto and many others. In the late 1930s, Talcott Parsons emerged as the great synthesizer of this tradition and, for the last fifty years, his writing has directed work on this perspective.

Parsons (1977) distinguishes sharply between legitimation and justification. Legitimation refers to processes which create and validate the normative order of a society. It ties together the resource mobilization system and labour consumption market. Legitimation refers to processes which bring cultural values to bear on the distribution of resources in society; whereas justification operates at a lower level of generality. It ties together the political support system and resource mobilization system. Justification, thus, presumes the existence of relatively codified cultural values and operates to demonstrate and ensure the congruence of particular allocative decisions with those values. For Parsons, justification is a technical problem administered by experts in particular fields of endeavour. The professions are seen as occupational groups particularly concerned with this class of problems.

Legitimation, the creation and validation of a normative order, is central to Parsons' theoretical approach. Human action, as opposed to reflex and mechanical

Table 11.1: Three perspectives on legitimation.

	Structuralist-Functionalist	Social Constructionist	Hegemonic
Key authors	Parons, Durkheim, Malinowski	Schutz, Weber, Berger & Luckmann	Marx, Gramsci
Perspective on legitimation	Mechanism for implementing social values	Process of giving 'meaning' to 'social facts'	Process of mystifying power
Imputed function	To ensure allocation of resources consistent with the 'functional imperatives' of society	To ensure intersubjectivity to allow social interaction and cultural continuity	To maintain stable power relations to advance the capital accumulation process
Source of value	Consensus driven by social functions	Consensus drive by social interaction	Elite ideology
Range of actions	Defined by functions	Defined by tradition	Defined by elite self-interest
Nature of link between action and values	Presumed to be unique and objective	Established discursively	False but believed by subordinates
Examples in accounting literature	Gambling (1977), Tiessen & Waterhouse (1983), Berry et al. (1984)	Boland & Pondy (1983) Burcell et al. (1985)	Tinker (1980), Cooper & Sherer (1984)
Research issues	Role of accounting systems in minimizing conflicts and helping cope with uncertainty	Role of accounting systems in cultural continuity and facilitating intersubjectivity	The role of accounting systems in creating, distributing and mystifying power

movement, can only occur where there is some normative order. Parsons regards the normative order of society as *a priori* to the existence of society. A normative order is presumed, for example, in both his definition of action and power. The creation of this normative order is based on a presumed consensus arising out of shared recognition of the functions which society must perform. This is not to imply that cultural values are immutable, they will change as the environment facing the society changes.

Parsons does refer, albeit briefly, to the concept of a 'moral elite' which acts to introduce and modify social values. The 'moral elite' would be those groups in society with superior scientific training and knowledge. In particular, as Durkheim observed, the professions and occupational guilds were suggested as the appropriate foci of the moral regulation of society. The professions, therefore, are seen as codifying and enacting the moral order of society.

Relevant Accounting Research

Accounting research implicitly using the structural-functionalist conception of legitimation treats accounting systems as technical devices which capture and implement the functional values of a given social system. Gambling (1977), for example, suggests that accounting serves a 'confidence-building and conflict avoidance' role in organizations. Covaleski & Dirsmith (1983) found that budgets in hospitals, relating to nursing costs, were used for two purposes: to advocate the cause of particular nursing groups (organizational subunits) and to control costs in that group. They also uncovered evidence that the advocacy role of budgets dominated and was decoupled from the control function. While Berry *et al.*'s (1985) work with the National Coal Board (NCB) indicated that accounting measures were used in this setting to buffer coal production from an uncertain and hostile environment.

The work of Mattessich (1978) and Thornton (1979) on the institutional aspects of accounting information is also consistent with the structural-functionalist approach to legitimation. They regarded institutions as objectifications of social values within which individuals interact. In agreement with Parsons' distinction between legitimation and justification, the value judgements or standards which are relevant are regarded as external to the practice of accounting such that accounting operates to justify relations within a set of institutionalized value constraints.

The Social Constructionist Perspective

A Theoretical Overview

The social constructionist perspective developed from German idealism and complementary work in symbolic analysis is based on ordinary language philosophy and sociolinguistics. This perspective focuses on symbols as reflective and constitutive attributes of social reality. The approach is based on the epistemological assertion that we can only know reality as a complex set of mental images or symbols. The source of these images is the society to which we are socialized and in which we interact.

The concept of legitimation from this perspective emerges as a central problem in the organization of knowledge of social reality including problems of cultural continuity and access to knowledge in society.

Berger & Luckmann (1966) suggest that social reality is constructed through a dialectical process involving three moments: externalization, objectification and internalization. First, our conceptions of society reality are given a tangible form, externalized, in our performances, rituals, symbols and artifacts. Second, these conceptions of reality are then given an objective status in our life. We begin to accept things that we have constructed as immutable parts of our reality. Finally, the objectivated constructions of past action are internalized through socialization processes (e.g. education) and become further divorced from the processes which created them.

Berger & Luckmann distinguish four levels of legitimation. The first level is linguistic. The second level consists of 'theoretical propositions in rudimentary form' (Berger & Luckmann 1966: 112). This category includes myths, stories and other forms of anecdotal evidence which are used to justify certain social events or relations. The third level consists of explicit theories linked to particular institutional contexts, for example, marginalist economic theories in the economic sphere. Finally, the highest level of legitimation consists of symbolic universes which are able to tie together different institutional environments and explain their interrelation. This level of legitimation typically provides the means by which social and individual biographies may be 'rationalized' and given meaning. Rites of passage from one stage of life to another are specified within symbolic universes.

Berger & Luckmann recognize that the maintenance of the legitimating apparatus of society typically becomes the domain of particular occupational groups who not only maintain and expand the legitimating symbols of society, but also may engage in 'therapy' to ensure that individuals conform to the official version of reality.

Relevant Accounting Research

Belkaoui's (1978, 1984) work on the linguistic relativity of accounting argues that the way in which accounting represents reality can affect the perception and behaviour of users of accounting information.

Burchell *et al.*'s (1985) study of the use of value added accounting in the UK is another example. It begins by demonstrating that value added accounting has been used as a linguistic category without empirical referent allowing it to be used as part of diverse political programs. The authors attempt to identify the manner in which value added arose as a focus of interest. Value added is presented as emerging out of an institutionally embedded debate combining a concern for industrial democracy and industrial productivity.

In a similar manner, Hopwood (1984) suggests that accounting is being used in the public sector to symbolize the new emphasis on efficiency by the state and, simultaneously, to provide a rhetoric which will bring about a change in operating procedures. Accounting provides selective visibility to particular issues, and perspectives on issues, which results in the 'creation of the significant' within the bureaucracy.

Meyer (1986) has provided a general framework for the analysis of accounting's social role from a social constructionist perspective. He suggests that accounting is part of the legitimating apparatus of society. The amount of accounting which organizations actually undertake will depend upon the demand for rationalized accounts in society. Simultaneously, however, accounting contributes to the construction of society as a set of rational interactions. Accounting thus fulfils two roles. It is a means by which organizations may signal their rationality and meet the expectations of society and it is implicated in the process by which these values come to be clarified and codified as social expectations.

The Hegemonic Perspective

A Theoretical Overview

The hegemonic perspective is derived from Marx's reversal of the German idealic position that reality is constructed according to mental conceptions. It holds that the relations among men are structured by modes of material production and consciousness is formed as a consequence of those modes of production. The evolution of Western society is seen as being driven by the demands of capital accumulation by a small group who control the productive assets of society. This group is also seen as controlling, through the intellectual strata of society, the consciousness of the society in order to mystify the power relation between the 'propertyless' workers and themselves.

The current status of ideology in society within radical sociological theory is largely due to the extensions of Marx by Antonio Gramsci. He argued that the class basis of society could only be maintained through 'moral leadership' or hegemony (the potential for physical coercion is always in the background), which structured the way in which people perceived social reality. The essence of politics and culture, he argued, was the struggle between different 'hegemonic forces' or political consciousness.

Gramsci rejected the definition of class based on the individual's position in the productive process. Instead, he substitutes the concept of a 'historical bloc', which represents a coalition of individuals of like mind although not necessarily of the same class in a Marxian sense. Hegemony is regarded as a material aspect of society and not a 'superstructure' to be derived from economic relations.

The nature of hegemony in a society could shape events independently of relations of production. Gramsci also asserted that hegemony was a strategy used by all ruling classes including the proletariat. He, thus, called on the proletariat to undermine the hegemony of capitalist interests and establish a working class hegemony rather than focusing on control of the labour process.

Gramsci identifies the intellectuals as the group through which hegemony is mediated. He differentiates, however, between organic and traditional intellectuals. Traditional intellectuals are 'functionaries' with close allegiance to their own tradition and craft. They consider themselves to be independent of all social interests and practice under a rhetoric of autonomy. Organic intellectuals, on the other hand, develop from within a particular social group and retain primary allegiance to that group.

The traditional intellectuals are the most important legitimating institution in maintaining hegemony. If they can be 'captured' by a particular group, their rhetoric of independence serves to legitimate the world view supported by that group. Organic intellectuals who interact with traditional intellectuals on their own ground are seen as the most effective means of 'capturing' the traditional intellectuals.

Relevant Accounting Research

This perspective has generated a number of articles critical of existing accounting practices and theories. Cherns (1978) argues that accounting, as a form of measurement which objectifies humans and human values, serves to alienate man from his labour. Tinker (1980) uses a hegemonic perspective to suggest that accounting numbers must be interpreted, not as a measure of economic efficiency, but as an outcome and reflection of conflicts and negotiations among various social interests. Tinker *et al.* (1982) suggest that accounting has been 'captured' by capitalist interests due to accountants' reliance on marginalist economics, and that accounting has come to serve as a legitimating institution for those interests. Lehman & Tinker (1984) examine the response of accountants, as represented by accounting literature, to changes in the 'official' ideology of the state surrounding the election of right-wing governments in the UK and USA. They contend that this literature mirrors the changes in social ideology, therefore contributing to the state's ability to maintain control.

Loft (1986) provides a further illustration of research from the hegemonic perspective. She analyses the rise of cost accounting techniques and associations in the UK surrounding the First World War. The data suggest that cost accounting arose primarily as a compromise between the need to establish a 'command' economy to meet the needs of war, while allowing capitalist interests to continue 'business as usual'. It continued to develop after the war to mediate conflicts between the populace and capitalist interests.

Hopper *et al.* (1986) argue that accounting is used in the NCB to assure the compliance of labour with the management's wishes. Through the manipulation of transfer prices among nationalized companies, the state is able to realize surplus value in different areas of the economy.

The studies focus on the position of accounting within a framework of social tensions and conflict. They use society as the unit of analysis, but additional insights have been gained by tracing the effect of these social tensions within the organizational area.

Conclusion

A fundamental distinction between natural and social phenomena is that an understanding of social phenomena requires an appreciation of the meanings attributed to those phenomena by individuals affected by them in addition to an understanding of the observable outcroppings of these phenomena. The values connoted by social actions are a crucial aspect of the manning of those actions and, therefore, individuals' behavioural and affective response to actions.

The three perspectives outlined above are attempts to conceptualize the means by which values or interests become embedded in knowledge and are enacted in day-to-day social practices. Each of these perspectives posit the existence of occupational groups in society, which mediate the relationships between values and action. They differ, however, on the source of values, the range of conceivable actions to which values can be linked, and the nature of the mapping between values and actions.

References

Belkaoui, A. (1978). Linguistic relativity in accounting. *Accounting, Organizations and Society*, 97–104.

Belkaoui, A. (1984). A test of the linguistic relativism in accounting. *Canadian Journal of Administrative Sciences*, 238–255.

Berger, P., & Luckmann, T. (1966). *The Social Construction of Reality*. New York: Penguin.

Berry, A.J., Capps, T., Cooper, D., Ferguson, P., Hopper, T., & Lowe, E.A. (1985). Management Control in an Area of the NCB: Rationales of Accounting Practice in a Public Enterprise. *Accounting, Organizations and Society*, 3–28.

Boland, R.J., & Pondy, R.J. (1983). Accounting in Organizations: A union of natural and rational perspectives. *Accounting, Organizations and Society*, 223–234.

Burchell, S., Clubb, C., & Hopwood, A. (1985). Accounting in its social context: towards a history of value added in the United Kingdom. *Accounting, Organizations and Society*, 381–413.

Cherns, A.B. (1978). Alienation and accountancy. *Accounting, Organizations and Society*, 105–114.

Cooper, D.J., & Sherer, M.J. (1984). The value of corporate accounting reports: Arguments for a political economy of accounting. *Accounting, Organizations and Society*, 207–232.

Covaleski, M.A., & Dirsmith, M.W. (1983). Budgeting as a means for control and loose coupling. *Accounting, Organizations and Society*, 323–340.

Gambling, T. (1977). Magic, Accounting and Morale. *Accounting, Organizations and Society*, 141–153.

Hopper, T., Cooper, D., Capps, T., Lowe, E.A., & Mouritsen, J. (1986). Financial control in the labour process: Managerial strategies and worker resistance in the National Coal Board, in Managing the labour process, H. Willmott & D. Knights (eds). Aldershot: Gower, 109–141.

Hopwood, A.G. (1984). Accounting and the pursuit of efficiency, in A.G. Hopwood and C. Tomkins (eds). *Issues in public sector accounting*. London: Philip Allen.

Lehman, C., & Tinker T. (1984). The great moving right show. Paper presented to the American Accounting Association, Reno (August).

Loft, A. (1986). Towards a critical understanding of accounting: The case of cost accounting in the UK, 137–170.

Mattessich, R. (1978). *Instrumental Reasoning and Systems Methodology*, Dordrecht/ Boston: D. Reidel.

Meyer, J.W. (1986). Social environments and organizational accounting. *Accounting, Organizations and Society*, 345–356.

Parsons, T. (1977). *Social Systems and the Evolution of Action Theory*. New York: Free Press.

Thornton, D.B. (1979). Information and institutions in the capital market. *Accounting, Organizations and Society*, 211–234.

Tiessen, P., & Waterhouse, J.H. (1983). Towards a descriptive theory of management accounting. *Accounting, Organizations and Society*, 251–267.

Tinker. A.M. (1980). A political economy of accounting. *Accounting, Organizations and Society*, 167–200.

Tinker, A.M., Merino, B.D., & Neimark, M.D. (1982). The normative origins of positive theories: Ideology and accounting thought. *Accounting, Organizations and Society*, 167–200.

Chapter 12

Letting the Chat Out of the Bag: Deconstruction, Privilege and Accounting Research[1]

C. Edward Arrington, *The University of North Carolina*
Jere R. Francis, *The University of Iowa*

There are signs on the intellectual scene that we are moving out of an era in the social sciences termed modernism — a belief that separating fact from value, truth from falsity, is just a matter of applying the right version of method. The purpose of this paper is to introduce accounting researchers to a movement termed 'deconstruction' which reflects the postmodern view that modernism is an untenable philosophical position. Postmodern thought in general and deconstruction in particular demand self-reflection and abandon any desire to somehow 'ground' knowledge in an external and transcendental metaphysics like the positivist's faith in observation or the Marxist's faith in historical determinism. Deconstruction differs from the academic tradition in which competing metaphysics attack each other with their different dogmas. Instead, it works from within a research paper (text), taking an author's *own criteria* for privileging his or her work, and then de-constructs the text by pointing out how the author violates his or her own system of privilege.

In this study, we both introduce deconstruction and apply it to Michael Jensen's 'Organization Theory and Methodology' [*The Accounting Review* (April 1983): 319–339], a text which would suggest that positive theory in accounting should be privileged over other ways of knowing and writing accounting discourses. We show through deconstruction that positive theory and the empirical tradition are not entitled to the kind of epistemic privilege and authority that they have enjoyed in silencing other kinds of writings about accounting. Deconstruction is a moment of resistance to the reductionism of modernism and its desire for knowledge closure. It resists metaphysical author[ity] and restores life to its original difficulty before our obeisance to metaphysics.

---

[1]Reproduced (in an abridged form) from C. Edward Arrington and Jere R. Francis, 'Letting the Chat Out of the Bag: Deconstruction, Privilege and Accounting Research', *Accounting, Organizations and Society*, 1989, vol. 14, no. 1/2, pp. 1–28, with permission of Elsevier.

The purpose of deconstruction, then, is to subvert the attempt to get closure around knowledge production — the attempt to silence other voices by illicitly claiming to possess a superior awareness of 'truth'. The subversive impulse makes deconstruction polemical, a political act designed to critique and dismantle intellectual elitism. Felperin says:

> Its [deconstruction's] polemic is directed not against one school or another, but against the purist or imperialist tendency of them all, their motivating belief that persistence in theory (their own in particular) will resolve the problems that have beset and debilitated past practice rather than throw up new ones just as debilitating (1985: 1).

Our purpose in introducing deconstruction to accounting is two-fold. First, we believe that accounting has the capacity to construct realities in a manner that dictates the conditions of human life and that current theories of accounting are infused with unexamined commitments to particular moral and social orders. Thus, the practice of accounting and theorizing about that practice are always and already informed by ethics which help to *create* the material conditions of human lives. To deny the value-ladenness of one's theorizing is to deny responsibility for the consequences of one's theories. Deconstruction can serve as a practice oriented toward forcing those value commitments to the surface of our 'scientific' practice and lead us to question our research on ethical grounds.

Our second purpose is to subvert the pretensions of positive theory as a theory of knowledge production. We argue that this school of accounting research exercises undue influence on the production of accounting knowledge. This influence is due to many factors; among them: (1) accounting scholars' unwillingness to critically examine the political, ontological, metaphysical and epistemological assumptions that underlie research, and (2) specific institutional arrangements for the production and dissemination of accounting knowledge which form a 'market' for accounting research that is driven by factors beyond the intellectual competence of the research.

Thus, accounting research is less expansive and less intellectually rigorous than it could be because of the disciplining forces of a hegemonic academic elite. The theories proposed by this elite also reflect an extremely conservative political perspective on the role of accounting in producing the social order. Our dual purposes, then, are designed to hold positive theory intellectually accountable and to make clear the fact that knowledge production is always a political act. We find deconstruction a useful praxis for these purposes, just as Foucauldian historical exegeses are useful in subverting the notion of accounting as a technical rational tool at the disposal of progress.

The Metaphysics of Presence

The attempt to externally ground or *originate* knowledge prior to its production through language and human purpose is what Derrida (1976) terms metaphysics of presence, a 'logocentric, ultimately religious, superstitious, or nostalgic, impulse to ground or center discourse in an originary author, response in a unitary subject, and textuality on a re-presentable world, when all are nothing other than effects and functions of linguistic differences' (Felperin 1985: 35). For purposes of deconstructing positive theory, the grounding of 'textuality on a re-presentable world' (empirical testing of the 'data' as grounding the 'truth' or 'falsity' of a theoretical discourse) is the relevant metaphysic or presence.

The notion of linguistic differencing that is central to deconstruction originates from the pre-eminent concern with language in twentieth century thought. With a few exceptions, accounting researchers have paid little attention to the role of language in the production of knowledge, and, as a result, it is necessary to provide a brief background before moving on to deconstruction.

A second important historical moment is the predominantly French intellectual movement, structuralism, which grew out of Saussure's (1916) pioneering work in linguistics. Saussure's work dealt with spoken and written language and the distinction between words (signifier) and concepts (signified). For Saussure, a signifier and a signified (the mind image) combine to constitute a 'sign'. Saussure rejected the mimetic grounding of sound signs in concepts to which they referred; rather, he argued that signs operate by differencing themselves form other signs.

Deconstruction as Exegesis and Subversion

While structuralism moves us to knowledge as a process of differencing among signs, deconstruction goes further. For Derrida, structuralism is itself an attempt to occupy the center rather than extend its own awareness of the 'free play' of signification to its limit. In Derrida's terms, to play out the limits of structuralism while giving up the desire for the center is to recognize the infinite possibilities of language and knowledge.

Deconstructive readings of texts reveal how unruly and unstable meaning is and efface the veil of linguistic law and order we place over texts. By contrast, modernist accounting discourses deny their discursive textuality, deny their constructivist origins, and present themselves as originating outside themselves mimetically representing 'nature'.

Attempts to occupy the center, to privilege one's discourses, make knowledge production always and already a violent and political act designed to 'arrest' the other. This battle for the center is a history of one system using its own arguments to attack the arguments of another system. Deconstruction, in contrast, takes an author's own system of grounding and reveals how his or her text violates that system — it bores from within; it implodes.

The positive moment of deconstruction, then, lies in restoring life to its original difficulty which modernism and metaphysics have veiled and caused us to forget. As Ryan (1984: 8) says, 'To affirm the abyss deconstruction opens in the domain of knowledge is politically to affirm the permanent possibility of social change'.

Organizational Theory, Deconstruction and Accounting Research: A Case Study of Michael Jensen's 'Organization Theory and Methodology'

This paper will apply basic concepts of deconstruction to Michael Jensen's (1983) text which we believe is reflective of the most powerful claim to 'the center' in US accounting discourse. This is a text that prescribes research discourse and privileges a specific libertarian microeconomic empirical vision as representative of 'the way the world is'. The deconstruction will proceed through a close reading of this text and demonstrate that the positive theorists' claim to privilege is both illicit and dangerously capable of closing off the conversational space of accounting research. Jensen's text holds out the possibility that all of the complexity surrounding organizations can be robustly represented with the microeconomic arguments that he advances.

This section of the paper will utilize Derrida's concepts of aporia, *differance*, supplementarity and trace to show how Jensen's text violates itself by deviating from its own premises. As with any text, which grounds itself in some external criteria, which privileges itself as a dispenser of rules, deconstruction will take the author literally and reveal how the text dismantles itself in the light of violations of its own rule system. In this case, Jensen's positive theory vanishes through revealing those 'extra-positive', or 'supplementary', rhetorical moves Jensen must make. We have structured this deconstruction around a select set of these rhetorical moves that we believe capture, but do not in any way exhaust, the ways in which Jensen's positive theory rests on a bed of figural language and rhetorical argument. The point here is not to discredit empirical accounting research. Rather, it is about the rhetoric which positions Jensen's brand of positivism as a privileged epistemology and philosophy of science. For the reader not familiar with Jensen's text, it should be read prior to the remainder of this paper.

The Rhetoric of Revolution and the Aporia of Positive Theory

Jensen (1983) sets out to describe a positive theory of organizations, one which represents the foundations of a 'revolution in the science of organizations' (p. 39). He speaks of the development of '*a*' theory of organizations as if there isn't one (or many) already and of the accomplishments of his own theory in the future tense as if inevitable; indeed, as required — 'Because such positive theories as these are required for purposeful decision making, their development will provide a better scientific basis for the decisions of managers, standard-setting boards, and government regulatory bodies' (p. 319).

Clearly, the data for such a theory of decision making in organizations must come from observation of existing decisions which are not yet purposeful, since they can only become purposeful, with the development of the positive theory. Thus, the data-generating process is not capable of providing evidence from 'the way the world is' to support, in its scientific sense, the theory of organizations that Jensen has in mind. Further, these 'nonpurposeful' decision makers must be either making their decisions randomly or already acting upon incorrect 'normative' theories since they are awaiting the development of a positive theory. Alternatively, if they are using their knowledge of 'the way the world is', then they either do not need a positive theory or they already have one.

The discussion above demonstrates how the privileging of the positive over the normative in Jensen's theory engenders its own contradiction. Positive theory relies for its privilege upon observation of the way the world is; that is, it will study actual decisions. But this positive theory is required for purposeful decision making. Thus, decisions are not yet purposeful. So we will develop positive theory from a population of unpurposive decisions. Then, decisions will become purposeful. Such is the conclusion based on Jensen's own positivistic insistence on literalness, on the correspondence of sensations (visual awareness of things, words, etc.) with a 'presence'.

The text constructs its own aporia. Jensen's concept of the 'real', the 'positive', has only rhetorical (normative?) not literal (positive?) certification. It depends foremost upon an act of faith that Jensen can go outside of the data and find a 'normative' structure to convert 'the way the world is' to the way that he would like it to be. The 'positive' is useful only to the extent that it provides evidence that things are not quite right in 'reality', but some view of 'rightness' must lie within Jensen's values and is both necessary and normative.

The Normative/Positive Dichotomy and Differance

Derrida views the privilege attached to the superior term in a binary opposition as a rhetorical move required to carry an argument through in the face of the argument's inevitable failure to ground itself outside of the text. 'One of the terms dominates the other, occupies the commanding position. To deconstruct the opposition is above all, at a particular moment, to reverse the hierarchy' (Derrida 1981: 56–57). In our case, it would reverse the positive/normative by pointing to the normative within the positive; that is, it effaces the dichotomy. It uses the negative space created by the normative, to show how the positive exists only parasitically. Its affirmative status exists only because of its denial of the normative.

In establishing the normative/positive dichotomy, Jensen states that 'Answers to normative questions always depend on the choice of the criterion or objective function which is a matter of values' (p. 320). He then completes the privileged side with 'Answers to positive questions, on the other hand, involve discovery of some aspect of how the world behaves and are always potentially refutable by contradictory evidence' (p. 320). For Jensen, then, the presence of objective functions (goals, values, etc.) always and already places one in the domain of normative theory. Thus, to remain independent of normativeness, positive theory must deny itself objective functions (goals, values, etc.). What would such positive theory look like? With no goals, no values, no objective function, the researcher would have no basis to decide what 'aspect of how the world behaves' to investigate.

Supplementarity: Bandaging the Aporetic

The inability of positive theory to stand alone causes Jensen to inject all sorts of what Derrida terms 'supplements' into his analysis. Observation, supposedly complete in itself, must be supplemented by Jensen with 'definitions' and 'tautologies'. This is not to suggest that such supplements can be avoided; they are always necessary. Rather, it is to point out that privilege claimed by authors for positive theory (or any other theory) becomes questionable with the presence of supplements. From a Derridean perspective, there is no unsupplemented, primary, first principle, only a (normative) desire for it, or a myth creating it. Specifically, it is difficult to determine why some definitions and tautologies are acceptable for Jensen while others are not except on normative grounds. What are the boundaries on the inevitable definitions and tautologies that could possible tell us when we have a positivist and when we have a normativist?

Survival of the fittest and minimization of agency costs within Jensen's positive theory of 'how the world is' act as supplements which ensure that his theory leads to the kinds of conclusions that follow from his political and economic beliefs. In lifting tautology out of its 'scientific' context of analytic philosophy and appropriating it for positive theory, he [mis]uses science that is championed as a privileged way of speaking (writing). This is particularly so, since tautology is essential to the early twentieth century work in analytic philosophy that was designed to clean-up the nineteenth-century brand of naïve positivism which comes closest to Jensen's own view.

Self-interest and Survival of the Fittest as Normative Ethics

Jensen shares with other positive accounting theorists a faith in self-interest, Adam Smith's invisible hand, as the motive for human behavior that has 'good' social consequences. Self-interest is a panchreston, a universal panacea, a term so broad that it is meaningless. But, most importantly, it is impossible to falsify, to demonstrate its absence; thus, it is impossible to build a positive theory around it — it defies refutation.

Jensen re-writes self-interest as survival of the fittest and says it 'completes most of the major building blocks of the analytical framework for creating a theory of organizations' (p. 331). Analytical? Self-interest and survival of the fittest have at least as much ethical import as they do 'analytical' import. As an ethic, it conjures the ghost of Thomas Hobbes and the law of the jungle.

Economists are fond of studying cases in the limit in order to glean their generalities. We might look for positive evidence of a society that is grounded in a limit case of self-interest. Turnbull (1972) tells of such a society. There is a Ugandan mountain tribe, the Ik, whose morals, whose humanity, extend only to taking whatever they can in order to survive. 'Economic interest is centered on as many individual stomachs as there are people, and cooperation is merely a device for furthering an interest that is consciously selfish...the Ik have dispensed with the myth of altruism, but they have also largely dispensed with acts that in reality served at least mutual interests' (Turnbull 1972: 157). 'Luckily the Ik are not numerous...so I am hopeful that their isolation will remain as complete as in the past, until they die out completely. I am only sorry that so many individuals will have to die, slowly and painfully, until the end comes to them all' (Ibid.: 285).

We doubt that positive theorists would find such a society desirable, but this society has very successfully both minimized agency costs and based itself on the other 'useful tautology', survival of the fittest. The point is that, from a deconstructionist perspective, what kinds of ethical supplements are necessary to positive theory in order to take us away from the limit case of the Iks?

More Supplementarity: Licensing Poor Science

Just as Jensen is unwilling to accept responsibility for his use of tautology, he wants exemption from the demands intellectual history places on the use of an important term like positive. He again appeals to the term positive within the mysterious black box of usage 'in the social sciences' (p. 320). In a related footnote he states 'The use of the term 'positive' in this context has had the unfortunate effect of linking accounting researchers who have been engaged in the effort to develop 'positive' theories with 'logical positivism', a school of thought in philosophy which has been controversial. The proposal to focus on positive theories of accounting does not commit those who propose it to logical positivism' (footnote 1, p. 320). But this disclaimer leaves one washed ashore between an earlier positivism, approximated by Jensen's view, and the later logical positivism, a system which at least addressed the epistemic implications of the language problem. It is as if we are expected to return to granting licences to avoid the linguistic and rhetorical. Logical positivism is neither an irrelevant nor a controversial supplement to positivism as is implied by Jensen. It 'corrected' the mistakes of early positivism and did much to set twentieth-century philosophy on its linguistic course. Jensen thus denies responsibility for both language (writing) and the implications of language for the knowledge claims that his positive theory would assert.

Behavior and Organizations: More Aporia and Differance

Much of Jensen's theory depends upon contracts; contracts provide the operational metaphor for the kind of evidence necessary to support his theory.

He is, however, concerned with organizations and views contracts as constitutive of organizations.

So Jensen argues that 'real', 'literal', 'positive' behavior of people (agents within the organization) can be observed not by the black box of economic theory but by the observation of contracts (both 'written' and 'unwritten', p. 326). The point here is that neither contracts nor organizations literally 'behave', nor are Jensen's contracts necessarily even observable if they are 'unwritten'.

To privilege contracts is just as vacuous as speaking of the behavior of the firm. Having pointed out the anthropomorphic character of the economic theory of the firm, Jensen simply supplants it with his own anthropomorphic 'nexus of contracts' view: 'The *behavior* of a complex contractual system made up of maximizing agents with diverse and conflicting objectives' (p. 327, emphasis added). A 'nexus of contracts' no more 'behaves' than an organization does; nor is it more 'observable', or less concerned with 'motives'. Nothing is really changed; he wants to slide in 'contracts' for 'people'. The unit of analysis is a select set of contracts, certainly not people.

Yet More Supplements: My Science and Everybody Else's

Jensen's text moves throughout with appeals to the status of science to distance itself from other (presumably) nonscientific theories. The words 'science', 'scientific', or 'scientists' are used 31 times. But the text's failure to adhere to its own notion of science appears when a plea is made (pp. 332–333) for a separate standard of evidence, a different epistemology, to validate the knowledge claims of positive theory. 'By its nature, much of this institutional evidence cannot be summarized by measures using real numbers. We simply do not know how to aggregate such evidence... Statisticians and econometricians are likely to react because it violates a long and venerable tradition of formal testing' (p. 332).

This appeal for an extra-science evidence standard is a supplement. If positive theory is good science, then it should be judged by the criteria of good science. While grounding positive theory in science, Jensen wants different grounds, a supplement, to prop-up the evidence, to hasten its acceptance, to quicken the 'revolution in organization theory'. That this appeal for a scientific theory to excuse itself from science is even made suggests that the theory may not be particularly persuasive when compared to others.

Yet in Jensen's hands, it seems little more than a rhetorical ploy to have one's cake (the privilege of science) and eat it too (without going through the 'rigor' of scientific practice). The sort of 'science' Jensen preaches more closely resembles Feyerabend's (1975) dictum of 'anything goes' than the law and order of rational scientific inquiry to which he appeals. The extra-science appeal subverts the rhetoric of Science which he uses to ground and privilege positive theory over the presumably nonscientific theories he is in competition with.

Deconstruction, the Politics of Discourse and Accounting 'Texts'

In *The Post Card*, Derrida (1987) focuses upon subversion of [phal]logocentric discourse through a series of love letters which speak allegorically to knowledge production through a language of seduction rather than a language of rational discourse. The letters are written to a voiceless lover and dispatched through various postal networks as Derrida proceeds from university to university delivering lectures.

In US accounting, the 'positive-empirical' code has the largest postal network, with minor postal services operating on a much smaller scale. It is our belief that the *poste* of accounting knowledge has become dangerously centered upon this technology of naïve empiricism. Further, the dominance of this view cannot be explained in terms of the intellectual competence of the arguments which it uses to privilege itself, and the deconstructive exegesis of those arguments bears this out. Instead, this view survives because of the political economy of accounting research. It has always been in the interest of those with the most wealth and power to make appeals to 'the market' as the arbitrator of 'quality', and we suspect that this is the argument that will be used against the more sinister view of the *poste* presented in this paper. Along with the Foucauldian critics, we would join in questioning the uncritical acceptance of 'the market' for knowledge without investigating the extent to which the archaeological structure of that market can be described as egalitarian and fair.

If the production of knowledge proceeds through postal rules which are biased, then serious consequences may emerge for the nature of knowledge generally. In fact, this is the key to Derrida's battle against the constraints of Western metaphysics. We argue that the combination of accounting research being prescribed as a positive science and the absence of intellectual credibility for this view is sufficient evidence for concluding that 'the market' for accounting research is governed by factors other than the quality of contributions to knowledge.

For Derrida, the real tragedy is that claims to privilege lead other voices (other research perspectives) into the dead letter box. It is this 'dead lettering' that stops conversation, that censors, that keeps us always in the transmission of right answers. However, deconstruction is about language and offers much more than a strategy for the critical reading, re-writing and decentering of accounting research texts and the opening up of academic discourse. Accounting itself, accounting practice, is a way of writing a certain kind of economic text about organizations, about 'organizations' of economic meaning. The meaning circumscribed within these accounting texts is presented as facticity and as transcendentally signified beyond the text itself. The metaphor 'the bottom line' speaks to the grounding of accounting in a metaphysics of presence and facticity, and usage of the metaphor beyond its accounting context reveals just how firm the grounding is. Accounting, then, produces an economic centering and privileges a particular type of economic visibility and calculation in the writing of texts about the organization. To deconstruct these texts, then, is to dislocate accounting's arbitrary power to circumscribe and close off the further possibilities of economic meaning about the organization.

Conclusion

This paper introduced the writings of Derrida and used deconstruction as a means to reflect upon the claims to privilege by positive theorists. The point here is not destruction, not the dumbwitted response of those who would shout irrationalism or irresponsibility. Nor is the point to replace positive theory with another privileged one. Rather, deconstruction wishes to operate on the pretexts of texts in order to dismantle their pretensions. Traditional critiques are based on attacks from 'outside', from a different view of Truth. These critiques are Blitzkriegs, bombs dropped to explode one clerisy and replace it with another. Derrida's critiques work from the inside, they bore from within, they implode claims to privilege.

References

Derrida, J. (1976). *Of grammatology* (Trans. by G. Spivak). Baltimore: Johns Hopkins University Press.

Derrida, J. (1981). *Positions* (Trans. by A. Bass). Chicago: University of Chicago Press.

Derrida, J. (1987). *The post card: From Socrates to Freud and beyond* (Trans. by A. Bass). Chicago: University of Chicago Press.

Felperin, L. (1985). *Beyond deconstruction*. New York: Oxford University Press.

Feyerabend, P. (1975). *Against method*. London: Verso.

Jensen, M. (1983). Organization theory and methodology. *The Accounting Review*, 319–339.

Ryan, R. (1984). *Marxism and deconstruction: A critical articulation*. Baltimore: Johns Hopkins University Press.

Saussure, F. (1916). *Cours de linguistique generale*. Paris: Payot.

Turnbull, C. (1972). *The mountain people*. New York: Simon & Schuster.

Turnbull, C. (1981). The post-age. *Diacritics*, 39–56.

Part II

Contemporary

This section includes articles representative of more recent contributions that have followed in the footsteps of those in the Classical section. As such, each has 'pushed the envelope' of the various paradigms in important ways making a valuable contribution to the body of research regarding accounting and the social.

The first four articles follow up on the radical structuralist paradigm initiated by Tinker (1980) and Cooper & Sherer (1984) as well the radical humanist paradigm suggested by Laughlin (1987). Hopper & Armstrong (1991) mount a labour process critique of Johnson & Kaplan's management accounting 'relevance lost' thesis that attracted a host of acolytes globally in the late 1980s and early 1990s to show how 'relevance was found' by corporations who harnessed management accounting systems, wedded to Tayloristic scientific management techniques, to weaken labour union gains and cheapen wage labour. Arnold (1998) demystifies 'the new management accounting techniques' and 'the rhetoric of cooperation and employee empowerment' at the plants of three large multinational corporations who used them instead to eliminate jobs, weaken trade unions, and virtually destroy the community of Decatur, Illinois. Cooper & Taylor's (2000) historical labour process based study reveals how capitalist interests relied on scientific management techniques, deskilling and dummying down of clerical office workers to progressively relieve them of autonomy and dignity in their working lives. And Macintosh (1990), along the lines of Laughlin's (1987) radical humanism trail, presents an analysis of IBM's depiction of women in the computerized workplace as 'happy slaves' and suggests avenues for their enlightenment and eventual emancipation.

Three articles follow up on the introduction by Hopwood (1986) and Miller & O'Leary (1986) of Foucauldian analysis into management accounting literature. Ezzamel's (1994) study of a university's management regime illustrates how the administrators' attempt to inflict disciplinary bio-power on its faculty was met with a successful concerted resistance effort. Hopper & Macintosh (1993) show how the management control system, used at ITT Inc. during Harold Geneen's reign as CEO, accorded closely to Foucault's principles of surveillance and punishment by disciplining spaces, time, and bodies within a panopticon-like control watchtower. And Ezzamel, Carmona & Guitérrez (2002) present a genealogical historical account of the changes in disciplinary and surveillance practices that ocurred in a tobacco factory in Seville in the mid-1700s.

Several articles pick up on Hedberg & Jönsson's (1978) pointer reading regarding the way individual cognitive maps can come into play in an accounting information processing sense. Pihlanto (2000) presents a holistic concept of man using a theatre metaphor for conscious experience as a sophisticated way to understand users' accounting information processing characteristics. Shearer & Arrington (1993) extend the cognitive maps terrain by presenting a radical feminist perspective that was previously negated and neglected in the accounting literature. Jönsson & Macintosh (1997), picking up on issues of how individuals communicate, think about their actions, and choose to do what they do, especially in the context of trusting accounting systems, make the case for more ethnographic research.

The Roberts & Scapens (1985) introduction of structuration theory as a powerful way to understand management accounting systems inspired many follow up articles. Macintosh & Scapens (1990) present a detailed exegesis of the dimensions of structuration and illustrate its power as a sensitizing device for understanding the social side of management accounting systems with their analysis of the struggle over a university budgeting system waged by State officials and university administrators in Wisconsin. Baker (1999) focuses on the morality dimension of structuration and presents a framework for researching the ethical and philosophical dimensions inherent in accounting systems. Jones & Dugdale (2001) show how expert systems such as accounting regimes are disembedded and reembedded across time and space by global corporations allowing them to take action at a distance in controlling their vast Latourian-like networks. Busco, Riccaboni & Scapens (2002) offer a detailed field study of these processes by presenting a detailed field study of the General Electric Corporation's (GE) takeover of the Italian Nuovo Pegone (NP) firm. They vividly illustrate the concepts of how expert systems, such as GE's expert system of management controls, can be disembedded, transported across time and space, and reembedded within its vast global network to effect control-at-a-distance and make radical changes in local cultures.

In the final article in this part, Dillard (1995) draws together many of the threads in the articles in this part by, first, presenting three perspectives (technical-empirical, historical-hermeneutic, and critical) for researching accounting information systems, and then offering an auto-critique of each by drawing on Bruno Latour's knowledge accumulation cycle metaphor.

Chapter 13

Cost Accounting, Controlling Labour and the Rise of Conglomerates[1]

Trevor Hopper, *University of Manchester*

Peter Armstrong, *University of Leicester*

Traditional management accounting history has been fixated on a search for origins, on the questions of who did what first, and when. Preoccupied with invention, rather than diffusion and application, writings in this genre are rich in narrative but neglect important linkages between phases of accounting development and their socio-economic context. If this perceived deficiency needs to be addressed, then the recent marriage between accounting antiquarianism and doctrines of liberal economics constitutes a definite theoretical advance. Premised on the notion that business organization and control systems are driven by searches for efficiency in competitive environments, accounting development is an integral part of this evolutionary process. Johnson & Kaplan's *Relevance Lost* (1987) is the most thorough-going exemplar to date of this new tradition. Given the impact of this work in academic, consultant and practitioner circles, there are good reasons for subjecting its historical and theoretical adequacy to close scrutiny, not least because this may bear importantly on the prescriptive message which Johnson & Kaplan draw from their version of accounting history.

In conformity with their evolutionary model, Johnson & Kaplan (1987) portray the initial phases of cost accounting development as a steady accretion of knowledge and technique achieved by practising engineers and managers in seeking efficiency. As a result of this process, they argue, virtually all contemporary techniques of management accounting were in operational use by about 1920. Johnson & Kaplan then depart from their evolutionary model to argue that the achievements of this 'Golden Age' have subsequently been stifled by the influences of financial reporting and academic teaching. This theoretical twist enables the authors to launch an attack, from the historical ground of the 1920s, on the inefficiencies resulting from the contemporary teaching and practice of management accountancy. Accounting information systems of questionable relevance are said to be used in a mechanical

---

[1]Reproduced (in an abridged form) from T. Hopper and P. Armstrong, 'Cost Accounting, Controlling Labour and the Rise of Conglomerates', *Accounting, Organizations and Society*, vol. 16, no. 5/6, pp. 405–438 with permission of Elsevier.

fashion by a generation of American executives brought up to manage 'by the numbers'. This is held responsible for a decline in the international competitiveness of American businesses, especially in relation to the Japanese. This message evidently strikes a chord with many practising managers, perhaps because the inroads made by Japanese manufacturers are indisputable, perhaps because there is some truth in the thesis of accounting stagnation, but also, perhaps, because of the implicit daemonization of academics and financial accountants.

Despite the respect in which Johnson & Kaplan's work must be held, the argument of this paper is that their theory is flawed, their history partial and some of their prescription neglectful of the socio-economic conditions on which the achievements of the 1920s depended. In contrast to the social harmony and self-equilibrating behaviour of individuals, firms and markets assumed in the transaction cost framework employed by Johnson & Kaplan, many historical events in the thesis of their *Relevance Lost* book are better understood through a 'labour process' approach to economic and industrial history. Recognizing the need for a broader, more critical, institutional analysis of capitalistic development, the core presupposition of this perspective is that social and economic conflicts arising from modes of control which characterize particular phases of capitalistic development stimulate the creation of new forms of control intended to eliminate or accommodate resistance and to solve associated problems of profitability. These new forms of control, in turn, decay, partly because their competitive advantage disappears as a consequence of their generalization and partly because they give rise to new contradictions and forms of resistance. Thus, a labour process approach stresses crisis rather than continuity; contradiction rather than internal consistency; social and political conflict rather than harmony; the monopoly power of corporations rather than self-equilibrating competitive markets; patterns of class formation in specific economies rather than an atomized view of the individual; and human agency in its cultural and institutional setting rather than economistic reductionism.

A re-examination, along these 'labour process' lines, of Johnson & Kaplan's chosen exemplars of efficiency-driven development indicates that mid-nineteenth century cost accounting systems were employed to intensify labour in response to increased competition as well as to stimulate searches for efficiency. It reveals accounting's implication in the tightening of managerial control through the destruction of subcontracting and craft controls later in the century, and it shows that a major feature of the General Motors system of the 1920s was the insulation of shareholders' dividends from economic fluctuation by throwing the costs of this onto the workforce. Because such usages of accounting information depended upon a lack of resistance from organized labour, it is by no means accidental that Johnson & Kaplan's apogee of management accounting development fails to recognize that this took place in an age of anti-union violence and espionage. The contemporary implication is that the 'relevances' of 1920s accounting control systems can only be resurrected in contexts where the resistance of labour is weakened.

A labour process approach is also useful in reassessing Johnson & Kaplan's thesis of accounting stagnation, according to which the influence of financial accountants and academics was sufficient to arrest the development of management accountancy for over sixty years within the most dynamic economy in the capitalist world. Here, the historical record suggests that the post-1930s decline of interest in accounting for process efficiencies was actually the product of the New Deal era, when trade unions were able to resist lay-offs and the speed-up, and the increasing industrial concentration which enables employers to displace costs of welfarist employment strategies onto semi-monopolized product markets. In this new socio-economic context, the relevance of budgetary controls may have changed, rather than declined. Cost accounting came to be used for monopoly pricing policies designed to protect a partial accord between capital and certain sectors of the labour force. How far this accord will persist into the 1990s is an open question, but to the extent that it does so, there may be resistance to Johnson & Kaplan's call for a reassertion of accounting for process efficiencies.

Relevance Lost is not considered here from the standpoint of managerial prescription. Rather, the concern is with the partial interpretations of history that underlie its thesis. Since this problem stems, in part, from certain inadequacies in the transaction cost framework employed by Johnson & Kaplan, it is necessary to review these before proceeding to matters of historical substance.

Most of the problems stem from the assumption in transaction cost theory that changes in organizational forms and control systems are universally driven by searches for efficiency, whereas it is an elementary feature of capitalist economic life that there are also gains to be made from the extension and intensification of labour and from the monopolization of product markets. [In fact, it is only fair to point out that the fine detail of Johnson & Kaplan's history often *does* acknowledge issues of labour intensification and monopoly.]

This fanciful and individualistic genesis notably glosses over why economies in transaction costs should be achieved by assigning the right to fill in gaps in employment contracts to capital ownership, in the person of the employer, rather than, say, to elected representatives of the workforce. More, it buries all gains to capital from the right to direct labour within a neutral-sounding reduction of transaction costs.

The transaction cost view of management as a search for process efficiencies has consequences for Johnson & Kaplan's conception of the managerial role of accounting information as data fed into a rational decision-making process. Thus, the quality of managerial decisions on production processes and resource allocation is seen as depending fairly straightforwardly on the timeliness, accuracy and relevance of cost information. Within this schema, cost data are seen in realist terms. Johnson & Kaplan write frequently of the 'accuracy' of costs or, on the negative side, of their 'distortion'. Whilst stressing that cost data need to be appropriate to the decisions to be taken, they nevertheless believe that, within the parameters of relevance, the quality of cost data is determined by its accuracy.

If, on the other hand, management is taken to be about the control of labour and of junior managers, the issue looks different. From this perspective, accounting information is to be judged by the results achieved, rather than its notional accuracy. Given the monopoly power of certain American corporations before the panic over Japanese competition, for example, product costings may have been more significant for pricing policy than for manufacturing strategy. Moreover, even where competition places cost reduction on the agenda, there is something to be said for the inaccuracy of traditional full-costing systems, since these serve to direct managerial efforts to cut unit labour costs of labour-intensive processes, which are where resistance from labour is likely to be at its weakest.

Explaining Accounting Stagnation

Much of the rhetorical force of Johnson & Kaplan's version of management accounting history derives from a contradiction. If the search for reduced trans-action costs drove the evolution of organizational forms and accounting systems up to the mid-1920s, why did this process cease thereafter? Necessarily answers have to be imported from outside the transaction costs framework. Johnson & Kaplan find them in the imposition of financial reporting conventions on management accounting technique by professional accountants and a takeover of research by academics interested only in abstract simplified problems. Thus, Kaplan's diatribe against the shortcomings of current management accounting is reconciled with Johnson's (1975) optimistic view of the autonomous evolution of corporate forms and accounting technique. Into the bargain, plausible culprits are produced. Since, not even their best friends could pretend that accountants are not preoccupied with financial reporting or that academics are not academic.

   Whilst this may constitute a solution to the logical problems created by framing accounting history within transaction cost theory, there remains an air of unreality about it. To reduce accounting problems to accountants, be they academics or practitioners, seems to be a case of blaming the monkey rather than the organ-grinder. We are asked to believe that the comparatively minor vested interests of accountants and academics could impose their intellectual habits upon manage-ment practice in America's giant corporations for over sixty years, to the detriment of their profitability. In fact, the independent influence of accounting profession-alism on corporate practice may have been minimal.

   In examining the questionable thesis of financial accounting dominance, it is important to consider the possibility that the cost accounting systems which stand accused of failing American enterprise actually persisted because they had some offsetting managerial advantage beyond the grasp of transaction cost theory.

Social Transformation and Management Accounting Technology: Towards a Labour Process Approach

Johnson & Kaplan are not unaware of the relevance of the capital–labour relationship to the operation of accounting information systems. Noting that early cost accounts were concerned with labour control, they remark that 'arguments about the causes, costs, and possible benefits to workers of surrendering control over their labour in return for a fixed income have abounded since Ricardo and Marx' (Johnson & Kaplan 1987: 22). But political economy is cast aside when they self-consciously limit their remit to 'the implications for accounting of the complications that factory managers faced once workers were employed at a wage' (Ibid.: 22). The implication is that the problems of securing compliance from the workforce are sufficiently addressed through the institution of the wage relationship, leaving managers free to search for process efficiencies. The notion that the problem of extracting work from the workforce *cannot* be solved on a once-for-all basis, and that it actually lies at the root of many of the 'complications' for accounting, is thus excluded from consideration.

It is this questionable intellectual procedure which underlies Johnson & Kaplan's theorization of changes in management control and capitalistic development through transaction cost theory. In this vein, it is stated as fact that 'the goal of the scientific management engineers, such as Frederick Taylor, was to improve the efficiency and utilization of labour and materials' (Johnson & Kaplan 1987: 10). This is demonstrably partial, since Taylor himself stated that his system was a means of eliminating 'systematic soldiering' (group output restriction) by the workforce (Taylor 1903). More generally, the notion that searches for efficiency under the pressure of competitive markets were the primary drive behind the development of capitalistic organizations and scientific management is highly contentious and has been strongly disputed by historians and radical political economists, many of whom reject technological determinism and economic imperatives as a satisfactory basis for explaining changes in management controls. In contrast to the assumed self-equilibrating behaviour of firms and markets and the social harmony implicit in transaction cost research, they describe how social conflicts were embedded in historical changes and how institutions, such as the state and trades unions helped shape controls at the point of production. Transaction cost theory tends to deflect attention from such issues rather than shed light on them.

It also portrays technological change (in this case, of management accounting systems) as the product of a continuous evolutionary selection of more efficient forms, rather than as discontinuous, and crisis-driven. Johnson & Kaplan portray accounting developments up to the mid-1920s as a steady accretion of knowledge and practice spurred on by firms and individuals operating within competitive and self-equilibrating markets. Such assumptions are called into question by the accumulating evidence that new technologies and organizational forms are partly responses to problems of capital accumulation and labour control.

A Labour Process Approach

In contrast to Johnson & Kaplan's approach, writings in the labour process tradition emphasize that much of the gain in profitability from the early factory organization of production came, not from increases in the technical efficiency of the conversion process, but from the ability of owners/entrepreneurs to intensify labour through close disciplinary control and to extend the working day.

Many early English factories employed the same production technology as the handicraft system which they displaced, indicating that their initial competitive advantage stemmed not from economies of scale, technological innovation or some conjectural reduction of transaction costs, but from an enhanced ability of owner–managers to discipline and drive labour in the factory setting.

In this phase of capitalist development, labour processes remained for the most part untransformed. In the Marxist terminology of labour process writers, labour became *formally* subordinated to capital in the sense that workers were now employees, but there was, as yet, little *real* subordination in the sense that production processes were designed and controlled by employers and their agents.

Since workforces were accustomed to the rhythms of agricultural production, the ability of early factory regimes to increase labour productivity depended on a harsh discipline of time and task. Thus factory work was unpopular and the supply of labour frequently depended upon a lack of alternative sources of livelihood. Some early American textile mills, for example, recruited whole families from the depressed agriculture of New England on the so-called 'Rhode Island system'. The Boston Associates, on the other hand, owed much of their success to the provision of company dormitories for single 'Yankee farm girls' willing to work for a short period to supplement the family income before returning to marriage and the land. Besides serving to attract labour, this system also exhibited features of 'total institutions' creating the conditions for a disciplinary regime which extended deep into what would nowadays be considered to be workers' private lives.

Whilst Johnson & Kaplan are too competent as historians to be unaware of these features of the organizations, or to ignore the potential of accounting records for increasing effort levels, their interpretation is distorted by their commitment to transaction cost theory. Mills also offered incentives and controls to mitigate slack behaviour that might otherwise dissipate the productivity gains inherent in mechanized, multiprocess systems (Johnson & Kaplan 1987: 31). Thus, an intensification of labour is represented as an implicitly costless reduction of 'slack behaviour' and the productivity gains therefrom are credited to mechanization and integration.

The facts bear a different interpretation. The accounts in question date from the mid-nineteenth century, a period when the Boston Associates were faced with falling prices and rising inventories of unsold cloth as a result of intensified competition from England. In 1834, acting in concert, they imposed a wage cut of about 18% in all their factories, so precipitating an abortive strike. In 1836, there was a similarly unsuccessful strike against an increase in the price of boarding and lodgings. By the time further wage cuts were imposed in 1837 and 1840, the 'Yankee farm girls', having alternative means of survival, began to leave the mills and, from 1840 onwards, their place was increasingly taken by Irish immigrants who had little choice but to accept the worsening conditions.

It is not clear from Johnson & Kaplan's account whether their interpretation of the uses made of accounting information in Lyman Mills is based on records similar to these, or on others. What *is* clear, however, is that *some* of the accounting information in the Boston Associates' factories of the mid-nineteenth century was clearly implicated in the intensified exploitation of labour with which the employers responded to increased competition.

Once it is established that accounting information is used to redistribute the rewards from productive labour, rather than to increase the efficiency with which it is employed, it needs to be seen in the context of other labour process controls, since such a redistribution may well be resisted. For example, records which indicate where piece-rates 'should' be cut are of little use unless the possibility of acting on the information has already been established.

Scientific Management and the Homogenization of Labour

The second major phase of management accounting development occurred roughly between 1870 and 1920, as firms sought to maintain profitability through a series of economic recessions. The period was also characterized by intensified competition in consequence of the geographical expansion of markets, following the creation of a national rail network offering cheap freight rates.

Firms responded in two basic ways. Attempts to intensify the labour process took the form of further assaults upon internal subcontracting and craft labour controls. At the same time, companies sought to protect themselves from competition and the prospect of bankruptcy through a series of mergers, culminating in the great merger movement of 1898–1902. In the space of twenty years, the structure of American industry was dramatically transformed. The small, owner-managed and essentially self-financing firms of the late nineteenth century were swept up into giant conglomerates, controlled by external financiers through pyramid holding companies and the concentration of voting rights into small proportions of the total equity (Berle & Means 1933).

In a commanding synthesis of labour histories of the period, Montgomery (1987: 45–46) describes both of the above developments in the American iron, steel and metal-working industries between 1870 and 1930:

> By the turn of the century, the steelmasters' quest for greater and more secure profits had led them not only to integrate 'backward' for every operation from the iron or coal mine to the rolling mill but also to attack the menace of workers' control in any part of those operations and ultimately to search for ways in which to cut the taproot of nineteenth century workers' power by dispossessing the craftsmen of their accumulated skill and knowledge.

Where Johnson & Kaplan follow the transaction costs, orthodoxy in arguing that the appearance of vertically integrated companies resulted from entrepreneurial perceptions of possible efficiency gains, Montgomery (1987: 179) points out that it is difficult to point to cost savings for the large metal-fabricating firms, since these enjoyed few economies of scale, if any. Similarly, whilst Wells (1978) concurs with Johnson & Kaplan that developments in cost accounting were closely associated with the efficiency movement centred on the American Society of Mechanical Engineers, he explicitly denies their presumed imperative of efficiency as a cause, noting that, 'Contrary to the common view that competition provided the stimulus to the introduction of costing systems, a notable feature of the American mechanical engineers was a lack of competition' (Wells 1978: 51). In parallel with the theme of this paper, Wells notes that by the 1920s 'With the advent of efficiency experts, the emphasis [of costing systems] shifted to control' (Wells 1978: 53).

The increases in the size and complexity of industrial organizations following the merger movement, and employers' efforts to develop systematic means of labour control, created a need for complex managerial hierarchies to administer the paper bureaucracy which increasingly replicated and controlled the productive processes (Braverman 1974). However, these systems did not appear overnight. Initially, the labour process was managed through the agency of foremen, and efforts at intensification were relatively unsystematic. Later, however, this aspect of the foreman's role was increasingly taken over by the industrial engineers, who began to undermine craft controls through process redesign and the creation of effort standards under the slogan of 'Scientific Management'. These formalized production methods and effort (cost) standards were to play a crucial role in the developing bureaucratization of industrial organization (Littler 1982).

Overhead Allocation and the Targeting of Secondary Sector Labour Costs

Johnson & Kaplan argue that allocating indirect costs on the basis of direct labour costs is arbitrary and makes labour-intensive processes appear more costly than they are, with consequent distortions in firms' manufacturing policies. Leaving aside the question of how indirect costs should be allocated, it can be argued that present practice fits well with a feature of core corporations in the era of labour segmentation. As noted above, a segmentation of labour markets has taken place *within* some corporations, with primary and secondary sector conditions coinciding roughly with capital and labour-intensive processes. On the whole, workers on modern labour-intensive processes tend to be unskilled (or defined as such), are easily substitutable from external labour markets and, in consequence, are weakly unionized. The bargaining position of workers on capital-intensive processes, on the other hand, is much stronger, either because of their extensive training or because of their responsibility for expensive plant. In consequence, the latter are less vulnerable to managerial attempts to intensify their labour and downgrade their employment conditions.

In this situation, it makes capitalistic sense to incorrectly allocate costs to pressure managers of labour-intensive processes to minimize direct costs disproportionately — for these are where the resistance of labour to further intensification and casualization is likely to be weakest. Information on the costs of capital-intensive process, on the other hand, may be relatively useless, since there may be little scope for the reduction of costs by technical means in an up-and-running system, and whose primary sector labour is likely to be highly resistant to attempts at intensification.

In other words, if cost information is regarded primarily as a means of directing effort, rather than as a representation of reality, it can be argued that distortions of contemporary cost accounting systems make managers focus their cost reduction activities precisely where they are most likely to yield results. True to their realist conception of cost information as a basis for rational economic decision making, however, Johnson & Kaplan argue that overestimates of costs of labour-intensive operations may lead managers to abandon these unnecessarily in the face of overseas competition. Whilst this may be true, it is equally possible that the threat of doing so may enable these same managers to drive secondary sector labour costs even lower than necessary to meet the competition. Where initiatives of this type are successful, corporate management cannot be expected to be greatly concerned if the information on which they are based is accurate, or if the consequent increase in overall profit is incorrectly attributed to capital-intensive operations. As for the effect on product pricing policy, given the relative absence of competition in many American product markets between 1930 and 1960, finely tuned product costs for strategic decision-making purposes may have been a secondary consideration in primary sector corporations. Of course, this situation changed with the rapid growth of Japanese and other Far-Eastern competition, and much of the present-day relevance of *Relevance Lost* derives precisely from that fact.

Social Transformation and Cost Accounting Today

Relevance Lost seeks to inform current accounting problems through historical analysis through the lens of transaction cost theory. The intention of this paper has been to establish that instead there is a prima-facie case for considering accounting developments in the light of labour process histories of capitalist organization. The paper has argued that there is a relationship between systems of accounting information and phases in the evolution of capitalist control of the labour process. Systems of control both entail costs and provoke characteristic forms of resistance which, under competitive conditions, render them increasingly ineffective as means of capital accumulation. These contradictions build into crises of control, especially in times of economic recession, and this leads to a search for new systems of controlling the labour process, either directly or through its immediate management.

Thus developments in accounting for direct labour costs were implicated both in the employers' liquidation of internal contract and in the curbing and focusing of the power of the salaried foremen who replaced them. Standard costing systems were pioneered as an aspect of the fragmentation and deskilling of craft labour, which had hitherto resisted employers' attempts at intensification through piecework payment systems. Once American industrial engineers had gained control over working methods, they could make 'scientific' decisions on the pace of work, and to issue these in the form of standard costs.

As organizations grew in size and complexity, the problem of securing middle management commitment to the demands of capital ownership for secure dividends was addressed by the development of the return-on-investment measure. A re-examination of the General Motors case reported by Johnson & Kaplan indicates that the effectiveness of this measure depended, at least in part, on the 'drive system' of employment and anti-union campaigns which secured the freedom of middle managers to throw the costs of economic fluctuation and recession directly onto the workforce.

Subsequently, the drive system ran into, and partially created, the American recession of the 1930s, from which there emerged a resurgent labour movement and a government committed to some measure of legislative support for trade unionism and employment stability. In these circumstances, the relevance of the accounting systems of the 1920s was indeed lost. Managements became less able to *act* on accounting information which told them where, and by how much, to cut direct labour costs. Instead, large corporations, aided by the monopoly positions they increasingly enjoyed, began to employ budgets for the very different purpose of preserving an accord with their core labour forces by means of monopoly pricing policies. Johnson & Kaplan describe an early prototype of this strategy in their case study of DuPont, though the purpose there was apparently to keep manufacturing plant fully occupied rather than to provide stable employment. When used as an instrument of monopoly pricing, apportioned indirect costs became relevant in cost accounting systems, as opposed to the prime costs relevant to management decisions on manufacturing methods.

In the phase of capitalist development described by Gordon *et al.* (1982) as one of 'segmentation', this accommodation with labour was restricted to a primary sector of core operations within core corporations. Elsewhere, in the competitive sector of the economy and amongst small suppliers to core corporations, secondary sector employment conditions continued. Indeed, by throwing the effect of economic fluctuations and downturn onto secondary sector firms, core corporations could use the insecurity and low wages of secondary sector employment to subsidize their accommodation with their labour force.

There are signs that the boundaries of this accord are being redrawn. Whilst parts of the independent primary sector of managers and professionals remain protected, the bureaucratic and costly apparatus of control in large core conglomerates that emerged in more benign economic conditions than the past fifteen years or so, is increasingly being questioned with consequences for the control and employment prospects of lower levels of management. Similarly, conditions in the subordinate primary sector of skilled manual workers are increasingly under attack. Anti-union drives and threats of plant closure have enabled employers to claw back previous trade union gains on wages and employment security. Edwards (1979: 157) argues that the accord with subordinate primary sector labour came under pressure in the early 1970s when the oil crisis precipitated a series of economic and social crises. Under these circumstances, 'For the firm, bureaucratic control threatens to become a pact with the devil that, while offering temporary respite from trouble, spells long-term disaster. The reason is simple: bureaucratic control speeds up the process of converting the wage bill from a variable to a fixed cost'.

The present may turn out to be a period of exploration from which new forms of control of the labour process and its immediate management may emerge. There are parallels with the British context, in which debates on 'Japanisation' (*Industrial Relations Journal* 1988) and 'flexibility' (Pollert 1991), both tacitly predicated upon the destruction of current trade union rights, now clog the academic and practitioner journals. In this context, current accounting research obsessions with agency theory, downscaling and financial rewards, far from being irrelevant to real-life problems as Johnson & Kaplan believe, make sense. Agency theory, in particular, offers a new 'scientific' rationale, and some practical guidance, for tying the rewards of managers to their success in rolling back the previous gains made by labour and treating it as a variable and expendable cost. Likewise, the attraction to firms of activity costing may lie in its potential for questioning the continued need for bureaucracies and bureaucrats whose functions originated not in the quest for corporate efficiency but in the search for a labour/capital accord and associated modes of control now perceived as redundant.

In the American context, the inroads of Japanese manufacturers have been such that Harvard Business School itself, so long the high temple of strategic management, is now the headquarters of a sect which reasserts the centrality of manufacturing policy. The work of Johnson & Kaplan, with its concern to adapt management accounting to new manufacturing technologies and Japanese systems of organization, is part of this intellectual ferment. It is likely that *Relevance Lost*, with its resonant assertion that management accounting systems are to be judged solely by their relevance to managerial decisions on manufacturing processes, however historically inadequate, may turn out to be an important moment in the search for a leading role for accounting in new forms of control of the labour process.

On the other hand, there are reasons for expecting the influence of financial reporting on management accounting systems to increase rather than decrease. Burawoy (1985) sees the present intensification of international competition and the potential mobility of capital in multinational conglomerates as creating the conditions for new regimes of corporate control in which financial reports are used to reassert the primacy of capital accumulation at the level of operating subsidiaries. Thus, plant-level accommodations with primary sector labour (regimes of 'factory hegemony' in Burawoy's terminology) may be preserved through the common interest of plant-level management and labour in preventing the flight of capital. At the same time, these may be subjected, through financial accounting reports, to the discipline of internal capital markets. If Burawoy is correct, and this hegemonic despotism is the map of the future, corporate-level management accounting may continue to pay little attention to the prime costs of production and regard these as an internal matter for establishment-level managements competing for investment capital. If this perpetuates the games of financial entrepreneurship currently played with overhead allocation by the managers of operating subsidiaries (and much decried by Johnson & Kaplan), the result may be a continuation of the loss of relevance to manufacturing policy of management accountancy. However, because individual companies may evade the consequences by astute policies of acquisition and divestment, the costs may ultimately appear in the US balance of payments figures rather than in the balance sheets of the companies concerned.

References

Berle, A.A., & Means, G.C. (1933). *The modern corporation and private property*. New York: Macmillan.

Braverman, H. (1974). *Labour and monopoly capital*. New York: Monthly Review Press.

Burawoy, M. (1985). *The politics of production: Factory regimes under capitalism and socialism*. London: Verso.

Edwards, R. (1979). *Contested terrain: The transformation of the workplace in the twentieth century*. London: Heinemann.

Gordon, D.M., Edwards, R., & Reich, M. (1982). *Segmented work, divided workers*. Cambridge: Cambridge University Press.

Industrial Relations Journal (1988). Special issue on the Japanese employment relationship.

Johnson, H.T. (1975). Management accounting in an early integrated industrial: E.I. Dupont nemours powder company 1903–1912. *Business History Review*, 184–204.

Johnson, H.T., & Kaplan, R.S. (1987). *Relevance lost: The rise and fall of management accounting*. Boston: Harvard Business School Press.

Littler, C.R. (1982). *The development of the labour process in capitalist societies: A comparative study of the transformation of work organisation in Britain, Japan and the USA*. London: Heinemann.

Montgomery, D. (1987). *The fall of the house of labour: The workplace, the state, and American labor activism*. Cambridge: Cambridge University Press.

Pollert, A. (1991). *Farewell to flexibility*. London: Routledge.

Taylor, F.W. (1947). *Shop management*. (1903). Re-published in *Scientific Management*. New York: Harper and Row.

Wells, M.C. (1978). Influences on the development of cost accounting. *The Accounting Historians Journal*, 47–59.

Chapter 14

From the Union Hall: A Labor Critique of the New Manufacturing and Accounting Regimes[1]

Patricia J. Arnold, *University of Wisconsin, Milwaukee*

This study presents the critique of new manufacturing regimes that is emerging out of debates within the US labor movement over the merits of union/management cooperation as a strategy for revitalizing American manufacture. The research focuses on the labor histories of three union locals in Decatur, Illinois and their critique of new forms of factory governance such as teams, quality circles and employee participation programs. The paper examines the implications of the labor critique for management accounting's attempt to establish its relevance within contemporary manufacturing environments.

Introduction

A new conventional wisdom has found its way into management accounting theory and practice. Accounting academics, industry consultants, the media, trade journals and accounting textbooks now almost uniformly accept that traditional cost accounting, with its emphasis on controlling production workers, is no longer relevant to contemporary management and manufacturing strategies.

According to this new received wisdom, globally competitive or world class manufacturing is achieved by some combination of new manufacturing technologies, such as flexible specialization, lean production, just-in-time production, design for manufacture, synchronous manufacture, computer integrated manufacture and cell manufacture. Competitiveness also demands new management philosophies, notably, total quality management (TQM), continuous improvement, team building and union–management cooperation.

Labor and management, the story goes, benefit jointly from the introduction of these manufacturing and management regimes. Some jobs may be lost initially as companies retrench and re-engineer and union concessions may be required to eliminate rigidities such as job classifications and contractual impediments to

---

[1]Reproduced (in an abridged form) from P. J. Arnold, 'From the Union Hall: A Labor Critique of The New Manufacturing and Accounting Regimes', *Critical Perspectives on Accounting*, 1999, vol. 10, pp. 399–423, with permission of Elsevier.

Accounting, the Social and the Political
N. Macintosh and T. Hopper (Editors)

employee participation programs. Nonetheless, academics, government and business spokespersons and many union leaders assert that labor-management cooperation is essential if US manufacturers and manufacturing jobs are to survive in an increasingly competitive global economy.

The revitalization of American manufacturing is thus portrayed not merely as a strategy for corporate profitability, but as a strategy for national economic competitiveness. For labor, the new manufacturing regimes promise not only secure jobs, but also good jobs — a decentralized work place where multi-skilled workers function in teams, rotating jobs and controlling their own work; where workers' knowledge and creativity are valued; and where employees at all levels participate in decision making to continuously improve manufacturing processes and quality.

The critical accounting literature, however, has taken exception to such un-questioning acceptance of such conventional wisdom on manufacturing reform. Oakes & Covaleski's (1994) history of profit sharing plans in the 1950s and 1960s demonstrates that previous attempts to wed accounting techniques and union–management cooperation programs failed to deliver on their promises to labor. The claims made for contemporary manufacturing regimes and accounting reforms have also been called into question. Hopper & Armstrong's (1991) histor-ical analysis of activity based costing suggests that the revival of interest in accounting innovation since the 1980s and 1990s is related to the changing patterns of labor relations, including the declining strength of trade unions, which enabled companies to eliminate categories of indirect labor that were previously protected. Hammond & Preston (1992) and Ezzamel (1994) question the applic-ability of contemporary Japanese management practices to other organizational and social contexts. Williams *et al.* (1994) employ value added accounting measures to show that structural constraints rather than outmoded management practices lie at the root of the auto industry's competitivity crisis. Yuthas & Tinker (1994), simi-larly, argue that the optimism of those who advocate manufacturing and ac-counting reform will prove unsustainable in the face of the instabilities of late of capitalism.

This study extends the critical accounting literature by presenting a critique of the new manufacturing regimes, employee participation programs, teams, quality circles and new technologies that are being articulated on the shop floors and in the union halls by trade unionists who have experienced the new manufacturing regimes.

This study focuses on the experiences of unions at three plants in Decatur, Illinois, a midwest town that became the center of US labor struggles in the 1990s. The research draws extensively from interviews with union officials and rank and file members of three union locals in Decatur. They include the United Auto Workers (UAW) Local 751 representing workers at Decatur's Caterpillar plant; the United Paperworkers International Union (UPIU) Local 7837 representing workers at A.E. Staley and the United Rubber Workers (URW) Local 713 representing workers at the Bridgestone/Firestone plant in Decatur.

The War Zone

In the mid-1990s, striking trade unionists and the labor press referred to the midwest industrial town of Decatur, Illinois, as a 'war zone'. The east end of Decatur had more industrial workers on picket lines than at work and the city was drawing national attention as a center of rank and file opposition to corporate offensives against unionized labor. After working for three years without a contract, United Auto Workers (UAW) at the Caterpillar corporation went on a nationwide strike over unfair labor practice violations on June 21, 1994. Striking auto workers from Caterpillar's Decatur plant joined the picket lines with union members who had been locked out by the British-owned A.E. Staley Company since 1993. On July 12, 1994, workers at Decatur's Bridgestone/Firestone plant walked out when the United Rubber Workers (URW) called a national strike. The conflicts continued into 1995 with nearly 2000 workers from the three Decatur plants either on strike or locked out.

In each case, the corporations demanded concessions that threatened to dismantle hard won protections and attempted to enforce those demands with lock outs or permanent replacements. The unions found themselves negotiating and ultimately striking to preserve basic contractual guarantees such as eight hour days, seniority rights, health and safety provisions and job security provisions.

In all three cases, the companies took aggressive positions in contract negotiations. Hostilities mounted when Caterpillar and Bridgestone/Firestone attempted to break union strikes by hiring permanent replacements. Although a 1938 Supreme Court decision gives US employers the right to hire permanent replacements during a strike, the practice was virtually non-existent until the 1980s when President Reagan fired some 11 000 striking air-traffic controllers and replaced them. Several companies, including Phelps Dodge and Greyhound, followed suit in the 1980s. Caterpillar's attempt to break its 1991–1992 strike by hiring permanent replacements, marked the first attempt to use the strategy against one of the United Auto Workers' core auto or farm equipment contracts.

Models of Labor-Management Cooperation

Such hostile labor relations would seem the antithesis of the manufacturing workplace envisioned in the recent management accounting literature. Yet all three cases were, in fact, implementing variations of cooperative management philosophies, such as quality circles, employee participation programs and union-management teams prior to or coincident with taking offensive postures in contract negotiations.

In the 1980s, Caterpillar adopted a conciliatory stance in its labor relations and sought UAW cooperation in implementing a multi-billion dollar plant modernization program, known as the Plant With A Future (PWAF). The Decatur plant was one of the plants modernized. Advanced flexible manufacturing equipment, robotics and computer integrated machinery were installed. The plant was reorganized into multi-purpose cells, machine operators were designated as 'cell proprietors', and a customer-driven quality program, known as the cell certification program, was implemented. Accounting expertize was essential to Caterpillar's manufacturing reforms. New accounting techniques, such as competitor cost analysis, bundle monitoring of capital projects, activity based costing and predictive costing were employed and the plant modernization was implemented with the assistance of the consulting division of the accounting firm of Deloitte, Haskins and Sells.

In their 1986 contract, the UAW members agreed to reductions in job classifications and endorsed an employee participation program, called the Employee Satisfaction Process (ESP). In the Decatur plant alone, some 985 UAW workers participated in 100 ESP teams that developed suggestions for improving the manufacturing processes. Nationwide, the union–management cooperation program was estimated to have saved Caterpillar $50 million.

To an observer in the 1980s, any of these three cases might appear to be a textbook model of employee involvement in improving manufacturing processes. Viewed in the context of their subsequent labor histories, however, a pattern emerges where the adoption of employee participation programs in the 1980s is followed by assaults on union contracts and bitter labor disputes in the 1990s. How do we reconcile the new management philosophies which supposedly recognize workers' skills and knowledge as essential elements of programs to continuously improve quality, with the willingness to permanently replace the entire union labor force?

The answer cannot be found by blaming union intransigence. Union opposition to participation was not a factor in any of the Decatur labor disputes. In all three cases, the union members actively participated in the 'jointness' programs. At A.E. Staley and Caterpillar, union–management cooperation began as a union initiative. At Caterpillar, the company's consultants, Deloitte, Haskins and Sells, credited the union with being more 'on board' and with factory modernization than some managers. And at Bridgestone/Firestone, there was a waiting list of people volunteering to participate in Process Improvement Teams.

While initially accepting union–management cooperation programs, trade unionists in Decatur became disillusioned and increasingly critical as they experienced the contradiction between the rhetoric of 'empowerment' and the actuality of outsourcing, downsizing and concession bargaining. While many international unions continued to endorse the concept of union–management cooperation as a strategy for national economic competitiveness, a substantive critique of the rhetoric of cooperation emerged among the rank and file trade union members and local union leaders in Decatur. The critique of the new manufacturing regimes voiced from Decatur's union halls and the progressive labor press, such as *Labor Notes*, challenged conventional wisdom.

Labor's Critique of the 'New' Manufacturing Regimes

The labor conflicts in Decatur destroyed any illusion of 'trust' that figures so prominently in the discourse on flexible manufacturing and continuous quality improvement. In fact, many Decatur unionists argue that all the 'talk of trust in the 1980s' exacerbated the bitterness and betrayal people felt when they were locked out or permanently replaced in the 1990s. In retrospect, Decatur workers who embraced union–management cooperation became extremely skeptical of participation programs, teams, and quality circles, seeing them as vehicles for appropriating workers' knowledge, intensifying work and weakening unions, rather than as strategies for saving manufacturing jobs.

Appropriating Knowledge

> One of the first things they do in participative management is that they get people to write up operating manuals. They get people to write up JSAs (jobs safety analyses). Once the operators write those up, they have given their heart and soul to the company. And, once they have given that heart and soul, all the company has to do is plug that heart and soul into the machine.

> Staley Worker, UPIU Local 7837

The Rhetoric of Cooperation

> The real danger of any employee program is that you get people lulled into a false sense of security that the company is their friend. That you are not equal partners, but they are actually your friend.... Once they get you down to where you're 'old buddy, buddy,' it takes people a long time to get the will to fight ... or think they'll actually do this to us. 'No they wouldn't do this to us ... They wouldn't close this plant'. Yes, they would. They would do it in a heartbeat.

> Union Representative, UAW Local 751

In retrospect, labor leaders in all three Decatur unions characterized employee involvement programs as a strategy to weaken or eliminate unions. The tension between independent unionism and company-sponsored employee teams is evident at both the national and local levels. On the national level, President Clinton's Commission on the Future of Worker–Management Relations (the Dunlop Commission) sought to promote employee participation in 1995 by recommending the weakening of labor laws that prevent company-dominated teams from negotiating working conditions. Historically, company-sponsored or company-dominated workplace organizations have been used to undermine independent unionism and some trade unionists fear that teams may represent the first step in an attempt to establish company unions.

On the plant level, Decatur's trade unionists contend that the psychological ramifications of cooperation programs and their accompanying discourse constitute the greatest threat to independent unionism. The rhetoric on revitalizing American manufacturing, which frequently portrays unions as an outmoded constraint on national competitiveness, rather than a constraint on how profits are distributed within firms, contributes to declining public support for unions. More importantly, a managerial strategy that claims to respect workers' ideas and to value their contributions can serve to convince workers that their interests are aligned with management and that unions are unnecessary anachronisms from an era when labor relations were adversarial. This is implicit in the language that constructs rubber workers at Bridgestone/Firestone 'associates' and machine operators and assemblers at Caterpillar as cell 'proprietors'. Trade unionists view the use of such language as purposive and strategic. As one UAW trade unionist described it, 'this is control — social and psychological'.

Because of the importance attributed to the rhetoric surrounding the new manufacturing regimes, labor is contesting and redefining the meaning of the terminology and concepts that have become so common in management accounting. In their union guide to participation programs and re-engineering, Parker & Slaughter (1994: 69, 89) state that the terminology 'is carefully crafted to trigger strong positive responses: teams, teamwork, job rotation, empowerment, multi-skilling, job security', but these terms provide a misleading description of today's manufacturing workplace. In their translations 'continuous improvement' means 'continuous speed-up'; 'flexibility' means 'eliminating job classifications'; 'outside contracting' means 'job loss'; 'design for manufacturing' means 'design for deskilling'; 'worker empowerment' means 'more power for management'; and 'competitiveness' means 'worker against worker'. By contesting the language, meanings and normative judgments conveyed by the dominant discourse on manufacturing reform, labor's critique demonstrates that the conventional wisdom on new manufacturing and accounting technologies is neither neutral nor disinterested, but rather a contested ideological terrain.

Theoretical Alternatives

The Decatur case poses a theoretical challenge to a management accounting literature that neglects history and politics. The dominant research paradigm views the development of managerial accounting and control systems as market driven efficiency adaptations, i.e. as responses to market imperatives and changing technologies. This reliance on the explanatory power of markets is evident in *Relevance Regained* (1992), where Johnson argues that manufacturers must adopt customer-driven TQM strategies and concomitant changes in cost accounting systems in order to survive in an increasingly competitive global marketplace. Although his conclusions advocating a TQM-type transformation from 'top down management' to 'bottom up empowerment' are non-traditional, the argument remains essentially a traditional market efficiency argument premised on the neo-classical notion that the market-driven search for 'competitive excellence' alone will force companies to adopt manufacturing strategies that emphasize quality, skilling and worker autonomy. This conclusion, in turn, rests on the unquestioned and perhaps untenable assumption that these outcomes can be obtained via the rational operation of 'minimal economic institutions', namely market competition and corporate hierarchies.

The contradiction between the rhetorical claims of workplace reform and empowerment and the reality of management assaults on wages and working conditions in Decatur can be understood within this political-institutional context. The US political economy in the 1980s and 1990s was marked by neo-liberal economic policy, weakened trade unions, the ascendancy of the New Right and the absence of any coherent industrial policy that might have curbed structural imperatives for corporations to increase profit by cutting labor costs. Given the relatively impoverished institutional structure of the US economy and the comparatively weakened position of US trade unions in the 1980s, it is not surprising, from a political-institutional perspective, that experiments with employee participation and quality programs failed to deliver the promised empowerment, security and job enrichment. Nor is it surprising that 'reform' efforts in the plants examined in this study were accompanied by efforts to cut costs by eliminating jobs, increasing work intensity and dismantling contractual job security, safety and benefit protections. For as Streeck (1992) would argue, without socially embedded institutional constraints on managerial prerogatives to unilaterally rescind their promises, there is no basis for trust.

Similarly, there is little reason to expect that quality and participation programs, such as those at Caterpillar, A.E. Staley and Bridgestone/Firestone, would necessarily curtail the deeply ingrained practice of treating labor as a cost or the rationality of reducing labor costs in the interest of increasing profits. Caterpillar destroyed years of union–management cooperation when it came to the bargaining table in 1991 armed with an accounting analysis of competitor costs to demand the end of pattern bargaining in the interest of cutting labor costs. At A.E. Staley, after a maintenance worker lost his life in an industrial accident in 1990, a company executive testified before the *United States Occupational Safety and Health Review Commission* (1995, p. 8) that Staley analyzed safety decisions on a cost-benefit basis, weighing the cost of an OSHA citation against the cost of taking corrective action, and opting for the 'cheaper course of action regardless of employee safety'. Such blatant violations of the vision of a new role for cost accounting strongly suggest that, in the absence of socially imposed constraints on opportunism, market competition will not provide sufficient inducements for companies to maintain commitments to the principles of quality improvement and employee empowerment when confronted with opportunities to cut labor costs.

The management accounting literature has not sufficiently concerned itself with the question of how production patterns are socially and institutionally embedded, much less with the problem of how techno-economic changes can be directed toward the goals of job enrichment, employment security and worker empowerment by reforming socio-political institutions. Instead accounting has been preoccupied with the problem of techno-economic response, i.e. how can management accounting practice respond to changing production technologies and management strategies? This approach ignores political and institutional context and avoids the issues of economic regulation and non-market governance. Underlying this approach is a tacit assumption that techno-economic changes, such as new manufacturing technologies and cost accounting practices, are themselves a sufficient basis for manufacturing reform. The fact that this assumption was not borne out in the Decatur case, suggests a need to explore alternative theoretical approaches such as those offered by the regulation and governance schools.

Conclusions

The manufacturing work place is being affected by new technologies from just-in-time to computer integrated manufacture as well as by associated shifts in factory governance — teams, quality improvement and employee participation. In characterizing the role of accounting expertise and new accounting technologies in relation to these manufacturing regimes, the accounting literature has generally portrayed the shift in workplace governance with its emphasis on quality, customer satisfaction, teams, and worker empowerment in positive terms, echoing the conventional wisdom that these new manufacturing regimes serve the mutual interest of corporations, labor and the nation.

Within the US trade union movement, there is no such consensus, but rather a serious debate over the issue of whether union cooperation with management programs to 'revitalize' manufacturing will benefit or harm labor. Rank and file trade unionists, like those in Decatur, Illinois, who have experienced the negative impact of the new manufacturing regimes, offer a very different interpretation of quality circles, participation programs and union–management cooperation than that given by the conventional wisdom. They view shifts in factory governance as mechanisms for appropriating knowledge, intensifying work, eliminating jobs, dividing the work force and weakening unions. Labor's accounts of intensified Taylorism, returning supervision and declining interest in teams once new technologies or processes are fully operational, challenge the rhetorical claims that saturate the contemporary discourse on manufacturing reform.

The implications of this critique for management accounting as it attempts to reconceptualize the role of accounting within these emerging manufacturing regimes are twofold. First, the contradiction between the theoretical conceptions of the new manufacturing workplace, and the experience of Decatur's workers poses a challenge to accounting theory. In the absence of institutionally imposed constraints on corporate opportunism, the employee involvement and quality programs implemented in the three plants examined in this study not only failed to deliver the promised job security, workplace autonomy and empowerment, but actually culminated in the opposite — job eliminations, intensified Taylorism, strikes, lockouts and permanent replacements.

Second, the labor critique draws attention to the fact that much of what is taken for granted in contemporary discourse about teams, quality circles, participation and the redesign of work is being contested and challenged in local union halls and the progressive labor press. The view of factory life portrayed by trade unionists in the United States who are challenging the conventional wisdom about new modes of factory governance contradicts the conventional wisdom portrayed in accounting textbooks and trade presses. In their view, the rhetoric of manufacturing 'reform' with its emphasis on teams, high wage/high skilled jobs and worker empowerment not only fails to describe the reality of the contemporary US workplace, but, more importantly, represents a form of subjective social control — an attempt to convince workers that their interests are aligned with the management, which enables managers to appropriate knowledge and weaken trade unions.

Labor's challenge to the rhetoric of cooperation, teams and the redesign of work cautions against uncritically adopting that rhetoric into accounting research and pedagogy as if that language were neutral or disinterested. At the very least, the history of labor relations at the Decatur plants cautions against positioning discussion of new accounting and manufacturing technologies within an ostensibly progressive discourse about national competitiveness, job security and worker empowerment. For accounting to adopt such a discourse without regard for the critique that is being mounted against it from within the labor movement is to collaborate in a project of constructing not only a new conventional wisdom, but a new workplace ideology.

References

Ezzamel, M. (1994). From problem solving to problematization: Relevance revisited. *Critical Perspectives on Accounting*, 5(3), 269–280.

Hammond, T., & Preston, A. (1992). Cultural, gender and corporate control: Japan as 'Other'. *Accounting, Organizations and Society*, 795–808.

Hopper, T., & Armstrong, P. (1991). Cost accounting, controlling labour and the rise of conglomerates. *Accounting, Organizations and Society*, 405–438.

Johnson, H.T. (1992). *Relevance regained: From top-down control to bottom-up empowerment*. New York: The Free Press.

Oakes, L., & Covaleski, M. (1994). A historical examination of the use of accounting-based incentive plans in the structuring of labor-management relations. *Accounting, Organizations and Society*, 19(7), 579–599.

Parker, M., & Slaughter, J. (1994). *Working smart: A union guide to participation programs and reengineering*. Detroit: Labor Notes.

Streeck, W. (1992). *Social institutions and economic performance: Studies of industrial relations in advanced capitalist economies*. London: Sage Publications.

United States Occupational Safety and Health Review Commission. (1995). Notice of Decision in Reference to Secretary of Labor v. A. E. Staley Manufacturing Co, OSHRC Docket No. 91-0637 and 91-0638, January 27.

Williams, K., Haslam, C., Cutler, T., Johal, S., & Willis, R. (1994). Johnson 2: Knowledge Goes to Hollywood. *Critical Perspectives on Accounting*, *5*, 281–293.

Yuthas, K., & Tinker, T. (1994). Paradise regained? Myth, milton and management accounting. *Critical Perspectives on Accounting*, *5*(3), 295–310.

Chapter 15

From Taylorism to Ms Taylor:
The Transformation of the
Accounting Craft[1]

Christine Cooper,   *University of Strathclyde*
Phil Taylor,   *University of Stirling*

The history of professionally qualified accountants and their regulatory processes command considerable attention in the academic accounting literature. This is the case even in the *critical* accounting literature. In contrast, 'non-qualified', clerical employees have been virtually excluded from serious accounting research. In the UK in 1998, 78% of the accounting labour force of 1.3 million were 'clerical' as opposed to 'professional'. Of the 'clerical' stratum, 76.5% were women. There is still no thoroughgoing analysis of this majority employee experience. This paper aims to overcome this serious deficiency in the academic literature. It is centrally concerned with the changing work practices of non-professionally qualified workers in accounting clerical roles.

Adopting a long term perspective, the paper charts the changing work practices of accounting clerks from the mid-nineteenth century until the publication of Braverman's *Labour and Monopoly Capital* (1974). It continues where Braverman left off in 1974, by studying the skills required by employers of accounting clerks from 1974 until 1996 through a longitudinal analysis of job advertisements and other contemporary changes within the accounting industry. The framework used in the paper to analyze the work practices of accounting clerks draws strongly on the theoretical foundations of Marx and subsequent development by Braverman. Braverman contended that in the monopoly capitalist era, Scientific Management is used both to deskill workers and to progressively relieve them of autonomy in their working lives.

[1]Reproduced (in an abridged form) from Christine Cooper and Phil Taylor, 'From Taylorism to Ms Taylor: The Transformation of the Accounting Craft', *Accounting, Organizations and Society*, 2000, vol. 25, pp. 555–578 with permission of Elsevier.

Accounting, the Social and the Political
N. Macintosh and T. Hopper (Editors)

Braverman and the Labour Process

When Braverman's *Labour and Monopoly Capital* (Braverman 1974) first appeared a quarter of a century ago, no one could have imagined the breadth and intensity of debate which this pathbreaking account of the capitalist labour process would stimulate.

The explanatory power of Braverman's analysis lies in the appreciation of the *long-term* consequences of the separation of conception and execution in the labour process and the accretion of management control. If one comprehends the 'deskilling' thesis as an overall tendency and if one disregards its application as a 'universal law' applying in all cases at all points in time, and finally, if one adopts a broad temporal perspective, then Braverman's essential validity comes into view. Over a period of, not years, but decades, one would expect to find, if Braverman is correct, that work in the majority of occupations has become progressively deskilled, subdivided into routine and fragmented tasks, subject to increasing amounts of managerial control.

A broad historical perspective also informs the most effective theoretical analysis of class structure. Given the central importance of a person's place in the relations of production, three groups of white collar workers must be distinguished. At one extreme there exists 'a small minority who are salaried members of the capitalist class, participating in the decisions on which the process of capitalist production depends' (Callinicos & Harman 1987: 7). Secondly, occupying managerial and supervisory positions between labour and capital, which might be termed 'contradictory class locations', there is the 'new middle class' of well-paid salaried employees. Thirdly, there are the majority of white-collar workers, whose numbers have grown massively this century. This latter group includes the mass of clerical workers and those in the 'lower professions' (Callinicos & Harman, 1987: 17).

We would argue that the mass of accountancy workers must be regarded unequivocally as part of the working class. These workers who constitute the clerical ranks are distinguished, firstly and obviously, from senior accountants who may be part of, or close to, the capitalist class. They are distinguished also from qualified professional accountants, who as a 'contradictory' layer performing managerial and supervisory functions, stand above the mass of clerical accounting labour.

Accountancy workers, as distinct from accountants, neither own the means of production nor can exist without selling their labour power. They will be subject to control by senior management or, more likely by managers and supervisors who directly execute policies on behalf of owners and senior management. If Braverman is correct, then we would expect to find the mass of accountancy workers to have been effectively divested from control over their labour process. We would further expect a progressive, if not wholly linear, tendency for deskilling to have occurred over a long time span. Our belief in the centrality of the deskilling aspects of Scientific Management to the contemporary work practices of accounting clerks and bookkeepers requires that we spend some time explaining its concepts and principles.

The Introduction of Taylorism and Scientific Management

Frederick Winslow Taylor was the key figure in the Scientific Management movement which began in the last few decades of the nineteenth century. Basically, Scientific Management's task was, and is, to find ways of controlling labour in rapidly growing capitalist organizations. Capitalism is central to Scientific Management because the antagonistic social relations created by capitalism are taken by Scientific Management as *natural* and inexorable.

This paper takes the view that Scientific Management played and *continues to play a central role* in shaping the capitalist work process. We do not believe that Taylorism or Scientific Management have been superseded by newer 'management schools' or by Human Resource Management.

Scientific Management is very much more than a straightforward study of work to produce efficiency gains. The self-use of experimental methods in the study of work by the craftsman is, and probably always has been, part of the practice of the craft worker. But the study of work by *managers* developed with the growth of the capitalist system and is wholly concerned with wresting control over work practices from labour. Capitalist managers, from the outset were interested in controlling workers. Burrell (1987) describes how workers were physically removed to factories where they could be more readily surveyed and controlled. But Taylorism took capitalist control to an entirely new level by asserting that an absolute necessity for adequate management is the dictation to the worker of *the precise manner in which work is to be performed*. Taylor insisted that management could only be a limited and frustrated undertaking so long as workers were left with any discretion in the implementation of their work. To totally alleviate management's frustration, Taylor developed a revolutionary division of labour.

To Taylor there were two basic factors which prevented workers from producing a fair day's work. The first was pure laziness (or *natural soldiering*) and the second was more conscious, deliberate, collective and universal (*systematic soldiering*). Taylor was less concerned with laziness than with systematic soldiering, which was created by workers' relationships with each other. Systematic soldiering was carried out with the deliberate object of keeping management ignorant of how fast work can be performed. Taylor recognized that since wage rates were determined chiefly by market, social and historical factors, that there was no incentive for workers to work harder. Pre-Taylorist management had introduced piecework systems in an attempt to improve the work rates. But Taylor found that it was under piecework systems that workers produced the most advanced types of systematic soldiering.

The historical antecedents of skilled workers or craftspeople being repositories of knowledge spanned from earliest times to the Industrial Revolution. In each craft, the worker was presumed to be the possessor of a body of traditional knowledge, and methods and procedures were left to his or her discretion. The apprenticeships of traditional crafts ranged from 3 to 7 years. Taylor recognized that it would not be easy to take control of these skilled workers' knowledges but this was the task he set himself. Taylor set out three principles which underpin his system and which are seldom publicly acknowledged.

First Principle

Braverman described his first principle as the *dissociation of the labour process from the skills of the workers.* Taylor demonstrated this principle with both simple and complex tasks and found that it was possible in either case for the management to collect at least as much information as is known by the worker who performs it regularly. The manner of obtaining this information brought into being new methods that can be devised only through the means of systematic study.

Second Principle

Braverman's second principle held that 'all possible brainwork should be removed from the shop and centred in the planning or laying-out department...' (Taylor 1903: 98–99). This removal of brainwork, the separation of conception from execution, is perhaps the cornerstone of Taylor's work. In short, management must take control of the worker's actions. Clearly if a worker's execution is guided by his or her conception, then the management will be unable to impose its own efficiency norms. Thus, work always had to be studied by the management and never by workers themselves. There was never a question of having *scientific workmanship* rather than *Scientific Management.* Braverman makes the telling point that not only has capital become the property of the capitalist but *labour itself thus becomes part of capital.* The advent of the Industrial Revolution ensured that workers lost control of the means of production. Taylor then compounded this by ensuring that they also lost control over their own labour and the manner of its performance.

Third Principle

Braverman's third principle holds that 'the most prominent single element in modern Scientific Management is the task idea. The work of every workman is fully planned out by the management at least one day in advance, and each man receives in most cases complete written instructions, describing in detail the task which he is to accomplish, as well as the means used in doing the work...' (Taylor 1911: 63 and 39, cited in Braverman 1974: 118).

Thus, the third principle involves using the knowledge taken from the worker to control each step of the worker's day. Thus, Taylorism ensured that as crafts declined, workers would sink to the level of general and undifferentiated labour power, adaptable to a large range of simple tasks, while as science grew, it would be concentrated in the hands of the management.

A Brief History of the Labour Process of Bookkeeping

Clerks of the mid-nineteenth century were the predecessors of modern middle management rather than the army of clerks found in the modern workplace. In the prosperous decades of the nineteenth century, the socio-economic position of clerks was relatively secure. Clerks formed a small, homogeneous group differentiated from the mass of the urban working class at the bottom of the social ladder. These clerks were men. Kirkham & Loft (1993) note the practical and ideological struggle that women of this period faced if they wanted to become clerks. The masculine qualities required of clerks 'contrasted markedly with the image of the weak, dependent, emotional "married" woman of mid-Victorian Britain' (Kirkham & Loft 1993: 516).

Clerical work in its early stages had the characteristics of a craft. Master craftspeople like bookkeepers maintained control of their work, which essentially consisted of keeping the current records of the financial and operating condition of the enterprise, as well as its relations with the external world. Moreover, clerks were *trusted*.

The antecedents of contemporary clerical labour arrived in the late nineteenth and early twentieth century with the creation of a new class of clerical workers, which had little continuity with the mid-nineteenth century small, masculine, homogeneous and privileged clerical stratum. For the bookkeeper, the significant change from mid to late nineteenth century was the massive increase in the number of jobs. Anderson (1976) believes that part of the reason for the reduction in relative pay and change in the gender composition of clerks was increased education brought about by the Education Act of 1870. Better education meant a rapid increase in the number of female and young male clerks all equipped with the basic skills of clerking. The proportion of women clerks rose from 1.1% in 1871 to 18.2% in 1911.

While the gender composition of the new clerical layer moved from men to women, bookkeeping clerks on the whole tended to be men, with men taking bookkeeping classes and women studying shorthand and typing. Even with the huge influx of women into clerical positions during the First World War (from 500 000 to 930 000), many into skilled accounting roles, few women sat for their Institute of Bookkeeper's examinations. Women had long been barred from sitting the examinations of professional accounting bodies. From their formation these bodies had adopted practices which would serve to exclude 80 or 90% of the population (i.e. those without funds to pay for the training and membership premium and women) from their membership.

It was not at the top but at the bottom end of the clerical labour market that women made their impact. In the early twentieth century for working class men, becoming a clerk was seen as an opportunity for upward social mobility. Their competitors for clerical posts were typically well educated middle class women. Since the 'marriage bar' which required women to leave work upon marriage was in operation at this time, women employees were not given long and expensive training which would be lost to the employer upon their marriage. With the rapid feminization and growing working class composition of clerks, their salaries and status were driven down. Notwithstanding the early twentieth century clerk's ideological alignment with management, Victorian clerk's pay did not keep pace with their industrial counterparts and by the 1950s US clerical workers' pay was less than the pay of manual workers.

The change in the gender and class composition of clerks continued throughout the twentieth century. For many years, the outrageous price women had to pay for very small promotions and meager financial independence was the renunciation of marriage and children. During the 1930s, clever working class girls who had been given opportunities of schooling after the age of 14 provided a ready supply of recruits to lower level clerical jobs. Women have been increasingly channeled into the lower-level repetitive, or Taylorized work with few promotion prospects. It could be argued that feminized work in offices meant Taylorized work.

The Growth of Paper 'Controls'

With the advent of larger scale organizations and monopoly capitalism in the late nineteenth century, the accounting functions of control and appropriation, expanded enormously. An accounting function which could exactly 'shadow' the *real* production process became increasingly important. This was partly due to the coordination and control of new productive processes through accounting and its paper trail and partly due to the removal of 'trust' as an expected clerical skill. The dishonesty or laxity of employees made double entry bookkeeping particularly appropriate.

The increased importance of bookkeeping was also tied to the drive to maximize profits in accordance with an economic system which encompassed demand-led calculations of value. This meant that, in effect, the actual type of commodity being sold became obscured by the net gain appropriated from that commodity. The value form of commodities separates itself out from the physical form as a vast paper empire which under capitalism becomes as real as the physical world. Thus, a portion of the labour of society must therefore be devoted to the accounting of value. Indeed, as capitalism becomes more complex and develops into a monopoly stage, the accounting of value becomes infinitely more complex.

With the rapid growth of companies and their paper trails, office work changed from something merely incidental to management into a labour process in its own right. The characteristic feature of this period was the ending of the reign of the bookkeeper and the rise of the office manager as the prime functionary and representative of higher management. Office management developed as a special branch of management in its own right. As a consequence of the operations side of business growing to employ hundreds of clerks and bookkeepers, rather than half a dozen or so, companies were compelled to investigate whether or not clerical employees were producing 'a fair day's work'. Given the historical context, this inevitably meant considering the application of Scientific Management methods to the office.

The first practitioners of Scientific Management applied Taylor's concepts to the office. This resulted in the dissolution of work arrangements which had allowed clerks to work according to 'traditional methods, independent judgement, and light general supervision, usually on the part of the bookkeeper' (Braverman 1974: 307). New work practices were prescribed by office managers. Work methods and time durations were to be verified and controlled by management on the basis of its own studies of each job. The role of the office manager in terms of supervision was a key to the increased productivity of clerks brought about by the implementation of Taylorism.

It is worth noting that the implementation of Scientific Management in offices around the turn of the century worked (as did Taylor) with existing technology (which typically consisted of typewriters, although the instruments for adding, dictating and ledger posting by mechanical means had already been devised). The mechanization of the office still lay far in the future.

The Technical Division of Accounting Labour

Management's solutions to the problem of how to control large offices were found firstly in the technical division of labour and secondly in mechanization. In industrial terms, the work processes of most organizations could be described as 'continuous flow processes'. With the advent of large scale activity and organization, and the application of Scientific Management, the process was subdivided into minute operations, each becoming the task of a worker or group of workers. One necessary division was the introduction of various ledgers (sales, purchases, nominal). The essential feature of this parceling out of individual processes was that the workers involved *lose comprehension of the process as a whole and the policies which underlie it*. The indefinable element of judgement and intuition based upon skill, experience and a comprehension of several stages in the process had been removed. Moreover, clerical processes could now be controlled at various points by mathematical checks with, for example, the measurement of the number of invoices posted per day per worker or the quantification of mistakes made by an individual clerical worker, operating possibilities.

The Advent of Mechanization and Large Scale Computerization

Office mechanization has further accelerated the process of deskilling of accounting labour. Significantly, this has meant the deskilling of feminized accounting labour. Remington's first typewriters of the 1870s were met with rather a cool reception. But by 1890, Remington were selling 65 000 typewriters annually. Selling around the concept of 'The Remington Girl', the new techno-logy promised emancipation for women, entry into the male world of business with pay, conditions and above all status well above those in factory or domestic work. Like computer systems several generations later, typewriters and other machines speeded up work processes and reduced labour costs by allowing the (more expensive) male correspondence clerks to pursue the more analytical side of clerical work.

The computer's early applications were for large scale repetitive and routine operations which, before the advent of computers, were typically performed mechanically, or almost mechanically by cumbersome machines. Such tasks would consist of payrolls; billing; debtors and creditors; mortgage accounting; stock control, actuarial and dividend calculations and so on. But computers were also applied to other tasks, for example, management accounting, sales reports and so on up to the point where companies' books of record were put into computerized form. Once computerization had been achieved, the pacing of data input became available to management as a weapon of control. The reduction of office information to standardized 'bits' and their processing by computer systems and other office equipment provided management with an automatic accounting of the size of the workload and the amount done by each operator, section or division.

Clearly, this increased output due to computerization would have two implica-tions for management. They would be able to get by with less labour. The labour which they needed could be less skilled (and therefore cheaper).

A recent account of the clerical labour process in diverse locations in both the public and private sector spells out the consequences of the introduction of IT to the office; an increase in intensification of effort and the speed, volume and intensity of work, as subdivided tasks become subject to unprecedented levels of monitoring and target setting.

But what about the myth that with the advent of computerization companies would need better educated labour? This myth was quickly recognized as such by the management. But, it is true that during the transition period from manual or machine based accounting to computerized accounting a degree of upskilling occurred. Bookkeepers with knowledge of both computerized and manual systems, could for a while, demand higher salaries. But once the new computerized systems had passed through their initial trial period, the necessity for highly skilled bookkeepers diminished.

The junior-most bookkeeping staff were most severely affected at first by the advent of large scale computerization. Their jobs were degraded and frequently transformed into pure data processing jobs with no promotion prospects.

Enid Mumford and Olive Banks in a study of bank computerization reported that personnel managers were 'recruiting girls of too high intellectual caliber for the new simple machine jobs' (Mumford & Banks 1967: 190).

The position of more skilled bookkeepers was also weakened by the advent of computerization. Braverman cites the example of an US multibranch bank which reported that within 18 months of installing electronic bookkeeping machines, the bookkeeping staff of 600 had been reduced to 150, and the data processing staff had grown to 122. This was in line with the experience of most banks which achieved labour reductions of between 40 and 50%. Many bookkeeping staff were replaced by machine operators, punch card operators and similar grades of workers (US Department of Labor Statistics 1966: 247). The removal of the 'conception' part of a clerk's work is one of the key elements to the implementation of Taylorism in an office.

Deskilling of Accountancy Workers: The Glasgow Evidence

In order to chart the changing skills of bookkeepers we have chosen job advertisements as the primary source. All job advertisements for accountancy workers from 1974 to 1996 were copied from the appointments sections of the Glasgow *Herald* newspaper. Typically, the jobs recorded were those for the more general categories of bookkeepers and accountancy assistants as well as for the more specifically designated ledger clerks and cashiers. A representative sample for each year was then selected giving a total of 1024 separate advertisements for the 23-year period.

Gender Composition of Job Advertisements

For the first 3 years of our sample (1974, 1975 and 1976), *The Herald* had separate job columns for men and women. Almost 81% of the bookkeeping jobs appeared in the women's columns. The most common job titles in the women's columns were Bookkeeper or Clerkess (to trial balance). The men's job titles were more varied including Assistant Accountant (with experience), Bookkeeper, Accounts Clerk and Accounting Assistant. There were salary differentials between the two. For example in 1974 the range of salaries for jobs advertised in the women's section was £1500–1700. The men's salaries ranged from £1750–1900. With the advent of the Sex Discrimination Act, these separate columns disappeared.

In the periods after 1976, employers managed to 'gender' their jobs and offered lower pay by various means. The descriptor clerkess was frequently replaced by clerk/ess. Clerk/ess appeared as late as 1996, the last year of our survey. Employers also placed advertisements for bookkeepers under the Secretarial Job Section rather than the Accountancy Section to denote the gender of their job. Some employers were more blatant about their gender requirements.

Computer Knowledge and Experience

There is clear evidence of the developing requirement for computer 'knowledge' and experience over the 23-year period. The proportion of job advertisements which explicitly require computer expertise successively rise across each of our four time periods. The greatest increases in requests for computer experience occurred between the first and second periods and between the second and third periods. What is most striking, however, is the massive change between the first and last period. Between March 1974 and November 1979, only 6.7% of job advertisements requested computer knowledge and experience, while between March 1991 and December 1996 almost two-thirds of job advertisements (66.3%) explicitly requested computer experience.

The clear evidence from these figures hardly does justice to the qualitative impact of computerization upon the labour process of accountancy workers. Firstly, the arrival of computers marks the virtual extinction of older machine technologies like the comptometer. Secondly, and more profoundly, they signify the progressive deskilling of a range of accountancy jobs. As computers arrive, the range of specific skills requested in job advertisements declines.

Advertisements in the early years of our survey make specific mention of a range of skills and abilities. Typically, an advertisement for a 'bookkeeper' or an 'accountancy assistant' might explicitly require an applicant to be able to take books 'to the trial balance stage', to be experienced in the sales, nominal and purchase ledgers and, additionally, to demonstrate expertise in double entry bookkeeping.

Whilst the ability to take to trial balance is still a skill required by a sizeable, if progressively, shrinking proportion of employers, the broader abilities once associated with this process have been, in part, reduced to the manipulation of computer-based software packages. But gradually the number of organizations requiring a broad knowledge of accounting has declined.

Our survey of advertisements also seems to indicate a decline in the desire of employers to engage a layer of accountancy workers able to perform their tasks with levels of discretion and autonomy. The level of discretion and autonomy held by key accountancy workers also has diminished. If the labour process is more subdivided, regulated and computerized, then the need to have key individuals who act as the repository of accumulated informal knowledge and expertise will decline as a consequence.

Without explicitly posing a direct causal relationship between the onset of computerization and the decline in required skill requirements, it may be useful to display in graphical form the increase in requests for computer skills and experience against the reduction in requirements for general and specific skills (Figure 15.1).

Pay

Many of the advertisements were silent about the level of pay although they might have included vague assurances that salaries would be 'competitive' or 'good' or 'according to age and experience'. However, a significant, though declining,

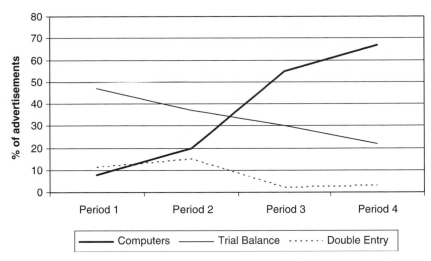

Figure 15.1: Relationship between computerization and accounting skills.

proportion did include information about salaries. While we would not claim that our figures represent a broad ranging UK salary survey, the salaries mentioned in the advertisements do suggest that bookkeeping/clerical salaries have fallen in real terms.

Falling real wages adds weight to our arguments surrounding deskilling. If, with the advent of computerization employers were simply using different language to demand the same set of skills, we would at least expect to see wages remain stable. Falling wages are the realized potential of Taylor's systems. Taylor himself stated that the potential of his system

> will not have been realised until almost all of the machines in the shop are run by men who are of smaller caliber and attainments, and who are therefore, cheaper, than those required under the old system (Taylor 1903: 105).

In the early years of the study, a knowledge of computers would have increased salary levels by at least one third. For example, in 1975, typical salaries ranged from £1600 to £1800 pa. But, in the 9% of the advertisements which mentioned that knowledge of computing would be an advantage pay ranged from £2300–2700. Again in 1976, typical bookkeeping salaries ranged from £1600–1800; whereas in the 10% of 'computerized' jobs, salaries were significantly higher, in one case the salary mentioned was £4000. As companies went through the process of computerizing their accounts, they typically required 'skilled bookkeepers with a knowledge of computing'. Indeed, companies frequently ran manual (or accounting machine) systems, alongside new computerized ones. But it seems as if once companies had gone through the process of computerizing, bookkeeping salaries tended to fall.

The difference between skilled bookkeepers and professionally qualified accountants' salaries in the late 1970s was surprisingly small. The skilled bookkeepers in the earlier period were likely to have been 'repositories of organizational knowledge', and an important source of information for both those within their organization and those outside of it, for example auditors. Today, qualified accountants tend to earn three times as much as bookkeepers. We would argue that several factors account for this. Firstly, due to deskilling, bookkeepers in the late 1990s do not have the same prestige, skills and usefulness to employers as their 1970s counterparts, and this has driven down their salaries. In addition to this, the prestige and 'professionalism' of qualified accountants (along with their images and so on) has probably increased professionally qualified accountants' salaries in real terms. Very few bookkeeping job advertisements mentioned management accounts but the ones that did tended to offer significantly higher salaries. This may be because the jobs required bookkeepers who would also play a 'lower' management role.

Implications and Conclusions

In this paper, we have presented a study of the transformation of the bookkeeping craft from the mid-nineteenth century to 1996. The transformation is a dialectical process which seems to take on several (quantities) of changes before undergoing a fundamental qualitative transformation. The transformed 'bookkeeper' of the 1990s is likely to be a young woman (hence the use of Ms Taylor in the title), working in a repetitive, deskilled job, with relatively low pay and little prospects of promotion.

What is the implication for the accounting professional of the removal of the concentration of information and decision-making capacity from the minds of key bookkeeping personnel? Our work gestures towards some important conclusions which are concerned with the future of professional and nonprofessional accounting labour. Neither of these can be considered in a vacuum and need to be set within the context of other contemporary changes confronting the accounting industry.

The history of bookkeepers presented in this paper is intended to give a space to the many workers in the accounting industry who have to date been rendered practically invisible by the academic accounting literature. The paper serves to highlight the continuing importance of Braverman's theoretical position and his analysis of Taylorism in the 1990s and gestures towards a future which will remain under the ongoing influence of scientific management. Despite the rhetoric by politicians of all political persuasions surrounding the need for a 'skilled workforce' the dehumanizing long run impact of Tayloristic deskilling is impacting on the majority of the accounting workforce. It may, in the near future, begin impacting on 'professional' accountants. For the individual bookkeeper, the future is grim. The next stage in computer technology is likely to be cheap voice data entry systems. In some senses this was poignantly predicted by Braverman 25 years ago.

> The progressive elimination of thought from the work of the office worker thus takes the form, at first, of reducing mental labour to a repetitive performance of the same small set of functions. The work is still performed in the brain, but the brain is used as the equivalent of the hand of the detail worker in production, grasping and releasing a single piece of 'data' over and over again. The next step is the elimination of the thought process completely — or at least insofar as it is ever removed from human labour — and the increase of clerical categories in which nothing but manual labour is performed. (Braverman 1974: 319).

Bookkeepers in large factory-like institutions and perhaps outsourced accounting companies may well find themselves working in sick buildings, in totally surveyed teams, reading lists of incomprehensible numbers into computers with no promotion prospects and extremely low pay.

References

Anderson, G. (1976). *Victorian clerks*. Manchester: Manchester University Press.

Braverman, H. (1974). *Labour and monopoly capital*. New York: Monthly Review Press.

Burrell, G. (1987). No accounting for sexuality. *Accounting, Organizations and Society, 12*(1), 89–101.

Callinicos, A., & Harman, C. (1987). *The changing working class*. London: Bookmarks.

Kirkham, L., & Loft, A. (1993). Gender and the construction of the professional accountant. *Accounting, Organizations and Society, 18*, 507–558.

Mumford, E., & Banks. O. (1967). *The computer and the clerk*. London: Routledge and Kegan Paul.

Taylor, F.W. (1903). *Shop management*. American Society of Engineers.

Taylor, F.W. (1911). *The principles of scientific management*. New York: Harper and Bros.

Chapter 16

Annual Reports in an Ideological Role: A Critical Theory Analysis[1]

Norman B. Macintosh, *Queen's University*

> Under the peculiar logic of accountancy, the men of the nineteenth century built slums rather than model cities because slums paid (Keynes 1933).

Accounting, as Keynes observed more than sixty years ago, occupies a significant position in the functioning of society. In organizations and in society alike, what is accounted for shapes participants' views of what is important, sets the agenda, and determines how institutions function. Recently, there has been a resurgence of the idea that the symbolic, non-rational roles of accounting, including ceremony, power distribution, value clarification and political manoeuvring, should be the subject of research. This paper reports the results of a critical theory analysis of a case study of IBM's annual reports in terms of their construction and reconstruction of an ideology of an inferior role for women in the computer workplace.

Critical Theory

'Critical theory' (or 'critical philosophy') was chosen as the analytical methodology for this study. Critical theory is aimed directly at investigations of societal and institutional ideologies and so is ideally suited for the research problem of this paper. Critical theory was developed by a group of philosophers, known as the 'Frankfurt School', including Horkheimer, Gadamer, Adorno, Marcuse and Habermas. Critical theory takes a stance between philosophy and historical sociology. It argues that most societies are permeated with 'objective illusion'. This objective illusion stems from ideologies which individuals and groups (that is, agents) have a hand in creating, or at least legitimizing, but subsequently come to treat as the handicraft of others. The consequence of this is that agents suffer from self-inflicted delusion

---

[1] Reproduced (in an abridged form) from Norman Macintosh, 'Annual Reports in an Ideological Role: A Critical Theory Analysis', in D. Cooper and T. Hopper (eds). *Critical Accounts*, 1990, pp. 153–72 with permission of Palgrave Macmillan, Basingstoke, UK.

Accounting, the Social and the Political
N. Macintosh and T. Hopper (Editors)

(that is, false consciousness) and a fettered existence (that is, coercion). Critical theory aims to effect a transition of society to a state where agents are free from false consciousness (enlightened) and liberated from self-imposed coercion (emancipated). The transition, critical theory contends, can take place only through introspection and self-reflection.

'Ideology', the essential concept in critical theory, is used in the sense of a world view held by agents in a society. Agents have more than just a bundle of randomly collected beliefs, attitudes, life goals and artistic endeavours. Rather, they have a coherent social knowledge whereby each piece fits into a package in which the parts are related, albeit in a complex way, to each other. This package is called an ideology and has a characteristic structure, deals with central issues of human life, is shared widely by all agents, is central to agents' concept of society and has a deep influence on their behaviour. In this sense, it is a form of consciousness which legitimizes social practices and institutions. Ideology is seen as a major social force in the process whereby society produces and reproduces itself.

In addition to its descriptive meaning, ideology also is conceived of within critical theory to have a pejorative sense. Here ideology is thought of as a false form of consciousness whereby individuals delude themselves about their personal true interests, their position in society and society in general. In this case, the aim of crucial theory is to demonstrate to agents that they are deluded. This is accomplished by showing them why they hold particular beliefs and attitudes, how these lead to false consciousness and how society imposes 'surplus repression' on its members by frustrating their preferences more than is needed for society to maintain and reproduce itself. Ideology in the pejorative sense involves the criticism of consciousness that incorporates false beliefs, functions in a reprehensible way or has a tainted origin.

Critical theory also defines ideology in a positive sense. Here the critical theory, itself a form of ideology, includes the actions agents take to understand how they are deluded, to sort out what their real interests are, to rid themselves of false consciousness and to free themselves from self-imposed coercion. In this positive sense, critical theory provokes self-reflection and hence induces enlightenment and emancipation.

From the critical theory perspective, it is necessary to identify and analyze a society's ideology (in the descriptive, pejorative and positive senses) in order to understand the beliefs knowledge agents hold about their society. This means, paradoxically, that a full-fledged critical theory must include an account of itself if it is to produce an exhaustive understanding of this knowledge. The logic is that a critical theory is itself part of the objective domain of the belief system of any society. (This contrasts with natural sciences such as particle theories of physics, where the theory itself is not a particle in motion.) So critical theory is at least partly about itself and so must be reflective and self-referential.

The self-reflective nature of critical theory calls for a unique type of evidence for its confirmation. Whereas scientific theory relies on empirical observation and experiment for corroboration, a critical theory must be 'reflectively acceptable'. A critical theory is acceptable only if the agents to whom the theory is addressed would freely agree to the ideas in the theory under conditions of perfect information: full freedom, and thorough consideration of the views expressed about freedom and coercion. (Perfect information in the sense that the information available is believed to be true by all parties. Full freedom in the sense of full implementation of normative expectations as to equality, order and consensually acceptable rules.) Such conditions are labelled the 'ideal speech situation'.

Paradoxically, then, a valid critical theory must contain its own criteria of confirmation. Confirmation, however, is paramount to the theory. It acts as the grindstone to set free the utopian kernel of beliefs and values of any society, a kernel embedded in the false consciousness of both privileged and disadvantaged agents. The goal of a critical theory is to present the possibility to agents in society that they can explicitly recognize their true aims and can form correct views about their real interests.

Women in the Workplace

The specific ideology selected for analysis for this paper is that of the role of women in the computer workplace. This is seen as a particularly important issue, given the dominant role given today by organizations to harnessing the new information technology. Women today comprise over 40% of the workforce of Western capitalist nations. Yet, throughout history they have been routinely underprivileged through consignment to the secondary sector where low-paying, specialized, deskilled jobs and insecurity are the order of the day.

A widely accepted view is that this inferior position is the result of a major ideological theme of Western society whereby women are considered a 'reserve army' labour pool to be called upon to fill the voids whenever males are unavailable, particularly in times of crisis. For example, in the fourteenth century in Britain, when peasant women in the feudal era were obliged under the Statute of Labourers (1349) to work in the fields due to the shortage of men as a result of the Black Plague.

For the next few centuries, women became a readily dispensable industrial reserve army to be pulled in or tossed out of work as required by the owners of the shops and factories. Just as women entered the factories in increasing numbers in the eighteenth and nineteenth century, they were recruited into the office in the late nineteenth and early twentieth centuries, particularly during wartime economies.

The office, for example, originally had been the purview of men. The post of office secretary was a prestigious job. It entailed administrative work such as composing important letters, recording and payment of accounts, dealing with routine meetings with suppliers and customers and managing all correspondence on behalf of the owner. In addition to the mundane clerical chores, men were apprenticed in these jobs in preparation for advancement in the executive hierarchy, partnership and even ownership.

With the advent of mechanization, however, office work was reshaped in a pattern which paralleled that of the factory — specialization, deskilling, low wages and the employment of women. The men staked out the higher, skilled, thinking positions, while the new deskilled jobs became the purview of women. Social domination, as before, proved to be accompanied by economic ascendancy as male incumbents in the thinking positions enjoyed considerably higher salaries than their female counterparts in the manual jobs. The pattern developed in the factory had repeated itself in the office.

This change was driven by an enormous increase in the quantity of paperwork necessitated by the huge expansion of the economy, in industry, commerce and government. The ever-increasing volume of paperwork required a permanent battalion of foot soldiers for which the reserve army of women were ideal recruits. Once again the work was specialized and deskilled as clerical chores were separated from administrative work. Men moved out of secretarial work into sales, advertising and administration, and women were hired to fill the specialized, deskilled and low-paying white-collar service jobs. By 1910, over 80% of these jobs in the US were filled by women, compared to an insignificant fraction a mere thirty years earlier. The outer office, a clean and respectable place to work, became, and remains today, the purview of women.

A Case Study

IBM's annual reports were selected for a case study of their ideological theme regarding women in the computer and information system workplace for obvious reasons. IBM, the largest of the new information-technology firms in the 1950s, operated globally, employed nearly 375 000 people, and anticipated industry-wide sales of over one trillion dollars by 1993. IBM's image of the role of women in the workplace may prove critical to the historical evolution of women's struggle for a more equitable stake in the workplace.

The research problem was to identify and analyze the ideological message contained in IBM's annual reports, as they shape and legitimize the role of women in the computer and related information-workplace. For this purpose, a panel of twenty judges, graduate students in economics and management, examined a sample of pictures (with captions) from IBM's annual reports. Seven annual reports from 1957 through 1982 were selected at random. From these reports all pictures, eighty in total, showing people involved in using, designing, manufacturing, installing and repairing information-technology products were included. The judges first identified every person in each picture as either male or female and then categorized each of them in terms of one of three types of work: (1) creative-thinking; (2) technical-supervisory; and (3) routine-repetitive (or routine-menial). The results of the judging, shown in Table 16.1, indicate that males in the pictures dominated

Table 16.1: Results of judges's classifications.

Category	Male	Female	Total
Type I (routine-repetitive)	239 (36%)	403 (64%)	642 (100%)
Type II (technical-supervisory)	460 (66%)	238 (34%)	608 (100%)
Type III (creative-thinking)	172 (70%)	71 (30%)	243 (100%)
Undecided	–	–	17
	871	712	1600

the creative-thinking and technical-supervisory categories, while females dominated the routine-repetitive group.

A Critical Theory Analysis

Against this background, a critical theory analysis of the role of women in the computing and information systems workplace might proceed as follows. Under conditions of perfect information, full freedom and thorough consideration, it seems plausible that agents in society, both male and female, would opt for a world where members of both sexes had opportunities to participate equally in all segments of the computer and related information-technology workplace. Now the ideology, in the descriptive sense, expressed in IBM's annual reports, differs distinctly from this normative world view. It contains a false form of consciousness and so deludes some of the agents involved. What is required, then, is reflectively accept-able action which will alert agents to their delusion, help them identify the real interests, and free them from false consciousness and self-imposed coercion.

Four possible major types of coercion for females can be identified in the IBM case. The first case, known as 'ideological delusion', occurs when individuals in society are fully satisfied and show no signs of hidden frustration, because their social institutions are so powerful and effective that they cannot even formulate desires which are not available to them under the present institutional framework. The result, nevertheless, is delusion, shallowness and a dull, impoverished existence. Here a critical theory can extract, from the cultural tradition, standards of the good life and then compare these to the current state of existence of the deluded members. Even though parts of the good life may be utopian, and thus, unattainable, critical theory can enlighten agents about how much more of their traditional good life remains to be realized. In the case of women in the computer and informa-tion systems workplace, a critical theory analysis enables them to compare their existence in the menial-routine segment with society's ideal that all individuals, regardless of sex, should have an equal opportunity to attain and hold jobs in the other segments. Even though this ideal may not be available, they will understand that the impediment is society's patriarchal ideology.

The second case is the 'society of happy slaves' who are genuinely content with their chains. Under these conditions, social control is so effective that members are prevented from even forming desires which cannot be easily satisfied. This would be the case if the women in the menial and routine job resist, due to ideological delusion, understanding their plight, and cannot see that they are under the influence of social opiates (for instance, clean, modern working conditions; considerate bosses; company bowling leagues and picnics; short working hours; pension plans and so on) that bind them to the present organization of society.

In this instance the women actually believe the descriptive ideology and are bonded to a set of false modes of gratification. Consequently, they are immune from emancipation. Critical theory here can at least invoke the principle of 'free assent' and point out that an opiate mode of gratification is appropriate only if the women themselves would have agreed, under an ideal speech situation, that the current state of affairs is in their own true interests.

The third brand of coercion comes into play when individuals realize they are suffering, but have either no theory or a false one. Here critical theory aims to make agents aware of the source of their coercion. For women in the computer and information workplace, it is necessary for them to understand that the source is the patriarchal ideology which permeates much of organizational life. This understood, they can either set aside false biological theories (such as, women are physically more dextrous and so better suited to this type of work, and by nature more adaptable to repetitive, boring work, than are their male counterparts) or, if they have no theory, fill the vacuum with a critical theory. Either way they come to realize the true source of their frustration. In both instances, critical theory is committed to the existence of the 'true' causal relationship between a powerful social institution and the agents who are suffering under it.

The fourth type of coercion occurs when the agents know fully well what they want — an abatement in coercion and suffering — and they know which social institution is the prime cause. What they do not know, however, is that they could act in a legitimate and rational way, one which is compatible with the pursuit of their real interests, in order to relieve their suffering. Here critical theory shows them what can be done by confronting head-on the particular social group that fosters, promotes and has every reason to resist the abolition of the patriarchal society. And it makes clear that active engagement by agents in society is required in the form of women's movements lobbying for legislation, making sure laws are followed, and confronting the coercing agents.

The critical theory, it should be underlined, must be aimed not only at women in the workplace, but also at their male counterparts. The goal in this instance is first to reveal to male agents their major 'objectification mistake'. Objective illusion occurs when any particular interest group produces a realm of social 'objects' and then fails to recognize it as a result of their own doing. If the society is to reproduce itself, most agents must make this objectification mistake. This ideological form of consciousness, it is important to understand, serves to legitimize the social institution and its resultant action.

In the case of the ideology depicted in IBM's annual reports, it seems highly plausible that one group in society (the males) are entwined in an objectification error. The pictures clearly suggest that the majority of women work in (and should work in) the routine-menial segment. The normal explanation for this is that this is a physical (that is, natural) fact. A count of the actual number of females in public information issued by IBM regarding 'Equal Opportunity and Affirmative Action Programs' confirms that males dominate the managerial and professional positions and women dominate the office and clerical jobs. Thus, it is easy for males to make the objectification error by merely pointing to the statistics and concluding that 'this is the way the world is as I experience it'.

This line of reasoning, however, obviously fails to recognize that the working world is dominated by males, and that this domination requires an ideology which legitimizes it and serves to reproduce social relations at work whereby women are disadvantaged. This ideological delusion, of course, works to the benefit of the male members of the workforce. It seems better, within the current social order, to be a member of the dominant group. Ideological delusion helps this group to have as much normative ideological power as possible.

Discussion

Critical theory here can become the self-consciousness of a successful process of emancipation and enlightenment for the male group. The first step is to extract from them their views about the good life in terms of their notions of freedom, truth and rationality as embedded in their normative knowledge of the world. The normative kernel for most males would be a workplace, where all individuals and groups are permitted equal access to all segments of the workplace.

The next step is to confront the male group with the discrepancy between their ideal of the good life and the realities of the workplace. This makes it possible for them to see that it was subjectively rational for them to acquire a patriarchal ideological form of consciousness. They then have a chance to realize how this seems to allow them the personal development, expression and satisfaction of their basic desires within their normative framework, yet is really self-destructive because it frustrates members of the dominated group from developing and satisfying those same desires. Once this is understood, both the advantaged and disadvantaged groups are enlightened, and the emancipatory process can take place whereby the underlying genuine human wants, needs and aspirations of the entire society can be separated and recovered from their mode of expression in the patriarchal ideology.

In the case of women in the computer and information system workplace then, a critical theory analysis attempts not only to expose the false consciousness of both groups, but also through a reflective process, to bring all agents into a new set of social relations whereby males and females can participate in the computer and information systems workplace in accordance with the essence of society's normative views about freedom, truth and rationality.

One major criticism of critical theory is that it pays too little attention to economic processes of capital accumulation and to the role of the state in managing a viable equilibrium, at least in Western capitalist nations, amongst capital, labour and the middle classes (Gramsci 1971; Althusser 1971). As a consequence, it downplays the importance of what Weber and others saw as the ever-increasing rationalization of social life as embodying an ideology of the main tendencies of capitalist development. While critical theory places primacy on the subjective nature of social relations, it tends to deprecate the importance of objective empirical forms of social coercion and domination. Many sociologists would argue, following Marx's later writings, that emancipation is only possible when a widespread class consciousness, one that exists in a more positivistic sense outside any one individual, emerges and is used by the subordinate class to attack the dominant class and its world view. From this latter perspective, women in general will not be free merely by understanding the source of their oppression, but rather they must take collective action to become free from the structural male domination.

Conclusion

A major aim of this paper was to investigate the role of accounting in shaping and supporting important societal ideologies. This type of research demonstrates how accounting reports can play an important part, wittingly or unwittingly, in shaping important social relations. Accounting reports are seen as more than neutral objective documents providing investors with economic information about the financial affairs of the entity. They are, in and of themselves, phenomena that can be analyzed and interpreted as texts to reveal their essential and significant social meaning (Tinker & Neimark 1987). They are a permanent expression of those social issues which top management regard as important and wish to communicate to shareholders and the public, and so are a record of the entity's historical social consciousness. Accounting as a social action is an important arena for investigation.

Investigations of accounting in its social role, however, require a different type of analytical methodology than, say, economics. Rather than develop testable hypotheses based on theory, and devising objective tests to support or falsify them, critical accounting aims to bring basic attitudes, beliefs and behaviour patterns to full consciousness in order to change them if they appear undesirable or false. It holds the potential to take the current appreciation of accounting-systems design to new important levels.

Critical theory investigations can be used, as shown, to expose the role accounting plays in masking contradictions and tensions amongst classes in society. The women in the pictures performing the menial-routine jobs appear happy, contented and natural. Yet, a critical theory analysis unmasks the contradictions and tensions between a male-dominated managerial class and a female-dominated working class, and exposes how accounting reports serve to mystify these unequal arrangements. Similarly, Tinker's (1980) reconstruction of the accounts of Delco Company Ltd. exposed the contradictions between the European owners and the native workers who performed the underground production work. And Tinker & Niemark's (1987) analysis of General Motors' annual reports over a period of sixty-one years revealed ideological themes that treated women as a reserve army of production workers to be called up or discharged as circumstances dictated.

Who knows, studies such as this one may even provide a logic of accountancy whereby men of the twentieth century build model cities instead of slums because model cities 'pay'.

References

Althusser, L. (1971). *Lenin and philosophy*, London: New Left Books.

Chua, W.F. (1986). Radical developments in accounting thought. *The Accounting Review*, 601–632.

Gramsci, A. (1971). *Selections from the prison notesbooks*. London: Lawrence and Wishart.

Keynes, J.M. (1933). National self-sufficiency. *Yale Law Review*, *22*, 755–763.

Tinker, A.M. (1980). Towards a political economy of accounting: An empirical ilustration of the Cambridge controversies. *Accounting, Organizations and Society*, 147–160.

Tinker, A., & Neimark, M. (1987). The role of annual reports in general motors: 1917–1976. *Accounting, Organizations and Society*, 71–88.

Chapter 17

Organizational Change and Accounting: Understanding the Budgeting System in its Organizational Context[1]

Mahmoud Ezzamel, *University of Cardiff*

Introduction

Researchers are becoming increasingly involved in studying the dynamic processes of organizational change, and in exploring the extent to which accounting systems, both influence and are in turn influenced by these processes. Organizational change typically involves the internal redirection of resources which is mainly achieved through the corporate budgeting system. Expert knowledge of accounting can help to mobilize support for change initiatives. Alternatively, accounting knowledge can enable the mobilization of successful resistance by organizational members opposed to change. Changes in the organization's mission or structure can also impact on the budgeting system.

Power/Knowledge Relations

The relevance of Foucault's work to organizational analysis is gaining increased recognition. The 'conventional' view on power assumes that power is possessed by unitary, 'sovereign' political forces so that the will of the sovereign is power. Foucault invites us to pursue an alternative view by shifting our focus away from the concept of sovereignty towards the effects of the exercise of power.

Foucault has developed two distinctive concepts of power which, he argues, have been prevalent in modern institutions such as universities, secondary schools, barracks and workshops from the early nineteenth century onwards. The first is what he calls 'disciplinary power' and the second is 'bio-power'. 'Disciplinary power' is targeted at rendering specific individuals or groups of individuals orderly and

---

[1]Reproduced (in an abridged form) from M. Ezzamel, 'Organizational Change and Accounting: Understanding the Budgeting System in its Organizational Context', *Organizational Studies*, 1994, vol. 15, no. 2, pp 213–240 with the permission of Sage Publications, Inc.

regimented through the use of methods of assessment and surveillance. These disciplinary practices became widely disseminated through state institutions and ultimately found their way into the factory. 'Bio-power' is aimed at the subjugation of human bodies and the control of populations by defining 'what is and what is not "normal", and what is and what is not available for individuals to do, think, say, and be ... Bio-power normalises through discursive formations of psychiatry, medicine, social work, and so on' (Clegg 1989: 155–156). The main purpose of the technology of the body or bio-power, is to render a human being a 'docile' yet productive body.

Power according to Foucault is historically constructed via practices, it is 'neither given, nor exchanged, nor recovered, but rather exercised'. The exercise of power is a means by which certain actions modify others, i.e. it is an action upon an action whether present or future. Two elements are indispensable to the emergence of power relations: (i) the subject over whom power is exercised is a person who acts, and (ii) a wide array of responses, reactions and results is available. The exercise of power in itself is neither predicated on violence nor on engineering renewable consent, instead 'it incites, it induces, it seduces, it makes easier the more difficult; in the extreme it constraints or forbids absolutely ...' (Foucault 1982: 220).

Power and knowledge are dimensions of the same practices and social relations. Power informs knowledge and produces discourse, it unintentionally achieves strategic effects through methods of discipline and surveillance. These methods of discipline and surveillance are a form of knowledge constituted not only in texts but also in definite institutional and organizational practices. Therefore, disciplinary practices are 'discursive practices'. Knowledge constitutes discipline, and discipline is an effective constitution of power. Knowledge, so defined, is practical and disciplinary; it yields obedient bodies, regulated minds and ordered emotions in a manner that creates a new basis for order. Knowledge is embedded in the struggle for domination; knowledge and power are not external one another.

The formation and implementation of relations of power depend upon the production, circulation and functioning of discourses of truth, but truth is linked in a circular relation to the systems of power which promote it, and to the effects of power which truth itself generates. Truth is not perceived as a universal concept which traverses all human societies, rather it is local and politically constituted through practices which define what is false and what is true. The mechanisms of power are thus related to two points of reference: to the rules of right which outline the formal limits of power, and to the effects of truth which are produced and transmitted by power. These elements combined form Foucault's triangle: power, right, truth.

Resistance emerges at the point where power is exercised and 'can be integrated in global strategies' (Foucault 1980: 142). To understand power, forms of resistance within different expressions of the exercise of power should be taken as a starting point. Resistance can be used as 'a chemical catalyst so as to bring to light power relations, locate their position, find out their point of application and the methods used' (Foucault 1982: 211). Resistance is immediate in the sense that people oppose instances of power which are closest to them, and the target of such resistance is the effects of the exercise of power. More critically, resistance asserts the right of the individual to be different but, at the same time, opposes attempts to separate the individual from others; resistance is a struggle against the 'government of individualization'. Further, it is an opposition against the privilege of knowledge, secrecy and mystification (Foucault 1982).

Accounting and Power/Knowledge Relations

Accounting can be deployed as a powerful disciplinary regime in modern organizations. Accounting can operate in this way because of its ability to render human performance visible and calculable as a rational economic action. Accounting has a capacity to create visibility which encourages new areas of discourse, by generating and incorporating in its formal reports alternative courses of action. Although the disciplinary power of accounting is exercised through its invisibility, accounting imposes compulsory visibility on those it subjects to its calculus, and it is through this visibility that their subjection is maintained. Through the application of a concise yet powerful metric, accounting functions as a calculative practice, certain courses of action and complex work technologies are rendered calculable and hence more visible. Accounting techniques enable social fields to be represented as areas of rational economic action.

Accounting is a form of power/knowledge only available to the experts. Those who master accounting knowledge can bring the activities of others, no matter how fluid, detailed and distant, both temporally and geographically, under an instant and constant disciplinary gaze. To many of those who are unfamiliar with its techniques, accounting is held in some awe. Its calculations are perceived to be not only competent and authoritative, but also mysterious and beyond reach. Those who are suspicious of accounting calculations but who, at the same time, are ignorant of its techniques have little option but to mobilize local, non-accounting, knowledges to resist the effects of accounting. Those who are invested with accounting knowledge can mount more effective resistance by ruthlessly exposing the arbitrariness and selectivity of accounting procedures and the incompetence or partiality of accounting practitioners.

Accounting as a Disciplinary Regime

The research reported next utilizes Foucault's framework of power/knowledge relations. The analysis is based on a field study in which a change initiative was developed by top policy-makers (the Centre) in a UK university against a background of reduction in funding by the state. The budgeting system is perceived to have relevance in this context at two levels: (i) as the vehicle through which reallocation of resources is effected, and (ii) as a means that provides actors with technical knowledge which can be utilized in the context of power relations. The analysis demonstrates that the Centre failed to deploy the budgeting system as a disciplinary regime in the sense of making it possible for the proposed resource reallocations to be implemented. The analysis also shows how the groups opposed to the proposed change: (i) through their technical knowledge successfully deployed arguments from within the accounting discipline to render the Centre's calculations 'incorrect' or at best debatable; (ii) combined these technical accounting arguments with arguments from outside the accounting discipline to cast strong doubts on the ethical and professional underpinnings of the Centre's proposals; and (iii) evolved, and promoted, a 'more viable' strategy to cope with the reduction in funding at the Centre's university.

The university Centre, under considerable financial pressure due to a government three-year nation-wide resource funding cut, proposed differential cuts (ranging from 8.5 to 36%) across budgetary groups. The latter were given 24 days to come up with coping plans, including names of staff to be made redundant, otherwise the Centre would make the decreases for them.

Foucault has discussed strategies of surveillance and discipline that are manifest in the deployment of definite forms of power and knowledge. The Centre's strategy for change encapsulated in the recommendations of the Budget and Development Committee's Strategy Document [B&DII] had a disciplinary intent. The discipline was rooted in the accounting power/knowledge wielded by the Centre, which sought to demonstrate that the viability and future success of The University depended upon major restructuring. Such disciplinary power has been perceived in previous literature to be endowed with many of the attributes that accounting calculations have come to symbolize for their users; technical expertise, rationality, clarity and authority. The context of the case study reported here gives rise to some interesting questions about the role of accounting as a disciplinary regime: why was not the disciplinary regime of accounting widely perceived to exhibit those attributes? Why was it that, far from rendering members of The University docile, the disciplinary regime of accounting engendered mistrust in the Centre and a spirit of resistance? And how was resistance so effectively mobilized against that regime?

The Centre sought to impose a regime of accounting discipline against a background of a well-ingrained tradition of job security, academic freedom and liberal work practices. Such organizational 'myths' embedded key assumptions concerning the *appropriate* domain of activities of The University and the *proper* way of organizing them. In Foucault's terms, established power/knowledge relations were well entrenched. The robustness of the 'myths' was reflected in the 'momentums' they developed which were not susceptible to management manipulation through the deployment of the disciplinary power of accounting, but, rather, acquired truth-like qualities. Job security, academic freedom and liberal work practices were all parts of The University's 'general politics of truth' and locally constituted discourses. Collectively, they formed the rules of right that defined and confined the formal limits of power. Those resisting B&DI were able to mobilize this highly entrenched regime of truth and to network their opposition with the accounting-based discourse. It was because of this triangle of power, right and truth that opponents could reject B&DI as divisive and cruel.

In the face of proposed budget abatements, six members of a disadvantaged Faculty produced a document called an Alternative Viable Strategy (AVS). The emergence of resistant rather than docile actors was triggered by their high degree of economic and professional dependence upon The University. The economic dependence, it seems, was one crucial factor, even though in much of the discourse it was carefully masked beneath what were thought to be more substantive arguments, such as those related to The University's culture and its work practices. National mobility in the academic labour market, at least at that time, was highly constrained and the financial repercussions of job losses were severe. The discourse (mostly financial) sought to establish unambiguously the dependence of staff on The University as an employer.

Initial response by The University to the resistance was manifest in the resolution that further discussion of B&DI be delayed by one week so that the B&D Sub-Committee would meet the authors of the AVS to discuss in detail and clarify the alternative views and to identify areas of common ground. These resolutions reflected the Centre's recognition that the authors of the AVS wielded considerable support within The University. A series of acrimonious meetings took place between the AVS side and the Centre. New documents, including accounting calculations, were prepared by both sides as ways of coping (such as using cash reserves and selling property). A Joint Policy Committee (JPC) was set up which eventually supported the original B&DI. The AVS's counter-proposals, now more widely visible, were gradually endowed with fact-like and truth-like attributes. This 'effective sociology of translation' tactic prompted considerable opposition against the Centre's proposals.

Eventually, the Senate rejected compulsory redundancy (by a narrow majority) and recommended to Council (a higher authority) to follow suit. The Council eventually rejected the B&DI and passed a motion to the effect that 'compulsory redundancy should be used as a very last resort and after all other avenues have been explored', thereby reinforcing Senate's corresponding resolution. Through the effective translation of interests and mobilization of resistance by the AVS proponents, the B&DI became formally discredited as a University strategy; natural wastage and voluntary redundancy became 'preferred' solutions. The time scale for determining a definite policy was extended sufficiently to allow more lobbying and to consider alternative solutions.

So the technical accounting knowledge available to the AVS authors allowed them to undermine all attempts by the Centre to endow B&DI with respectability. The 'disadvantaged' groups in The University could, through their knowledgeable agents, challenge and refute the Centre's calculations and offer an alternative set of accounting calculations. For them, the accounting calculations contained in B&DI were neither assertive nor clear-cut, but were perceived to be at best politically determined and even 'unprofessionally' produced. It is against such background that the role of accounting in organizational change can be more fully understood. The case study demonstrates both the capacity and limitations of accounting in its creation of a visibility that may foster the development of new areas of discourse, in its functioning as a calculative practice by rendering the visible calculable, and in its ability to create an area of economic action.

It seems that the Centre had expectations that its accounting system would facilitate transition to change. Certainly, accounting endowed the Centre's proposals with visibility by translating them into formal reports. Accounting rendered the Centre's proposals calculable through the judicious use of methods of asset valuation and recognition, and also of particular heuristic decision models (e.g. the magnitude of the proposed differential cuts). Finally, accounting re-presented The University as a distinct arena of economic action to which the economic concepts of efficiency and rationality were applicable. Yet it was through an alternative within the accounting discourse (the AVS) that the visibility which was initially created for the Centre's policy was discredited, that the apparent objective calculability of the Centre's proposals was challenged, and that the area of economic action was undermined and then denied. By challenging the decision parameters and methods of asset valuation and recognition underlying B&DI calculations, and by offering alternative (more defensible) accounting choices, the authors of the AVS succeeded in rendering the accounting arguments of B&DI 'incorrect' and 'unprofessional'. The duality of the potential of accounting in terms of both enabling and constraining change renders the understanding of accounting more problematical. However, the relationship between knowledge and power, as demonstrated in this particular case by the accounting technical know-how, is not deterministic in the sense of knowledge leading to power.

Also, the familiarity of the AVS group with the structural arrangements of The University helped to bolster resistance. Such familiarity was deployed to identify what were deemed to be crucial arenas for struggle, and to gain full appreciation of the temporal attributes of University events. To challenge B&DI successfully, the deployment of the accounting-inspired discourse was carefully timed to coincide with the scheduled meetings of critical committees and forums. Further, the AVS group made skilful use of delaying tactics to invalidate the Centre's timetable.

Conclusions

This paper examined the power/knowledge relations concerning an attempt to supplant an incremental budgeting system by a comprehensive Planning, Programming and Budgeting System (PPBS) in a university facing a financial crisis. The budgeting system was involved in power relations at two levels. First, it provided a vehicle through which the proposed reallocation of funds was translated, communicated and given initial visibility. Second, it provided a basis for much of the discourse that took place between the various constituencies: monitoring the activities of The University; formulating the alternative strategy; shaping the arguments put forward by those opposed to the change and the counter-arguments made by the Centre; and expressing the 'compromise' solution in the form of the new set of allocations which were ultimately approved.

By evolving alternative technical arguments from within accounting and by combining them with other arguments relating to well-entrenched 'truth-like' local practices such as job tenure and academic freedom, organizational constituents opposed to change were able to resist the disciplinary intents of the initial budgeting proposals. While the arguments from outside the accounting discourse helped to strengthen and galvanize resistance, the evidence points to the central importance of accounting knowledge in situations of struggle. Such importance was manifest in the manner by which the AVS gained ascendance over alternative strategies which lacked technical accounting knowledge, and by the way in which the accounting terminology came to dominate the dialogues that took place within and outside The University committee system. The accounting-based discourse was expressed by experts with technical knowledge of methods of asset recognition, asset valuation, costing and risk quantification, and was deployed in such a way as to cast severe doubts over *other* accounting calculations, thereby rendering the latter subjective, inaccurate and even unprofessional.

References

Clegg, Stewart R. (1989). *Frameworks of Power*. London: Sage.

Foucault, M. (1980). *Power/Knowledge,* C. Gordon (ed.). Brighton: Harvester.

Foucault, M. (1982). The subject and power, in H. L. Dreyfus & P. Rabinow, (eds). *Beyond structuralism and hermeneutics*. 208–226. New York: Harvester.

Chapter 18

Management Accounting as Disciplinary Practice: The Case of ITT under Harold Geneen[1]

Trevor Hopper,   *University of Manchester*

Norman B. Macintosh,   *Queen's University*

> We are much less Greeks than we believe. We are neither in the amphitheatre, nor on the stage, but in the panoptic machine... Is it surprising (then) that prisons resemble factories, schools, barracks, hospitals, which all resemble prisons? (Foucault 1979: 217, 228)

This paper has three main intentions. It extracts a model of the main principles of discipline and control from '*Discipline and Punish: The Birth of the Prison*', Foucault's most celebrated piece of writing. It then illustrates, using ITT as a case history, the model's relevance for providing a broader understanding of management accounting and control systems than traditional views. The paper argues that a Foucauldian approach to management accounting is neither incommensurate nor discordant with the labour-process view and both can be used in a complementary way to provide a critical edge to studies in and of management accounting and control.

Foucault's Principles of Discipline and Control

In his classic book *Surveiller et Punir: La Naissance de la Prison*, Foucault detailed the emergence from the Classical era of an all-encompassing disciplinary drive that became ubiquitous during the Modern era. Foucault identified three general principles underlying how the disciplinary society functions: the principle of enclosure; the principle of the efficient body; and the principle of disciplinary power. The enclosure principle includes concepts like the cell, useful sites and rankings. The efficient body principle stems from ideas of timetabling, manoeuvres

---

[1]Reproduced (in an abridged form) from T. Hopper and N. Macintosh, 'Management Accounting As Disciplinary Practice: The Case of ITT under Harold Geneen', *Management Accounting Research*, 1993, 4, pp. 181–216 with the permission of Elsevier.

and dressage, and the exhaustive use of time. The principle of disciplinary power includes concepts such as: hierarchies, panopticons, normalizing sanctions and examinations.

Disciplining Space: The Enclosure Principle

Discipline proceeds initially, according to Foucault, by the careful distribution of heterogeneous individuals over space–time locations. In the first instance there is general confinement. This involves specifying special purpose, self-enclosed locations (*clotures*) inside which individuals can be contained and sheltered in a monotonous disciplinary state. Monasteries, poor houses, schools, military barracks, factories, prisons, hospitals and even universities are examples.

Partitioning   Enclosure, however, is insufficient to achieve disciplinary spaces. It is also necessary to partition enclosures to make them amenable to discipline. Partitioning involves dividing up to the general enclosure into as many self-contained locations or 'cells' as there are elements (bodies) to be distributed. This makes it possible to know, master and make useful to each and every individual. The principle of enclosure can be traced back to the monastery of the Classical era where each monk had his own cell.

Enclosure, confinement and partitioning were the necessary first steps for turning a heterogeneous mass of humans into a homogeneous social order. With each individual in his or her own space and, importantly, each space with its own individual, troublesome aspects of large transient groups and their confused collective dispositions could be avoided.

Functional Spaces   Enclosure and partitioning make it possible to effect the 'rule of functional sites'. Initially, each site is defined by the specific function performed there. Then it is necessary to distribute the individual partitions in a legible way so they are linked to form a permanent grid of functional, useful, serialized spaces.

Thus, each site is converted into a functionally useful place where tight control could be exercised over each individual. 'Particular places were designed to correspond not only to the need to supervise, to break dangerous communications, but also to create *a useful space*' (Foucault 1979: 143–144). This distribution and partitioning of disciplinary space, Foucault observed, not only achieved specialization within the production process, but also fragmented and de-skilled labour power. Here Foucault is in concordance with Marx's notion of the de-skilling and commodification of labour. Within a disciplinary grid, each space and every individual could be analyzed, measured and assessed according to criteria for the strength, skill, promptness and constancy of the individual occupying that space.

The criteria arose from the requirements of the production machinery. Thus, the body could be matched perfectly with the machine.

Ranking Another important aspect of enclosure involved ranking each disciplinary space. Everyone is defined by the rank he or she occupies in the hierarchy and by the space that separates each rank from the one immediately below and above it. Individuals are not only distributed across a network of relations, but also moved up or down or across the network. Ranks remain permanent, but the individuals change according to their most recent assigned rank. What is important is the place the individual occupies in the ranking.

Spaces so constituted are real in a *material* sense, as they dictate the distribution of physical objects like buildings, rooms, machines and furniture, but they are also *idealized* spaces, being constituted by their function, their relationship to other spaces, and their rank within the power hierarchy. The effect is to create a *tableau vivant* that transforms '... the confused, useless or dangerous multitudes into ordered multiplicities...' and so is the basis of '...a microphysics of what might be called a "cellular" power' (Foucault: 148–149). The individual's obedience is almost guaranteed.

The Principle of Enclosure at ITT

The principle of enclosure and its counterpart, responsibility center accounting, is illustrated vividly in Geneen's story. Once installed as CEO, Geneen quickly reorganized the company, replacing the old functional/geographic organizational structure with decentralized profit centers. Managers became responsible and accountable for financial performance. By 1977, ITT's line operations consisted of nearly 400 000 employees enclosed in 250 profit centers. Following the principle of enclosure, each space had its own manager; and each manager had his or her own space.

Having neatly partitioned the company into profit centers, Geneen made each responsibility center analyzable through what he called 'the discipline of the numbers'. For most people, he postulated, numbers are easier to read than words. Numbers use unambiguous symbols which measure the tasks and operations of the organization and, most importantly, they inform upper management about what is happening.

The financial control system provided Geneen with continuous, functional surveillance of each enclosed responsibility center. For Geneen, this was absolutely essential if ITT were to become a disciplined and productive company. From his autobiography, it is apparent that Geneen was deeply influenced by his educational experiences, his knowledge of control systems at General Motors, his attendance at Harvard Business School courses and his accounting background. All relied heavily on the principle of enclosure inherent in the management accounting axiom that organization should be divided up into responsibility centers headed by an accountable manager.

Disciplining Time: The Efficient Body Principle

With individuals enclosed in identifiable, ranked, serialized and functional spaces, the principle of the efficient body can be utilized. This is realized through three additional disciplinary practices: the timetable; the articulation of body and machine; and the exhaustive use of time. Just as the principle of enclosure disciplines space, the principle of the efficient body disciplines time.

The Timetable   The timetable is the first stage in disciplining time. It articulates each functional partition in terms of when specific activities and routines are to be performed. It establishes a rhythm and a regularity to actions. It can be formulated in terms of days, hours, minutes and even seconds. It defines a time '...without impurities or defects; a time of good quality, throughout which the body is constantly applied to its exercise' (Foucault 1979: 151). The timetable effects a clockwork-like world of daily repetition and regular cycles of 'useful' activities. It programs each individual in a chain of detailed, minute actions for the entirety the individual occupies that space.

Foucault traces timetables back to the strict regimen of monasteries in Europe. Regimen and routine led to a 'disciplined disciple'. Other institutions readily adapted the monastery timetable to make time penetrate the body rendering it docile, but efficient.

While the timetable specifies when the activity is to be performed and defines the general framework within which it operates, the 'temporal elaboration of the act' goes further by specifying precisely how it is performed. Foucault cites the transmutation of the correct way of marching for French soldiers as an example. Efficient body movements and the timetable, however, are necessary, but not sufficient conditions for fully achieving the principle of the efficient body. It is also necessary to systematically and meticulously mesh the body to the specific object — pen, rifle, wagon, machine or whatever.

The Exhaustive Use of Time   These techniques, however, were insufficient to effect the principle of the efficient body. In addition, time had to be used exhaustively. As Foucault explains, in the Classical era, the principle of non-idleness prevailed. Since God counted time and men paid for it, to waste it was a mortal sin in the eyes of God. Moreover, it was economic dishonesty in the eyes of society. During Modernity, however, this negative conception took on a positive economy of wasted time represented by demand for continual increases in the utilization of time. Concern with the efficient use of time could provide a competitive edge. For example, it was a strategic advantage in the mid-1700s for the Prussian army under Frederick II whose brilliant victories caught attention throughout Europe. Armies in other countries soon followed suit — as did schools, hospitals, workshops and universities. The principle spread throughout society and the 'educated, useful body' becoming commonplace.

The exhaustive use of time also calls for the incorporation of highly trained individuals in a body-machine system. Consequently, *bon dressement* ('dressage' or 'correct training') emerged as an important disciplinary technique. The disciplined soldier, for example '... begins to obey whatever he is ordered to do; his obedience is prompt and blind; an appearance of indocility, the least delay would be a crime' (Foucault: 166). In the school, a signal from the teacher — a word, a clap of the hands, a bell, a glance or a single gesture — attracted children's attention making them instantaneously attentive to its implicit but clear command. More importantly, dressage automatically triggers a reflexive response from the disciplined body. It places the individual in a world of signals, each with its unique response and its moral imperative. Dressage not only restrains the subject, but also links individuals together and so multiplies their usefulness.

It is important to realize that the efficient body principle, for Foucault, is not a celebrated, triumphant power. Instead, it works in a modest, calculating and constant fashion. It must be exercised gingerly in order not to weigh too heavily on the individual. Nevertheless, its effects are remarkable. It forms an otherwise mobile, confused and useless mass of individuals into obedient objects whose deportment can be counted on to conform to the prescribed actions.

For Foucault, these new techniques of subjection — the timetable, the temporal elaboration of the body, the articulation of body and machine and the exhaustive use of time — led to a metamorphosis of the treatment of the body. It became a target to be manipulated, to be exercised in correct movements, and to be available for the imposition of ever more knowledge. Thus subjugated, the individual functions as an obedient, docile and willing body.

The Efficient Body Principle at ITT

Geneen's financial control system at ITT bears correspondence with the principle of the efficient body. In terms of timetabling, each profit center manager and staff divisional head submitted their annual budget and business plans in February for review at both the local level and at headquarters. Then, in November and December, Geneen and other key headquarters officials met face-to-face with each manager and his or her own staff to discuss, review and finalize the plans and budgets. The finalized budget, now 'carved in stone', became the benchmark for performance in the ensuing year.

Geneen required each profit-centre manager to sketch out 2, 3 and 5 year profit plans as well as anticipated capital expenditures. He did not, however, put a great deal of stock in long-range, qualitative strategic plans but instead focused on the current year.

The cornerstone of the financial control system was the monthly operating report. Each profit center manager submitted to headquarters, by the fifth working day of each month, reports containing detailed information on: sales, earnings, inventory, receivables, employment, marketing, competition and R&D along with any current or anticipated problems. The manager also reported on the current economic and political situation in his or her territory. Divisional comptrollers also made a monthly financial report to the headquarters comptroller. Moreover, all head-quarters staff division heads (engineering, accounting, marketing, R&D, etc.) sent Geneen a monthly report about the situation in their specialized area, as did the product line managers. Geneen and his headquarters staff personally scrutinized each and every report. He summed up his surveillance network as: 'Information flows up the chain and orders flow down. Everyone knows his or her own place and responsibilities in the hierarchy. Logic and order are to reign supreme' (Geneen 1984: 85).

The profit-centre philosophy trained managers to act like 'individual entrepre-neurs'. Geneen selected each manager carefully to ensure that only persons who fitted his predetermined mould got the job. He did not want geniuses who could not communicate with ordinary, hard working people. Nor did he want people who got by on their good looks, smooth talk or family connections. Instead, he looked for people who shared his enthusiasm for hard work. Intelligence, knowledge and experience were necessary, but not sufficient characteristics. Each manager also had to display 'an enthusiasm for labouring'. Geneen's normalizing mould was clear for all.

More specifically, information in financial controls became the basis for the dressage-like training of ITT's managers. The on-site, monthly meeting with 150 European General Managers and 40 headquarters staff managers quickly became Geneen's 'training grounds'.

> We sat around a large U-shaped table, covered in green felt, facing one another, and I asked questions based upon the notes I had made on their monthly operating reports. Why were the sales down? Was he sure of the reasons? Had he checked it out? How? What was he doing about it? What did he expect in the month or two ahead? Did he need help? How did he plan to meet or outdistance the competition?

Geneen came armed with a series of 'red-ink queries'. He exhorted others to do likewise:

> Not only I but anyone else at the meeting could say anything, question anything, suggest anything that was pertinent. Each man had a microphone in front of him. With the figures on the screen, we could all see how each profit center measured up to its budget commitments, its last year's performance and whatever, in sales, earnings, receivables, inventory, etc.' (Geneen 1984: 96).

Differences and queries were handled on the spot so everyone learned from each other: 'It was at times almost group therapy' (Geneen 1984: 97). The financial control system and the monthly meetings trained ITT managers in correct manoeuvres. The signals from Geneen and the financial control system automatically triggered the required proper behaviour. ITT managers performed as efficient bodies. Back in their own subsidiaries, they inflicted the same regimen on their underlings.

The Principle of Disciplined Bodies: The Means of Correct Training

The third principle in Foucault's model is the principle of disciplined bodies or the means of correct training. This final link in Foucault's chain of disciplinary power involves the use of hierarchical surveillance, normalizing sanctions, examinations and the panopticon. These 'instruments of organization', he believed, led to the successful imposition of the principles of enclosure and efficient bodies.

Hierarchical Surveillance   Hierarchical surveillance emerged in the eighteenth century as a special kind of 'looking on' or 'gaze' that constrained the individual without the watchers being seen or even without them looking. This discreet art of close watching consisted of '...the minor techniques of multiple and intersecting observations of eyes that must be seen without being seen; using techniques of subjection and methods of exploitation, an obscure art of light and the visible was secretly preparing new knowledge of man' (Foucault 1979: 171). The gaze constrained as it watched.

The disciplinary gaze was not complete, however, without systems to relay information. This required a pyramid-like administrative network, discreet enough not to appear to weigh too heavily on individuals in the hierarchy, yet sufficient to be a brake or obstacle upon each individual's activities. The pyramid was decomposed into small but precise units of surveillance and the levels and numbers of administrators increased. The disciplinary gaze could have no missing links.

As factories became larger in the nineteenth century, close surveillance became essential. A disciplinary gaze was necessary to monitor specific activities of the workers; observe their skills, knowledge and how they went about their tasks; measure the speed of their work observe their zeal for work and monitor their general comportment while on the job. This called for a vast hierarchy of subalterns, administrative underlings, controllers, inspectors, foremen and straw-bosses. Hierarchical surveillance, with its cadre of administrators, emerged to meet this need as a separate, but essential function of discipline and control. This hierarchical gaze was to be writ large later in the form of the 'master budget'.

Foucault saw hierarchical surveillance as one of the most important social inventions of the eighteenth century. Aimed at the individual, it functioned as a complete network of relations from top to bottom and from side to side. Following the laws of optics and principles of mechanics, it enabled an uninterrupted, calculating, disciplinary gaze to play out over the surface, lines and fibres of organizations. Importantly, however, it functioned without force, excess or violence. It imposed its new power, not through corporal punishment, but more insidiously, as an infliction on one's cerebral and erudite sensibilities. Anonymous, automatic and indiscreet, hierarchical surveillance became an integral part of the economic and social order of Western society (Foucault 1979).

Normalizing Sanctions   Hierarchical surveillance, however, required a system of rewards and penalties. Consequently, the new layer of supervision developed a system of 'normalizing sanctions' which moved into spaces not covered by general statutes of the state. It produced its own laws, ranges of proper behaviour, rules for solicitous judgements, designated infractions and appropriate sanctions for deviance. It operated like a miniature legal and prison system. Surveillance and sanctions spread throughout society. In workshops, schools, the military, bureaucracies, etc. deviant behaviour was ferreted out and appropriately sanctioned. Everyone was enmeshed in an *ex legalis*, punishable-punishing world.

Disciplinary sanctions, Foucault emphasized, were basically corrective. Alongside the regular punishments of the legal system (fines, whippings and solitary confinement) a different series of punishments were erected — drills, long and arduous apprenticeships, repetitive exercises, etc. — to sanction and reduce non-conformity. In school, for example, a student whose behaviour was deemed 'uncooperative' was made to memorize long passages by heart or to write repeatedly one or two lines of verse. Punishment was not for avenging an outraged law, nor for expiation or repentance, but to correct behaviour and minimize non-conformism — it lay outside the legal, juridical systems.

Most normalizing sanctions, importantly, were not punitive: penalties were avoided if possible. Instead, the master, teacher, boss or reformer applied positive recompenses more frequently than painful ones. Superordinates believed that lazy individuals are more motivated by desires to receive the same rewards as diligent peers than the fear of penalties. A judicious mixture of gratifying and negative sanctions — along with drilling, repetition and correction — made improper behaviour all but impossible.

These new techniques of sanctioning, however, were not mere carbon copies of legal and official tribunals, but entered spaces previously unobservable, unfettered by any rules, or untouched by formal and legal regulation. This point is important because it is one of Foucault's great insights. Disciplinary punishment colonized areas not already ruled by society's judicial system, i.e. spaces which were until then the only 'natural' places left for the individual. The soldier, for example, who did not raise his rifle to the required height during drill, or the student who did not remember the catechism from the previous lesson, or the worker who did not hold his tool correctly, found themselves victimized as the object of a series of penalties. Under the normalizing gaze, domains previously indefinite and non-conforming, became penalizable.

Moreover, these gratification-penalty structures were readily quantified. Behaviour was calibrated along a continuum with positive and negative ends. Individuals received points for their behaviour on the continuum, making an on-going, real-time accounting table (*grande tableau*) possible for each individual. The military, workshops and schools soon employed these 'personal accounting' systems. Portioning, ranking, sanctioning, promoting and demoting were integrated into a cycle of complete knowledge about individuals. Each teacher, officer, master, overseer or reformer was required to perform the essential surveillance, ranking, and punishment functions, and to keep a written record of subordinates' progress and comportment. The record served as a rationale for distributing sanctions, promotions and demotions. Each person was not only completely known, but also completely 'written'. This constant 'accounting' for the individual completed the 'cycle of knowing'.

The art of punishment within the realm of the disciplinary power gaze, Foucault observed, was neither retributive nor restitutive. Rather it put into play five other processes: it set up an entire field of comparisons for individual actions; it differentiated each individual in terms of his or her minimal, average or optimal rule following behaviour; it measured, quantified, ranked and valued each person according to his or her capacity, ability and 'general nature'; it introduced the constraint of conformity through the valorization of specific activities and behaviour; and it defined extreme limits or frontiers of the abnormal. Differentiation, hierarchy, homogenization and exclusion combined to effect a ubiquitous, penalizing gaze on each subject. Through the disciplinary gaze came the power of the normalizing sanction.

The Examination The next element of the principle of disciplinary power is the 'examination'. As with other techniques of discipline and control, it developed into a major vehicle of power in the late seventeenth century. The examination incorporated aspects of surveillance, hierarchization, measurement and normalization. Through its ceremony of power, it established 'the truth' about each individual, and became one of the most effective instruments of discipline and control in Western society (Foucault 1979).

Schools became a vehicle for continuous examination. This brought a double burden on the subject — learning and undertaking examinations. Educational institutions changed gradually from a place where students played and competed with each other to one where they were constantly compared, measured, discussed and sanctioned. The story was repeated in the military. The examination came into its own as a mechanism to transform the economy of visibility into the exercise of power.

The examination also left behind a perpetual, detailed, archival documentation of each individual, which provided material for databases to calculate national averages and to construct norms for the entire population. This made it possible to compare and classify individuals and segments of the population, according to predetermined 'desirable' features. Seemingly trivial techniques of data collection, notation, registration, files and the compilation of tables and columns provided raw material for developing new 'sciences of man' which, according to Foucault, placed everyone in a state of perpetual subjugation. Constantly in the light, each individual could be seen, examined, categorized, rated, sanctioned and normalized.

The examination and its ensuing database also gave birth to the 'case study'. The social scientist, now an expert, measured, described and compared each case against the 'normal' individual. This enabled the expert to judge each case and to determine the proper correction, exclusion or detention. The space, so to speak, between normal (average) behaviour and the individual's actual behaviour became an area for investigation, study, theory and research. Real lives were turned into 'accounts' or 'texts' of lives and a new technique of power emerged — the writing, or more appropriately, the 'righting' of the person. The new clinical experts measured, described and normalized the individual.

The Panopticon   These 'techniques of correct training' — hierarchical surveillance, normalizing sanctions and the examination — worked best within the panopticon. Originally designed for prisons, the panopticon features a unique architecture. A central tower looked out in all directions into layers of solitary cells arranged in the periphery ring. The cells, or cages, acted as tiny theatres, putting each inmate on the stage, alone and individualized, but with uninterrupted visibility from the central tower. The inmate, although constantly aware of the outline of the central tower, could never be sure at any given moment whether or not he or she was being watched. The central tower was designed with venetian blinds, specially angled partitions, and zig-zag internal openings that could scan in different directions. As a result, the presence or absence of a guard or director in the central tower was unverifiable from the cells. Spectacular manifestations of power in the old dungeons gave way to anonymous but constant surveillance.

An advantage of the panopticon was that anybody would do in the central tower — a friend of the director, a relative, a servant or just a passer-by. The inmate could only catch an occasional glimpse of a shadow. Nor did it matter what the person's motives were — curiosity, malice, research or just the pleasure of spying — as long as there was occasional movement in the tower. In fact, Foucault observes, the panopticon worked all the better when there was a variety of temporary, anonymous observers, as the inmates' anxiety rose making them more liable to conform to prescribed 'normalization'. The panopticon, a highly efficient seeing-machine and laboratory of power, was the ideal means for knowing and disciplining space, time and the body.

The Principle of Disciplined Bodies at ITT

Geneen's account of his financial control system at ITT typifies many aspects of disciplinary power. One of his first, but perhaps most critical, moves in reorganizing ITT was to restructure the comptroller's organization. Under the old system, field comptrollers reported directly (solid line) to field managers and only indirectly (dotted line) to headquarters. Geneen changed this to a solid-line reporting to headquarters *and* a solid (but weaker) line to the field general managers. Initially, this met with stiff resistance.

Geneen completed his system of hierarchical surveillance by setting up a cadre of technical staff and product managers in his central headquarters 'panoptic tower'. Technical personnel, experienced and proficient in all aspects of ITT's activities (such as telecommunications, electronics, consumer goods, engineering, accounting, marketing and personnel) were organized into specialized headquarters staff offices. These managers reviewed and analyzed the monthly reports and could go to an ITT location without invitation to investigate anything within their expertise. On site, they asked questions, got answers, and reported their findings back to Geneen. Before reporting to Geneen, however, the staff people had to tell the local manager involved, as well as their own boss, exactly what they were doing and what findings they came up with. Thus, the manager had a chance to correct (normalize) the situation. This part of the hierarchy played its normalizing, disciplinary gaze over the surface, lines and fibres of the entire line organization.

Geneen also initiated a system of ranking every responsibility center in ITT. A typical example is the rating system he set up for comptrollership units. In the late 1970s, ITT employed nearly 23 000 persons in the comptrollership activities, including 325 corporate headquarters staff. Each field controller was examined and rated by an effectiveness score based on 30 identified areas of comptrollership including, for example, intercompany accounting, budgets, cost accounting, capital expenditures, payables, debt and foreign exchange management, the comptroller's monthly operating and financial review and the comptroller's interface with both the unit general manager and the director of financial controls.

These ratings were displayed on a massive colour-coded 'Comptrollership Grid'. The grid listed each of the 250 comptroller field units on the vertical axis and each of the 30 areas of comptrollership on the horizontal one. As a result, Geneen and other top executives could see at a single glance how well any field controller was performing as well as getting the picture for any specific function. Newly acquired units and units featuring a 'high situation complexity' (unfavourable business environment, inadequate staff, degree of multiple operations, trouble-some governments or tricky foreign exchange transactions) frequently received poor ratings. Here, the measure of the unit comptroller's effectiveness was the time he or she took to remedy the situation. The comptroller's exact actions were detailed in minute fashion. The Comptrollership Grid provided an exhaustive, automatic examining, portioning, ranking, sanctioning and promoting or demoting of the comptrollers. The result was obedient, disciplined and willing comptrollers.

Such disciplinary practices prevailed throughout the company. Each line and staff manager received a similar dose of surveillance, discipline and sanctions. Each operating and staff manager included in their monthly report a brief description of significant problems they were facing, a clear statement of the action recommended, the reasoning and numbers used to analyze the problem and a brief opinion statement regarding the resolution of the problem. These problems remained 'red-flagged' until they were solved. They also became part of the agenda at the monthly face-to-face meetings:

> If the man knew [of a problem] and was reluctant to put the facts in the open, my questions would force him to admit what he was trying to hide. If the man did not know or understand his own lines, which was often true because he had not written them, then my questions,

> doubly embarrassing, would force him to do his homework (Geneen
> 1984: 100).

While Geneen's disciplinary grid provided hierarchical surveillance, the numbers were the most critical part of it. In fact, 'the numbers make you free' became his famous credo.

As the budget year unfolded, a similar set of numbers flowed into headquarters each month, or weekly in the case of red-flagged units. Geneen scrutinized every piece of information searching for anything that might be off plan. He believed fervently that 'unshakeable' facts, along with hard-headed, hard-hitting cross-examinations, were essential to instill the requisite degree of discipline into the organization.

> It is discipline that is built into the credo management must manage.
> Part of that discipline is recognizing that the first answer you receive is
> not necessarily the best one. That is why I put so much emphasis upon
> probing for unshakable facts (Geneen 1984: 123).

Geneen insisted on receiving timely, detailed and accurate information from every nook and cranny of the organization. He was convinced that if executives looked closely at the numbers, any company could slowly but surely emerge as a well-managed enterprise. If, however, they did not keep at the numbers constantly, they would soon slide downhill.

Rather than using committees Geneen preferred to 'examine' the managers of the operating units himself. The notorious monthly meeting in Brussels of 150 of ITT's top executives served as Geneen's examinatory:

> The invited 150 officers hear introductory remarks by Geneen, an
> operations report from Dunleavy, and reports on such matters as
> inventory levels and receivables. Then the action begins. The heads of
> the bigger companies and the line group vice-presidents responsible for
> the others track the performance of their operations against
> their budgets. Anybody attending can ask questions and make
> suggestions.
>
> Some former employees complain that the big meetings reek of
> Kafkaesque courts, of volleys of verbal invective fired at under-
> achievers. 'Many of us have frankly left the organization for having
> been spit upon publicly', says a former European unit manager.
> Geneen, by contrast, views the meetings as open, business-like forums,
> at which participants try to help one another (*Business Week*,
> November 3, 1973).

This examinatory practice, featuring an alphanumeric-inquisitional process of reading, examining and re-writing each manager as a text, was seen by the managers not so much as a 'helping' session, but a 'hell' session.

Geneen was also a master of 'dressage'. Each manager had to at least posture as a user, and more importantly, a believer in 'managing by the numbers'. They were trained to meet face-to-face, to look into each other's eyes, to listen carefully to the tone of other's voices, and to pay attention to their 'body language'. Telephone or telex would not do. You had to see the other person's reactions.

Geneen's management accounting and control system mirrored the ideals of the panopticon. From the central headquarters office, the accounting system cast its constant normalizing gaze into every responsibility center. At a glance, it could monitor any part of ITT. It effected a continual flow of both formal and informal information into Geneen's office. Individual managers, however, never knew when Geneen was 'gazing' directly at them through the windows of the numbers, or if not him personally, then some other member of the anonymous headquarter's staff. Within this accounting and control panopticon, the line organization anxiously conformed to the 'prescribed normalization of the numbers'.

Geneen's credo — 'the numbers will make you free' is the antithesis of Foucault's message. For Foucault, they would be a critical part of the 'prison' which incarcerates managers in their responsibility centers. 'For the disciplined, as for the believer, no detail is unimportant, but not so much for the meaning it conceals within it as for the hold it provides for the power that wishes to seize it' (Foucault 1979: 140).

Reflections

Not all of these empirics, however, fitted neatly into Foucault's model. Foucauldian analysis, if it is to provide a basis for full theorization, may need extension and refinement. This was apparent in three respects. First, whilst accounting controls in ITT effected a disciplinary gaze upon management, their features did not exactly mirror the principles of discipline and control detailed by Foucault. Moreover, accounting controls evolved and changed in ITT over time; accounting was not always the principle mode of control and it did not take a single form. If accounting is an expression of modernity then Foucault's bi-polar turning point for change of pre- and post-modernity cannot explicate subtle shifts in the means of control within ITT. Second, whilst Foucauldian analysis picked up the significance of discourse and disciplinary power, it failed to encompass other important factors affecting modes of control within ITT, especially financial markets, corporate relations with states and technologies. Third, panoptical control is not absolute, resistance within and without ITT helped shape its transformation.

Whilst Foucault explicitly accepted that materialist factors could shape disciplinary controls, he did not explicitly explore how this occurred in *Discipline and Punish*. Consequently, it is not surprising that some research found Foucault's methods neglected how external factors bore on controls, especially financial markets, government bodies and nation states. Economic factors did shape events at ITT. Moreover, Geneen never regarded himself as a free agent but rather saw himself as a willing servant of stock markets. Geneen's concerns were well founded, for stock market pressures were paramount in precipitating key changes in senior management personnel and policies, including the demise of Behn and Geneen's own rise and fall.

Thus, Foucauldians compete with transaction cost theory and labour process approaches for an explanation of accounting change. The latter would both argue that in their different ways they incorporate economic and social factors in a superior fashion.

The Chandlerian/transaction cost approach to management accounting history attributes the rise of accounting controls in organizations to their superior efficiency in coordinating activities *vis-à-vis* market transactions. The underpinnings of this approach are intertwined with influences upon Geneen's ideas including Sloan's accounting innovations and Harvard Business School course material. Moreover, it reconciles his potentially conflicting beliefs in market imperatives and the unique efficiency of his management techniques.

Whilst markets helped precipitate accounting change in ITT, it is not conclusive that these techniques increased stock market returns or increased the efficiency of all parts of the business. The financial superiority of Geneen's methods is unproven and problematical. In addition, relationships with states, not mediated by normal market forces, were a critical factor in ITT's development. If the economic imperatives claimed by transaction cost theory are not well supported empirically, then it is open to accusations of being a pseudo-scientific mode of theorizing which retrospectively translates events in line with managerialist beliefs: such knowledge was the very object of Foucault's scorn.

Labour process approaches work somewhat better. Hopper and Armstrong (1991) argue that management accounting in large USA corporations was a consequence of the labour–capital accord that emerged from the 1930s, involving corporations, unionized labour and the state. The emergence of large corporations, high industrial concentration and Fordist production from the early part of this century were consequences of merger activities to address financial crises and the abandonment of internal control through craft workers and subcontractors. The resultant vacuum in control, initially unsuccessfully filled by foremen, came to be filled by a large and growing managerial cadre to administer bureaucratic planning and control systems. Management accounting was important not only for planning and controlling operations, but also for controlling the new class of managers themselves. The breakdown of the accord in the 1970s, marked by declining corporate profitability and social and industrial conflict, began to wreak changes in management accounting systems resonant with post-Fordist themes.

The chronology of events in ITT are reasonably consistent with this account. ITT emerged early in this century with few formal management accounting controls, but in the 1950s, due to increasing size and complexity, it imitated and then refined the management accounting methods pioneered by large corporations such as General Motors and DuPont. A strength of this political economy approach is that it explains accounting change and discontinuity in a manner that recognizes the interdependence between accounting and other controls in the context of state actions and markets, though without subscribing to the linear efficiency imperative of transaction cost theory — all pertinent issues in our study of ITT.

However, no material gathered on ITT directly connected changes in its accounting systems to changes in labour processes at the point of production and attendant labour conflicts. Rather it revealed a continual concern by ITT in controlling managers. Whether this is a consequence of the secondary sources used, which were mainly managerial, financial and strategic, or because it was not a significant factor requires further study. This is critical to any judgement of labour process theory *vis-à-vis* Foucauldian approaches as labour process theory ultimately rests upon conflicts in production relations as a motor of change. Foucauldian theory on the other hand is suspicious of any generalization from a meta-narrative. Whatever, labour process research to date, in the context of this Foucauldian study, appears neglectful of management as a distinct phenomena and the emergence of managerial knowledge and how it provides managers with a self-conception of their mission.

References

Foucault, M. (1979). *Discipline and punish: The birth of the prison.* New York: Vintage Books.

Geneen, H. (1984). *Managing.* New York: Avon.

Hopper, T.M., & Armstrong, P. (1991). Cost accounting, controlling labor and the rise of conglomerates. *Accounting, Organizations and Society, 16*(5/6), 405–438.

Chapter 19

The Relationship between Accounting and Spatial Practices in the Factory[1]

Salvador Carmona, *Universidad Carlos III de Madrid*

Mahmoud Ezzamel, *University of Cardiff*

Fernando Gutiérrez, *Universidad Pablo de Olavide*

During the eighteenth century, tobacco production in the Royal Tobacco Factory (RTF) of Spain moved from the San Pedro Factory located in downtown Seville to the purpose built New Factories outside the city walls. This paper examines the relationship between accounting practices and spatial practices in these two radically different factory premises. The paper explores how the intervention of detailed accounting calculations into spatial configurations and the intertwining of accounting and spatial practices provide discipline in the factory by yielding calculable spaces and accountable subjects. The spaces produced by architects in the New Factories were subsequently mediated through administrative arrangements that rendered enclosure and partitioning more disciplinary. Moreover, accounting practices were developed as a coding system to reconfigure factory space by classifying it into cost centers, quantifying activities carried out in these cost centers and rendering spaces visible and subjects accountable. In this context, we argue that accounting practices have the capacity to function as time–space ordering devices, and through networking with spatial practices, provide the scope for managers/administrators to enhance employee surveillance and overall factory discipline.

From the sixteenth century, the tobacco industry in Spain was organized around small-sized family-owned workshops which by the latter part of the seventeenth century became a state monopoly co-ordinated and controlled by the Tobacco Agency. In 1684, a Royal decree awarded the city of Seville the right to produce tobacco in the San Pedro Factory. As the consumption of tobacco (snuff and cigars) in Spain rose from 1.1 million pounds in 1701 to 3.2 million pounds in 1740, steps were taken to increase the production capacity of the San Pedro Factory by buying or renting additional buildings. However, these measures proved insufficient for meeting the rising demand for tobacco. Moreover, because the Spanish Crown became increasingly dependent upon tobacco revenue, both the Tobacco Agency

---

[1]Reproduced (in an abridged version) from S. Carmona, M. Ezzamel and F. Gutiérrez, 'The Relationship Between Accounting and Spatial Practices in the Factory', *Accounting, Organizations and Society*, 2002, vol. 27, no. 3, pp. 239–74, with permission of Elsevier.

and the administrators of the RTF were concerned to prevent tobacco theft, which was rife in the San Pedro Factory and to improve overall factory discipline. Hence, in 1724 the decision was made to build new factory premises. The New Factories, with a production capacity two and a half times that of the San Pedro Factory, started operations in 1758 reaching full production in the late 1760s. As cigar production depended upon highly skilled operators who were monitored and motivated by a piece rate pay system accounting and spatial practices were fairly similar in both Factories. Hence, in this paper we will focus our discussion on the intertwining of accounting and spatial practices in snuff production, for it is there where we note the most significant differences between the San Pedro Factory and the New Factories. Numerous accounting practices were developed in the New Factories to monitor the various stages of snuff production more effectively.

Snuff was processed in five production stages known as *beneficios* (profits, benefits, value added). These stages were extremely difficult to distinguish in the San Pedro Factory and it was not until production was spatially reorganized in the New Factories that these stages became clearly visible. The first *beneficio* was known as *Azotea*, the factory terrace, where tobacco leaves were dried after being prepared. Bundles of tobacco leaves were separated into individual pieces which were then classified into piles on the basis of the quality of raw tobacco and the season of year. The second *beneficio* consisted of grinding and sifting the tobacco leaves in *Monte*. It required milling the leaves in horse-driven mills until the leaves were turned into snuff. This snuff was then sifted through different kinds of cloth depending on the particular class of tobacco [fine or exquisite].

Moja, the third *beneficio*, consisted of toilet watering the snuff and mixing it with other ingredients (e.g. fruit) to obtain different flavours in order to prepare snuff for subsequent production stages and to differentiate each class of snuff according to its colour and smell. The fourth *beneficio* was called *Entresuelos* where snuff was ploughed and turned over until it dried fully. In *Repaso*, the fifth *beneficio*, snuff was milled and sifted further using jasper stones to make it finer. These phases were followed by *Fermentación* and *Distribución*. *Fermentación* was performed in large warehouses with wooden floors. Snuff sacks were kept half opened in the warehouses from 1 to 3 days (higher quality snuff was kept for longer periods). Once the sacks were sealed, higher quality snuff was kept for 25 days while lower quality tobacco was kept for 15–20 days in the warehouses. *Distribución* was the warehouse for storing finished snuff.

Space Configuration and Accounting Control in the New Factories

Architect Ignacio Sala's design was considerably influenced by the views of Carlos Mirail, General Superintendent of the RTF, contained in a memorandum sent to Sala. First, the new building should separate the five different *beneficios* (snuff production steps noted earlier). Second, a central patio should constitute the core of the building and be the site of the tobacco weighing machine. Third, warehouses for raw materials should be located close to the relevant production stage in order to ensure easy access and the *Entresuelo* (drying) should be situated on a diaphanous (transparent) floor so that with the construction of light walls it would be easy to distinguish different *Mojas* (watering and mixing) of tobacco. Finally, the *Azotea* (terrace preparation) space should have a high wall so that tobacco leaves left to dry are not lost or destroyed in windy conditions. A separate quarter was to be devoted to cigar making.

Sala's plan embodied the notions of enclosure, partitioning and discipline. Concerning enclosure, the factory building was to be situated outside the city walls, away from the city. Two patios were designed, the main central one was intended to control operators of both the snuff and cigar factories upon leaving the RTF. The plans were such that once operators passed the main patio, partitioning would come into effect so that 'it will not be possible [for different groups] to be in contact with each other'. Partitioning, however, was not restricted to communications of operators of different factories. It also applied to operators in the different stages of snuff production. Sala stated: '[I have kept contact between operators] to a minimum; ideally, I should have isolated every area so that factory security increases. We have to minimize the reasons for which operators have to move around the factory, which compromise tobacco security'. Sala's design allowed the Superintendent easy access to any part of the Factory: the upper *Azoteas* should not be connected to the rest of the factory, except through the house of the General Superintendent to give him the opportunity to 'monitor the whole Factory from his house as he told me'. In designing the location of the mills, Sala followed the principle of the diaphanous grid so that, as Morales Sánchez (1991: 123) notes, the *Monte* production phase was the repetition 'ad infinitum' of a cell formed by four pillars and one dome.

The building was divided into two parts following the East–West axis. The Northern part incorporated the façade, administration offices and apartments for senior RTF officers. The Southern part contained the shopfloor, workshops and warehouses. The North–South axis included the venues for communication: the main gate; the internal street; and the central patio. Concern for monitoring was evident in the space configuration of the building. Unlike in the San Pedro Factory, in the New Factories the offices of administrators and accountants were located close to the main gate with a view over the central patio.

Other architectural procedures were followed to maximize the visibility of production activities; the vantage view enjoyed by the General Superintendent from his apartment allowed him to observe the location of bodies in space as carefully arranged spatial entities while not being seen, hence the disciplinary power of the Panopticon was extended to him. The apartments of the Stables Supervisor and his foreman were located so as 'to allow the observation and monitoring of the operators of the stables'. The design of the workshops was based on a grid formed by the numerous repetitions of domes in order 'to house the machines but also to allow the patron, as well as those concerned with monitoring activities, easy control over all the tasks'.

While the construction of a linear and clear street made communication between the factory gate and the central patio easy, this was finely balanced against the desire to ensure the enclosure and coding of employees in space. What were perceived to be idle movements by employees between different locations were eliminated; hence we concur with the assessment of Morales Sánchez (1991: 206): 'the connections that existed between different departments were awkward. This made it easier to monitor each work unit'. The grid structure used for housing the mills was highly flexible, making possible the construction of light partition walls to produce new space by rearranging previous partitions whenever needed in order to enhance discipline. The clear demarcation of space not only revealed operators' presence and absence and facilitated their supervision, it also created a greater scope for accounting coding in the form of quantifying reporting, comparing and monitoring the performance of individual operators (in the cigar factory) and types of raw materials, specific tasks (e.g. production of tins) and *casillas* (cost centers) in the snuff factory. The labour force and cost centers can now be systematized, differentiated and hierarchized. These accounting practices represented a major departure from the San Pedro Factory by providing supervisors and foremen with a systematic and detailed mechanism, combining physical and monetary measures, for monitoring the flow of tobacco in the factory. Hence, once the accounting series devoted to manufacturing in the New Factories are considered in their totality, a far more extensive and accounting-centric surveillance scheme swims into view. These practices were developed at a time when there was substantial pressure on the RTF administrators to increase output significantly by using factory space more efficiently, to drive the cost of production down and to improve product quality.

The premises of the San Pedro Factory were not purpose-built in a manner that facilitated monitoring or the intervention of detailed accounting calculations. As more enlargements were made, new problems emerged in relation to controlling and policing a larger number of more dispersed buildings and operators. Control was rendered more difficult because the cigar and *rollo* buildings were located outside the main factory complex in the City center and the snuff production stages were not clearly differentiated. Accounting practices simply focused on house-keeping arrangements, cash flow movements, and reporting on production in the most aggregate manner. Factory space remained primarily a 'closed' space, as activities, operators, and supervisors eluded detailed accounting-based monitoring that could link them to specific times or spatial locales.

The configuration of space and development of administrative and accounting practices in the New Factories was significantly mediated by several concerns. These were providing for greater production capacity; ensuring high quality production at the lowest possible cost; instilling better work discipline on the shopfloor; and minimizing tobacco theft.

The Production and Control of Malleable Space

The space produced in the New Factories embodied new, and carefully thought out configurations which were closely linked to the discourses and practices of Spanish construction ideals. The redesign of the factory floor is implicated in changes that go beyond the boundaries of the plant such as political ideals. The New Factories came to reproduce the quadrangular model perfected in city design for the Spanish American colonies. This geometrically precise model was constituted by the *Orders for Discovery and Settlement*, published in 1573, which was arranged under the codes of discovery, settlement and pacification. The model provided a strict hierarchical organization of space, gradually proceeding from the town center, beginning from the *ciudad* (City) and reaching out to the surrounding *pueblos* (towns). Starting from the *Plaza Mayor* (Main Square), a grid extends indefinitely in every direction, as mirrored by the grid reproduced in the New Factories extending from the central patio, where each space was assigned a function and each function a space in a geometrically precise and hierarchically organized construction.

The symbolic relationship between the exterior (façade) and interior space was striking. The Northern elevation of the New Factories was the 'palace' whereas the Southern elevation was differentiated as the factory. This demarcation of exterior and interior space is significant, as is the demarcation between back region and front region. For while demarcation of this type helps to bring certain attributes into sharp relief (such as the symmetry or beauty of the façade), for outsiders it may mask other attributes, such as the strict discipline exercised over the shopfloor.

For space to be controlled, it has to be conceived as something 'usable, malleable' (Harvey 1990: 254). In the New Factories, space was conceived as usable and malleable (e.g. the partitioning of the *Entresuelos* diaphanous nave through the use of light walls, the partitioning of the mills grid) and amenable to administrative action. The new mapping of factory space and snuff production in the New Factories entailed changes in locations and spatial movements. The enclosure and partitioning used in the New Factories yielded new configurations of space that made it possible to assign specific spaces to individuals and individuals to spaces and, through the intricate coding of accounting, spaces were rendered calculable and individuals accountable fragments of mobile space.

The grid used almost to perfection in the New Factories capitalized upon the disciplinary potential implied in repetitive spaces which, as Lefebvre (1991: 75) has suggested 'are the outcome of repetitive gestures (those of the workers) associated with instruments which are both duplicable and designed to duplicate'. As spaces become repetitive, it becomes possible to develop disciplinary accounting practices, as reflected in the partitioning of the *Entresuelos* into repetitive cells susceptible to accounting calculations, thereby allowing control over activities. Thus, in the New Factories the Superintendent was able to assign operators to *beneficios* (as different spatial locations) and then, through the intervention of accounting, to exert control over their daily activities. He could link performance to operators at various locations, ensure direct observation of operators by foremen and of foremen by himself.

Foucault (1979) has emphasized the idea that any reorgnization of space is simultaneously a reorganization of the framework through which social power relations are practiced; hence space is a container of social power. The reconfiguration of space in the New Factories was the culmination of the intertwining of power relations spanning several interested parties. These included state organs and the Tobacco Agency, who were propelled by the desire to maximize tobacco revenue and reinforce the power of the Crown, and the amalgam of architects, RTF administrators and accountants each with their own technical affiliation and specific, expert knowledge. As new space is produced through enclosure, partitioning and coding, new power relations are constituted. This fragmentation of space creates the perception of total control and domination. For those in higher administrative positions rest assured that: 'The diversity of peoples could be appreciated and analyzed in the secure knowledge that their "place" in the spatial order was unambiguously known' (Harvey 1990: 250).

Against the fragmentation of space in the New Factories comes the idea of the panopticon whose disciplinary effects are established through greater visibility from a vantage point. The organization of production along the design of a grid and the location of certain crucial activities in centrally located spaces such as patios and the location of the Superintendent's apartment, rendered the New Factories visible as one unit. Superiors, such as the Superintendent, could instill discipline in the workforce by virtue of being able to see them, while he himself not being necessarily seen, thereby extending the locales assigned to them into his private space to command a 'global' view of factory activities as a known totality. This was reinforced by the comprehensive mapping of accounting practices upon space which, while fragmented and coded that space into smaller centers of calculation, maintained and conveyed the 'global' view of the RTF by also providing aggregate, factory-based calculations (e.g. cost of a pound of snuff).

The 'emptying' of space in the New Factories reflected some variation from the factors identified by Giddens (1991). On the one hand, the design of the New Factories made possible the production of new spaces and the substitutability of different spatial units, thereby satisfying one of the forms of 'emptying' space identified by Giddens. The flexibility of the *Entresuelos* architectural design allowed more partitioning of space through the use of light walls, and the use of the grid structure also facilitated the production of new space through the repetition of production cells. The new structure also enhanced the mobility of individual operators across factory space. For example, the 1761 Regulation stipulated that 'Supervisors should check if there are daily absences in the offices. If absences were found, they should select a corresponding number of operators from either *Moja* or *Entresuelos*. [Such arrangements will be made] on a leave basis'.

On the other hand, the representation of many spaces in the New Factories privileged distinct vantage points, such as the apartment of the RTF Superintendent and the offices of other superiors who could observe from these locations production activities and tobacco transactions being made on the central patio of the New Factories. In this regard, accounting practices helped to turn these spatial locations into scrutinized spaces whereby accountability is assigned to operators inhabiting these locations. The production of space in the New Factories was therefore strongly influenced not only by the ideals of the less visible and distanciated *Orders for Discovery and Settlement*, but also by the local factors as represented by the technical expertise and interests of the architects, tobacco experts, administrators and accountants.

Thus, functions or offices deemed crucial to the activities of the RTF were located in strategically designated spaces. The administration buildings were located close to the main gate of the RTF so that accounting staff could directly observe the inflow and outflow of tobacco materials and finished goods. The tobacco sales patio was located outside, yet close to, the factory premises and a small office for the sales accountant was provided close by. A number of considerations were taken into account in selecting the location of the Cash Office. First, to enhance security over cash, the location of the Cash Office was selected in what was deemed the safest part of the building. Secondly, to ensure easy access for monitoring purposes, the Cash Office was situated close to the office of the RTF Superintendent and to the Accounting Office. Thirdly, to make it easy for operators to collect their wages on the way out of the factory, the Cash office was located close to the main gate of the RTF. Houses provided for the Stables Manager and his Deputy were designed and located in such a way as to allow them to exercise visual control over stable operators. Finally, the grid of diaphanous spaces used in the workshops rendered them suitable to accommodate machinery, but simultaneously facilitated direct control over operators by foremen.

The Intervention of Accounting into Space

We have argued that snuff production activities in the San Pedro Factory were scattered across different locations and that accounting practices treated the whole factory as one closed space rather than monitoring these activities in any detail. This would suggest that there are certain limits as to the extent of accounting intervention into factory space. If space is configured in a ramshackle and haphazard way, this may militate against the possibility of its partitioning into what may be deemed meaningful centers of calculation from an accounting perspective. In the San Pedro Factory the same production stage (e.g. drying tobacco leaves) was repeated, but not necessarily in exactly the same way, across numerous scattered houses, rather than being confined within the same space. This spatial diversity created major uncertainty for accountants and administrators as to first, gaining an understanding of the logical flow of production activities and second, developing appropriate ways to draw accounting boundaries around *beneficios* in order to render them calculable.

Another possibility for the proliferation of accounting practices in the New Factories could be that the Spanish monopolies at the time were subjected to such intensification of accounting as part of a state initiative to render monopolies more profitable. These changes resulted in a substantial increase in tobacco sales to £3 126 936 in the 1760s and £3 486 138 in the 1770s.

As early as 1727, the RTF administrators were aware of the importance of clearly separating the five different phases of snuff production. Why then was this not undertaken in the San Pedro Factory? We would argue that possibilities to partition the San Pedro Factory into smaller centers more amenable to the intervention of detailed accounting calculations may have appeared daunting for two reasons: any partitioning of that space was likely to be rather crude given the spatial problems discussed earlier and whatever benefits to be had from space partitioning may have been perceived to be outweighed by the cost of doing it given the short time horizon over which these benefits would have accrued before the move to the New Factories. What we are suggesting here is a twin argument. Firstly, the haphazard way of configuring the factory made it difficult for any detailed and systematic accounting intervention to occur. Yet, even when spatial configurations are not especially malleable, it is likely that some degree of detailed accounting intervention is possible. Hence, secondly, it is possible that a more detailed intervention of accounting was rendered by the RTF administration undesirable because of expectations such as high costs compared with benefits and the short time horizon over which the intervention would be effective. This argument has some support by the finding that soon after the move to the New Factories, new supervisory posts were created and many more detailed accounting series were implemented. We would suggest that some of these new supervisory and accounting arrangements were already known while production was still located in the San Pedro Factory, but they were not deployed there because the conditions, discourses and rationalities prevailing at the time were not conducive to their introduction.

Ways of organizing and ways of calculation frequently develop together. Once production moved to the New Factories, it became possible to forge strong links between the economic motives of the various discourses and practices that sought to organize space (and time). As Harvey (1990: 229) has suggested 'If money has no meaning independent of time and space, then it is always possible to pursue profit (or other forms of advantage) by altering the ways time and space are used and defined'. The interest of the Spanish Crown in extracting greater revenues from the tobacco monopoly was an important reason why new, larger and purpose-built factories became a priority. Modifications of the configurations of factory space were seen by the tobacco administrators as the means for enhancing profit, through the expansion of production capacity, the improvement of employee discipline, the emphasis upon high quality products and the drive for cost reduction. Once the connection between the money/profit incentive and the design/use of space in the RTF had been forged, a relationship between accounting and space was simultaneously established through the production of calculations of target and actual costs and profits. In the case of the New Factories, the new accounting practices made possible the generation of detailed calculations of the cost of each production stage. Through these cost calculations each production stage became more visible, in quantitative and monetary terms and hence susceptible to administrative intervention. Moreover, the classification of products into 'good' and 'reworks' shows how accounting coding through the charge/discharge system has explicit accountability and disciplinary implications.

Although the new accounting series developed for the New Factories could be viewed as a mapping of accounting practices onto existing configurations of factory space, accounting practices in turn partitioned factory space into new centres of calculation and locations of visibility. Accounting is adept at creating abstract spaces (e.g. cost centres) that are amenable to quantification and measurement as calculable spaces, which may not correspond to physical locales. The new costing system developed in the New Factories re-presented each of the snuff and cigar factories as a constellation of individual, quantifiable cost centres which were mapped onto production activities to produce a new spatial configuration of the New Factories. Compared with the San Pedro Factory where only one charge/discharge system was used, we observe a partitioning of the New Factories through several charge/discharge systems, one for each cost centre.

The mapping of production activities onto the newly produced space in the New Factories rendered the now much clearer production stages, the spaces allocated to individuals and the individuals allocated to spaces, all amenable to the intervention of accounting. An alliance was forged, we would argue, between spatial and accounting practices where the administrators of the RTF saw an opportunity to intensify discipline (both materially and symbolically) over the workforce and this alliance created much scope for the proliferation of accounting practices.

More detailed and temporally frequent measurements were combined with new configurations of space and novel monitoring practices in the New Factories to yield a highly potent regime of surveillance. These new spatial configurations were more conducive to the detailed intervention of accounting calculations, hence the proliferation of accounting practices aimed at the level of individual production stages in the snuff factory. We have also suggested that accounting practices used in the New Factories functioned as 'time–space' ordering devices and facilitated some form of 'time–space' distanciation by reducing, but not eliminating, the need for face-to-face interaction for monitoring purposes. The accounting practices introduced in the New Factories measured spaces and operators, either quantitatively or financially, and converted them into seemingly precise metrics to be compared and assessed. In this way, enclosure, partitioning and coding assumed new meanings and greater significance not possible without the intervention of accounting. This influx of accounting practices which reached deeper into factory space than ever before demonstrates the remarkably powerful role that accounting practices can play in organizations.

References

Foucault, M. (1979). *Discipline and punish: The birth of the prison.* New York: Vintage Books (Translated by A. Sheridan).

Giddens, A. (1991). *The consequences of modernity.* Cambridge: Polity Press.

Harvey, D. (1990). *The condition of postmodernity.* Oxford: Blackwell.

Lefebvre, H. (1991). *The production of space.* Oxford: Blackwell (translated by D. Nicholson-Smith, French edition 1974).

Morales Sánchez, J. (1991). *Arquitectura, territoria y ciudad en la sevilla del siglo XVIII.* Sevilla: Colegio Oficial de Arquitectos de Andalucia Occidental.

Chapter 20

Decision-making in the Theater of Consciousness: A Theater Metaphor for Conscious Experience and the Holistic Concept of Man in Understanding the User of Accounting Information[1]

Pekka Pihlanto,   *Turku School of Economics and Business Administration*

Introduction

This article suggests the holistic concept of man (HCM) as a basic model for dealing with human nature (Rauhala 1986; Pihlanto 1989, 1990; Carr and Pihlanto 1998; Vanharanta *et al.* 1997). This concept is basically phenomenological. It is completed here with a Theater metaphor for conscious experience (TMCE) presented by Baars (1997). The aim is to deepen the area covered by the HCM with the newest inventions of brain research, by combining related models. In this way, it would be possible to better understand the characteristics of the user of accounting information. Also, the contribution of the models to each other is dealt with. The following first briefly introduces the HCM and secondly, the main features of the TMCE are analyzed in relation to the HCM. Finally, the models are discussed with an accounting context in mind.

The Holistic Concept of Man

The HCM consists of the following basic modes of the existence of man, which together form a holistic entity: (1) consciousness — or existence as a psychical-mental phenomenon — as experiencing; (2) situationality or existence in relation to

---

[1]An article published in T. Reponen (Ed.), Management Expertise for the New Millennium. In Commemoration of the 50th Anniversary of the Turku School of Economics and Business Administration. Publications of the Turku School of Economics and Business Administration, Series A-1: 2000. This abridged version reproduced by permission.

reality or personal situation; and (3) corporeality — or existence as a set of organic processes — as a body.

Consciousness as the totality of human experience consists of the following processes: (1) an object in the situation (reality) provides the consciousness with meaningful content; (2) a *meaning* emerges in the consciousness, as a consequence of this content becoming referred to an object located in the situation; (3) meanings are accumulated in the consciousness; the sum of all these meanings is termed the *world view* of an actor; (4) the world view is constantly redefined, as new meanings emerge on the basis of new content from the situation.

All this occurs in terms of *understanding*. Understanding is complete only after a *meaning* is generated. This occurs when an actor knows, believes or feels what an object in his or her situation implies. As to the nature of meanings, they might be even unclear, ill-structured, distorted or erroneous, but nevertheless they are meanings.

Everybody has relationships with something. *Situation* is that part of the world with which an individual gets into a relationship. *Situationality* is the totality of the relationships of a person to his or her situation. The situation of an individual consists of *concrete* or *ideal* components. The former includes all varieties of physical factors, while the latter is comprised of values, norms and human relationships as experienced contents, etc. The situation and situationality of every actor are *unique* and accounting information provides only one of the components of situation.

As to the possible relevance of situation and situationality in accounting studies, there has been a great interest in the notion of the *context* of accounting — both organizational and social. In addition, when accounting makes a certain action in a form visible to an actor, this action becomes, in a specific form, part of the situationality of the actor(s) concerned.

Corporeality, i.e. existence as organic processes — even if not the most essential element in an accounting context — should not be totally dismissed, because all the three modes of existence appear inseparably linked: when something occurs in one mode, there is invariably a corresponding occurrence in the other two. While situation is the 'place of the game' in which corporeality is 'located', corporeality realizes the physical side of existence of an actor and makes the other two possible.

Structure of the Theater Metaphor for Conscious Experience

In the following, the different elements of the Theater metaphor (TMCE) — the stage, the players, context operators behind the stage and the audience — are analyzed and related to the HCM.

The Stage   The basic idea in the TMCE presented by Baars (1997) is that conscious experience of a person is strictly limited by capacity. Conscious experience is realized on the 'stage of the theater, in the spotlight of attention', while the rest of the stage corresponds to immediate working memory (see Appendix 1).

The spotlight on the stage corresponds fairly well with the process of understanding phenomena by a person in the consciousness, as presented in the HCM. Thus meanings formed in the consciousness from the objects in the situation, are born 'on the lit spot of the stage'. Clearly, the notions of the stage and spotlight in the TMCE help the reader to better imagine the birth of meanings in the HCM.

On the other hand, the TMCE does not accentuate *the* consciousness, but defines consciousness in a brain-centered way — as a faculty of the brain. In the HCM, the corresponding personal experience is defined as a separate dimension from the brain, even if intimately inter-linked with it.

The Players   In the TMCE, the players appearing on the spotlight of the stage are defined as the contents of conscious experience. Conscious contents emerge when the spotlight of attention falls on a player on the stage. Keen competition and cooperation occur between the different players trying to reach the stage. The players are of three types: inner and outer senses, and ideas. Outer senses involve the forming of seeing, hearing, feeling, tasting and smelling sensations about different objects. Inner senses introduce such players as visual imagery, inner speech, dreams and imagined feelings. Inner speech is what a person hears himself saying, and visual imagery what a person sees with the 'mind's eye'. Ideas consist of imagined and verbalized ideas as well as fringe consciousness and intuitions. The fringe consciousness includes such experiences as feelings of knowing, familiarity, beauty and goodness.

In terms of the HCM, all these players are types of *meanings* appearing in the consciousness. Sensations are meanings from objects in situation. Inner speech and imagination correspond to meanings usually recalled from the world view, i.e. created before and scrutinized anew at a later time. Inner speech-type meanings are 'heard' in speech form in the consciousness. Correspondingly, visual imagery represents meanings experienced in a visual form and fringe images are feeling-type of meanings. All these players complete the notion of meaning in the HCM.

Context Operators   Behind the scene there are executive processes — *context operators* — such as *director*, *spotlight controller* and *local contexts*. They set the background against which the 'brightly lit' players play their roles. Context is defined as any source of *knowledge* that shapes conscious experiences, without itself being conscious. Baars does not separate *director* and *spotlight controller* clearly enough. Therefore, we apply these concepts synonymously using the term *director*. The director performs executive functions and maintains long-term stability in a person's experiences.

In terms of the HCM, *context operators* refer to certain unconscious content of the world view. The role of world view is defined in quite the same way as context: the previous understanding shapes and guides conscious experience.

New understanding is based on previous understanding and the latter therefore sets the background against which the new understanding (meanings) emerge, exactly like the players play their roles influenced by context operators in the TMCE. According to the HCM, however, the unconscious nature of the previous experience in the world view is not accentuated to such a degree as in the TMCE. In the latter, context operators are unconscious, but if violated they become conscious.

In terms of the HCM, the director may be interpreted as self or the feeling of self-consciousness. According to humanistic psychology — which shares an intimate link with the HCM — the human capacity for self-consciousness is what distinguishes us from all other beings (Rauhala 1986). Director seems a useful notion, since the HCM does not contain a clear 'steering unit' for actualizing the processes of the consciousness. According to the HCM, however, the will steers the action of an individual, but will does not sound permanent enough to form the necessary control unit. From the point of view of the HCM, however, it is important to stress that director is realized in the form of meanings and does not represent any separate instance in the consciousness. Instead of will, the meanings in question are called director, in order to accentuate their active function in the consciousness.

The Audience   Players in the spotlight are the only ones capable of disseminating information to the audience consisting of specialized experts, who represent the unconscious resources of memory, knowledge and automatic mechanisms. Members of the audience share a vast network connecting each to each, enabling them to carry out routine tasks without consciousness. It is likely that these routine collaborations between separate automatic units were created in the past with the aid of consciousness. These include *memory systems, interpreting conscious contents, automatisms* and *motivational systems*. These are triggered when their 'calling conditions' appear: for instance, a visual experience may trigger a linguistic analysis or object recognition.

To sum up, the connection between the stage and audience functions as follows. The spotlight selects the most important events on stage, which are then distributed to the audience consisting of unconscious routines and knowledge sources. The audience may hiss or applaud, asking to hear more or less from any given player. Audience members can also exchange information among themselves and form coalitions to bring other messages to the stage.

In the HCM, the audience can be located at world view — the cumulative inventory of previous understanding in the form of networks of meanings. Objects in the situation are understood in relation to this previous understanding, e.g. the above 'separate automatic units created in the past with the help of consciousness'. The unconscious contents of the world view or audience can be retrieved into the spotlight and dealt with by mental and reflective conscious activities. The notion of audience offers additional evidence for the HCM that unconscious meanings in the world view may be changed and combined without the person being aware of it.

The Combination of the Theater Metaphor and the Holistic Concept of Man in Understanding the User of Accounting Information

What then is the relevance of the combination of the TMCE and HCM in understanding the decision-maker in an accounting context and how the models complete each other?

The TMCE accentuates the limited capacity of the spotlight or the conscious experience: people are aware of only a small fraction of information at a time. On the other hand, the HCM points out that the decision-maker, in using accounting information, experiences the world in terms of meanings which are formed in relation to a subjective world view. In this light, searching for information and comprehending it is not a simple task. This feature is worthy of consideration by those preparing accounting reports and planning accounting systems: the decision-maker is seriously limited by his or her attention to information and subjective in understanding the phenomena.

The *players* on the spotlight of the stage were defined in the TMCE as the contents of conscious experience. In terms of the HCM, then, the players are simply different types of meaning in the consciousness and by definition they *mean something* to the person in question. There is keen competition and intimate cooperation between the players or types of meaning as they try to reach the stage. For instance, when analyzing the chances of the contents of an accounting report to reach the stage, the 'struggle' between different players is relevant. The message should be offered in such a way and form that the possibilities for 'wrong' players to reach the stage — i.e. 'wrong' meanings to emerge — are minimal.

The existence of 'creations' of *inner senses*, such as visual imagery, inner speech, dreams and imagined feelings — as well as imaginable and verbalized ideas — offers the impression of a decision-maker who has a rich inner life. A decision-maker may 'see inner pictures', silently 'discuss by him- or herself', dream and imagine things, etc. when concentrating on a message. This play of meanings in the consciousness may support the message, but may also prevent its appearance on the stage. Further, the existence of *fringe consciousness* stresses the possible deficits in the decision-maker's awareness of information. All this, as considered by the people planning accounting systems and preparing reports, may make them learn to create unambiguous information, which effectively rouses the user's interest and minimizes the possibility of dreaming or irrelevancies.

The *context operators* behind the stage — especially the director — point out that the user of accounting information is a voluntary person not totally determined by situational factors, for instance, a report. Therefore, the producer of the report should realize that people are not easily influenced, and refrain from wasting their time in order to obtain uninteresting or overly complicated information. Further, the local context refers to the fact that the user is a 'prisoner of his or her past', i.e. the previous experiences accumulated into the individual's world view during his or her lifetime up to that point in time.

The *unconscious audience* — or contents of the world view representing various forms of 'skill and meaning inventory' — deepens the picture of the user of the accounting information towards the notion of a many-sided processor of routine tasks triggered by the players. The players entering under the spotlight — among them meanings derived from accounting information — trigger tasks by members of the audience. Everybody may know the existence of these tasks, but by accentuating them explicitly and linking together with other parts of the TMCE and HCM, they are shown in a different light: as part of the total picture about the decision-maker, which appears surprisingly complicated and many-sided.

As to the details of the unconscious audience, first the notion of *memory system* accentuates the fact that a user of accounting information is in constant contact with unconscious sources of information in the world view. These include lexicon, semantic networks, memories from the person's own past and deeply rooted beliefs. Second, the role of *interpreting conscious contents* by a user of the accounting report can be described in the same way: previous meanings in the world view have a crucial role in interpretation or forming new meanings. In this process, a person understands objects (e.g. recognizes figures) that he or she 'picks up' as meanings from the report to the spotlight. All this happens not only in the brain but in the consciousness as well. What makes interpretations highly problematic is the great personal variability of the interpretative process, due to varying personal experiences in the world view.

Third, *automatisms* complete the reactions and actions of a person, for instance, those resulting from seeing a report. Automatisms realize the skills and operations needed in reading and thinking, etc. Paradoxically, even if the user is a voluntary person, he or she is — at the same time — an automation as well, who does not need to be aware of all the detailed actions and processes necessary in completing a task triggered by the report: they just happen. Moreover, different people have different automatisms within world views and therefore interpretations are individual.

The fourth element in the audience, *motivational systems*, stresses the user of accounting information as an intentional and free-willed person. The user has in his or her consciousness — in world view — deeply rooted and highly individual meanings representing goals. With the help of these, the meanings appearing in the brightly illuminated spotlight of attention derived from objects — such as an accounting report — are put under an unconscious relevance check. In the case of inconsistency, an attempt is made to resolve goal conflicts in the consciousness. Also emotional responses, facial expressions and preparing the body for action represent the area of responsibility respective to motivational systems. All this happens when a decision-maker reads an accounting report.

This unconscious audience points out that the accounting information user possesses a rich unconscious mental and physical life. Therefore, the accounting information user is not a 'tabula rasa' when under an influence of a message. Instead, the user is a living system possessing rich information in the form of meanings in the world view, providing substance and direction to his or her reactions towards the message.

Discussion

The combined model resulting from the examination seemed logical, as it was possible to attach all the features of the TMCE to the framework of the HCM, without problems worth mentioning. The HCM gained important additional aspects and details from brain research, but still preserved its clear structure and philosophical nature. Perhaps the most important feature in the TMCE is the notion of the spotlight of conscious experience. It stresses the limitations of human experience and consciousness. The attention-directing task of accounting actually means trying to get accounting information to appear as meanings called 'players' in the spotlight of attention of relevant decision-makers. For instance, only when an important deviation represented in a report enters the spotlight and triggers a relevant reaction has the task of the accounting message been completed.

Particularly, the idea about players (created with the help of outer senses, inner senses and ideas) who compete for access to the stage of consciousness, clarify the definition of meaning in the HCM. Further, the great relevance of unconscious — the kind of instinctive — processes called members of unconscious audience in the TMCE, offer valuable ideas for the HCM in understanding the behavior of the decision-maker. This notion completes the knowledge about the contents of the world view in the HCM. Similarly, the director defined in the TMCE seems a useful amendment to the HCM, as the latter does not contain a clear 'steering unit' responsible for initiating the processes of the consciousness.

In this new philosophical environment offered by the HCM, the TMCE gained additional features and explanations. One of them is the view about the basic nature of human experiencing or understanding: instead of being a purely brain-centered phenomenon, it is based on meanings formed in the consciousness (in reference to the world view about objects in the situation). By accentuating the brain, the TMCE belittles the independent and individual role of the decision-maker as a free-willed person.

Furthermore, the situation and situationality of an individual stressed by the HCM are ignored in the TMCE. The relationships represented by situationality are extremely important precisely because they 'feed' the consciousness with observations or those players — termed outer senses in the TMCE. Without these concepts, the TMCE is essentially a closed system. With the help of situationality, it is possible to realize that the particular situation in which the decision-maker is located dictates, to a substantial degree, what other outer sense-type players are possibly competing with accounting information for access to the spotlight.

To conclude, the TMCE can be seen as a complementary description of some important features of the consciousness (including world view) defined in the HCM.

However, because the TMCE assumes these as features of the brain, corporeality is therefore accentuated. However, as the HCM accentuates consciousness and situationality, the end result is a fairly complete total view about a decision-maker. Taking the models together, it is clear that a decision-maker in a firm is by no means at all times such a conscious and rational actor, as assumed in the literature.

References

Baars, B.J. (1997). *In the theater of consciousness: The workspace of the mind.* Oxford: Oxford University Press.

Carr, A., & Pihlanto, P. (1998). From homo mechanicus to the holistic individual: A new phoenix for the field of organisation behaviour? in M. Afzalur Rahim, Robert T. Golembiewski and Craig C. Lundberg (eds). *Current Topics in Management*, vol. 3, 69–91. Stamford: JAI Press.

Pihlanto, P. (1989). Holistinen ihmiskäsitys ja johdon laskentatoimen aktorinäkemys [Summary: The holistic concept of man and the notion of an actor in management accounting research]. *Liiketaloudellinen Aikakauskirja [The Finnish Journal of Business Economics]*, *38*(2), 117–141.

Pihlanto, P. (1990). The holistic concept of man as a framework for management accounting research. *Publications of the Turku School of Economics and Business Administration*. Series Discussion and Working papers, 5.

Rauhala, L. (1986). Ihmiskäsitys ihmistyössä (The concept of human being in helping people). Helsinki: Gaudeamus.

Vanharanta, H., Pihlanto, P., & Chang, A.-M. (1997). Decision support for strategic management in a hyperknowledge environment and the holistic concept of man, in Ralph H. Sprague Jr. (ed.). *Proceedings of the Thirtieth Hawaii International Conference on Systems Sciences,* Vol. 5, 307–316, Advanced Technology Track. Los Alamitos, CA: IEEE Computer Society Press.

Appendix 1: The theater metaphor for conscious experience.*

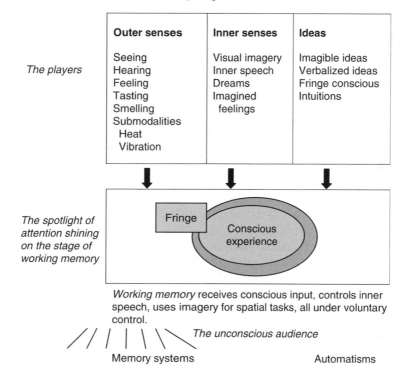

Context operators		
Director	Spotlight controller	Local contexts

Competing for access to consciousness:

Outer senses	**Inner senses**	**Ideas**
Seeing	Visual imagery	Imagible ideas
Hearing	Inner speech	Verbalized ideas
Feeling	Dreams	Fringe conscious
Tasting	Imagined	Intuitions
Smelling	feelings	
Submodalities		
Heat		
Vibration		

The players

The spotlight of attention shining on the stage of working memory

Fringe

Conscious experience

Working memory receives conscious input, controls inner speech, uses imagery for spatial tasks, all under voluntary control.

The unconscious audience

Memory systems   Automatisms

Interpreting conscious contents

Motivational systems

* Baars (1997).

Chapter 21

Accounting in Other Wor(l)ds: A Feminism Without Reserve[1]

Teri L. Shearer, *Queen's University*

C. Edward Arrington, *The University of North Carolina*

Sexual identity, like economic identity, is a product of historical systems of discourse and representation; that is, sexual identity is produced culturally and linguistically. In this sense, even the body itself is not pre- or acultural. Instead, it is a socially inscribed 'sexed' body, a body often constructed and made meaningful as either phallic (the masculine) or castrated (the feminine). Viewed in this light, sexual identity is not essential or biologistic. Instead, it is an artifact of morphology, produced through discursive effects.

Because such discursive effects are not neutral, they embed a sexual politics. Within Western culture, that politics privileges a phallic, male identity — an identity parasitic upon and dominant over female identity. To the extent that accounting is one of the dominant discursive practices within Western culture, it too is both situated within and helps enact this domain of sexual politics. A major task of this essay is to speculate upon possibilities for comprehending a feminist accounting through discernment of the sexual politics embedded within accounting's extant shape, rationality and practice.

It may seem odd to conflate domains as apparently diverse as sexual identity and accounting, though there is at least one study which does so (Burrell 1987). But accounting is a socially constructed practice that does not exist in isolation from other social practices. Its history is fluid, contingent and inextricably bound up with a range of complex moral, economic, social and discursive phenomena both inside and outside of accounting.

This essay is not concerned to advance a liberal humanist perspective. First, liberal humanist feminism becomes suspect since, teleologically, it stops at mere assimilation. Taking assimilation as its telos, liberal humanism leaves the shape, rationality and functions of accounting and its institutions intact. While liberal humanism may retain the hope that women who enter accounting may transform its practice, that 'hope' is neither theorized nor articulated. The critical challenge to

---

[1]Reproduced (in an abridged form) from T. Shearer and C. E. Arrington, 'Accounting in Other Wor(l)ds: A Feminism Without Reserve', *Accounting, Organizations and Society*, 1993, vol. 18, no. 2/3, pp. 252–272, with permission of Elsevier.

liberal humanism then becomes: 'Why would one desire assimilation into the selfsame institutions that sustain the exclusionary practices that make assimilation an issue in the first place'? Feminism easily becomes libertinism here — sharing in institutionally grounded rights to exclusionary power and oppression, becoming like the oppressors. Without a disruptive vision with respect to the institution, assimilated 'women' participate in that oppression, thereby dooming those who come after to repeat the process of victimization. In our view, this assimilatory liberalism is not 'women's' business, nor should feminist theory be used as a means to privatize ends of libertines (having a penis is not a prerequisite to be a libertine). Feminist theory ought to do more than focus on accounting's membership roster.

Hopwood (1987: 67) suggests a second approach to feminist theory and accounting, an alternative to liberal humanism. From this perspective, feminist theory becomes — 'a tradition of scholarship which seeks to explore the functioning of influential social practices and bodies of knowledge'. Such a perspective on feminist theory and its relation to accounting is consistent with the task of this essay inasmuch as we view accounting as a body of knowledge, a discursive field within which sexist pathologies might be revealed.

Accounting, Philosophy and Woman: A Poststructural Rendering of Sexual Identity

Irigaray (1985a, b, 1987) calls philosophy the 'discourse on discourse' — it is, for her, the language (the code) which articulates all the honorific categories of all the disciplines. It is in philosophy that one looks for the origins and the arguments to sustain terms like rationality, logic, order, theory, science, etc. Accounting uses these terms often, primarily because it is from philosophy that the intellectual justification for the social contracts that give rise to institutions and public life emerge; and, accounting is a discourse that serves those social contracts. Thus, there are two reasons why a feminist theory of accounting ought to deal with philosophy — accounting takes the meaning of its terms from philosophy and it takes its telos from the social contracts that emerge out of philosophy. If, as Julia Kristeva (1981) says, woman is all that has been excluded from the symbolic order (language) and the social order (social contracts), then philosophy is central to feminist theory as well as to accounting. The French feminists in general and Irigaray in particular have devoted a great deal of attention to the construal of woman in philosophy.

The *Genesis* myth is exemplary of woman's status within philosophy. It is also a fairly efficient way to narrate accounting. Adam is the *imitatio Dei*, made in the image of God, the corporeal mirror-image of all that is positive, good and legitimate. Eve, born from the gift of a rib, is always and already once removed from God, from the positive, good and legitimate, displaced and dispossessed even at the level of her corporeality. Her originality is Evil; original sin. She is woman as the untamed, natural and even evil opposition to man, God and culture (the Covenant). She is the seductive temptress that stands outside of the Law; that is, that stands on the side of nature rather than culture. Because of her 'sin', Adam, God and culture are granted sovereignty over Eve, Satan and Nature. The Law (the Covenant, the written word, the logos) exercises dominion over her. She has no voice in the matter. This myth is repeated throughout the history of philosophy. Its thematics are the granting of priority to men over women; the negation of nature; and the privilege of the word (of culture, of the abstract, of form, of order and of Law).

Accounting is the covenant, the law, of economic participation. It disciplines and controls the unruly (Eve). It grants the law priority over nature. It is hierarchical; it enforces a social order where superordinates and principals (Adams? Gods?) are granted priority over subordinates and agents (Eves? Woman?). On what grounds? Holy ones, managerial ones?

In pre-Platonic philosophy, the Pythagorean table of opposites repeats the phallocentric myth: ten contrasts, where the first term is superior to the second, are offered — limit/unlimited, odd/even, one/many, right/left, male/female, rest/motion, straight/curved, light/dark, good/bad, square/oblong. Pythagoras suggests that the first term in each exemplifies the 'superiority' of determinate form, while the second is negated as 'formless'. The Greek understanding of sexual reproduction confirmed this priority of the male as form. The father provided 'the formative principle, the real causal force of generation' and the mother provided '*only* the matter which received form or determination' (Lloyd 1984: 3, emphasis added). There was then a 'scientific' link between *sexual* priority and the priority of the 'masculine imaginary' over discourse (philosophy).

Plato's *Symposium* (where the only woman present was 'the little flute girl',) repeats the story of Adam and Pythagoras — the honorifics of the logos were the same: rationality, order, clarity, logic, form, unity, culture and closure over and against chaos, ambiguity, nature, openness, dispossession, preservation, content, the unknown and the concealed, negated attributes that philosophy has always found usefully described with the metaphor of 'woman'.

Prior to the seventeenth century, the hierarchy of male and female was somewhat taxonomic. But, through the philosophical discourse of those like Bacon, Locke and Hobbes nature becomes something to be conquered, transformed and commodified for 'human' purposes. Nature is to be tamed by man, made to be transformed through her subjection to the philosophies and 'social contracts' of the Enlightenment. It should not be surprising, then, to find the Eve myth repeated: in *The Masculine Birth of Time* (a title not unnoticed), Francis Bacon sets the Enlightenment agenda and indicates her gender — 'I am come in very truth, leading you to Nature with all her children to bind her to your service and to make her your slave' (quoted in Lloyd 1984: 12).

There are countless other examples like these. We want to point out two reasons why the negation of woman in the history of philosophy might be important to feminist theory in accounting. The first set of reasons is institutional; it has to do with parallels between philosophy's exclusion of woman and accounting's. This is of interest to liberal humanist work. The second set of reasons is discursive. This is of more interest to the kind of feminist theory that we seek for accounting.

Like philosophy, accounting is a highly specialized language of expertise — elitist and monopolized by men. There are few 'little flute girls' present to the 'conversation' of accounting and this has consequences that make a liberal humanist drive toward assimilation naïve. As Crompton (1987) points out, accounting is double coded. From the outside, there is a highly visible domain of policies, rules and expectations for accountants (policy manuals, written documents, training programmes, etc.). These are the 'official lines'. But from the inside, there is a second code, an invisible code that drives promotion and advancement. In Crompton's terms, this is 'organizational knowledge', and it has much to do with the exclusion of women that is a hallmark of accounting.

Crompton is correct, and one can look to the 'history of philosophy' — look back across two-and-a-half millennia to see just how 'deeply ingrained' exclusionary practices are as they relate to the acquisition of knowledge — philosophical, organizational or otherwise. But the question that Crompton does not address is this: 'Should the task be to seek organizational knowledge or to try and (re)imagine an alternative? Should one, like Irigaray, seek to (re)write philosophical texts (and accounting institutions) or merely seek access to them? Is the goal to participate in exclusionary practices or to subvert them? And what sort of difference does it make if women have access to clubs, schools and director's dining rooms? Men know the rules so well they don't have to rehearse them; they have been taught them since they were small boys. And, if they need to rehearse them, they certainly will find other places to speak those rules if women's presence becomes a threat. Feminist issues are for the benefit of women (of both sexes); they are not for libertines who simply want access to the reins of exclusionary power and violence.

Our second point about the relation of accounting to philosophy is more complex. It has to do with recognizing that the discourse of accounting is part and parcel to the discourse of philosophy; and, as we have seen, the meanings of the terms of that discourse embed a sexual politics. Consider first how nature, like woman, is something that is subjected to the Law of accounting; accounting assigns no value to nature until it is tamed, harnessed, commodified and (through the income calculus) literally *negated*: Nature has no value in economics (John Locke) or accounting until accounting 'makes her its slave', That is a condition of accounting and its rationality that is so deeply ingrained in our language and our practice that it seems hardly to demand reflection. But one would have to be dead today not to see how Nature is trying to speak for herself, for her own value and for 'man's' violence against her. There are no sanitizing euphemisms here — Nature has become the shitpile of an appropriative rationality (exemplary in accounting's income calculus) called global capitalism. We are not trying to lay the blame for that violence solely on accounting, but we are claiming that accounting is a discourse that contributes to that violence and we are claiming that there is no reason why the discourse of accounting has to commodify and negate nature. If that seems preposterous, we would argue that it is no more preposterous than clinging to a seventeenth-century theory of value which holds that nature *qua* nature is valueless until submitted to the commodifying and appropriative mastery of the hu[man]. We would argue that it is no more preposterous than a radical subjectivism that derives value only from a cogitating ego and its desires to appropriate utility from nature. Feminist theory (French or otherwise) contains a massive literature that aligns the negation of nature with the negation of woman and (re)imagines possibilities for value other than appropriative ones. We return to this theme later.

The priority of form over matter in philosophy is relevant to accounting's fetish for abstraction and reification. Woman has always been associated with 'coarse materiality' and formlessness and man with the abstract and ideational priority of form. That form displaces materiality from itself. Many accounting examples are available — accounting's fixation on number, its fixation on order, control and discipline, its preference for an abstract and binary calculus, one that reduces the complex materiality of economic experience to a quantifiable duality and its abstract representation of human performance in the abstract technicist jargon of norms, standards and deviance. Accounting imposes form over matter at every turn, granting positivity to abstract objectifications and diverting materiality to the negative space left in the wake of such abstractions.

This priority of form in accounting also reifies material, sensual relations between humans and between humans and their labor. Through accounting, relations between humans lose their materiality, indeed their sensuality, as they are transvalued into abstract and hierarchical relations that take on meaning only instrumentally, only in the context of the production of profits as inscribed through the calculus of accounting. All relations become instrumental, even relations to the *self*: accounting 'tends to reproduce in those subject to it a similarly instrumental orientation not only to one's own and other's actions, but more completely to one's self and others' selves' (Roberts 1988: 5). And the product of labor, to rehearse an old but profound Marxist argument, is displaced from labor, to be replaced with the most abstract of forms, the money wage.

To conclude this section, we focus on how the relation of feminist theory to philosophy might be something of a guide to critical accounting theory. First, if one construes gender as the discursive construction of woman's place within the social order, then that place is the space of negativity that philosophy has carved out for woman, a place she shares with nature and all of its philosophical cousins — formlessness, irrationality, hysteria, ambiguity, openness, etc. Any critical theory works *from* and *through* negativity: its point of departure is anything that has been negated, defined as lacking, and repressed in the history of discourse. The focus of critical theories of accounting is typically upon labor, alienation, etc., all of which are thematics that theorists like Irigaray would read as intimately related to philosophical history. Critical accounting theories can benefit from attention to the way she and others reveal the discursive and philosophical construction of negativity. Second, liberal humanists should not make the mistake of assuming that 'gender bias' or 'women's exclusion' is just a matter of *access* to accounting. The forces at work to produce exclusion are deeply embedded in language, social philosophy and ordinary experience. Our analogy between philosophy and organizational knowledge seems to illustrate that embeddedness. Third, accounting might be a useful discourse for radical feminists outside of accounting to target — it is exemplary of the honorifics that philosophy has sustained by negating their opposites (woman). Accounting, more so than most discourses, values abstraction, law, order, discipline and form quite highly.

'Which Sexuality? Whose Accounting?'

We want to close with a critical reading of Burrell's claim that accounting and sexuality are fundamentally opposed, trying to make that claim problematic in light of what we have had to say about sexuality. Sexuality is, we can now say, the pleasure of difference, of its permanent possibility, of its unfettered imagination. At one level, we agree with Burrell; at another, we do not. The difficulty with an easy opposition between accounting and sexuality is the same as the difficulty with any simple and binary opposition — the margins between the terms are too tightly drawn; and, for that reason, both terms are circumscribed too narrowly, occluding both the multiplicity of differences and the multiplicity of similarities between them. This binary style is doubly interesting given that Burrell is critical of the particularism of other feminist work in accounting (his essay is a critique of Tinker & Neimark 1987). Indeed, as Irigaray has shown, sexuality (as the term is commonly understood and as it is understood by Burrell), can be read as exemplary of accounting — Freud produces a highly accountable sexuality. Burrell, in our view, does likewise.

Burrell appeals for inquiry into the ideological and structural mechanisms at work in accounting's repression of sexuality, a repression he documents empirically. In this sense, he correctly views accounting as a metonymic example of the history of phallocentrism and its exclusionary and negating effects. Using examples that range from Pacioli's theological negation of sexuality, to technical accounting controls over sexuality not only in the factory but also at home, Burrell constructs an opposition between accounting and sexuality:

> Desire is essentially resistant to rationality. It requires free time, free space and control of one's body. It often implies privacy and does not welcome the calculating gaze of the judges of normality. In short, one can make out a case that it is everything (at least potentially) that accountancy is not. In the absence of any basis for commonality, accounting appears to have suppressed sexuality wherever it is found. If this is forgotten or ignored one cannot fully understand the relationship between men and women in organizations (1987: 99–100).

On one level, this argument works well. As we have tried to show, the history of Western thought is a history of suppression and negation of all that stands outside of the rationality, order, form, abstraction and law that it imposes. Accounting is exemplary of that history. However, the coherence of the argument depends upon resisting the attempt to bracket desire, say, or sexuality — to resist bracketing all that is different and 'pre-discursive' (Irigaray's term) within a restricted economy of singularity, of closure, of the self-same. Terms like 'desire' and 'sexuality' can carry the history of phallocentrism just as easily as terms like accounting; and, in our view, Burrell urges 'desire' and 'sexuality' into the same order, closure and phallocentrism that he attributes to accounting:

> What is defined as 'sexuality', the range of emotion and activity it is deemed to cover and what is socially acceptable or seen as perverted may all vary in time and space but if one identifies sexuality with sexual intercourse, then the *maintenance of an 'essentialist' perspective which assumes a homogeneity of sexuality is just about possible* (Burrell 1987: 91, emphasis added).

We agree. If one assumes an essentialist definition of sexuality, then the result is indeed sexual homogeneity. What counts as sexuality and desire, what is excluded from sexuality and desire, in short, all difference is accountable to the sociologist's desire for closure, for a clear, precise, observable and operational term that accommodates itself to one's theory. One is left with a phallocratic rationality that differs hardly at all from accounting. By assuming singularity in what is meant by the sexual *act* (and perhaps desire and sexuality as well), Burrell silences difference. Difference requires an opening of space, not a closure. Why would one want an essentialist perspective on sexuality? In our view, Burrell falls prey to the same phallocentric rationality that he sought to critique — a rationality of discursive closure, a rationality of accounting.

In fairness to Burrell's text, he is aware of the difficulty that radical difference (and a radical feminist theory like Irigaray's) poses. Using the term 'disciplinary mode' where we use phallocentric discourse, he points out the pathological way in which critique adds energy to the growth of discipline (adds to the phallocentric):

> But does this mean that the newer radicalized versions of accounting theory must also contribute to the growth of discipline?... The paradox here is that discourse, the discussion, analysis and critique of writings and lectures, itself is part of the development of the disciplinary mode. To dissect existing literature and to replace it with one's own, even if it is self-consciously anti-disciplinarian, is to add to the volume of discourse on accounting and to enhance its capacity to subject us all to its gaze. For alternative judgements of normality... are still judgements on normality. They continue to outline correct behaviour and to criticize existing standards. They classify, standardize and conceptualize in ways which add to 'power-knowledge' (Burrell 1987: 98).

Again we agree. But it strikes us that orienting desire and sexuality toward essentialist definitions so that critical work can follow the protocols of acceptable social science is more guilty of this denegatory normalization than, say, deconstructive techniques like Irigaray's — techniques which are the antithesis of essentialism, of closure and of hard evidence, techniques which problematize whole categories by blurring the epistemological matrix that partitions science, literature, philosophy, art, etc., ways of writing that, to borrow from Derrida, disrupt the 'apartheid' of the modern university — a place that keeps scientists, artists, poets, accountants, sociologists, etc. in their assigned regions, that keeps them accountable. Some writings do not, in fact, 'outline correct behavior'.

Burrell raises similar questions with respect to the Tinker and Neimark text that he critiques:

> Academics in the profession [accounting] are unlikely to debate the issue and may even be blind to it. It is an occupational hazard and suggests that Tinker and Neimark's neglect of sexuality...may have its origins in their immersions in their own professional arena (Burrell 1987).

And we might ask the same question of sociologists perhaps? It seems, for Burrell, that 'the only way out from discipline is to forsake academic discourse entirely — a state of affairs few of us would welcome unreservedly' (Burrell: 99). Really?

Why not challenge the authority of the university to impose such discipline? Why grant the academy license over what counts and what does not count as academic discourse? After all, some of the finest work comes from those excluded from the academy either voluntarily (e.g. Wittgenstein) or violently (most of the Jewish tradition between the wars). What is so precious about that tradition that one must participate in it all the while denying its truth value, all the while recognizing its complicity in victimization? Why not, like Derrida or Irigaray (who quit the university) stand in the tradition of Socrates, Nietzsche, Heidegger and others that to differing degrees refused the rules of the game (of all of the games?). The problem is not that two accountants (Tinker & Neimark 1987) trying to write a paper on socialist feminism are blind to sexuality; the problem is that academic discourse (including sociology) cannot make room for difference, cannot resist the phallocentric urge to hold all difference (desire? sexuality?) accountable.

Hope

> Hope cannot aim at making the mutilated social character of women identical to the mutilated social character of men; rather its goal must be a state...in which all that survives the disgrace of the difference between the sexes is the happiness that difference makes possible (Theodor Adorno 1967: 82).

> I am trying...to go back through the masculine imaginary, to interpret the way in which it has reduced us to silence, to muteness or mimicry, and I am attempting, from that starting point, to (re)discover a possible space for the feminine imaginary (Irigaray 1985a: 164).

References

Adorno, T. (1967). *Prisms.* Cambridge: MIT Press.
Burrell, G. (1987). No accounting for sexuality. *Accounting, Organizations and Society*, 89–101.
Crompton, R. (1987). Gender and accountancy: A response to tinker and neimark. *Accounting, Organizations and Society*, 103–110.
Hopwood, A. (1987). Accounting and gender: An introduction. *Accounting, Organizations and Society*, 65–69.
Irigaray, L. (1985a). *This sex which is not one* (translated by C. Porter). Ithaca: Cornell University Press.
Irigaray, L. (1985b). *Speculum of the other woman* (translated by G.C. Gill). Ithaca: Cornell University Press.
Irigaray, L. (1987). Sexual difference, in *French feminist thought: A reader.* Oxford: Blackwell.
Kristeva, J. (1981). Women's time. *Signs: Journal of Women in Culture and Society*, 13–35.
Lloyd, G. (1984). *The man of reason: Male and 'female' in western philosophy.* Minneapolis: University of Minnesota Press.
Roberts, J. (1988). The possibilities of accountability. Paper presented at *The Second Interdisciplinary Perspectives on Accounting Conference*. The University of Manchester.
Tinker, T., & Neimark, M. (1987). The role of annual reports in gender and class contradictions at general motors: 1917–1976. *Accounting, Organizations and Society*, 71–88.

Chapter 22

CATS, RATS and EARS: Making the Case for Ethnographic Accounting Research[1]

Sten Jönsson,   *University of Gothenburg*

Norman B. Macintosh,   *Queen's University*

Trust (Sten)

Suppose you had just completed the field phase of a study of a 'lean' production control system. A team of friendly managers had provided you with a host of system specifications, definitions of variables, design and frequency of reports, incentive mechanisms — everything. You were just packing up to leave, convinced that you had all the material you need to write a perfectly logical and publishable article, even if it was based on a case. In the objectivist view the test of knowledge gives the observer epistemological privilege. Knowledge is to be able to describe a phenomenon in a way that fits theory by using concepts and definitions provided by that theory.

Then, when you turn towards the door your principal informant says: 'Of course it wouldn't work if we did not trust people'! You say, 'Yes, of course'! and leave. You think about what she or he said on your way home. You talk to a colleague who says: 'Yes, of course! Any lean production model is built on the assumption that people can be trusted. Otherwise you couldn't be sure that decisions are carried out as intended...and even if they were not, this lean production control system is designed to monitor performance so that corrections can be applied quickly. Otherwise the effects of deviations would spread'.

Your colleague hesitates, realizing that the argument assumes that which it is supposed to provide. Now you are convinced that you have to find out what your friendly informant means by the statement that 'It wouldn't work without trust'. You talk about trust and your informant is adamant that it is possible to know whom to trust and that with some people it is an insult to check up on them if what

---

[1]Reproduced (in an abridged form) from S. Jönsson and N. Macintosh, 'CATS, RATS and EARS: Making the Case for Ethnographic Accounting Research', *Accounting, Organizations and Society*, 1977, vol. 22, no. 3/4, with permission of Elsevier.

they tell you is true. It is also a principle with your informant that one must never betray given trust. The cost would be prohibitive.

'But surely', you say, 'if the system shows that a trusted person does not perform to standard ... Then I would suspend judgement until I was very sure of that ... But, you said that the whole idea with this lean production control system was real time and that deviations could be dealt with quickly! ... Well you can't interfere with people you trust, not without good reason ...'

You decide to make a study of whether trust is good for the system or vice versa, and which direction — trusting or betraying trust — is the primary one in real organizational life. You want to design a study to understand how trust is created and betrayed in the use of a lean production control system.

Only after such a study has been carried out is it possible to write that article about lean production control systems in use! But then you realize that you want to know not only the principles necessary to give an account of how trust relations work, you also need to know how to enter into a trusting relationship with the operators of a lean production system. You want to be able not only to give an account of the essential features of the practices, an *opus operatum*, but also of the generative principles of the practices, their *modus operandi*.

In short, trust seems to be a concept that can only be described in terms of examples and discourse. It relates closely to responsibility, competence, interaction, roles, expectations, sincerity, etc. It seems reasonable to try to record interaction and analyze, together with the participants, how actions and responses affect trust in order to get a first approximation of the phenomenon. Objective, scientific measurement seems hardly possible.

Ethnographic Research (Norman)

What Sten is saying is that maybe the best way to research trust is to conduct an ethnographic study. Ethnographic research in general involves intensive, face-to-face participant observation in natural settings over long time period. The aim is to produce a systematic narrative of the behavior and idea systems of the actors in a particular culture, organization, profession, or community of some sort including their conceptions, discursive practices and interrelationships with each other. The central idea is to get as close as possible to the participants in the community that the research is going to describe. This means the researcher must 'live-in' with members of the community for some time to experience in real time and space the ebb and flow of their social existence. So the resulting narrative is based on the first hand involvement by the researcher in the social setting being described. It provides a rich and thick portrayal of a way of life, a narrative that can be read and understood by people outside and inside the community. 'Walk their walk, talk their talk, and write their story' is the researcher's motto.

So, the hallmark of ethnographic research is that it is *representational, interpretive* and *rhetorical*. Representational means to tell stories, narrate lives and provide context in a thick and substantive way. Interpretive means to set forth categories, make comparisons and interpret symbols and rituals. While rhetorical means to bring the distinctive social world into some sort of textual order that not only pleases the reader but, more importantly, produces a concrete, sharp and complex portrait of life in the community, one that persuades the reader that the narrative can be trusted and that '...this is life as it is lived by real people, in real time and in real places' (Putnam *et al.* 1993: 224). The narrative's validity rests not only on any specific theory or data base, but on its plausibility and aesthetic appeal.

The final distinguishing feature of ethnography is that the researcher, unlike his or her critical or rational theory counterpart, does not set out particularly to enlighten or emancipate members of the community from coercive and exploitive social relationships. (Although if this occurs as a result of the narrative, all the better.) This does not mean, however, that the poor, the voiceless, the dispossessed, the stigmatized or the disinherited are ignored. Merely that the underdog does not necessarily get center stage. The reason for this is that the research goals emerge in the field as the study progresses. There are no pre-given aims except to write a thick and convincing description.

Ethnography, however, is by no means a coherent, unified and monolithic research genre. In fact there are several different brands each of which has somewhat different aims and focuses. Silverman (1985) offers a useful typology consisting of three types — cognitive anthropology, symbolic interactionism and ethnomethodology. If the signature of cognitive anthropology is a focus on the communicating habits of the natives (intercourse and speaking), the hallmark of the interactionist is the attempt to zero in on their shared thinking (symbolic constructs), while the stamp of ethnomethodology is a concentration on their doings (social practices). Key characteristics of each are summarized in Table 22.1.

Table 22.1: Distinguishing features of three main ethnographic genres.

Research Characteristics	Cognitive Anthropology	Interaction	Ethnomethodology
Main concern	How actors communicate	What actors are thinking — how they make their actions meaningful	How actors choose to do what they do
Particular focus	What counts as communicative competence	The concepts and symbols actors use to conduct their social life	The orderly patterned character of actors' every day social practices
Describe in detail	The natives' speaking and listening habits	The actors' inter-subjective or shared symbolic world	The form of the actors' sense assembly equipment

Cognitive Anthropology

Cognitive anthropology is concerned primarily with the individual's communicative competence within a particular culture. So, the cognitive anthropologist aims to describe everything an actor needs to know and believe in order to communicate in a way that is acceptable to the other actors in the culture. The researcher tries to comprehend the culturally appropriate concepts through which the members conduct their social life and write a story (a narrative) about the essence of the actors' communicative competence, including both the implicit knowledge of the language that the actors use as well as what constitutes adequate performance in speaking or writing that language. Both knowledge and proper use of language are needed in order to cope socially in the culture. The cognitive anthropologist's narrative, straddling two cultures by first making sense of observations in one culture and then reporting in a way that makes sense in the other culture, tries to capture that native communicative knowledge of 'the beaten track' — what one has to know about language in order to communicate, speak and write effectively in that culture.

Frake's (1964) study of the beer drinking ceremony of the Subanun pagan community in a remote part of the Philippines is vintage cognitive anthropology. The ceremony is a mandatory part of any festive gathering. Participants take turns in drinking from a large jar of fermented mash keeping the jar topped up with water which picks up large amounts of alcohol. The ceremony involves several stages — jar talk, appreciating the beer, gossip about the community, serious deliberation on important issues and finally displays of singing, verbal skills and artistry. The most skilful players become *de facto* leaders in the community and are trusted to settle disputes and rule on important community decisions. 'In instructing our strangers to Subanun society how to ask for a drink, we have at the same time instructed him how to get ahead socially' (132). The most skillful drinkers are trusted in the community to take on leadership roles.

Interactionist Sociology

Interactionist sociology is at base concerned with providing rich descriptions of the way in which the actors in a culture create, reproduce and at times change the culture's symbolic order by way of social interaction. If the hallmark of cognitive anthropology is a concern for forms of communication, then the distinguishing feature of interactionist sociology is its concentration on the ordinary aspects of the social system under analysis, particularly the small talk and other normal daily social interactions of the ordinary actor. The interactionist researcher focuses on capturing the process, not the form, by which the actors construct meaning since social reality is taken to be continually established symbolically during interaction. Interactionists take the viewpoint of the social actors and describe the situated character of their interactions over time and the meanings they share.

Becker *et al.*'s (1961) ethnography of first-year medical school is considered a classic interactionist study in which the students defined and redefined their symbolic order over several stages. The students entered the program in a highly idealistic frame of mind. This soon collided with the realities of a crushing workload and a relentless round of lectures, labs and exams. At this stage, the student community shifted to a 'learn it all' mentality featuring hard work, long hours and neglect of family and social life. Students saw themselves as 'learning machines'. This phase soon faded as the student community's values shifted to a resentful survival mentality of playing cat-and-mouse with the faculty. They divided up work chores, copied assignments and shared crib notes. The final stage saw the students coming together in a united front where medical school symbolized finding out what the faculty wanted and learning it in the most efficient way. At the same time, importantly, the students did not lose their idealism—they merely put in on hold. Over time, then, trust in the faculty went from idealistic trust, resentful distrust, to trust yourself and play the game.

Ethnomethodology

Ethnomethodology overlaps in its aims with cognitive anthropology and interactionism, but it has important differences in terms of its methodological drive to base conclusions in observable data. Ethnomethodologists are more interested in describing what actors are doing socially than with what they are thinking (interactionists) or how they are communicating (cognitive anthropologists). They are interested in understanding how actors jointly define the character of an event and how they sustain (or change) those meanings. So they try to capture the ways in which actors achieve commitment, trust, or whatever 'is going on' in the social interaction under study. The aim is to discover the situated rationality of the actors' mundane, every day social practices in order to describe the sense-assembly equipment they use to construct and to sustain their daily procedures, practices and stocks of social knowledge. The goal is to produce particularistic accounts of the common sense procedures actors use in situated contexts.

Jönsson's (1982) study of budgetary behavior in a city government illustrates the ethnomethodological approach used in an accounting study. By scrutinizing the different budget documents, observing the ongoing debate in the decision-making body as background information, and getting weekly comments from one key informant (the chief budget officer) regarding recent events, the current situation, and the expected initiatives of actors, Jönsson mapped the 'budgetary game' played by the participants over three budget cycles. The concurrent comments by the inside informant allowed reliable observation of how politicians and department heads used the rules of the budget game to promote their own claims in a series where overplaying one's cards in one year resulted in the loss of trustworthiness and reprisals in the next, and of how the need for reformulating the rules grew as actors became adroit at the game.

A key finding concerned trust. In the second year, when the final budget negotiations took place during as well as after the election campaign, the participants experienced a decline in their trust of the rules of the game. A shift had occurred in the City Hall majority when the election was won on promises which the previous majority claimed were contrary to positions taken in the closed budget planning sessions. This was seen by the losing side as a betrayal of commitments. They felt they were taken by surprise during the last weeks of the campaign and, not surprisingly, later on experienced budget cycle 'disillusionment'.

In the third year, the new majority were able to implement a budget reform and increase taxes while claiming mismanagement by the old majority. Moreover, expenditure levels were on the increase and department managers were learning to use the new rules of the budget game to improve their own positions. The research indicated that the actors had learnt how to improve their performance in the budget game, but little evidence emerged to indicate that budgets were being used better in any reasonable sense.

In the foregoing sections, we briefly described three genres of ethnographic research. This methodology differs significantly from both CATS and RATS studies. In the next section Norman tries to set up a 'conversation' between CATS, EARS and RATS.

CATS, EARS and RATS (Norman)

CATS also focus on meaning construction and trust. In fact, CATS researchers are primarily concerned with the way accounting meanings get played out in organizations and institutions in the context of power relations. They describe how meaning comes to be politically mediated and how competing interest groups differ in their ability to produce and reproduce vital meaning systems, such as accounting ones, which construct social reality. This seems *prima facie* just the right approach for researching accounting and trust. But EARS argue against such a proposition. A brief review of the premises motivating CATS research will serve to put this rebuff into perspective.

The hallmark of CATS is its focus on the power acts of constructing and interpreting meaning in organizations and institutions by means of accounting and control systems. CATS attempt to show how these systems, with their power relations, produce a sense of closure for organizational participants who come to accept the *status quo* as natural and immutable. These researchers aim to strip back the veneer from the surface of what seems a stable social reality, one that participants take for granted, and to reveal the class and interest group struggles operating below the surface layer. The *status quo* is seen as a web of social relations erected on an invariant foundation whose structure a critical theory analysis can reveal and explain. The key research question is always 'Why that way of life and not some other'?

This question is posed in order to invoke the enlightening and emancipatory moves that critical theorists believe are mandatory and inevitable. So researcher interpretations are taken to be legitimate, only if they induce the agents in the social system to engage in self-reflection and re-evaluation of the conditions of their social existence. The stance is always critical of the *status quo*. The chains binding social relations *must* be uncovered and they *must* come off.

The other major characteristic of CATS is its presupposition of a foundational and commensurable theory. It is foundationalist in that it asserts that analysis of a social order must have a firm theoretical grounding and in that it posits *ex ante* the presence of ubiquitous deep structures running below the surface of daily social existence, which organize the reality of social relations and which produce a coercive and exploitive existence for most agents. The commensurability impulse refers to the belief that a critical theory should be brought under one set of rules which will allow researchers to reach agreement on every point in their narrative.

So CATS researchers aim to demonstrate how accounting systems are part of the control apparatuses of an exploitive and coercive social order. The ultimate goal is to enlighten academics, practitioners and students alike about this underside of the accounting world. Such an idealistic impulse holds out the hope of a more democratic, humanistic and less coercive world. While few of us would argue against such aims, CATS' epistemological and ontological presuppositions, EARS content, do not seem well suited for researching trust including the role accounting plays in moderating trustful relationships.

EARS on CATS

EARS see several major drawbacks to the CATS position. For ontology, the latter treat the vast majority of participants in organizations as people who lack the ability to understand, let alone express, the nature of their social existence at work and who do not understand the power relations which bind and exploit them. Moreover, most CATS research is conducted in the researcher's office at a comfortable and safe distance from the field. So they have no first-hand data of how participants actually feel and think about accounting systems and their related trust (or mistrust) relationships in the work place. The individual's being is simply presupposed to be in accordance with the commensurable set of rules of the particular critical theory at hand. For EARS, such presuppositions fly in the face of what participants actually say about their experiences in organizations.

The epistemological drawback is that the result of CATS research is always given before the research starts because the research story is built around a pre-given theory. Political economy and labor process accounting studies start out assuming that the capital accumulation process and capitalist forces of production determine the essence of social relations and the individual's being. Regarding trust, such theories dictate that the capitalists do not trust the workers (and so must appropriate for themselves the knowledge of both the technical and financial information regarding the production process) and they also use accounting information to press workers (who the capitalists believe cannot be trusted to do an honest day's work) for ever more output in order to usufruct the fruits of their labor. In return, the workers do not trust the owner's concerns for their welfare, or if they do, they are suffering from self-delusion and false-consciousness. That is the story, regardless of what any of these parties actually says, thinks, or does.

Another drawback EARS claim is that CATS assume that the monolithic capitalistic mode of production works in pretty much the same way in, say, Sweden, Canada, USA, Singapore and Israel as it does in Britain. One only has to look below the surface to unmask the indubitable infrastructure that induces a coercive, exploitative and class divided social terrain around the globe. Similarly for hegemonic CATS, the pejorative ideology of a powerful elite is carried in accounting reports to its destination — the agents in society—where it works to chain them to a set of tainted ideas and to delude them of their true interests. There is a reality out there and that reality is coercive and exploitive. All the researcher has to do then is, acting like an organizational psychotherapist, pull back this hypothetical tarpaulin and expose these deep structures that organize and structure the social terrain.

In consequence, the results of any CATS research tend to take on a commodified nature. They start with the same story, end with the same result, and so come across more like a prepackaged ideology than a theory. What leverage does such universalizing positivism give us for researching trust? Not a lot, EARS researchers warrant. We usually do not know anything more about trust and accounting after reading the results than we did before.

The CATS Come-back

CATS scholars, however, are usually little moved by these criticisms. So it seems unlikely that many of them will discard their foundational and commensurable theories and scramble for the field to produce thick descriptions of conversations with actors. It is more likely that they will invoke the traditional critique of EARS. After all, scholars are supposed to argue with each other. Two aspects of EARS are particularly acute for them.

The first worry concerns the method and grounds of knowledge upon which EARS researchers rely. The hard technical problem confronting EARS researchers is that they are compelled to use, as their sole research instrument, the very apparatus they study — language and conversation. So, they are vulnerable to the sort of hazard facing physicists ever since Heisenberg pointed out that the experimental method was not separate from the outcome, but rather that it determined the results (particles act like individual bits of matter or they act like waves — it all depends on the research experiment employed).

So, the closer EARS researchers come to understanding the problem under investigation, such as trust, the more they must manipulate the very mechanism with which they are researching — conversation and language. And just when they get close to some answer, they realize they must somehow trust the conversation they are engaged in with the agents. At this moment, the hermeneutic circle problematic kicks in and the answer gets blurry. Without some firm theoretical foundation upon which to ground the results, there is no way of telling whether or not the narrative is sense or nonsense. Rather, the results are merely an endless reiteration of the researcher's and the actors' subjective interpretations — an imbroglio of subjectivity.

The hermeneutic circle problem refers to the circular way knowledge and meaning get constructed by researchers in the hermeneutic sciences. Hermeneuticians begin with a particular text and a preliminary projection about its whole meaning. They then 'take offense' at the text when parts of it make no sense or are irreconcilable in terms of the preliminary projection of the whole meaning. This leads to a better understanding of what is there in the text and then the preliminary projection is revised accordingly so as to accommodate the offensive part. 'The circle keeps rotating' (Weinsheimer 1985: 23) as the hermeneutician penetrates further into the text's overall meaning.

Similarly, EARS researchers treat the collective subjectivity of the actors in the community under observation as a text and assume a priori that it has some whole meaning which is revised to accommodate insights gained from observations and conversations with particular actors. They too, as with the hermeneuticians, proceed in a circular way from a preliminary projection of the overall meaning to the parts (the actors' descriptions of their social world) which leads to a revision of the former. The circle continues until the parts, in the main, are reconciliable with and do not take offense at the whole meaning. This contrasts sharply with the linear method of the physical sciences where the researcher gets a theory, selects a hypothesis, sets up a decisive experiment, and either accepts (for now) the hypothesis or rejects it on the basis of the results. For CATS, by relying on the hermeneutic method, the narratives EARS produce about the collective subjectivity of the actors are little more than flotsam and jetsam on a circling sea of subjectivity.

Another closely related major epistemological issue concerns the assumption by EARS researchers that they can produce a neutral description of the 'way things are' for the agents in the social system under investigation. For CATS, the very idea that one can be a mere neutral recorder of the way others see the world is an impossibility. Like the proverbial monkey-on-the-back, theoretical presuppositions always come along for the ride. Moreover, these serve as value criteria which always ground interpretation. They are the material which makes possible the very act of constructing a narrative about social relations. So when an EARS researcher produces a compelling narrative, it has to arise from the way the researcher brings these inevitable theoretical presuppositions to bear. There is no neutral, objective, position to occupy. A story (text, narrative) of any kind, is inevitably theoretically and politically grounded. Storytellers must stand on some conceptual infrastructure, speak from some political power station, and (inevitably) enjoy some privileged status. Even if researchers do not realize it, EARS always involves more than just 'telling a good story'.

The same goes for the stories the actors in the community tell to each other and to the researcher. Meaning is more than just what gets manifested in a community's symbols, rituals, languages and discursive practices. It is also politically mediated. So, CATS contend, researchers must look closely at the relationship between the communicative practices of a particular social system and its power relationships with the wider world at large. Moreover, producing a narrative about a community's meaning system is never just an act of translating and interpreting the beliefs, actions and communication habits of the actors. It is first and foremost a political act. Words are power.

This criticism is the driving idea behind critical theory's literary turn. Meaning, CATS insist, gets played out in the context of power relations in which the various interest groups in the community differ in their ability to produce and reproduce discourses and systems of meaning, including accounting, that shape the organizational reality. Understanding the dynamics of a community's deep domination and legitimation structures, as a research goal does not simply appear in front of the researcher in the field. As with the truffle (that delightfully edible subterranean fungus coveted by master chefs and gourmets), the harvester cannot simply spot them lying on the forest floor; they must be sniffed out and unearthed by a trained (and muzzled) pig. Similarly, CATS assert, EARS researchers in the field will never find these domination structures unless they go looking for them as an explicit goal.

EARS on RATS

EARS also see RATS as trained by *ex ante* foundationalism with the issue of trust settled beforehand. In the case of agency theory, for example, the principal (owner) does not at all trust the agent (manager). The fundamental notion is that the agent will use private or hidden information opportunistically and with guile in obtaining and performing a contract with the principal.

Once under contract, the agent undertakes similar untrustworthy actions including the adverse selection, moral hazard, the excessive perquisite consumption and the shirking-on-the-job responses. The owner can circumvent these — but only at a cost — by acquiring trustworthy accounting information, sharing output or buying insurance. It also seems reasonable, although agency theory seldom addresses the matter, that the owner is also untrustworthy since she or he has access to private (hidden) crucial information and would be expected to use it strategically to pursue self-interest with guile in negotiating an enforceable contract which is sub-optimal for the manager.

Ironically, then, agency theory works on the basis of trust — both parties trust that the other party will *not* trust them. Both parties, however, do trust accounting information for monitoring the contract. What gets left out of the theory is that if the agent actually is trustworthy, does not exploit hidden information and does tell the truth, then transaction costs (e.g. buying information, bonding and output sharing) are incurred without benefit. Either way, however, trust — or rather *un-trust* — the basic presupposition in agency theory, is settled prior to the start of an agency theory research study.

CATS, RATS and EARS: Where to? (Norman and Sten)

While clearly there are fundamental differences between CATS and EARS, there are also important but often overlooked points of agreement. For one thing, both stand in opposition to the presuppositions of RATS such as those of agency theory in which mistrust and self-interest play a central role and are taken to be innate, self-regulating characteristics of managers who automatically and chronically misrepresent their abilities, hoard strategic information, consume perquisites excessively and shirk on effort.

In contrast, for CATS mistrust (and trust) is not in-born and inevitable but rather arises from social relations in a class-divided society. CATS also believe that all people have the human potential for trust and altruism whereby they regard others and themselves, as a principle, as capable of unselfish action. While for EARS, both trust and mistrust are human characteristics that stem from cultural norms and rights and which can be built-up or destroyed locally by agents in a particular culture.

CATS and EARS also stand in opposition to the RATS assertion that management accounting systems provide neutral, objective facts and data to managers who then use them to make rational (or at least boundedly rational) decisions. Such a picture is ruled out in favor of one that highlights how political, strategic and morality dimensions are brought into play to shape or even distort accounting reports. In this regard, CATS researchers argue that accounting is an important weapon in the hands of elite groups who use them to exploit and coerce the *hoi polloi*, while EARS tend to see accounting information as ammunition for competing groups in the inevitable political tug-of-war over ends and means. Both CATS and EARS pay particular attention to power and morality and the struggle over the rules guiding the *status quo* while RATS either take them as given or ignore them.

Another important similarity between CATS and EARS is that both give place of privilege to meaning construction, interpretation and language. EARS researchers see their craft as interpretive, figurative, representational and rhetorical. They '... tell stories, narrate lives, provide context, set forth categories, interpret symbols, and more generally, bring a more or less distinct social world into some kind of textual order...' and they consider their narratives to be valid and trustworthy if it persuades readers that '... this is life as it is lived by real people, in real times, and in real places' (Putnam *et al.* 1993: 224). Research must not be trapped in preconceived rigid theories about what drives the participants or what is good for them. The main concern for EARS is to understand how the actors construct meaning and interpret their social world.

CATS researchers also emphasize the importance of meaning construction and interpretation. They focus on the way meaning gets played out in the context of unequal power relations and how various interest groups and classes differ in their ability to control vital meaning systems, such as accounting ones, in order to shape and tilt organizational reality in their favor. For CATS, meaning is more than just what gets manifested in the organization's traditions, rituals, myths and discursive practices. Meaning is also the unfurling of power relations that underlie and shape these cultural elements. So it is not good enough that EARS researchers 'tell a believable story'. Any story, including those produced by EARS, is always politically and theoretically grounded. A theory-less and neutral story is an impossibility. Moreover, and crucially, the story may be false.

CATS and EARS, however, share the general ontological assumption that structures running below the surface of social existence shape actors' social interactions and actions including their communication patterns and discourses. For EARS, each particular culture has its own unique codes (blueprints) that organize (structure) social action and interaction as individuals draw on them by means of customary rules, norms and resources. (These codes are unique to each culture rather than universal as for RATS.) But for CATS, in contrast, these cultural codes always rest on top of deeper, more fundamental structures (such as the ideology of capitalism or the code book of the ruling elite) which hegemonically program the life world. Cultures are simply containers for these deep structures which EARS researchers have no way to uncover. So while RATS, CATS and EARS assume that underlying structures play a crucial role, they disagree on their basic nature.

What can Interpretive Studies do for Management Accounting? (Sten)

Bruner (1990) argues that we use two modes of ordering experience and of constructing reality — the paradigmatic and the narrative mode. The paradigmatic mode, followed by CATS and RATS, is rational and deductive. It involves deducing particular outcomes from general laws and well-defined concepts. It also involves discovery of new areas of application of those laws and, to a certain extent, testing and correcting the laws. However, experience tells us that empirical evidence seldom, if ever, is enough to disconfirm core assumptions in most theories on accounting and economic behavior. Logical argument and rigorous proof, the veneer of the scientific method, gives persuasive power to this mode.[2]

In contrast, the narrative mode constructs stories that give credible accounts of the world of actors' experience and how they maintain their roles and identities. These stories illustrate how human actors give meaning to their experience. So interpretive research provides reports about how actors feel and think and establish what is canonical in a given society — what is expected of a member.

This truth concept in the narrative mode should be looked upon as pragmatic (Mead 1934; James 1974; Rorty 1979). It relates to subjective interactionism in that if it works in your experience, if you are ready to act on this new insight after having been frustrated, then the information in the narrative has meaning and truth value in

---

[2]Ironically, however, as Lyotard (1984) observes, the scientific method of constructing knowledge only gains legitimacy by calling on a narrative. The irony is that while science was determined to get away from story-telling, it could only legitimate itself in virtue of its own metanarrative of science and rationality.

a pragmatic sense. If action fails, data will be reconsidered, but if it succeeds, this experiential confirmation will constitute learning and the portfolio of practices may even expand. Repeated successful action will 'prime' behavioral patterns of actors, organizations and cultures making them more likely to be evoked in similar circumstances in the future. They become what Giddens (1984) calls routine situations during which social structures are regrooved.

Given such a view of learning through narrativizing experience, it is not difficult to imagine what a traumatic experience reorganizations or changes of accounting and information flows can be for actors or groups of actors. As Mead claimed:

> In everyday life people freely create accounts of their world, but many of these accounts would not receive strong empirical support. Scientific accounts gain credibility only after they are tested repeatedly and demonstrate their usefulness. And even the most reliable of scientific accounts are accepted only as provisional truths, always open to reconstruction as new data and unexpected events emerge (Baldwin 1986: 22).

But unexpected events do happen a lot of time. So the narrative mode of accounting for them may be a useful way of developing the theory construction of an area without prior demolition of the whole structure. (It is assumed the theory has a consistent and integrated structure!)

This means that CATS and RATS formulation of trust in organizations and trust in accounting systems can be problematized by EARS studies forcing them to reconceptualize their theories and basic presuppositions. Make them get closer to the ground, so to speak. Thus, while interpretive studies usually do not claim generality of conclusions or even universality, they can introduce proposals for reinterpretation of theoretical claims, identify problems with current knowledge and propose prospects for new research.

An even more pervasive point about such accounting studies is that they typically generate narratives. So, their capacity to persuade rests with their internal consistency and the degree of interest in the 'message' they can arouse. And if EARS researchers can be induced to work close to current theoretical discourse, the likelihood that CATS and RATS colleagues will respond to presented narratives will increase along with their relevance to current theoretical discourse. In this way EARS research can enrich the vocabulary of the theoretical world.

Towards Interactive EARS–CATS Research (Norman)

What Sten is proposing is that we can use ethnographic studies to interrogate and even problematize critical theories. This research would enable accounting ethnographers to go beyond merely producing narratives about the 'natives' subjectivity to include insights into the way these subjectivities come to be constituted. Such an expanded narrative, Power believes, would 'need to be self-critical' (1991: 350) in regards to any claims made about the distorted communications alleged to have stemmed from some kind of ideological colonization of the natives' lifeworld. It would also have to remain constantly sensitive to the potential danger of the results being determined before the field work even begins by some pre-given critical theory. As with Power, we encourage researchers to try for some kind of dialogue between the story that emerges from the field research and currently on-top critical theories.

Our proposal also differs in one important respect. We advocate an extended research strategy whereby the field narrative is produced and then used to interrogate, reinterpret and perhaps alter current versions of critical accounting theories. Such a dialogue between natives' subjectivity and critical theories could enrich both.

Concluding Comments (Norman and Sten)

Returning, after this tour of possible EARS approaches, and having weighed their pros and cons against those of CATS and RATS, to the matter of studying how trust interacts with the intended use of accounting systems, a first conclusion to draw is that the main problem in discussions of whether this method is more or less 'scientific' than that one, is usually mixed up because people are unable to keep the demarcation between ontology and epistemology clear. What makes researchers believe in the superiority of this or that method seems to relate strongly to their ontological assumptions.

Assume that we take the statement 'that the management control system would not work without trust' seriously. If we let this ontological assumption constitute our study, we would bring 'trust' to the foreground. The intended decision support function for rational managers that guided the system designers would provide background. Alternatively, we could push the ontological assumptions of RATS about rational decision making to the foreground and use 'mis-trust' as a candidate explanation of irrational behavior. The conduct of inquiry would be quite different in the two cases.

Still, in the practical research situation, ontology would keep interfering with epistemology — figure the ground, as it were. This problem is confounded by typologists (like ourselves), who 'define' boxes where scholarly products and their producers are pigeon-holed. A real challenge for EARS researchers is to find ways to determine whether trust and accounting are phenomena on different levels of analysis and therefore should be studied in this figure-ground fashion or are mutually constitutive and thus something we, with Wittgenstein, should not talk about — at least until we know more.

In conclusion, it seems that narratives can be powerful tools for opening up new areas of inquiry in stabilized and well established fields of knowledge, especially when ontological assumptions are questioned. While the willingness to throw established theoretical systems overboard is limited, new complementary lines of research may be opened. And who knows, it may be possible to put together new genres of research into something like a critical ethnography entailing critical descriptions of accounting practices in today's organizations where such systems may be discussed as instruments of discipline and control while recognizing that they also act as necessary social bonding materials. So it is our hope that this paper clears some space for constructive conversations between CATS, RATS and EARS. Otherwise we will continue to pass like ships in the night.

References

Baldwin, J.D. (1986). George *Herbert Mead: A unifying theory of sociology*. Newbury Park, CA: Sage.

Becker, H.S., Geer, B., Hughes, E.G., & Strauss, A.L. (1961). *Boys in white*. Chicago: University of Chicago Press.

Bruner, J. (1990). *Acts of meaning*. Cambridge: Harvard University Press.

Frake, C.O. (1964). How to ask for a drink in Subanun. *American Anthropologist*, 127–32.

Giddens, A. (1984). *The constitution of society*. Berkeley: University of California Press.

James, M. (1974). *Pragmatism — And four essays from the meaning of truth*. New York: New American Library (original 1907).

Jönsson, S. (1982). Budgetary behavior in local government — a case study over 3 years. *Accounting, Organizations and Society*, vol. 7, 287–304.

Lyotard, J.-F. (1984). *The postmodern condition: A report on knowledge*. Minneapolis: University of Minnesota Press.

Mead, G.H. (1934). *Mind, self and society: From the standpoint of a social behaviorist*. Chicago: University of Chicago Press.

Power, M.K. (1991). Educating accountants: towards a critical ethnography. *Accounting, Organizations and Society*, vol. 16, 333–34.

Putnam, L., Bantz, D., Deetz, S., Mumby, D., & Van Maanan, J. (1993). Ethnography versus critical theory: Debating organizational research. *Journal of Management Inquiry*, 191–235.

Rorty, R. (1979). *Philosophy and the mirror of nature*. Princeton: Princeton University Press.

Silverman, D. (1985). *Qualitative methodology and sociology*. Aldershot: Gower Publishing.

Weinsheimer, J.C. (1985). *Gadamer's hermeneutics: A reading of truth and method*. New Haven: Yale University Press.

Chapter 23

Structuration Theory in Management Accounting[1]

Norman B. Macintosh,   *Queen's University*
Robert W. Scapens,   *University of Manchester*

It has been recognized for some time that the scope of accounting research should be broadened beyond traditional positivistic investigations with a technical-efficiency focus to include social and political phenomena. We propose Anthony Giddens' (1976, 1979, 1984, 1990) 'structuration theory' as one way to overcome or circumvent some of these difficulties. The main reason for this is that it contains two concepts — the 'duality of structure' and 'structuration' — that illuminate in a powerful way the various roles management accounting systems perform in organizations. The duality of structure means that social structures are both constituted by human action (agency) and at the same time are the medium of this constitution. Thus, structuration theory subsumes two fundamentally antagonistic theoretical positions, that of the structuralists who see social life as determined by impersonal, objective social structures and that of the hermeneutical humanists and interactionists who see social life as a product of subjective and intersubjective human activity. Similarly, the concept of structuration — the process whereby agents reproduce social practices across time and space, sometimes almost intact while in other instances in radically different form — provides some leverage on the longstanding debates between oppositional positions held by competing approaches within the corpus of social and critical theory.

Structuration Theory

In analyzing social systems, Giddens distinguishes between system and structure. For Giddens, social systems comprise discernibly similar social practices which are reproduced across time and space through the actions of human agents, while structure refers to the structuring properties which provide for the 'binding' of those social practices into social systems. To emphasize this distinction we can

---

[1]Reproduced (in an abridged form) from Norman B. Macintosh and Robert W. Scapens, 'Structuration Theory in Management Accounting', *Accounting, Organizations and Society*, 1990, vol. 15, no. 5, pp. 455–477 with permission of Elsevier.

Accounting, the Social and the Political
N. Macintosh and T. Hopper (Editors)

say that systems are not structures, but rather that systems *have* structures which are drawn upon in social interaction. However, it is only through action and interaction that structures are themselves reproduced. This is Giddens' notion of the *duality of structure* whereby structures are both the medium and the outcome of interaction.

Social Structures

Giddens suggests that for purposes of analysis we consider three dimensions of social structure — signification (meaning), legitimation (morality) and domination (power). Although separable analytically, these three dimensions are inextricably linked (see Figure 23.1). For instance, the domination structure which comprises the rules and resources drawn upon in relations of power are closely linked to the significant and legitimation structures. Command over the management accounting process, for example, is a resource which can be used in the exercise of power in organizations. Drawing on the domination structure certain organizational participants hold others accountable for particular activities. Management accounting is a key element in the process of accountability. However, the notion of accountability in management accounting terms makes sense only in the context of the signification and legitimation involved in management accounting practices. Organizational participants make sense of actions and events by drawing upon meanings embedded in management accounting concepts and theories. Furthermore, management accounting gives legitimacy to certain actions of organizational participants.

Thus, it could be argued that management accounting is implicated in the signification, legitimation and domination structures within organizations, and that accounting signification is an important resource in relations of power. However, it is important to emphasize that structuration theory itself is not primarily concerned with the nature of social structures; but rather with the relationship between structures and the activities of human agents. In other words, it is concerned with

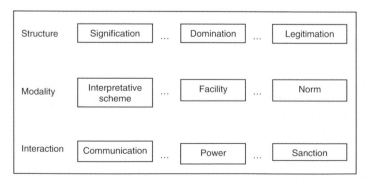

Figure 23.1: Giddens' structuration framework. (*Source:* (Giddens 1984: 29))

the way in which social practices both contribute to the reproduction of structures and are themselves shaped by those structures.

The Agent in Structuration Theory

Agency, for Giddens, refers to the actions taken by individuals in social settings. Agency takes place as a continuous flow of action (not a series of acts) and it involves the intervention of the acting subject in a flow of events which are potentially malleable. Agents intervene, not merely with automatic responses (in which case social structure would never change), but rather in a way that presents them with the possibility of acting in such a manner that social structures are sometimes modified or even radically altered. They do so to a large extent 'purposively' in that they know a great deal about why they act and what they do. They behave in a certain way recognizing they could have taken different action. Agents, if asked, will usually be able to explain (rationalize) the grounds of their social action, even if they are unaware of some of the consequences. Individuals are not just social dupes, but existential beings who reflexively monitor and provide rationales for the character of the ongoing flow of their social life.

This reflexivity, Giddens argues, is carried out at two levels of consciousness — discursive and practical. At the discursive level, agents can and do give reasons for and rationalize about what they do in social settings. Agents also reflexively monitor their own and others' social behaviour at the practical level of consciousness. Here, agents rely on implicit stocks of knowledge about how to act and how to interpret events and the actions of others.

These two levels, in turn, are seen to be the subject of motivations located in the agent's unconscious. Both the discursive and practical levels of consciousness are influenced, but not swamped by, a primary need lodged in the unconscious for ontological security. This picture of the agent's psychological makeup and its articulation to structuration, social structure and agency is shown in Figure 23.2.

Structuration Theory and Management Accounting

Signification Structure

Management accounting systems can be thought of as a vital signification structure. For example, management accounting provides managers with a means of understanding the activities of their organization and allows them to communicate meaningfully about those activities. As such, a management accounting system is an interpretative scheme which mediates between the signification structure and social interaction in the form of communication between managers. The signification structure in this case comprises the shared rules, concepts and theories which are drawn upon to make sense of organizational activities. They include the various

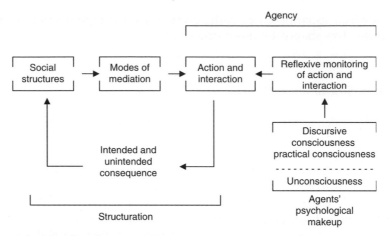

Figure 23.2: Agency in structuration.

notions of finance, economics, management science, etc. as well as accounting concepts, such as income, assets, costs, revenues and profits. These accounting concepts have signification prior to the interpretative scheme, in the sense that social actors will have shared understandings of their meanings which, although mediated by the management accounting system, are presupposed by that interpretative scheme. For example, the concept of profit is given specific time–space location through management accounting systems, but it exists outside time–space. It is instantiated only through the use of those systems in practice and it can be changed through such use.

Legitimation Structure

Legitimation involves the moral constitution of interaction. The legitimation structure is mediated through norms and moral codes which sanction particular behaviours. It comprises the shared sets of values and ideals about what is to be regarded as virtue and what is to be regarded as vice; what is to count as important and what is to be trivialized; what ought to happen and what ought not to happen. As such, the legitimation structure institutionalizes the reciprocal rights and obligations of the social actors.

   Management accounting systems embody norms of organizational activity and provide the moral underpinnings for the signification structure and the financial discourse. They legitimate the rights of some participants to hold others account-able in financial terms for their actions. They communicate a set of values and ideals about what is approved and what is disapproved, and what rewards and penalties can be utilized. As such, management accounting systems are not an objective and neutral means of conveying economic meanings to decision makers. They are deeply implicated in the reproduction of values, and are a medium through which the legitimation structure can be drawn upon in social interaction within organizations.

Domination Structure

Resources comprise the facilities through which agents draw upon the domination structure in the exercise of power. In specific time–space locations, the capacity to exercise power can be related to asymmetries in the distribution of resources. Giddens distinguishes two types of resources: allocative resources which arise from command over objects, goods and other material phenomena, and authoritative resources which arise from capabilities to organize and coordinate the activities of social actors. Both types of resources facilitate the transformative capacity of human action (power in the broad sense), while at the same time providing the medium for domination (power in the narrow sense).

   Power in its broad sense is the ability to get things done to make a difference in the world. Agency and power are related, in that agency entails the ability to act otherwise, to be able to intervene in the world, or to refrain from intervening. In a narrower sense, however, power is simply domination. According to Giddens, all social relations involve power in both the broad and narrow sense. But the exercise of power is not a uni-directional social process. All social relations involve both autonomy and dependence. Even the most 'subordinate' agents will have some resources (e.g. means of production, raw materials, information, contacts, position in society, etc.) which they can use to influence the actions of their 'superiors'. For example, subordinates may possess and choose to withhold information from their superiors. In this way, subordinates can exercise power in social interactions with their superiors. Giddens calls this *the dialectic of control*. The command over the management accounting system is a resource which can be used by both supervisors and subordinates in the exercise of power (in both the broad and narrow senses) in organizations. The management accounting system is a key element in the process of accountability in organizations and consequently a major facility for the mediation of the domination structure in relations of power.

The Agent's Psychological Makeup

The agent's psychological makeup as it is incorporated into structuration theory also holds implications for management accounting. One important implication is that management accounting systems can be a vital means of meeting agents' unconscious needs for ontological security. There also are implications for management accounting systems at the practical and discursive levels of consciousness. In the former case, it seems plausible that managers implicitly and tacitly rely on such systems and develop practical stocks of knowledge about how to respond to and utilize them. At the discursive level of consciousness, it is widely accepted that managers can give reasons about how and why they use management accounting systems as they do. The important implication is that management accounting systems can be vital to managers as they function at the discursive, practical and unconscious psychological levels.

Summary

Management accounting systems represent modalities of structuration in the three dimensions of signification, legitimation and domination. In the signification dimensions, management accounting systems are the interpretative schemes which managers use to interpret past results, take actions and make plans. In the domination dimension, management accounting systems are a facility that management at all levels can use to coordinate and control other participants. And in the legitimation dimension, management accounting systems communicate a set of values and ideals about what is approved and what is disapproved; justify the rights of some participants to hold others accountable; and legitimate the use of certain rewards and sanctions. The concepts, theories, values, ideals, rules, etc. upon which management accounting systems are based represent the structural properties of management accounting. Through the modalities described above, management accounting provides for the binding of social interactions in organizations across time and space. These social interactions represent the day-to-day use of management accounting systems; in other words, management accounting practice.

   In studying management accounting practice, it is important to recognize the way in which the three dimensions of structure described above are intertwined. By signifying what counts, management accounting provides a discourse[2] for the domination structure through which some participants are held accountable to others, while at the same time it provides legitimacy for the social processes which are involved. Thus, signification in management accounting terms is implicated in both the legitimation and domination structures, and as such is an important resource in structuring relations of power. However, the structural properties of management accounting are neither wholly explicit, nor unchanging. They can change as they are drawn upon and reproduced through the use of management accounting systems in the social interaction of organizational participants. We can now turn to a case study to illustrate the role of management accounting in the process of structuration.

The University of Wisconsin Budgeting System

The description of the University of Wisconsin budgeting system provided by Covaleski & Dirsmith (1988) provides a good illustration of structuration. Financing

---

[2]In this sense, a discourse can be said to be the 'outcome' of signification, or, in other words, its instantiation in practice.

for the University comes from State funds, and it is the relationship between the University and the State which is the subject of the Covaleski & Dirsmith (C&D) case study. The process of structuration can be seen very clearly in their case description. We will attempt to show that these social practices draw upon structures of signification, legitimation and domination and in particular that the signification structure is implicated in the relations of power. Specifically, the latter part of the case illustrates how a budgetary discourse can be used in the exercise of political power. It was only when the budgetary discourse was challenged by the University, that the State found it necessary to resort to other resources in the exercise of power. However, it is this resort to other resources when the budgetary discourse is challenged which exposes the importance of signification in relations of power.

In the following discussion, references to actions by the University of Wisconsin should be interpreted as referring to actions of University administrators. Similarly, references to actions by the State will refer to the actions of politicians and State administrators. In other words, the relations between the University and the State should be viewed as the social practices of human agents. As such, these practices represent the intended actions of knowledgeable, purposive human actors; although the actors may be unaware of the conditions of their actions and of all the consequences which flow from them, as we shall see later.

The placing of contextual boundaries on social interactions, such as between the University and the State, implies that institutionalized properties of such social interactions are assumed to be given. However, according to structuration theory all social interaction is structured by virtue of the duality of structure. In other words, the institutionalized practices which may be taken as given for a particular research study are themselves reproduced through the actions of human agents. In this case, we will analyze the strategic conduct of social actors in order to understand the ways in which they draw upon structures in their social relations. But it must be remembered that these structures are the outcomes of the social actions themselves. Furthermore, the particular context within which we will study strategic conduct is itself a part of a larger social context which again is reproduced only through the actions of social actors.

Structuration of Relations between the University and the State

The case study traces the origins of the budgeting system traditionally used in the State of Wisconsin, particularly the involvement of the University, and then describes the tensions which arose in the 1980s as a result of reductions in funding and the consequences for the relationship between the University and the State. The traditional budgeting system drew upon long-standing meaning structures through an accounting (budgeting) discourse which provided the interpretative scheme for making sense of the budgeting process. These meaning structures were central to the structuration of the social relations between the University and the State. They were drawn upon and thereby reproduced in the budgeting system.

Covaleski & Dirsmith trace the origins of these meaning structures to the 'progressive liberalism' of the turn of the century Progressive Movement led by Governor LaFollette. Embedded in these structures were beliefs of social efficiency and rationality emanating from the ideas of the Taylor school of scientific management. Within this framework, the role of the University was to provide a cadre of neutral, objective, apolitical, scientific experts (professors and graduates) to the State to secure and nurture a progressive liberal society for the citizens of Wisconsin.

In order to maintain a 'distance' between the politicians and the neutral experts within the University, an enrolment funding formula (EFF) was used to determine the amount of funding allocated to the University. Furthermore, the University was required to submit a great deal of quantitative information such as enrolment statistics for various programs and campuses, details of budget line items and specific funding allocations such as libraries, computing facilities and other support activities. The EFF and the supplementary information served three purposes for the State. First, it provided a mechanism for assessing funding needs which gave an appearance of rational and scientific choice. Second, it provided a readily understood rationale for determining the amount of funds to be approved. Third, it signified to the public at large that the University's needs and performance were being monitored.

In terms of structuration theory, the budgeting discourse drew on a signification structure which contained notions of the rationality of science, the neutrality of the expert, the efficiency of management science and the objectivity of accounting or more generally, the notion of budgeting as a rational, efficient and neutral allocation process. By continuing to use the EFF over many subsequent years, the University and the State reproduced this structure. In so doing, they continued to demonstrate to the public and elected representatives in the State legislature that the State was allocating funds on the basis of rational choice through a logical impersonal process and that the University was accountable for its use of those funds.

Conflict between the University and the State

During the 1970s, financial pressures on State resources meant that the funds available for higher education began to shrink, at least in real terms, and the State used the EFF to contract the funds allocated to the University. This contraction was achieved through the budgetary discourse and had the effect of reducing the space which had previously allowed the University to operate *internally* independent of the State. The problems came to a head in the early 1980s when it became clear that the prestigious Madison campus was consuming an increasing proportion of the available resources, at the expense of the other campuses.

In the years of sufficient economic resources, there was space for the University to have autonomy in its relations with the State. But as the available economic resources contracted, the University began to feel that it was losing its autonomy.

However, it did not lack resources which could be used in relations with the State. These resources included: control of local information used in the budgeting process; recourse to the media to challenge existing allocations; appeal to the wider public to challenge the legitimacy of existing budgeting procedures; and lobbying of elected representatives. The University's use of these resources in its attempt to regain autonomy provides a good illustration of Giddens' dialectic of control. In Covaleski & Dirsmith's description, we see conflict between the University and the State arising from the structural contradiction implied in using the budgetary process as both a means of control and a means of autonomy. By drawing on its resources within the structure of domination, the University attempted to bring about changes in the budget discourse.

The University submitted its 1983–1985 budget request, not in terms of the traditional EFF, but in the form of specific, qualitative program categories, labeled Decision Narrative Items (DINs). The DINs summarized the University's need for funds in three major budget categories: (1) for the modernization of instructional equipment in high technology areas, (2) for the expansion of programs in other vital areas and (3) to arrest the decline in library and information resources. The strategy behind the approach was to demonstrate the dire needs of the University, while at the same time allowing University administrators to retain control over internal allocations.

The new budget discourse included a qualitative rhetoric that placed emphasis on the role of the University in State-wide economic recovery and revitalization. It was, in effect, drawing upon the signification and legitimation structures in an attempt to replace one interpretive scheme (the EFF and supplementary quantitative information) with another (the DINs). In order to do this, the University used the resources at its disposal to challenge the traditional power of the State. For instance, it appealed publicly to the State citizenry for support to halt and reverse the decline in funding for higher education. The public responded sympathetically.

The new budget discourse, however, had upset the traditional division of responsibilities. Previously, the State had been able to reduce funding levels, but leave the specifics of the cuts to the University. The new budget discourse attempted to force the State into making this highly political decision, or alternatively, redistributing funds from other State agencies. University administrators felt confident that the general public and the University could combine to change the traditional budget discourse.

The new discourse challenged the moral order (or norms) embedded in the budgeting process. Under the old procedures, the State required the University to request funds in terms of the EFF and then held it accountable for its spending. The University met these obligations, not merely out of a felt positive moral commitment, but also because of the implied threat that failure to do so could result in a withholding of funds and interference in the internal allocation of funds. Faced with chronic underfunding, the University did not feel obligated to comply with these moral claims when it formulated its 1983–1985 budget request. It judged that the potential sanctions were less severe than the real effects of continued underfunding. Moreover, the new budget format implied a moral order in which the State would be accountable to the public and to the University for the underfunding of one or all of: high technology instructional equipment (DIN 1), expanded programs in vital areas (DIN 2) or library resources (DIN 3). The new procedures would not only alter the nature of the sanctions, but would reverse the direction of moral obligation.

The Governor and the State Department of Administration (DOA) refused to recognize the three separate DIN categories. Instead, they collapsed them into one budget category which they labeled 'Improving University Education'. This relieved the State from having to publicly choose amongst equipment, programs and libraries, and importantly shifted the budget discourse away from explicit political choices. The State acknowledged the general claim that resources for the University had decreased significantly, but argued that since it lacked any quantitative indicators, the magnitude of the problem could not be determined. Eventually, the DOA and the Governor in collaboration with the University administrators agreed to fund over 80% of the request.

This fund and the agreed increase in funding, however, was not to be part of the formal University operating budget of which salaries were the major component. These additional items were decoupled from the operating budget that was to be submitted at a later date.

Unintended Consequences

The University's attempt to change the budget discourse proved to be short-lived and had unintended consequences. As mentioned above, DOA officials were very concerned about the symbolic budget discourse. This concern surfaced when the University submitted its usual salary request in the Spring of 1983. University faculty are State employees and their salary budgets go, along with all State agency salary budgets, to the legislative Joint Committee on Employment Relations (JCOER) for recommendation to the Governor. The University asked for an 18% increase in the 1983–1985 salary budget, arguing that such an amount was essential in order to retain high quality faculty and maintain good morale.

In the summer of 1983, however, JCOER submitted a salary plan, which the legislature approved, freezing salaries for all University employees in the first year and providing for a 3.2% rise in the second year. The University responded with a request for a general supplement of one million dollars which JCOER approved, but which the Governor subsequently vetoed. It was only then that the University administrators realized that their attempt to change the budget discourse yielded unintended consequences. The large lump sum payment and the Star Faculty had been subsidized by the faculty themselves. As Covaleski & Dirsmith concluded, the Governor had, in the final analysis, not only beaten the University at the game of changing the budget discourse, but had turned it to his political advantage.

The Governor, with the support of DOA officials, had utilized the other resources at his disposal when the traditional budget discourse was challenged by the

University. He drew on the signification structure to argue that the University's procedure lacked rationality. In addition, he used his authoritative resources to combine the three DINs into a single budget category, and his allocative resources to withhold salary increases. These actions reinforced the rationality of the traditional budget discourse and limited the impact of the University's attempts to question its legitimacy and appeal to elected representatives and the wider public. The Governor succeeded in reimposing the traditional procedures. The relations of power which had produced (and were obscured by) the budget discourse were drawn upon more explicitly and very effectively to restore the traditional system and thereby perpetuate its use for the future. The University President resigned and for the next budget biennium, the State and the University returned to the traditional budget discourse.

Some Psychological Aspects

While Covaleski & Dirsmith's description and analysis focused primarily on social structures and political forces, there is a modicum of evidence, albeit indirect, that the traditional budgeting system served as a means of meeting some of the participants' needs for ontological security. For example, Covaleski & Dirsmith (p. 11) report: 'this historically rooted state/university budgetary relationship gave the USW [officials] a degree of comfort, even though it required the university to share a great deal of detailed, quantitative information with the State'; and elsewhere: 'The economic reality within which the UWS and State have lived had been traditionally defined using the accounting enrolment formula. The rules that had guided their requests for programs and pay, as well as governance, had been implicitly understood...The roles were defined and the actors found comfort within this budgetary relationship' (p. 19). The comfort provided by the traditional budgetary system could be seen as indirect evidence that the traditional budget was a source of ontological security for officials on both sides, while the implicit understandings are suggestive of their practical consciousness. Similarly, the attempt by the University officials to change the budget system in a radical way can be seen to be a cause of psychological anxiety, particularly on the part of State officials. Thus, the University budgeting system can be seen not only as modality in the reproduction of social structures, but also as an important means of meeting deeply rooted psychological needs for ontological security.

Discussion

The purpose of this paper has been to evaluate the potential contribution of Giddens' structuration theory for management accounting research. We have argued that structuration theory, its limitations notwithstanding, can be used to sensitize researchers to the social nature of management accounting practice. At the methodological level, structuration theory represents a set of concepts which provide a starting point for the development of substantive theory and empirical explanations in which management accounting is regarded, not as a natural phenomenon, but as a social construction. If researchers internalize these concepts, studies of management accounting practice will look to the relationship between day-to-day social action and the dimensions of social structure. This will involve locating accounting in relation to its social context and examining its historical setting. For example, it helps us explore how accounting is conditioned by the wider socio-economic system, how it provides a set of rules and resources which are implicated in the structuring of certain types of organizational behavior, how these rules and resources are themselves the outcome of social practices and how accounting systems might be a source of ontological security for the participants.

The paper also attempts, through the case analysis, to demonstrate how structuration theory can be used in management accounting research. At the theoretical level we argued that management accounting systems represent modalities of structuration in the three dimensions of signification, legitimation and domination. In particular, management accounting systems are the interpretive scheme which managers use to make sense of their day-to-day activities. Signification in accounting terms also provides a resource which can be drawn upon in the structure of domination, and a set of norms which can be drawn upon in the structure of legitimation. In the case study, we illustrated how this view of accounting could be used to make sense of relations between the University and the State of Wisconsin over a long period of time and in the specific context of a crisis incident.

Although structuration theory may enable us to make generalizations about the historical and spatial context of accounting practices, we must be very circumspect in making predictions about uses of accounting in the future. Nevertheless, it does provide a means by which we can understand the processes which determine future practices. Structuration theory is not, however, without its limitations and critics.

There is an important implication in this for our case analysis. We cannot say for certain whether or not the university administrators, in deciding to change the budget ritual acted in an unfettered, existentialistic way; or whether they merely followed the dictates of the prevailing social structures. Structuration theory does not automatically inform us in this regard. Our own perception, however, is that the answer lies close at hand and is to be found in Giddens' distinction between 'routine' and 'crisis' situations, a distinction underplayed or overlooked by many of the critics.

Routinization, Giddens (1984) points out, is fundamental to daily social activity. The routine is 'whatever is done habitually' and daily 'encapsulates exactly the routinized character which social life has as it stretches across time–space' (p. xxii). Daily routines are repeated recursively and so agents have no need to consciously think or speak about them. In addition to being functional, routines are also economical in that agents need not stop, devise and negotiate a new commonly agreed upon social code every time they meet. Under routine conditions human action, including the reproduction of social structures, flows continuously. Here, social codes are paramount.

In critical (or crisis) situations, in contrast, structuration works differently. A critical situation is 'a set of circumstances which — for whatever reason — radically disrupts accustomed routines of daily life' (Giddens 1984: 124). Conventions and social codes may be abandoned and new ones produced on the spot. 'The accustomed routines of daily life are drastically disrupted' (Giddens 1979: 125). Under crisis, agency comes to the fore, often reshaping prevailing social structures. All at once the orderly crowd at the general store turns into a lynch mob.

The distinction between routine and crisis situations informs our case analysis in an important way. It seems plausible that the traditional budgeting process was dominated by the structures of the progressive liberal ideology as State and University officials routinely carried out the budget ritual. By 1982, however, the University officials perceived the funding situation as a crisis. Acting consciously and deliberately they took action to change the budget discourse from the rational–quantitative one to a political–qualitative disquisition. The Governor, also acting consciously and deliberately, collapsed the three DINs into one, authorized a one-shot funding, and then restored the traditional budget discourse. Under crisis, although agency initially prevailed on both sides, in the final analysis it appears that the University proved relatively powerless to the deeply structural feature of the context in which the initial moral challenge was mounted.

Concluding Remarks

One aspect of structuration theory that stands out is its potential as a sensitizing device for researchers to understand the nature of management accounting and its role in organizations. As we attempted to demonstrate above, it can be used to make explanatory propositions about the way management accounting contributes to the existing social order as well as to changes in that order. For example, the role of accounting in the structuration process is most visible in times of crisis and in contests for control — as was seen in the Wisconsin case. But management accounting fulfils an important role in the maintenance of the social order at other times. Accounting discourse is the means by which sense is made of economic and business activities. It also is drawn upon to legitimate particular actions. As well, it is a resource for the exercise of power, both in the broad and narrow sense. Structuration theory, then, indicates the ways in which accounting is involved in the institutionalization of social relations. It is, in our view, a more focused, informative, integrative and efficient, yet comprehensive, way to analyze case studies of management accounting than many of the frameworks used in previous studies. Case studies by themselves are not enough to advance our knowledge of management accounting practice; they need to be informed by theory.

Structuration theory also highlights that the existing corpus of critical accounting studies has in the main neglected the agent's psychological functioning. From a structuration theory perspective, managers' reflexive monitoring of behavior in social settings, such as how they respond to and engage budgeting systems, is a function of their discursive and practical consciousness and their unconscious motivation for ontological security. While Giddens' construction of the agent remains problematic, it nevertheless highlights the fact that psychological factors need to be brought into the analysis. Just as structuration sometimes involves radical changes in social structures, it can also involve radical changes in the agent's psychological functioning.

References

Covaleski, M.A., & Dirsmith, M. (1988). The use of budgetary symbols in the political arena: An historically informed field study. *Accounting, Organizations and Society, 13*, 1–24.

Giddens, A. (1976). *New rules of sociological method.* London: Hutchinson & Co.

Giddens, A. (1979). *Central problems in society theory.* London: Macmillan.

Giddens, A. (1984). *The constitution of society.* Cambridge: Polity Press.

Giddens, A. (1990). *The consequences of modernity.* Stanford: Stanford University Press.

Roberts, J., & Scapens, R.W. (1990). Accounting as discipline, in D.J. Cooper & T.M. Hopper (eds). *Critical Accounts.* London: Macmillan.

Chapter 24

Theoretical Approaches to Research on Accounting Ethics[1]

C. Richard Baker, *Adelphi University*

The purpose of this paper is to identify theoretical approaches that have been taken toward research on accounting ethics and to examine how the approaches compare and in what ways they differ. To compare different approaches, a framework is proposed to characterize such research. This framework is based on the concept that ethics research may be characterized by the stance which the research takes with respect to two aspects of ethics. The first aspect deals with the epistemological status of the ethical question (i.e. how does a person know whether something is an ethical question?). The second aspect deals with the normative status of the ethical question (i.e. how does a person determine whether an act is good or bad?). A two-dimensional framework is proposed that incorporates an *epistemological* dimension and a *normative* dimension. The *epistemological* dimension characterizes research on accounting ethics according to whether the theoretical approach is closer to an *atomistic* view or closer to a *social* view. The *normative* dimension characterizes research on accounting ethics according to whether the underlying assumption of the research is closer to a *deontological* view or closer to a *consequential* view. Different approaches to research on accounting ethics are examined, and an attempt is made to show how the different approaches have been adapted from established paradigms in the disciplines of philosophy, economics, psychology, sociology, critical theory feminist theory, and postmodern theory.

The Philosophical Roots of Research on Accounting Ethics

The study of ethics deals with questions concerning what is morally good or bad, right or wrong (*Encyclopaedia Britannica* 1997). As a discipline, ethics focuses on questions similar to those raised in social science disciplines such as economics, psychology, sociology and political theory. At the same time, the study of ethics within philosophy, as Macintosh (1995) points out, may be distinguished from social science disciplines because the study of ethics is concerned not so much

---

[1] Reproduced (in an abridged form) from C.R. Baker, 'Theoretical Approaches to Research on Accounting Ethics', *Research on Accounting Ethics*, 1999, vol. 5, pp. 115–134, with permission of Elsevier.

Accounting, the Social and the Political
N. Macintosh and T. Hopper (Editors)

with empirical knowledge as it is with values; in other words, human behavior as it ought to be, rather than as it actually is.

The study of ethics within philosophy can be divided into two subdisciplines: metaethics and normative ethics. Metaethics centers on questions concerning the essential nature or ontological status of ethical concepts. In discussing metaethical issues, philosophers have taken distinctly different positions. Some have held that ethical concepts are universal metaphysical entities (e.g. Plantoic idealism). Others suggest that ethical concepts can only be understood in relation to the situation in which the ethical decision takes place (e.g. Aristotelian ethics). Still others assert that ethical concepts merely express attitudes or emotions which do not exist apart from the human mind (e.g. Hobbesian skepticism).

In contrast to metaethics, normative ethics is primarily concerned with establishing standards or norms for conduct and is commonly associated with general theories about how a person should live or behave. Traditionally, theories of ethics that judge actions by their consequences have been known as teleological, although the term consequential has in large part supplanted it. Another group of theories within normative ethics, referred to as deontological, judges actions by their conformance to some formal rule or principle (e.g. the Kantian categorical imperative). Having said that, the focus of this article is primarily on how a person comes to know about an ethical question (i.e. the epistemological dimension) and how a person determines the quality of the ethical act (i.e. the normative dimension).

The normative dimension of ethics is concerned with standards or norms of conduct. In general, there have been two approaches to normative ethics: the deontological and the consequential (see Figure 24.1). The deontological approach holds that there are certain ethical axioms that dictate the actions that a person ought to take regardless of the situation. Pursuant to the deontological approach, actions are seen as intrinsically right or wrong. Furthermore, it is typically not the individual who decides whether the acts are right or wrong, it is society as a whole, or more likely some external force, entirely separate and apart from human agency, which determines the rules that must be followed (e.g. God, natural law). There have been many philosophers who have taken a deontological approach to ethics. Macintosh (1995) suggests that the work of Plato can be characterized as

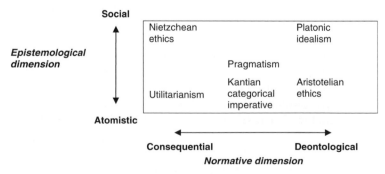

Figure 24.1: Philosophical approaches to ethics.

being deontological. Furthermore, because the knowledge of ethical decisions is universally determined within Platonic idealism, the Platonic approach to ethics can be characterized toward the social end of the epistemological dimension.

A consequential approach to ethics contends that rather than ethical acts being fundamentally right or wrong, there is a consequence of ethical acts which may be expressed in terms of the welfare of society as a whole, or the greatest good for the greatest number, or the welfare of the individual decision maker. Thus, the consequential approach to ethics is concerned primarily with the effects of ethical acts and decisions. Macintosh (1995) and others have suggested that the Aristotelian view of ethics is essentially a consequentialist position. 'For Aristotle, ethical knowledge always involves the concrete situation. It cannot negate the differences in the context of the action nor can it deny the reality of history' (Macintosh 1995: 297). Nevertheless, while Aristotle emphasized that the ultimate goal of ethical behavior is happiness, thus implying a focus on the consequence of ethical action, Aristotle also stressed that the proper means to achieve happiness was through cultivation of the virtues and that, moreover, there is a duty to act in an ethical manner. Because the emphasis on duty in Aristotle outweighs the emphasis on consequences, Aristotelian ethics might be best characterized toward the deontological end of the normative dimension.

The categorical imperative of Kant might be viewed as taking a deontological position. However, because the emphasis in the categorical imperative is on the consequences of failure to abide by the imperative, the work of Kant might also be characterized as having some elements of the consequential. In addition, because Kant's philosophy was fundamentally based in the Enlightenment worldview concerning the existence of individual free will, the Kantian categorical imperative can be distinguished from Platonic idealism in that it might be situated more toward the atomistic end of the epistemological dimension.

Utilitarianism is another form of consequentialism that focuses primarily on the outcome of ethical acts. The utilitarian approach might therefore be situated toward the end of the consequential position on the normative dimension and toward the atomistic position on the epistemological dimension. There have also been middle-range approaches to normative ethics. These middle-range approaches suggest that in their actual lives, persons are capable of evaluating the inherent rightness or wrongness of their acts and/or those of others and, simultaneously, are able to evaluate the consequences of their acts and/or those of others. Pragmatism, is essentially a middle-range approach. Because of its emphasis on democratic processes and practical solutions to problems, pragmatism may be situated toward the middle of the normative and epistemological dimensions.

The ethics of Nietzsche can be seen as anti-moral, in that he argues that the natural world is beyond good and evil and that morality is an invention of the weak to limit the strong. From this perspective, the individual is largely meaningless and powerless, while the survival of society is everything. Therefore, Nietzchean ethics might be characterized toward the social end of the epistemological dimension and the consequential end of the normative dimension.

Many of the theoretical assumptions underlying codes of ethical conduct in accounting tend to be normative in nature. The normative prescriptions contained in codes of ethical conduct are usually intended to be followed by all persons who are subject to the codes. There is no claim that a code of ethics may apply at a given time or given place and not apply at another time or place. In other words, ethical prescriptions are deemed to be essentially immutable and not relative to the situation in which the accountant finds himself or herself (i.e. a deontological view). At the same time, this normative view of ethics is concerned with the consequences of the ethical decisions that accountants may take (e.g. failure to act independently may lead to falsification of financial statements that would lead to a bad outcome for shareholders), and thus may be said to take a consequentialist perspective.

Recently, a virtue-based approach to ethics has appeared within accounting research. *Virtue ethics* argues that certain qualities such as honesty, concern for the economic status of others, and sensitivity to the value of cooperation ought to be emphasized by accountants. This theoretical approach to research on accounting ethics is essentially prescriptive in nature. Thus, it may be characterized toward the deontological end of the normative dimension.

It could be argued that the assumptions underlying most research on accounting ethics are deontological because it is often taken for granted that a distinction can be made between correct and incorrect ethical acts and that the correctness of a given act is not dependent primarily on its consequences. At the same time, the arguments that are raised in support of ethical behavior on the part of accountants are often couched in terms of the consequences that might arise from failure to abide by codes of ethical conduct, rather than the correctness of the acts in and of themselves. A deontological approach to ethics implies a transcendent nature for ethical rules and a concomitant necessity to explain the origins of this transcendence (i.e. derived from God, natural law or what?). Without an answer to this question, ethical prescriptions are subject to challenge by anyone who holds a different view. On the other hand, a consequential view of ethics implies that there is a method for measuring the goodness of the outcome of an ethical act. This perspective is also problematic in that there is no reliable means of arriving at an unequivocal determination concerning the degree of goodness of the outcome of an ethical act. This essential undecidability of ethical questions within philosophy has led many researchers to approach research on accounting ethics from a supposedly scientific perspective.

Social Science Approaches to Accounting Ethics

Economics-based Approaches

Theoretical approaches derived from economics underpin most accounting research. One example of an economics-based approach to research on accounting ethics is Noreen (1988). Noreen used agency theory to explain the existence of altruistic behavior in capitalist organizations. Noreen suggests that the existence of altruistic (i.e. ethical) behavior can be explained not only through biological (i.e. genetic) factors, the existence of religions and social control variables, but that ethics serves the function of lubricating the market.

Although theoretical approaches derived from economics underlie most accounting research, the vast majority of research on accounting ethics has eschewed economics-based theories. The principal reason for this lies in the criticisms that have been leveled at economics-based research. These criticisms have tended to focus on the fundamental assumptions underlying the economics-based research paradigm that adversely affect its ability to provide meaningful understandings of social reality. In addition, while attempting to comply with the strict rigor of the scientific method, economics-based research has placed emphasis on measurement for measurement's sake. Finally, research methods based on the analysis of quantitative data have been so exhaustively employed that they have reached a point of diminishing returns.

Bettner *et al.* (1994: 2–3) identify five basic assumptions underlying economics-based research in accounting and finance.

1. A cause and effect mechanism animates all [economic] activity. Connections exist between initial conditions and final outcomes.
2. The connections [between initial conditions and final outcomes] are determinable, and if conditions were to be completely specified, which it is in principle possible to do, then outcomes could be predicted with certainty.
3. The free will of the human being, by and for whom all [economic] activity is undertaken, can be ignored. All relevant human behavior is governed by the cause and effect mechanism.
4. All [economic] activity can be quantified, and the logic of statistical analysis and inference applies to all measures.
5. All human beings have equal access to the institutions and systems within which [economic] activity is undertaken.

While such assumptions may improve a model's mathematical tractability, they are rarely defensible. The use of these theoretical models have been frequently challenged. Yet, over a period spanning several decades, the implausible nature of these theoretical models has not been addressed in other than a superficial manner. Thus, economics-based approaches to research on accounting ethics have not been used in research on accounting ethics because of their inability to address the complexities of ethical decisions and actions (see Figure 24.2).

Psychological Approaches

Social science approaches to research on accounting ethics have frequently been conducted through methodologies derived from psychology. These methodologies assume that ethical acts are determined by attitudes, beliefs, values, personality

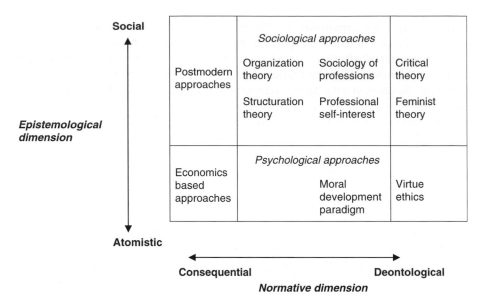

Figure 24.2: Social science approaches to ethics.

factors or levels of cognitive development that are inherent to a particular individual. The moral development paradigm focuses on an individual's ethical beliefs and how the individual's belief system controls conflict resolution and ethical problem solving in actual life. Kohlberg's (1981) studies of ethical beliefs in relationship to behavior were based on a psychological model derived from Piaget. According to Piaget (1932), a person's ethical sense develops through a series of stages over time as a result of social interactions. Kohlberg (1985) elaborated on the stages of ethical development as postulated by Piaget in order to explain the processes that appear to cause a particular individual to act according to a certain set of chosen ethical principles. Kohlberg developed a model of ethical development consisting of a series of cognitive steps. According to this model, a person's ethical judgment develops in stages. At any given point in time, a person is situated at a particular stage of ethical judgment and then proceeds to the next stage depending on the person's belief system.

Because of its grounding in the individual as the locus of ethical knowledge, the *Piagetian/Kohlbergian Psychology* approach to the study of ethics can be situated toward the atomistic end of the epistemological dimension. However, because the focus of this approach is fundamentally directed toward the encouragement of higher levels of ethical reasoning that benefit society as a whole, the Piagetian/Kohlbergian psychology approach can also be situated toward the deontological end of the normative dimension. The essential difficulty of approaches to ethics based in psychology is their emphasis on the atomistic aspect of ethical knowledge.

Sociological Approaches

Research on accounting ethics has frequently been based on theoretical approaches derived from sociology. Within the general framework of sociology, different researchers have taken very different approaches to ethics, ranging from the highly structural-functionalist theories put forth in the *sociology of professions* and *organization theory* literatures to the neo-Marxian approaches of *structuration theory* and *critical theory*. The sociology of professions literature focuses on identifying the social structures that define a profession and explains how these structures serve the functions of both advancing the profession and serving the public interest. The sociology of professions literature defines a profession as having (among other attributes): a defined body of knowledge, specific recognition by society, a code of conduct and a defined cultural tradition. Historically, persons have generally become members of professions by joining guilds or institutes that imposed codes of conduct on the members. These codes of conduct addressed both technical and ethical issues, and violations of the codes might constitute grounds for taking disciplinary actions against the offending member. Such disciplinary actions might range from warnings and reprimands to harsher penalties including expulsion from the guild or institute. Threats of expulsion from the professional guild or institute and the corresponding loss of status and income generally sufficed to cause the member of the profession to abide by the written and unwritten codes of ethical conduct.

The accounting profession is sometimes said to differ from other professions — while public accountants receive fees for services rendered to persons and organizations whom they refer to as their clients, public accountants also assume responsibilities to third parties and to the public generally. This unusual arrangement poses an ethical dilemma for public accountants.

Codes of ethics define the duties that professionals owe to their clients, to their profession, and to third parties and stipulate the sanctions that will follow from failure to abide by these duties. Even though the formal codes of ethics of a profession may be intended to assure appropriate ethical conduct on the part of professional practitioners, the ultimate question of how a profession functions in society rests on the conduct of its members. Nevertheless, the underlying assumption of the sociology of professions approach to the study of ethics is that the ethical dilemmas faced by accountants can be resolved by creating appropriate social structures such as codes of ethics. Therefore, the sociology of professions approach to the study of ethics can be situated toward the deontological end of the normative dimension and toward the social end of the epistemological dimension.

Another approach to the study of ethics within sociology is based in *organization theory*. In accounting research, there have been a number of studies that have approached the ethical conduct of accountants from an organization theory perspective. These studies have often focused on the ethical dilemmas faced by public accountants and discuss how organizational structure variables act to determine these dilemmas. These studies also argue that organizational and cultural factors have an impact on ethical behavior, regardless of the beliefs, attitudes, values, personalities or levels of cognitive ethical development of the actors. The general conclusion of this approach to research on accounting ethics is that the organizational and cultural settings in which the actors find themselves are determinative of their actual ethical behavior regardless of individual ethical beliefs. Because the underlying assumptions of the organization theory approach are based on the idea that organizational and cultural factors affect the decision-making behavior of actors, and that because of this the actors cannot completely exercise free will, the organization theory approach can be situated toward the social end of the epistemological dimension. Because the goal of the organization theory approach is to identify structures that work better, this approach can also be situated toward the consequential end of the normative dimension.

   Another approach to research on accounting ethics, which is grounded in sociology, is structuration theory. Structuration theory is based on the work of Giddens (1984, 1987). Macintosh (1995), suggests that Gidden's structuration framework, and particularly the idea of 'dialectic of control', is well suited for analyzing ethical issues in accounting. Giddens argues that morality, power and signification are inextricably intertwined in any social system. Focusing on morality alone offers only a partial understanding. A dialectic of control analysis reveals how morality is always inextricably intertwined with power and signification. While many approaches to ethics research tend to privilege human agency (i.e. an atomistic view) over social structures, structuration theory incorporates both social structures and human agency within its framework.

   For Giddens, the power aspect of ethics has a dual aspect in that:

> Sanctions only vary rarely take the shape of compulsion which those who experience them are wholly incapable of resisting, and even this can happen only for a brief moment, as when one person is physically rendered helpless by another or others. All other sanctions, no matter how oppressive and comprehensive they may be, demand some kind of acquiescence from those subject to them — which is the reason for the more or less universal purview of the dialectic of control (Giddens 1984: 175).

Some recent research studies within the broad category of sociological approaches to research on accounting ethics have taken a highly critical look at ethical issues in accounting and argue that *professional self-interest* may be the motivating factor behind these issues. The codes of ethics associated with professional guilds and institutes are viewed as mechanisms designed to enhance the interests of the members of the profession or to secure monopoly control of a particular economic activity. These attempts to influence the public perception of accounting may reflect a desire to enhance the economic self-interests of accountants. While the codes of ethics of the accounting profession have usually been expressed in terms of advancing the public interest, it can be seen that these codes are inextricably linked with the profession's private interests. Disciplinary practices for code of ethics violations have tended to focus on punishing acts such as: violation of prohibitions against advertising; driving while intoxicated; filing false tax returns; or embezzlement of funds; all of which, while important and deserving of disciplinary action, tend not to address the central issue of the conflict of interest inherent in the public accountant's role which arises from the need to serve the client's interests while simultaneously protecting the public interest. Thus, the professional self-interest approach can be situated somewhat closer to the atomistic end of the epistemological dimension than other sociological approaches.

Critical Theory Approaches

Critical theory approaches to the study of ethics are based on the idea that inherent contradictions within capitalism cause ethical issues to persist and that only the evolution of society away from the capitalist form of economic organization will allow a resolution of these ethical issues. Critical theory is founded on the principle that it is possible to change the nature of society to ensure a freer and more just life for all. The central thesis is that natural discourses of human beings create views about the world, about social relationships and about the status of individuals within the world (i.e. the life-world). Human discourses also create organizations and structures in society that reflect the life-world (i.e. systems). Finally, human discourses create mechanisms to help the systems reflect the needs of the life-world (i.e. steering media). As long as the systems of society and the steering media which control them are determined by the freely conducted discourses of human beings operating in the life-world, then society can move forward toward a freer and more just status. However, if the steering media take over, they can dominate the systems and control the life-world to the detriment of human freedom.

Recent studies reveal the complex interplay between accounting systems and the steering media of society. If accounting systems are not designed in an open and freely discursive manner (i.e. an ideal speech situation), then they are likely to be used by the steering media in a manner that reduces human freedom. The principal emphasis of critical theory may be characterized toward the deontological end of the normative dimension and the social end of the epistemological dimension.

Feminist Theory Approaches

Feminist theory is concerned with a critique of the gendered models that underpin most social science theorizing. Thus, it is not surprising that feminist theory has taken a critical view of research on accounting ethics. Feminists have critiqued Kohlberg's model by arguing that the model's stages of moral development contain a 'gender gap'. It is argued that the Kohlberg model and the various empirical applications of the model have de-emphasized the ethics of care and social responsibility in favor of an ethics of justice and rights. It is said that the scenarios used in the various psychological instruments that have been used to measure individual levels of moral reasoning ignore the contextual richness and complexity actors bring with them in making moral and ethical decisions. It is suggested that this produces a narrow focus to the study of ethics. Other feminist theorists have criticized the moral development paradigm for its utilitarian aspects and its implicit assumption regarding rationality on the part of decision makers.

As one of the leading feminist critics of the Kohlbergian moral development paradigm, Gilligan (1982) argues the Kohlbergian moral development paradigm excludes women's views of ethics and morality. She believes that the emphasis on care giving that is characteristic of women's views leads to universal moral judgments. Thus, the feminist theory approach to the study of ethics can be characterized toward the deontological end of the normative dimension.

For Gilligan, the Kohlbergian moral development paradigm results in an inadequate measure of women's level of ethical and moral development. In other words, if the psychological instruments that have been designed and used to measure levels of ethical and moral development took more consideration of women's values and views, then the measures of moral development scored by women would be higher.

In addition, from a feminist theory perceptive, it is argued that:

> The masculine personality tends to repress relational issues; males view themselves as more separate and differentiated individuals. The feminine personality tends to define itself in terms of external relationships, their retention, and continuity; females view themselves as connected to the world (Tolleson *et al.* 1996: 23).

An emphasis on connectedness to the world and group-based decision-making processes is a characteristic common to many of the research approaches within feminist theory. Feminist theory approaches to ethics may be characterized toward the social end of the epistemological dimension.

Postmodern Approaches

A *postmodern approach* is defined generally as a set of beliefs regarding the outmoded nature of modernity (Macintosh 1993). The first claim is that meta-narratives which constitute the underlying premises of modernity have lost their effectiveness and no longer represent reality. These meta-narratives generally concern the nature of reality and truth. The postmodern stance is one of incredulity with respect to meta-narratives. Second, postmodernism argues that modernity has not been uniformly progressive and emancipatory. Instead, the modern world has tended to produce a mechanized society which has reduced rather than enhanced freedom. Third, the modern era, spanning the nineteenth and most of the twentieth century, has been a period marked by increasingly deadly warfare and increased manufacture of weaponry. Fourth, the postmodern perspective claims that a new political order may be emerging which seeks to provide space for those who have been previously left out of the mainstream (e.g. women, minorities, etc.).

Finally, postmodernism argues that the development of new information technologies may open up new opportunities to truly democratize political and social life,
or they could become new instruments of coercion for the powerful. Postmodernism
essentially rejects the notion that there is such a thing as moral or ethical truth
and may in fact see arguments in favor of moral truth as merely another means
of controlling the less powerful in society and forcing such persons to act in a
certain manner.

Even though Foucault (1986) does not accept classification of his work within
the postmodern genre, he did address the question of ethics in an intriguing way
which may shed some light on the postmodern perspective. Foucault viewed
morality as a type of meta-concept that incorporates various subconcepts. These
subconcepts include: moral codes, moral behavior, and ethics. The moral code refers
to the set of laws, values and rules of action that are specified for individuals by
entities such as religious authorities, families, schools and so forth. The moral code
specifies the rules that must be followed on pain of sanction. However, these rules
exist within a 'complex interplay of elements that counterbalance and correct one
another, and cancel each other out on certain points, thus providing for compromises and loopholes' (Foucault 1986). In this sense, the moral code, as defined by
Foucault, may be compared to the deontological approach to ethics discussed
previously. However, because Foucault did not subscribe to the belief that the moral
code is immutable, nor is it necessarily the same moral code in all places at all
times, there is a difference between Foucault's definition of the moral code and a
deontological view of ethics.

Moral behavior, according to Foucault, consists of the actual behavior of
individuals in relationship to their moral code. The questions to be addressed
here are whether individuals comply more or less fully with a rule, the manner in
which they obey or resist an interdiction or a prescription, and the manner in which
they respect or disregard a set of values. From Foucault's perspective, ethics is
concerned with the kind of relationship a person ought to have with himself or
herself and the manner in which the individual constitutes himself or herself as a
moral subject. Thus, ethics is distinguished from moral behavior and the moral
code. Ethics concerns the manner in which a person conducts himself or herself in
order to become the 'right kind' of person. Ethics is concerned with disciplinary
practices of the self and self-formation as an ethical subject (Foucault 1986).

From an accounting perspective, the self-forming aspect of ethics is not as evident
in regard to the code of ethics as in respect to the various self-disciplining practices that commence early in the career of a prospective professional accountant,
ranging from difficult examinations in the introductory and intermediate accounting
courses, to the social rituals associated with accounting societies and other clubs,
and to the recruitment rituals of the public accounting firms. These ritualized
activities constitute self-forming and disciplinary practices that form the prospective
public accountant into an idealized ethical being — not an ethical being who
conforms to the code of ethics, but rather an ethical being who is disciplined and
self-formed into the idealized public accountant of the large public accounting
firm. The disciplinary and self-forming practices of the public accounting profession

are closely associated with the kind of person to which an individual aspires when he or she behaves in a moral manner. In accounting, this is the partner in the large public accounting firm who is an ethical being, not in the sense of conforming closely to the code of ethics, but one who is able to satisfy clients, bring in new business, be technically astute, all of this while simultaneously providing an image of action in the highest ethical manner (Baker 1977, 1993). What we find in a postmodern view of ethics in accounting is that the image of the large public accounting firm is dominating the public interest purpose of accounting. A postmodern view of ethics then might be situated toward the consequential end of the normative dimension and toward the atomistic end of the epistemological dimension.

References

Baker, C.R. (1977). Management strategy in a large accounting firm. *The Accounting Review, 52*(3), 576–586.

Baker, C.R. (1993). Self-regulation in the public accounting profession: The response of the large, international public accounting firms to a changing environment. *Accounting, Auditing, Accountability Journal, 6*(2), 68–80.

Bettner, M., Robinson, C., & McGoun, S. (1994). The case for qualitative research in finance. *International Review of Financial Analysis, 3*(1), 1–18.

Encyclopaedia Brittannica (1997).

Foucault, M. (1986). *The use of pleasure: The history of sexuality.* Volume 2, New York, Vintage Books.

Giddens, A. (1984). *The constitution of society.* UK: Polity Press.

Giddens, A. (1987). *Social theory and modern sociology.* Stanford: Stanford University Press.

Gilligan, C. (1982). *In a different voice: Psychological theory and women's development.* Cambridge: Harvard University Press.

Kohlberg, L. (1985). *The development of modes of moral thinking and choice in the years ten to sixteen,* unpublished Ph.D. Dissertation, Chicago: University of Chicago.

Kohlberg, L. (1981). *The meaning and measurement of moral development.* Worcester: Clark University Press.

Macintosh, N.B. (1993). A research proposal to investigate the possibility of poststructuralist accounting thought. Kingston, ON: Queen's University.

Macintosh, N.B. (1995). The ethics of profit manipulation: A dialectic of control analysis. *Critical Perspectives on Accounting, 6,* 289–315.

Noreen, E. (1988). The economics of ethics: A new perspective on agency theory. *Accounting, Organizations and Society, 13*(4), 359–370.

Piaget (1932). *The moral judgment of the child.* London: K. Paul, Trench, Trubner & Co. Ltd.

Tolleson, T., Merino, B., & Mayper, A. (1996). Applying behavioral models as prescriptions for ethics in accounting practice and education: Revisiting fish out of water and an experiment. *Research on Accounting Ethics, 2,* 21–49.

Chapter 25

The Concept of an Accounting Regime[1]

T. Colwyn Jones,   *University of the West of England*
David Dugdale,   *University of Bristol*

This chapter develops and illustrates the concept of an *accounting regime*. The concept is mobilized to explore the nature and power of accounting in totality and to identify its dimensions. Drawing on the work of Anthony Giddens, we portray an accounting regime as a set of social practices constructed through the disembedding and reembedding of accounting as an abstract system that interrelates institutions of modernity and modern forms of reflexivity. The regime simultaneously generates trust and skepticism, and displays recursive cycles of dissolution and reconstruction. Its power — although temporary, partial and fragile — depends on its ability to provide guarantees of expertise in the face of risk.

The Notion of an Accounting Regime

Background

Our interest in the concept of an accounting regime arose during field studies of management accounting. Much academic literature presented accounting as a highly powerful, often dominant, force in organizations. Our research into particular management accounting techniques — investment appraisal, costing systems — led us to doubt this view, but we had reservations about whether such a narrow focus on individual aspects of accounting was an appropriate approach to identifying the power of accounting.

There are two important issues here. The first concerns the construction of accounting as a *network of practices*. Each individual practice is related to sets of other accounting practices (both management and financial) that are themselves embedded in accounting knowledge as a form of economic discourse. The power of accounting may thus reside, not in any specific practice, but in the interconnectedness of the network of practices. The second issue concerns the *dimensions* over which

---

[1]Reproduced (in an abridged form) from T.C. Jones and D. Dugdale. The Concept of an Accounting Regime. *Critical Perspectives on Accounting*, 2001, vol. 12, pp. 35–63, with the permission of Elsevier.

Accounting, the Social and the Political
N. Macintosh and T. Hopper (Editors)

accounting operates. Accounting operates both more broadly and more deeply than appears immediately on the surface of specific practices. Accounting is embedded in (and constitutes) social relations and, in the UK, the relatively strong occupational organization of accounting, and the high rates of occupancy of senior positions by accountants, broadens its potential influence. This influence may be deepened when accounting is a distinctive way of thinking taken as an indicator that individuals have adopted an appropriate managerial (i.e. 'business-oriented') mindset. Thus, to identify the power of accounting it is necessary to capture not only its practices and the information generated from them but also its permeation of social relations and ways of thinking. It was in an attempt to do this that we turned to the notion of an accounting regime.

Terminology

The term 'regime' has a number of meanings and applications. Originally it was a version of 'regimen' and referred to personal practices, but soon it became applied to systems of governance. In contemporary social science it has acquired economic, rather than purely political, meanings. At the *macro* level, the concept of 'regime of accumulation' has been applied to the international economy where four major regimes have been identified in the development of capitalism: extensive accumulation — beginning in the eighteenth century; intensive accumulation without mass consumption (Taylorism/Scientific Management); intensive accumulation with mass consumption (Fordism); and an emergent post-Fordist regime (Hirst & Zeitlin 1992). At a *micro* level the term has been used in the form of 'factory regime' to apply to the political and ideological regulation of production relations (Burawoy 1985). At a *personal* level, a regime may be seen as 'a state of play rather than a permanent condition' but that nevertheless confronts actors 'as a social fact, which they have to come to terms with somehow' (Kessler *et al.*, 1987: 232). The way actors do this constructs a personal regimen — a mode of living.

Accounting and the Dynamics of Modernity

In considering the nature of an accounting regime we have found Giddens' (1990) analysis of modernity to be helpful. Giddens' analysis is informed by his extensive development of 'structuration theory' in which he attempts to replace the dualisms of agency and structure with the 'duality of structure' (Giddens 1973, 1984, 1992). Macintosh (1994: 172) offers a succinct summary of the main points:

> ... structuration theory is concerned with the interplay of agents' actions and social structures in the production, reproduction, and regulation of any social order. Structures, existing in virtual time and space, and drawn upon by agents as they act and interact

in specific time-space settings are themselves the outcome of those actions and interactions.

Giddens does not accord priority to either structures or action. Instead, he suggests we should study social practices that both socialize (constitute) individuals as actors, and realize (embody) structures. Thus structure and action are 'different ways of looking at the same thing: social practice' (Craib 1992: 34). The production and reproduction of society are seen as a skilled performance of its members who draw upon both *practical* and *discursive consciousness*. The former refers to our knowledgability about the world in a taken-for-granted way, the latter to our reflexive monitoring of action. 'Systems' are patterns of relationships that are structured and restructured in social practices: therefore systems have structures, but are not structures themselves. The three central structures in systems are 'signification', 'legitimation' and 'domination'.

> Signification creates meaning in social interaction, domination produces power, and legitimation provides for a system's morality. These three layers, while separable in the abstract for analytical purposes, are intimately entwined in reality (Macintosh 1994: 172).

Applying this to accounting systems, we can see that they consist of: signification codes and interpretative schemes for applying them; domination codes and resources (rights) used to draw upon them; and legitimation codes and norms for using them. When such systems are enacted in social practices of accounting — through communication, the exercise of power to mobilize allocative and authoritative resources, and the application of positive and negative sanctions — they generate meaning, influence and morality. Enacting these structures in routine situations reinforces them: but in crisis (or critical) situations the structures may themselves be transformed through action.

In this paper we are not so much concerned with structuration theory *per se*, but rather with the ways Giddens uses it in his substantive sociology of modernity, and to apply this to an understanding of accounting regimes. For Giddens, the 'dynamism of modernity derives from the separation of *time and space* and their recombination . . . *the disembedding of social systems* . . . and the *reflexive ordering and reordering* of social relations' (1990: 16–17, emphasis in original). He argues that these three dynamics fundamentally alter conditions of risk and trust in modern society. We explore each of these issues below and relate them to accounting.

Time and Space

In the pre-modern world time and place were firmly linked: we might characterize this as a concrete when–where. In modernity, time and space become separated and abstract. Time becomes standardized through the mechanical clock and universal calendar: space by uniform measurements and official maps. The separation of time and space involves standardization that 'empties' them of the necessity for a particular local physical setting for time–space that now becomes global. This 'distantiated' time and space can now be recombined through 'time–space ordering devices' (railway timetables are offered as an example). Giddens refers to this process as 'disembedding' which means 'the "lifting out" of social relations from local contexts and their restructuring across almost indefinite spans of time–space' (1990: 21). This is particularly evident in the way modern rationalized organizations connect the local and the global.

At core, accounting's contribution to disembedding is as a social practice that constructs information: concrete things and events are recreated as abstract values and exchanges. The lowest level of this is *measurement* — the production of data. This in itself is a complex social process and data 'are social constructions which emerge from a negotiated social order' (Jones 1995: 231). Accountants are aware of this and attempt to verify such data before they are accepted as accounting data — accountants deal with numbers but not 'any old numbers'. Since this activity is selective (not all data are checked), it involves the accountant as a knowledgeable actor — evaluating the trustworthiness of the persons and systems that supply data. The next level is that of *technique* — the creation of information from data. A variety of techniques are available that may be applied routinely or for particular purposes, and in some cases two or more techniques — producing different information — may coexist. Accounting also supplies *criteria* for the evaluation of this information against plans, targets and standards.

In the modern corporation such accounting information conditions the possibilities of 'acting at a distance' through its 'centers of calculation' which are flooded with inscriptions that are tabulated and totalled, and where new inscriptions construct a 'scale model' of distant time and space (Latour 1987). Accounting provides the mechanisms by which information on the local (e.g. operating units) is communicated to the global (e.g. head office) where it constitutes a means to act back into the local. In this process, accounting information is emptied of local (tacit) knowledge and changes its meaning. The resulting 'management by the numbers' involves particular recombinations of time and space.

Accountants do interesting things with time. Some practices are familiar, such as in discounted cashflow — where cash is visualized as streaming out into the indefinite future, being captured at some point, and then being hauled back to today as net present value. Other time practices are emerging in the struggle to create a conceptual framework for financial reporting standards that has led accountants to construct a scheme in which the benefits of past transactions (assets) and obligations in the future (liabilities) are to be brought together in the present to constitute the Balance Sheet.

Accountants also do interesting things with space. In financial reporting, a boundary is drawn around the 'accounting entity' which 'is an entity quite apart from its owners or proprietors...[which] owns its own assets and owns the claims (liabilities) against those assets' (Gee 1985: 155). Here the concept of 'the company' no longer refers to a group of individuals in physical proximity, but to a (deliberately fictional) construction of the enterprise, as a legal personality. Within the enterprise, accounting creates other 'abstract spaces' which are not defined by geographical location and that appear, for example, as profit or cost centers, and as direct and indirect locations. The relationships between spaces may be detailed in overhead allocations or transfer prices. These spaces may have no distinct physical, geographical identity: 'divisions' may operate on many sites and even span continents: 'ABC cost pools' may not exist as physical space at all — representing proportions of time and resources consumed in fragmented activities.

In such ways accounting redefines, separates and recombines time and space in abstract form. Accounting information, once created as a record, can move through time and space — it is durable and mobile. No longer attached to the particular circumstances of its construction it may be reconstructed by distant agencies. There may be long lines of translation where the original records are aggregated with others to produce consolidated accounts. They are combined with other records in new ways, perhaps with differential weightings, to provide new hybrid accounts — percentages, ratios, charts and graphs that combine summaries of different things. They can be compared across different localities as comparators that produce rankings. The most powerful of these become 'key performance indicators'.

The accounting record is a means of surveillance that informs the 'centers of calculation' (Latour 1987). However, the sanction that may be prompted by the record can remain undecided. The records are durable: but sanctioning is flexible (Munro 1997). Positive or negative response to the information is a matter of discretion and, importantly, this discretion may be deferred over time. What sanction, and whether or not it will be applied, is undecided for the moment: but at some unknown future date, by some as yet unanticipated actor, sanctioning may be activated — the accounts acting over time and space.

Disembedding Institutions

Giddens argues that the scope of 'time–space distantiation' is greatly extended by the development of *disembedding* institutions. He identifies two key mechanisms in this process, both of which are relevant to our discussion of accounting. First there is the development of *symbolic tokens*, in particular — money. Modern money exists both as cash and coins in everyday transactions and as disembedded symbolic token. It is a mode of deferral in time and implies a space between individuals and their possessions. Thus, it is 'a means of bracketing time–space by coupling instaneity and deferral, presence and absence' (1990: 25). The power of accounting rests to a considerable extent on its ability to re-present other forms of data and calculation in terms of money as pure information — thus linking itself to modernity's most potent symbolic token. Accounting claims to provide the ultimate translation — the bottom line.

Giddens' second important disembedding mechanism is the development of *expert systems*, described as:

> 'systems of technical accomplishment or professional expertise that organize large areas of the material and social environments in which we live today...An expert system disembeds by...providing "guarantees" of expectations across distantiated time-space' (1990: 27).

The layperson has little direct access to the knowledge that is inherent in such abstract systems and so the plausibility of these guarantees rests upon faith in 'the authenticity of the expert knowledge which they apply' (Giddens 1990: 28). Accounting is one such expert system that promises guaranteed economic information; a promise that appeals to the authenticity of accounting knowledge.

In the process of disembedding the nature of accounting discourse changes, and 'Theories, now made abstract and autonomous objects, float like flying saucers above the rest of science, which by contrast now becomes "experimental" or "empirical"' (Latour 1987: 242). The early development of financial accounting as a discipline and profession may be seen as the codification of existing practices so that it was the distillation of experience. However, once accounting was lifted from specific time–space localities it became an abstract system with its own internal logic and social relations, which could interact with other abstract systems.

Alongside, the academic shaping of accounting theory is the development of accounting principles and definitions within the professional bodies. In financial accounting, these are then crystallized in standard statements of practice: a process that has a particular politics of its own and is strongly influenced by the giant international accountancy firms. In management accounting, although the rules do not have statutory force, they may become established as 'best practice' — again with the active involvement of the management consultancy departments of accountancy firms — and be taken as a blueprint for action. These processes of academic and professional organization of abstracted knowledge are regulated by state (and/or supra-state) institutions. The academic and professional wings of abstracted accounting are then linked when accounting theory is laid down in syllabuses, textbooks and examinations that influence large numbers of students — in many parts of the world. Thus, disembedded abstracted accounting is operated on by many global factors and begins to be reembedded in local contexts.

Reembedding

Giddens argues that 'In conditions of modernity, larger and larger numbers of people live in circumstances in which disembedded institutions, linking local practices with globalised social relationships, organize major aspects of day-to-day life' (1990: 79). This everyday organization involves *reembedding*, which is 'the reappropriation of disembedded social relations so as to pin them down (however partially or transitorily) to local conditions of time and space' (1990: 79). At the local level actors have 'facework commitments' in conditions of co-presence with other actors, and 'faceless commitments' that relate them to the abstract systems (symbolic tokens and expert systems). This creates contexts of action that may support or undermine the disembedding mechanisms, and there are ambiguous relationships between facework and faceless commitments. Thus, 'Reembedding refers to processes by means of which faceless commitments are sustained or transformed by facework' (1990: 88).

Accounting as a process constitutes, and is embedded in, social and system relations. The reembedding of accounting is shaped by the social relations of local contexts while simultaneously shaping those contexts. Local time becomes organized around accounting periods — for example, structured by annual, quarterly and monthly reporting, or by longer term business plans. Accounting generates chronological cycles of planning, budgeting, performance monitoring and so on.

Accounting also applies to and restructures local spaces such as departments/divisions, cost pools, or manufacturing cells and establishes relationships between them through apportionment, allocation, transfers, delegation and control. Accounting thus regulates relations between individuals, between individuals and the wider organization, and between parts of the organization. A particular feature of the way accounting does this is the way it has become embedded not only in personal and organizational relations, but in computer technology through the software constructed around its principles.

This socio-technical institutionalization of systems leads to their extended reproduction over time–space — acting in specific localities but not limited to them. Conventional accounting has, in Latour (1987) terms, become a 'black box' that obscures the particularities of the origin of knowledge and represents it as universal truth. Thus accounting weaves itself into our thinking in particular forms of *accounting reflexivity* which present themselves as universal reasoning. The next passage explores the nature of this reflexivity.

Reflexivity

Giddens argues that modernity generates new forms of reflexivity. In early modernity, social change appeared as a move from tradition to reason. So, for example, Weber (1968) identified rationality as the defining feature of modern society. At first this seemed to promise the replacement of the certainties of traditional knowledge with new certainties of science. However, as modernity developed, it became clear that modern reflexivity subverts reason: the rational questioning of all things leads to questioning the assumptions on which the questions rest. In the constant monitoring of behaviour and contexts, of thought and action, all knowledge becomes unstable. Whereas some have identified this as the post-modern turn, for Giddens it is the working through of the modern ('radicalized modernity') as it comes to understand itself. In modernity, knowledge is always provisional, contestable and open to differing understandings. Since reflexivity becomes the basis for system reproduction, the instability of knowledge produces an unstable world.

Following this analysis we can identify shifts in the nature of accounting reflexivity. The first move is the secularization of accounting. This may appear surprising since modern accounting is usually regarded as an exemplar of rationality — for example in Weber's discussion. However, if we look to its pre-modern form we find it embedded in an inter-relationship of science and religion. For the monk Pacioli, at the end of the fifteenth century, double-entry book-keeping was part of a 'larger project to *re-emphasize a belief in order sanctified by God*' (Thompson 1994: 51, emphasis in original). In ninteenth century Germany, accounting could be seen as inscribing 'the soul of the middle class' reflecting a morality based on order and balance (Maltby 1996). Thus, the development of modern accounting as rational calculation involved a process of secularization — the purging (or at least obscuring) of beliefs and values.

The second move is the operation of modern reflexivity, with its self-doubting nature, on rational accounting. By the mid-twentieth century, in both the US and UK, an accounting regime had been established around the twin poles of the Profit & Loss Accounting and Standard Costing. Financial accounting was guided by the 'matching principle' for revenue and expense (Paton & Littleton 1940) with the P&L being privileged as the prime representation of financial reality — and the Balance Sheet being dismissed as 'a mausoleum for the unwanted costs that the double entry system throws up as regrettable by-products' (Baxter 1962, quoted by Tweedie 1996). In management accounting, heavily influenced by the Scientific Management movement, standard costing systems producing full absorbed costs and making careful distinctions between 'direct' and 'indirect' labour, were central to monthly routines of reporting 'efficiencies' and tracing 'variances'.

By the end of the twentieth century, both poles of 'traditional' and 'conventional' accounting had been destabilized. Financial accounting experienced a 'rationality crisis' (McKernan & O'Donnell 1998) that undermined the core concepts of established accounting practices. Academic accountants' response to this was that 'revenues and expenses' were to be decentered, and priority accorded to 'assets and liabilities', with the balance sheet instated as the prime statement of financial reality. Management accounting also faced a 'crisis of confidence' (Dent 1990) following identification of 'an acute failure of managerial expertise, and of calculative expertise in particular' (Miller & O'Leary 1993: 188). Following the declaration of the 'lost relevance' of management accounting (Johnson & Kaplan 1987) there was a development of a busy and crowded market for new accounting — e.g. activity-based costing, throughput accounting, target costing, economic value added — as traditional systems were condemned as producing irrelevant (mis)information.

What is at stake in this second move is not merely reliance on particular accounting techniques, but continued belief in the efficacy of accounting calculus in general for reporting financial performance and for 'managing by the numbers'. Modern reflexivity means that the powerful technologies of accountability and regulation are perpetually undermining themselves and require constant support and reaffirmation. Thus, at the same time as new forms of accounting were being created, accountants defended the validity of past accounting, and its continuity with the present — for example, by (re)defining financial reporting problems in terms of an 'expectations gap' or by identifying 'evolution not revolution' in management accounting.

Given that the knowledge of expert systems cannot be guaranteed, why then do people continue to rely upon them, to trust in them? Giddens argues that we make a 'bargain with modernity'. We are socialized to trust, so that as we learn science we also learn a respect for science as reliable knowledge. This spills over into respect for other forms of technical knowledge. This respect exists in conjunction with skepticism so that attitudes are ambivalent — a balance of respect and skepticism. In the modern world there is no escape from expert systems and

> 'attitudes of trust towards abstract systems are usually incorporated into the continuity of day-to-day activities and are to a large extent enforced by the intrinsic circumstances of daily life' (1990: 90).

Thus, we have a predisposition to trust, which is constantly being undermined, but lack of alternatives means we make pragmatic compromises that are woven into our routines. Giddens stresses that this does not necessarily imply 'passive dependence'. Instead, he identifies four possible adaptations: 'pragmatic acceptance' — just getting through it; 'sustained optimism' — reason will triumph in the end; 'cynical pessimism' — things will turn out badly whatever we do; and 'radical engagement' — participation in new social movements to change the world.

In constructing and applying pragmatic compromises in situations of ambivalency, accountants' reasons and reasonings are complex and influenced by technical, personal, social and political issues that are inter-related in the construction of an accounting rationality (Jones 1992). There are significant differences between forms of 'academic rationality' — applying to accounting in its disembedded form, and 'practitioner rationality' — when accounting is embedded in specific localities (Jones & Dugdale 1994). These rationalities are intertwined with *values* and *beliefs*. Here we identify values as concerned with the legitimacy of the ends to which accounting is directed: and beliefs as concerned with confidence in the means of pursuing them.

In much conventional accounting, the ultimate value is attached, to capital — the maximization of shareholder wealth — sometimes with a legitimating claim that this is a universal value. Against such views of the legitimate ends of accounting are the values of those who propose 'social responsibility' or 'green' accounting. In the latter, the accountants' overriding duty is to be 'a friend to the Earth'. Disagreement about value may also be detected in management accounting's treatment of costs. Whether labour should be treated as a 'variable' or a 'fixed' cost might be thought of as merely a technical issue, but for the strongest supporters of the latter view there are important humanitarian values at stake. These concern whether employees are to be treated as costs that must be reduced or eliminated, or whether organizations should — on moral and practical grounds — provide secure and satisfying employment for their members.

Disagreements over the ends to be pursued may be accompanied by very different beliefs about the appropriate means to be adopted. The last decades have seen successive waves of 'management philosophy' with their familiar acronyms (JIT, TQM, TOC, BPR, WCM) that offer very different views of what is to be done. Often the 'new' philosophy runs counter to 'conventional' wisdom. To move from one perspective to the other may require a fundamental shift in viewpoint. Thus, belief is more than the taken-for-grantedness of everyday life — it has to be established. Since the 1980s, such appeals to fundamental changes in view ('paradigm shifts') have been associated with the activities of 'management gurus'. Many observers of this phenomenon have noted the features of belief and faith in this and detected a similarity to spiritual or religious spheres of life.

Accounting not only responds to such values and beliefs, but also generates its own: that quantified information is superior to qualitative information and that it can be expressed in financial terms; that increasing shareholder wealth increases societal wealth; that accountability is necessary and that it can be achieved by monitoring and control.

Given the interplay between values and beliefs that lie below the surface of accounting, we can expect an emotional dimension to accounting reflexivity. This is a neglected feature of the social analysis of accounting. Nevertheless, we suggest that emotions are important in understanding accounting. Accounting may be associated with a wish for orderliness, balance and caution in life; but also with fear, pride and guilt. Accounting is something that people care about; and this occasionally comes into the light.

All of these ingredients — *rationality*, *values*, *beliefs* and *emotions* — construct an accounting mindset. By this we do not imply that accounting has constructed the subject — say as 'the governable person' (Miller & O'Leary 1987) — there may be consent, mediation and resistance to accounting as rules and resources for action. Rather, we point to ways in which the reflexivity of the 'knowledgeable actor' in an accounting regime is constructed from, and reconstructs, the rationality, values, beliefs and emotions of accounting. The ultimate power of accounting may reside in such a mindset — a 'bottom-line mentality' informing the reflexive monitoring of action.

Accounting, Risk and Trust

Central to Giddens' discussion of modernity is the rise of modern forms of risk and ways of establishing a sense of (limited) security in relation to them. In particular, he is concerned with the manner in which we trust expertise to identify and manage risk, whilst being aware that expert systems are themselves not fully reliable and generate new risks of their own.

Risk

Risk is identified as a characteristically modern phenomenon. In pre-modern societies, the relationship between dangers in the world and the human actor was seen to be governed by 'fortuna' (i.e. fortune or fate). When the term 'risk' was introduced in English (in the seventeenth century), it represented the modernist notion that unwanted results could be the consequences of the actors' own decisions and activities. Thus it becomes possible to speak about 'calculated risks' and 'acceptable risks'.

Giddens identifies increasing risk as a hallmark of the modern world. We have no guarantees that it will not all end in nuclear holocaust or environmental catastrophe; and we have no personal way of evading these possibilities. In modernity, risk increases in intensity, depends on an expanding number of contingent events and exists in created 'natural' environments and new institutional settings. We are aware of the risks we face (and aware of them as 'risk'), but recognize the limitations of our expertise in facing this environment. In the world which accounting inhabits these risks are demonstrated, for example, in the potential collapse of giant corporations affecting the lives of hundreds of thousands of investors, employees, pensioners and others (such as Enron's collapse in 2002), or in situations where the actions of a single trader in obscure financial markets far away might bring down a bank and threaten to destabilize the financial establishment.

Trust

Giddens identifies trust as a necessary condition for modern life. Modern forms of reflexivity have produced epistemological uncertainty — we can never guarantee our knowledge. Facing the pervading risks of the modern world this might put us in a perpetual state of existential anxiety (angst or dread). Yet, modern life is also characterized by ontological security: 'the confidence that most people have in the continuity of their self-identity and in the constancy of their surrounding social and material contexts of action' (1990: 92). At a cognitive level modern reflexivity means we can never be sure, but at an emotional level most of us are. Giddens identifies this as *basic trust*. Other forms of trust are built upon this basic level.

In pre-modern societies, *trust-in-persons* was constructed in localized contexts and embedded in social relations. In modernity, where social relations are disembedded, *trust-in-systems* becomes more important. Again trust is required because of ignorance — of the technical knowledge and the workings of abstract systems — but here trust rests upon a faith in the correctness of principles rather than the trustworthiness of individuals. Thus, in the modern world, social trust takes two forms:

> Trust may be defined as confidence in the reliability of a *person* or a *system*, regarding a given set of outcomes or events, where that confidence expresses a faith in the probity or love of another, or in the correctness of abstract principles (technical knowledge) (1990: 34, emphasis added).

The disembedding and reembedding of trust is illustrated in a number of accounting studies. Miller & O'Leary (1987) argue that the development of standard costing enabled the standardization of the 'normal' worker who could now be 'known' — made visible to the system — in new ways. Under Scientific Management, individual performances became abstracted to performance standards and workers could be known in terms of their 'efficiency' compared with the norm. Similarly, budgeting provided a means of making managerial performance visible. Accounting provided a calculative apparatus that lifted out performances from their local social relations to enable workers, managers, departments, plants and divisions to be monitored and compared. Ignorance of the local contexts of action gave rise to trust-in-systems at the global level.

The construction of trust-in-systems to replace trust-in-persons is also the central thrust of 'principal-agent theory'. Here, remote principles (e.g. corporate owners) are seen as contracting with their local agents (e.g. managers) with the aim of aligning agents' interests to those of principals. Accounting's contribution to this is to monitor the contract through the setting of targets, measurement of outcomes, and allocation of rewards — promising to constitute a trustworthy system. However, the problem with this is that monitors are themselves agents and would need to be monitored — which would lead to an endless (and prohibitively expensive) chain of regulatory relationships. At some point trust must be placed in persons and thus the inescapable issue is deciding who — not whether — to trust (Armstrong 1991). In Giddens' terms, abstract trust (in systems) can never be complete — it must be reembedded (in persons).

Access Points

Trust-in-systems and trust-in-persons interact when abstract systems are rembedded in specific contexts of action. These provide 'access points' linking personal and system trust, and individuals at access points normally go to great pains to show themselves to be trustworthy. At such access points, the expert represents the system — attempting to reinforce faith in its abstract capacities through personal performance ('facework').

One aspect of this is that:

> 'once rules are established and trusted, they define what constitutes a competent actor . . . [actors become trusted through] repeated demonstration of ability, willingness to live by the rules, and sincerity (Jönsson & Macintosh 1997: 369).

However, trust may require more than a technical performance. Harper (1988) describes the way that Chartered Accountants systematically acquire the attributes of appearance and demeanour appropriate to their public performances in presenting themselves and representing their profession. To succeed in their career, trainee accountants must convince both in their technical performance (especially in passing examinations) and in their social performance (looking and acting the part). Those that succeed find that their lives increasingly become played out as personal ambassadors for accounting. At the apex of the professional hierarchy, partners are almost never off-duty, and distinctions between public and personal life are abolished. As access points to accounting, these accountants have constructed an *accounting self* for presentation to others.

Simultaneously, laypeople present themselves for expert scrutiny, enabling knowledge of them in the manner in which the system constructs knowledge. For example, in putting forward investment proposals, proposers present themselves to investment appraisal. Senior managers' enquiries seeking to establish 'credibility', 'confidence' and 'faith' in proposals, are simultaneously interrogations to establish the trustworthiness of the proper. This trust may be based not so much in confidence in the 'probity' (moral uprightness, honesty) of the proposer, but that the proposer has adopted a business-oriented approach compatible with that of the senior manager. Here accounting practice operates as an embodiment of the abstract system, and a personal means of demonstrating an appropriate mindset. The proposer must present (must have learned to present) both a dextrous and convincing concrete application of abstract accounting principles.

Trust-in-systems, reinforced by trust-in-persons, may give confidence in the face of the risks of the modern world: but such confidence is never complete. There are 'design faults' in abstract systems, and persons are liable to 'operator failure'. Further, there are 'unintended consequences' that result not only from these two features, but also from the complex interrelationships of the modern world. Finally, the modern constant circularity of reflexivity and system reproduction means that these problems can never be closed: new knowledge creates new worlds. Thus, abstract accounting systems are simultaneously faced with trust and skepticism: always experiencing recursive cycles of dissolution and reconstruction.

The Concept of Accounting Regime

Drawing together the strands of our discussion of Gidden's theory of modernity, we now present a formal statement of our concept of an accounting regime.

An accounting regime is a system of governance that operates: at a macro level of national and international society, polity and economy; at the micro level of organization; and permeates the personal level where accounting constitutes both rules and resources for action. It encompasses an economic dimension (calculation of the production, distribution and consumption of value), a political dimension (regulation and accountability) and an ideological dimension (forms of accounting reflexivity). An accounting regime is socially constructed in recursive cycles of disembedding and reembedding that link the local and the global, the concrete and the abstract.

At the core, an accounting regime is composed of *sets of social practices* that generate information. This information is disembedded from local contexts to more global levels, moving through time and space, and changing meaning in this process. It is then used to act back upon the local level through processes of reembedding where again its meaning may be altered. In parallel with this, accounting practices are disembedded to become principles constructed within *accounting discourses*. These are socially organized at the global level in the production of accounting theory that is then reembedded in the form of standards or 'best practice'. In local contexts, accounting then constitutes, and is shaped by, *social and system relations* — structuring relationships between actors and between systems. At the access points between actors and systems, *accounting reflexivity* is constructed as a 'mindset' that both absorbs and acts back upon accounting discourses.

The power of an accounting regime depends on the strength of trust-in-systems that it can generate in construing the risks of modern society and presenting guarantees of the authenticity of its expertise in facing them. This trust is not absolute: it is constantly undermined by reflexive (epistemological) skepticism. Nevertheless, in acting in the modern world trust-in-systems is (ontologically) inescapable and so there are constant attempts to maintain and secure the abstract system, and to confirm it through trust-in-persons. The construction of such regimes relies upon the creation of networks that bind actors and intermediaries. These networks are formed by translations that — when strong — maintain and change them, but that — when weak or broken — can precipitate their collapse. Accounting regimes are temporary, partial and fragile — but no less powerful for that.

References

Armstrong, P. (1991). Contradiction and social dynamics in the Capitalist Agency Relationship. *Accounting, Organizations and Society*, *16*(1) 1–25.

Burawoy, M. (1985). *The politics of production*, London: Verso.

Craib, I. (1992). *Anthony Giddens*. London: Routledge.

Dent, J. (1990). Strategy, organization and control: some possibilities for accounting research. *Accounting, Organizations and Society*, *15*(1/2) 3–25.

Gee, P. (1985). *Spicer and Pegler's book-keeping and accounts* (19th ed.). London: Butterworths.

Giddens, A. (1973). *The class structure of the advanced societies*. London: Hutchinson.

Giddens, A. (1984). *The constitution of society*. Cambridge: Polity.

Giddens, A. (1990). *The consequences of modernity*. Cambridge: Polity.

Giddens, A. (1992). *The transformation of intimacy: Love, sexuality and eroticism in modern societies*. Cambridge: Polity.

Harper, R. (1988). The fate of idealism in accounting, *2nd Interdisciplinary perspectives on accounting conference*. University of Manchester: July.

Hirst, P., & Zeitlin, J. (1992). Flexible specialization versus post-Fordism: Theory, evidence and policy implications, in M. Storper & A.J. Scott (eds). *Pathways to industrialization and regional development*. London: Routledge.

Johnson, H.T., & Kaplan, R.S. (1987). *Relevance lost: The rise and fall of management accounting*. Cambridge: Harvard Business School Press.

Jones, T.C. (1992). Understanding management accountants: The rationality of social action. *Critical Perspectives on Accounting, 3*(3) 225–257.

Jones, T.C., & Dugdale, D. (1994). Academic and practitioner rationality: The case of investment appraisal. *British Accounting Review, 26*(1) 3–25.

Jones, T.C. (1995). *Accounting and the enterprise: A social analysis*. London: Routledge.

Jönsson, S., & Macintosh, N.B. (1997). Cats, rats and ears: Making the case for ethnographic accounting research. *Accounting, Organizations and Society, 23,* 367–386.

Kessler, S., Ashenden, D., Connell, B., & Dowsett, G. (1987). Gender relations in secondary schooling, in M. Arnot, & G. Weiner (eds). *Gender and the politics of schooling*. London: Open University.

Latour, B. (1987). *Science in action: How to follow scientists and engineers through society*. Milton Keynes: Open University Press.

Macintosh, N.B. (1994). *Management accounting and control systems: An organizational and behavioural approach*. Chichester: Wiley.

Maltby, J. (1996). Accounting and the soul of the middle class: Gustav Freytag's Soll und Haben. *Accounting, Organizations and Society, 22*(1) 69–87.

McKernan, J.F., & O'Donnell, P. (1998). Financial accounting: Crisis and the commodity fetish. *Critical Perspectives on Accounting, 9,* 467–599.

Miller, P., & O'Leary, T. (1987). Accounting and the construction of the governable person. *Accounting, Organizations and Society, 12*(3) 235–265.

Miller, P., & O'Leary, T. (1993). Accounting expertise and the politics of the product: economic citizenship and modes of corporate governance. *Accounting, Organizations and Society, 18*(2/3) 187–206.

Munro, R. (1997). Power, conduct and accountability: Re-distributing discretion and the technologies of managing. *Fifth interdisciplinary perspectives on Accounting Conference*, July.

Paton, W.A., & Littleton, A.C. (1940). *An introduction to corporate accounting standards*. Ann Arbor: American Accounting Association.

Thompson, G. (1994). Early double-entry bookkeeping and the rhetoric of accounting calculation, in A.G. Hopwood & P. Miller (eds). *Accounting as Social and Institutional Practice*. Cambridge: Cambridge University Press.

Tweedie, D. (1996). Regulating change — the role of the conceptual statement in standard setting, in I. Lapsley & F. Mitchell (eds). *Accounting and Performance Measurement*. London: Chapman, 18–35.

Weber, M. (1968). *Wirtschaft und Gesellschaft* (Tübingen: J.C.B. Mohr, 1922) Economy and society (Trans. G. Roth & C. Wittich). New York: Bedminster Press.

Chapter 26

Accounting, Learning and Cultural Integration[1]

Cristiano Busco and Angelo Riccaboni,   *University of Siena*
Robert W. Scapens,   *University of Manchester*

This paper draws on insights from a case study, combines empirical evidence and theoretical analysis to explore the interactions between performance measurement systems and the processes through which organizational cultures change. The focus is on the underlying nature and processes of learning and change.

Established in 1842 in Florence, Italy, Nuovo Pignone [NP] was originally a cast-iron foundry that developed the world's first gas-powered internal combustion engine, along with other products. In 1954, it was incorporated into ENI, the Italian government agency for hydrocarbons and began designing and manufacturing electrical turbines and rapidly achieved a reputation as a high-quality manufacturer of specialized equipment for process-based and energy-related industries. NP compressors, pumps and turbines are now world-class product leaders. Although, over the years, NP has had a 'fairly relaxed management style' (according to a senior manager at NP for more than 20 years), it has continued to be very profitable because of its excellent products and production systems.

NP had been a state-owned and largely bureaucratic company. It had to produce budgets and various reports for both the head office and the state. But the systems it used were not integrated into its management processes. NP was quite profitable, due largely to excellent products and production systems rather than to management and accounting controls. As an accounting manager pointed out, using a naval metaphor: 'To be a bureaucratic state ship, we were adequately equipped and armed. We didn't need to shoot, nobody asked us to find our limits, and there were no wars to fight'.

As part of the Italian government's wide-scale program of privatization in the early 1990s, General Electric Inc [GE] acquired more than 80% of NP equity shares in 1994. This percentage eventually increased to 91% in 1998, when a second major contract was signed for the Trans-Siberian pipeline.

---

[1]Reproduced (in abridged form) from Cristiano Busco, Angelo Riccaboni and Robert W. Scapens, 'When Culture Matters: Processes of Organizational Learning and Transformation', *Reflections: The Society for Organizational Learning*, 2002.

Accounting, the Social and the Political
N. Macintosh and T. Hopper (Editors)

The Role of Accountability Systems

Following the GE acquisition, NP implemented various restructuring programs of which the major change involved the concept of measurement. Whereas,
NP had no tradition of widespread performance measurement, GE's management
and organizational style relies extensively on measurement systems.

Changing NP

As one project engineer explained, 'When, in 1994, GE's integration team started to
arrive in Florence … one thing was clear to everybody: a revolution was going to
happen'. A finance manager sitting next to him added, 'We knew the world was
going to change. And the world has changed totally'! It was immediately clear to
everybody at NP that the company was undergoing a two-fold cultural change:
not only from an Italian to an American company, which was itself a big step,
but also from a bureaucratic state-owned company to one of the most intense,
business-oriented corporations in the world. It was also clear that, although the
process was described to the Italian staff as *integrating* NP within GE — introducing
GE's values while respecting NP's capabilities and promoting change rather than
forcing it — it was GE that was ultimately the new boss. Although a former ENI
director remained as NP's chairman, a 'GE man' was installed in the powerful
position as NP's CEO.

There were two major components to the organizational change that took place
within NP, both supplemented by intensive and extensive training programs.
The first component was the redesign of the company's systems of accountability
and the second was the subsequent implementation of a new measurement-based
quality program — the six-sigma program.

The Accountability Revolution

Redesigning NP's systems of accountability involved both major extensions of the
company's financial systems and a restructuring of the accounting and finance
function. This restructuring, which was essential for enabling the financial
systems to be extended, comprised a reorganization of the department traditionally responsible for cost accounting, setting up a new department of financial
planning and analysis for NP as a whole, and creating a new cadre of finance
managers. These managers were placed in the individual divisions and were
responsible for the supervision of budgeting and reporting at the operating level,
as well as providing financial support to the operating managers. As such, they
were able to help managers cope with the new systems of accountability and
performance measurement. In addition, managers at all levels were intensively
trained in the new systems to ensure that both the accountants and managers

understood them thoroughly. A finance manager who joined NP at the time of the acquisition explained:

> There had been no culture of measurement; at least, the attention towards those aspects was very poor. It wasn't a mere tools problem. Of course, several instruments were not adequate to the new requirements, but that didn't look like the key problem.... There was no emphasis on performance control mechanisms.... If no one asks you to make proper numbers, if no one checks your performance, you don't do it. You know you should achieve the targets, you try, but you are fairly relaxed.... It was a question of management a question of leadership. Ultimately, it was a question of culture.

Despite statements from GE's CEO such as: 'Don't focus on the numbers.... Numbers aren't the vision; numbers are the product.... I never talk about numbers', it was immediately clear within NP that financial measures and metrics of accountability had become crucial. 'Numbers became the core of our organizational life.... You need to achieve the targets, you need to show the numbers, and you must do it on a quarterly basis', explained a financial analyst. Now, reports, data, information, charts and so on flow continuously around the company, largely in response to the pressure to produce numbers, and good numbers, every three months. As a business analyst remarked, while nervously consulting his calendar, 'GE's headquarters need numbers to show Wall Street. Consequently, we need to be fast, reliable, and profitable. If not, the week after, tough inquirers start to cross the Atlantic...'.

The importance of producing the numbers has increased the status of the personnel directly or indirectly involved in finance and accounting. Furthermore, the need to incorporate operating processes into the accounting systems has prompted an extension of those systems. For example, a recent innovation has enabled these systems to permeate to the shop floor, which has allowed finance managers, who are physically located in the production sections, to monitor their operations daily.

Wearing the Finance Hat

To facilitate communication between accountants and engineers and between finance and project managers, the organization implemented a massive training program. Thus, it trained all NP engineers and skilled operatives in the fundamentals of financial measurement. In addition, it persuaded sales managers and other sales personnel to think in financial terms and to consider their customers as 'financial entities'.

An expressed concern for measurement and customer satisfaction were at the forefront of NP's cultural transformation. Management and control systems, comprising specific metrics of accountability and performance indicators, were essential tools for making the business measurable. 'Such an approach was ... very different from the past, but it was convincing .... At the end, it enhanced feelings of trust and respect', explained a salesman who then pointed to the relevant sections of an internal training manual on 'how to master financial selling'. 'If you're relatively new to finance, *relax* — it's not that difficult or complicated to get started. No, you don't have to be a CPA or financial wizard to use some of the fundamentals of finance in selling', reassures the introduction. The booklet emphasizes the importance of showing customers how GE solutions can affect the financial results of major segments of their business.

> Force yourself to continually think of your account as a 'financial entity' whose only goal is making greater profits, and your only goal is to help them do that via implementing GE solutions .... Stress GE's unique or powerful features as part of the financial selling process, then *translate* them into competitive financial reasons to buy .... We need to show our customers how these features translate into operational benefits — how they perform faster, more accurately, are less costly, and more efficient. Then, we can translate these features into *quantifiable financial benefits* with the help of our customers.

Following the massive training program, a new financial awareness emerged across the company. Describing NP's control systems before GE's acquisition, a management accountant emphasized, 'There were no pressures for financial improvements .... *The tools were there, the data were there, but they didn't look so interesting or "burning" as now.* I still have doubts that anyone bothered to read those documents carefully', he continued. But now, there are no such doubts.

The Six-Sigma Program

The six-sigma program played a major role in bringing about cultural change at NP. Six-sigma is a business philosophy, grounded in a quality improvement initiative, which has had a major impact on many large businesses during the past decade. At the core of the program is the process of *defining, measuring, analyzing, improving* and *controlling* all operations of the business — support operations as well as production operations. Furthermore, there are various six-sigma 'players', with titles such as *champions* (leaders who promote, approve and facilitate projects within their area of responsibility), *master black belts* (full-time six-sigma managers who lead teams dedicated to specific projects) and *green belts* (who work part-time on specific projects, while continuing their normal activities in the company).

NP implemented the six-sigma program at the end of 1996; it had an immediate impact on the company's organizational structure and human resources management. NP established a quality team, reporting directly to the CEO, to help the product divisions and functions implement their quality improvement plans and specific six-sigma projects, and appointed a master black belt for each business process or function. In addition, there was an extensive internal training program, with 1500 white-collar workers (of 3000) becoming green belts by the end of 1999. The emphasis on six-sigma was huge. It was considered the key common language to drive GE globally. As clarified by GE's vice president for the program: 'Without six-sigma, if you run a plant and I run a plant, it's tough to understand your numbers. Then you can say, 'Your ideas won't work, because I am different'. Well, cry me a river. The commonalities are what matter. If you make the metric the same, we can talk'.

Processes of Cultural Change

NP's organizational transformation went very deep, involving complex processes that combined rationality, successful experiences and feelings of trust. GE was so totally different from ENI that a massive cognitive redefinition was required. It was a matter of first unlearning the old culture and then relearning a new one. In general terms, people tend to resist profound cultural changes because unlearning processes is uncomfortable and produces anxiety (Schein 1999: 155). Nevertheless, possibilities for change increase when three factors are balanced: the mechanisms of disconfirmation, the creation of survival anxiety (or guilt) and the subsequent creation of psychological security to overcome learning anxiety. These factors contribute to *unfreezing* the values that inform the institutionalized organization culture, and as a result, cultural change becomes possible.

From the outset, the GE philosophy was imposed very aggressively throughout the company. GE's CEO, talking to a meeting of operating managers, categorized managers and employees in the following terms: *A Players*, who subscribe to the company's values and who have to be kept and rewarded; *B Players*, who still deserve to be trusted because they have the potential to improve their skills and productivity; and *C Players*, who do not subscribe to the company's values and, without remorse, deserve to be fired.

The changes at NP occurred quickly, and, despite its undoubted technical competence, speed was not a typical characteristic of the old NP. According to a B-ranked engineer, 'It wasn't a normal change; it was a shock! An earthquake in our daily way to think and behave. Take the example of human resource management; from a rather relaxed system mainly based on egalitarian principles, we suddenly faced the A, B, C ranking theory. I am not arguing it was right before, but this was scary'.

Within NP, the charismatic leadership of GE's CEO and the measurement-based training program were sources of disconfirmation, to which even the unions unintentionally contributed. As a result, all levels of the company recognized the need for change, which represented a new organizational credo. Although union leaders regarded local management's conduct as opportunistic and a betrayal 'by someone who has suddenly lost his memory due to being well paid'!

The 'GE way' seriously threatened the psychological security built during the era of ENI management. Most people at NP were aware of the company's past and present characteristics and knew its strengths and weaknesses. In view of GE's reputation, it was not difficult to predict the intensity of the integration process. Everyone was aware that 'scary' claims (like the A, B, C rankings) could and indeed would become reality.

The stories and the rhetoric that contributed to creating the myth of the 'GE way' had a powerful impact on established frames of meaning. The unions stated they were ready to fight the changes, but NP was already changing. Furthermore, workers' reactions to GE's values were quite rational. Interviews of lower level employees, while cataloguing the usual complaints, revealed quite clearly how much they cared about being part of a world-famous company. Thus, after initially creating survival anxiety or guilt, continuous waves of communication and training promoted an emerging sense of psychological security. The diffusion of a new business credo reinforced this feeling, which empowered people and gave them the trust needed to overcome learning anxiety.

...With Successful Experiences

After the unfreezing of NP's established frames of meaning, people's perception of 'new knowledge' was at a conscious level. Thus, possibly as a consequence of the need to align personal and collective values, beliefs and patterns of behavior with the new owner's vision, a certain degree of rational awareness characterized their motivations. 'We are building up the necessary kit for survival, aren't we'? asked a project engineer at the end of a financial training session.

Nevertheless, as organizational members gained experience in coping with the events that stimulated these conscious re-evaluations, their rational patterns of behavior tended to transform into more tacit, routinized behavior. More specifically, as the redesigned cognitive schema that underpin such routines work repeatedly over time (for example, in the six-sigma projects), they provide a sense of psychological security and are taken for granted. Furthermore, as the routines become socially validated, they become institutionalized and part of the stock of mutual knowledge.

Conclusion

Managing organizational complexity is undoubtedly one of the main challenges facing corporate leaders. In order to cope with problems of external adaptation and internal integration, many corporations are increasingly relying on measurement-based systems of management to align business processes with corporate strategy. In so doing, they are infusing organizational culture with metrics of performance measurement and accountability. In this article, we have illustrated how organizational culture and measurement-based systems can evolve simultaneously.

By translating external market-drive pressures into internal financial and nonfinancial targets, linked to specific production processes and business practices, these systems enable organizational leaders to transform broad, abstract strategies into visible (quantifiable and measurable) tasks, even at the lowest operational levels. As such, they provide objectives that individuals and groups can understand and enhance their identification with the organization's cultural values expressed by its leaders. From this perspective, the merging systems of measurement and performance accountability can be seen as socially constructed, validated practices through which organizational culture is created, stored and transmitted across space and time.

Management accounting and other performance measurement systems cannot be regarded as objective and value-neutral tools. By carrying, diffusing, validating and institutionalizing the taken-for-granted assumptions that constitute organizational culture, they can be seen as technologies deeply implicated in the production and reproduction of shared organizational knowledge and values. In the NP case, implementing such systems improved communication and integration by giving engineers and other nonfinancial personnel a common language of accountability based on financial and nonfinancial metrics. Furthermore, this shared vocabulary (the accounting language, the six-sigma metrics and so on) overcame the communication, cultural and operational boundaries between subsidiaries and divisions located in different parts of the world. For these reasons, we conclude that at NP, while the change of ownership opened the possibilities for organizational transformation, it was a measurement-based revolution that gave it direction.

References

Schein, E.H. (1999). *The corporate culture survival guide*. San Francisco: Jossey-Bass.

Chapter 27

A Termite Theory of Accounting Information Systems Research[1]

Jesse F. Dillard, *Portland State University*

Research in accounting information systems (AIS) can be categorized using three alternative perspectives: technical-empirical, historical-hermeneutical and critical. A fixation on technical solutions to complex organizational and societal problems has resulted in the dominance of the technical-empirical perspective. Generally, accounting information systems are portrayed as technique committed to the realization of rationalized technological systems and solutions. Drawing on Latour's (1987) metaphorical descriptions of the knowledge 'accumulation cycle', the inherent limitations in the three perspectives are illustrated.

Technological Imperative

The technological-empirical imperative is motivating and supporting the development and application of AIS within organizational settings. Modern organizations are viewed as the primary societal institution in the United States and organization management is committed to maintaining this privileged status. According to conventional organization theory, as the environment changes, the organization must react appropriately to these changes in order to survive. If the organization acts in ways that are inconsistent with the well-being of society, workers, or any other stakeholders, justification is required to rationalize and motivate continued cooperation and support. If organizations cannot legitimate their actions, they are in danger of losing their privileged position as custodians of society's resources, not the least of which are the time and efforts of those citizens working within the organizations. As the decision environment becomes more dynamic and complex, greater pressures are placed on organizations. Management finds it increasingly difficult to maintain adequate growth and profits. In the face of declining fortunes, it becomes more difficult to rationalize exploitative behavior and privileged positions.

---

[1] Reproduced (in an abridged form) from J. Dillard, 'A Termite Theory of Accounting Information Systems Research', *Advances in Accounting Information Systems*, 1995, vol. 3, pp. 163–180, with permission of Elsevier.

Accounting, the Social and the Political
N. Macintosh and T. Hopper (Editors)

To date, the primacy of the modern organization has been sustained by the general acceptance of the 'organizational imperative'. The acceptance of this imperative indicates that if the needs of the organization take precedence over the needs of the individual, the individual will be better off.

Given the increasingly competitive and international market environment, the current stewards of society's resources are finding it more difficult to sustain the legitimacy of the organizational imperative. As a result, management is appealing to redemptive technology in order to sustain its competitive and privileged position. However, the costs to stakeholders are not insignificant and must be justified.

This imperative holds that the individual must recognize that the good of the individual can come only from the organization whose good health depends on the development and application of advanced technology. The technological imperative represents one facet of a technological ideology that maintains all problems can be defined in technical terms and are solvable using advanced technology, reviving the Tayloristic principle of 'one best way'. 'The' solution is to be found through the application of scientific knowledge by technical experts. Experts are viewed as impartial problem solvers, above personal and political biases.

Resource allocation decisions are based on management's determination of the most pressing needs in light of strategic positioning, operational requirements and market demands. These decisions are increasingly being framed within a rather narrow, technocratic mind set. Innovation, cost reduction, quality improvement and flexibility are the principal justifications given for implementing advanced technology systems. Economic benefits are gained by replacing direct and indirect labor with capital. As processes become automated, information is directly and simultaneously entered into the information database, reducing the need for data entry personnel. At the lower and medium management levels, employees whose primary functions have been intermediate information processing are replaced by the powerful information processing capabilities of computer-based information systems. An extensive review of the extant work in the area identified the following general tendencies, within such environments:

• Polarization occurs among organizational groups as advanced computer-based systems are implemented;
• Technological complexity replaces organizational complexity;
• Higher abstract skill levels are needed to design and implement new systems;
• Lower levels of skills are needed to carry out the traditional organizational processes; and
• Wider gaps are opening among the groups.

While some recognize the displacement costs involved, the primary concern with respect to introducing advanced AIS systems is how to overcome the anticipated resistance.

Scott & Hart (1989) argue that the generally unquestioned acceptance of 'technological innovation' has come about as the result of a change in societal norms and values. Technical expertise and technology are viewed as untainted by political and economic interests, providing an objective and merit-based criterion for making resource allocation decisions. To challenge the technological perspective and the accompanying AIS, is seen as irrational, an indication of incompetence of political bias. As a result, the individual is subordinated by, and to, the technologically based system. Subordination prevents discourse whereby the legitimacy of actions can be debated and evaluative norms developed. As the organizational requirements come to dominate the evaluation criteria, objective forces deprive the person of his or her right to question, evaluate, accept, or reject the new workplace. The inability to reflect on and influence the circumstances within which one exists comes about as the technological imperative is internalized and becomes the individual's rationality.

The technological imperative provides legitimation for the implementation of systems designed to maintain the status quo. AIS can be seen as an integral part of the emerging technologies that are directed toward maintaining current power and social relationships. These new solutions are often unquestioned because they appear to be consistent with the prevailing ideology. AIS is supportive of, and determined by, the technological imperative. For example, the social and individual costs of deskilling as a result of automated manufacturing or an expert auditing system implementation are being justified by claiming the inevitability of technological change and the accompanying market pressures. Accounting information systems (AIS) are developed and applied within this context; therefore, the context cannot be ignored in AIS research.

The legitimation of AIS is based on the technological imperative that is allowing system implementation to proceed with little consideration for the negative implications of social costs. The question arises as to how an ideology becomes the unquestioned, and at times unrecognized, basis for action? This query leads to the second part of the discussion, which concerns how one uses, and does research into, accounting information systems.

Knowledge Networks

Accounting information systems are sociotechnical constructions of technique committed to the realization of rationalized technological systems.

Both the research and practice of AIS can be viewed as part of what Latour (1987) has called the 'accumulation cycle' that is being engaged in by 'centers of calculation'. The centers of calculation send out reconnaissance parties to gather information about the world. As these excursions cross paths with the 'natives', the intelligence gained is transported back to the centers of calculation. The ability to transport facts back depends on their mobility and stability. If the fact is not mobile or if it changes state (i.e. spoils) during the return trip, the fact cannot be faithfully transported back to the center.

The more trips, the more returns. The more path crossings with the 'natives', the more knowledge at the center. The more modern and complex the facts are, the more symbolic forms needed to transform existence outside the center of calculation into something that can be mobilized, gathered, archived, summarized, reassembled, simplified and ranked back at the center. The result of this process ultimately takes the shape of a flat surface (paper or computer screen) that can be archived, pinned on a wall or projected on a screen. The transformation of outside existence into symbolic forms allows the center of calculation to construct more extensive knowledge networks, establishing force fields between those who are controlled and those who control. As the asymmetry of knowledge gets larger, those in power will be better able to 'domesticate' those who are not.

The 'natives' do not generally wander into the center of calculation and, if they do, they are overwhelmed by the black box technology used to construct and maintain the knowledge networks. The assumptions underlying the calculations and the processing methods used are hidden under n level paper forms.

The center of calculation can be the headquarters staff of a strategic business unit or the laboratory of an AIS research team. Within these centers, extensive networks provide the context and means for searching, collecting and aggregating. In an organization, centers of calculation maintain control over the entity's resources. The extant techniques are justified, substantiated and sustained by a knowledge network that includes systems technology, calculative accuracy, accounting convention, control philosophy and management strategy.

In the research laboratory, theoretical justification in such areas as research design, measurement techniques and statistical analysis provides the foundations for AIS research studies. Within each area, extensive knowledge networks represent assumptions, theorems, functional relationships and rules for manipulation based on prior empirical and analytical networks. These networks, joined with the network of management accounting knowledge, result in AIS applications. The field progresses along this network as one study builds upon another, the latter being justified by the former. As the network develops, certain initial issues are no longer visible or subject to question. What was problematic becomes assumed and the current work proceeds along a path somewhat predetermined in its trajectory.

We creep along these networks giving very little thought to what immediately precedes the current object of consideration, and if we do happen to raise our heads and look astern, we are confronted with n levels of paper forms that have been produced by very capable people using very complex instruments. Thus, we assure ourselves that such backward looks are regressive, construed as irrational, and probably a waste of time since others with unquestioned qualifications have decreed the legitimacy of the work. The knowledge networks along which we travel are literally papered with the alleged representations of the phenomena of interest that have resulted from the accumulation cycle. Research, as we have come to practice it, cannot exist outside of such networks.

According to Latour (1987), research consists of closing a series of black boxes. Once the boxes are closed, it is difficult to reopen and examine them, to question their validity, or to eliminate their influence. At one level, an example of a Latourian black box is the application of the REA model as a valid means of organizing multidimensional data about economic events. At a more abstract level, an example of a Latourian black box is the technological imperative that represents an unchallenged assumption that provides the context for research and action. That the technological imperative provides the justification for such work as well as the allowable interpretative context is much less obvious, but much more pervasive and constraining. If the technological imperative is accepted as a legitimate socioeconomic manifestation and if the knowledge network description of Latour is accepted as a legitimate view of AIS research and practice, is there any way out of our narrow and biased networks? Probably not, but it might be helpful to investigate alternative network structures, each of which would result in different networks relative to the same phenomenon.

The Black Boxes of AIS

In this section, three research perspectives are briefly discussed to point out the associated black boxes that provide the methodological context for AIS research. Because different assumptions are made, different observations of similar phenomena are possible. These alternative perspectives will not eliminate the black-box-based knowledge mentality but they could foster an appreciation of alternative views.

The following discussion investigates AIS research and practice from three different perspectives:

• Technical-empirical;
• Historical-hermeneutical; and
• Critical.

The *technical-empirical* perspective is aligned with an objectivist tradition. The foundational research black boxes that underlie the technical-empirical perspective are summarized here:

• Reality is single, tangible and fragmentable;
• The researcher and object of study are, and remain, independent;
• Time and context-free generalizations are possible; there exist identifiable cause-and-effect relationships; and
• Inquiry is value free.

Two views prevail within this perspective. Both see computer-based systems as capital investments with the objective of reducing 'production' costs. One view is the traditional positivist view, embodied in the vast majority of AIS research and applications, which focuses on efficient and effective resource utilization through understanding and controlling instrumental means–end relationships. The legitimation for undertaking research and developing accounting information systems follows from the technological imperative and includes: improved quality, freedom from mundane tasks, more interesting work, reduced work time, improved documentation, increased effectiveness and reduced costs.

AIS have been shown to be especially effective in automating computational tasks which have prespecified rules and identifiable parameters. For example, spreadsheet programs have the propensity to greatly increase effectiveness and efficiency. The user can be freed from low-level, repetitive tasks, allowing one to engage in tasks where higher levels of analysis and judgment are needed. On the other hand, the need for technical and managerial skills may be diminished by the technology. As a result, there may be a reduction in opportunities for employment, skill enhancement and advancement, as well as costs.

The other technical-empirical view seldom encountered in the AIS literature takes a traditional labor process view, focusing on system design and implementation as they impact the worker/user. As such, this view points to the possibility of AIS accelerating the development of elite groups of narrowly focused experts accompanied by a general deskilling (or not-skilling) of the labor force (Tinker & Yuthas 1995). This view tends to question the acceptance of the technological imperative in light of the possible negative impact on the worker/user groups. As one black box is pried open, another is created. The technological imperative is replaced by the 'class struggle', which assumes that reality is to be framed in terms of the antagonistic social relations that underlie capitalist economic imperatives. The technological imperative is characterized as a false imperative instigated by the societally powerful groups and designed to maintain the prevailing power relationships. For example, AIS systems have been found to codify and reinforce prevailing power and control structures (Orlikowski 1991).

The *historical-hermeneutical* perspective is aligned with the naturalist or interpretivist tradition. The foundational research black boxes that support this perspective are:

• Reality is a contextually specific construction possibly taking many forms;
• The researcher and the object of study are interactive and inseparable;
• Generalizations are time and context bound; a state of mutual simultaneous shaping exists so that it is impossible to distinguish cause from effect; and
• Inquiry is value constrained.

The historical-hermeneutical perspective postulates that reality is constructed through language, conversation and context. The single-reality black box is replaced by a more pluralistic and malleable socially constructed one. Winograd & Flores (1986) focus attention on the system design limitations that arise because of the centrality of dialogical situatedness in understanding. An example of how this perspective might be useful in AIS research undertakings would be a reinterpretation of the Kerr & Murthy (1994) study that investigated group decision support systems (GDSS) and cooperative learning. As a result of their experiment, the authors concluded that GDSS are beneficial to learning or, more precisely, to acquiring technological knowledge when compared to face-to-face group activities and to acting alone. They also reported higher levels of dissatisfaction for the GDSS treatment group. The conclusion reached was that GDSS should be used to enhance performance and that better technology (i.e. interfaces) should be developed to overcome the dissatisfaction — a recommendation consistent with the technical-empirical perspective but somewhat at odds with a historical-hermeneutical one. A technical perspective is limited to technical knowledge. It seems that Kerr & Murthy's subjects were also telling them that interpersonal intereactions and context add richness and quality. Taking only a technical-empirical perspective severely limits the 'variables' considered.

The historical-hermeneutical perspective transcends the 'one best way' claim of the technological imperative by recognizing the subjectivity of understanding our reality. Human agency is central and action is predicated on the intentionality of human behavior, which contradicts technological determinism. The foundational black box assumptions again engender limitations. Generally, the position taken describes reality as that perceived by the individual(s). As a result, the ability to address external conditions that give rise to certain meanings and experiences is limited. With intentionality as a fundamental premise, unintended consequences, some of which have a strong influence in shaping social reality, are not addressed. Privileging human agency also obscures structural conflicts within society and organizations, ignores contradictions endemic in social systems and does not consider historical change. Further, there is no transformative dimension associated with the historical-hermeneutical perspective.

The *critical* perspective generally embraces the black box assumptions of the historical-hermeneutic perspective with two exceptions. First, the critical perspective attempts to open the sociocultural and political black boxes surrounding the interpretivist position through critical evaluation using particular theoretical frameworks that go beyond the self-understanding of the participants. The societal forces motivating such phenomena as the technological imperative and its implied deterministic nature are taken into account. Second, praxis is the objective of critical evaluation. Not only are the researcher and the researched interactive, but it is also the responsibility of the researcher to influence the researched in overcoming debilitating social relationships and practices that provide the basis for alienation and domination. The ability and desirability of change based on a critique of the status quo is a central tenet of the critical perspective. The purpose of critique is not to develop causal models, but to clarify the social tensions so as to facilitate emancipatory understanding and action.

Dillard & Bricker (1992) have used a critical perspective in investigating the application of knowledge-based expert systems in public accounting firms. Using a framework proposed by Habermas (1984, 1987), expert systems are seen as a manifestation of the technological imperative. While these systems have potential for enhancing audit — efficiency, quality and technical competency, an equally likely outcome is a negative effect on the development of expertise and value judgments. Reducing the auditor's public sphere may also reduce the quality of the work environment. If objective actions are the only ones permitted, one loses touch with normative and subjective dimensions, leading to distorted understandings and ultimately to distorted actions. As technical rationality dominates, value and ethical considerations are omitted as primary decision criteria and action is justified solely in terms of efficiency and effectiveness.

Though at a level different from the prior two perspectives, there are limiting black box assumptions associated with the critical approach. Through rational reflection, one is presumed to be able to discover rational self-clarity and a sense of collective autonomy, which will result in happiness. A major assumption holds that emancipation from oppressive conditions can be achieved by overcoming false consciousness through reflection, recognition and understanding. The notion that ideas are the sole determinant of behavior is dubious. Further, structural and physical restraints, such as those imposed by authoritarian regimes or monopolistic labor markets, limit the extent to which reflection and enlightenment can lead to resistance and freedom.

Network Constraints

Regardless of the perspective, Latour's (1987) knowledge networks provide at least a thought-provoking metaphor for visualizing how AIS research and practice are carried out. We, as actors, creep along the knowledge networks giving little thought to what immediately precedes the current action item under consideration, and if we happen to raise our heads and look back, we are confronted with *n* levels of paper forms and cultural legitimacy. We have not the time or the expertise to delve into the justifications of the paper forms that allegedly represent the object under consideration. And, in fact, it would be viewed as irrational to do so. By accepting the knowledge network (and realistically, we have little choice), we are constrained by the network. Accounting information systems techniques cannot exist outside the network and they cannot be understood outside the network. All activity extends the network and the dominance of the center of calculation. Transformational shifts are extremely difficult.

This description conjures up images of vast amounts of activity along these knowledge networks, not unlike what one might visualize within a colony of termites. Accountants, systems designers, managers and researchers build their enlightened networks using calculative techniques, giving the outside the same paper representation as their techniques inside. Termites build their galleries with a mixture of mud and their droppings. In both cases, the result is the same. One can travel great distances without ever really leaving home.

References

Dillard, J., & Bricker, R. (1992). A critique of knowledge based systems in auditing: The systemic encroachment of technological consciousness. *Critical Perspectives on Accounting*, 205–224.

Habermas, J. (1984). *The theory of communicative action*. Vol. 1. Trans. T. McCarthy. Boston: Beacon Press.

Habermas, J. (1987). *The theory of communicative action*. Vol. 2. Trans. T. McCarthy. Boston: Beacon Press.

Kerr, D., & Murthy, U. (1994). Group decision support systems and cooperative learning in auditing: An experimental investigation. *Journal of Information Systems*, *8*(2).

Latour, B. (1987). *Science in action.* Cambridge: Harvard University Press.

Orlikowski, W. (1991). Integrated information environments or matrix of control? the contradictory implications of information technology. *Accounting, Management and Information Technologies,* 9–42.

Scott, W., & Hart, D. (1989). *Organizational values in America.* New Brunswick. NJ: Transaction.

Tinker, T., & Yuthas, K. (1995). Unsettled frameworks: Voluntarism and dialectics of MIS research. in *Advances in Accounting Information Systems*, S. Sutton (ed.). Greenwich. CT: JAI Press.

Winograd, T., & Flores, F. (1986). *Understanding computers and cognition: A new foundation for design.* Norwood. NJ: Ablex Publishing Corporation.

Part III

Beyond

The articles in this part go beyond those in the contemporary and classic in that they gesture towards several promising directions for future research regarding accounting and the social. In the lead article, Lukka & Mouritsen (2002), challenge the idea of a hegemonic, homogeneous and monolithic economics-based accounting research program, as say, that advocated recently by Zimmerman (2001). They make a strong case for heterogeneity in accounting research, reasoning that homogeneity would not only silence epistemological and ontological debates, but also put a gag on scholarly freedom thus silencing any sort of critical stance. The articles that follow illustrate the richness of their call for heterogeneity.

The first three of these develop theories along the lines of the linguistic turn, advocated by the likes of Ludwig Wittgenstein and Richard Rorty, a path followed to great advantage by most of the social sciences and humanities for many decades. In the first of these, McGoun (1997) argues that today's postmodern financial capital market can no longer be usefully depicted as a 'rational institution' responding to the 'real' economic performance of corporations, as the conventional view would have it. Rather, McGoun argues for a perspective that sees the stock market as an ungrounded hyperreal game where financial assets have no 'true' value but are simply tokens (i.e. simulacra) that capital market players use as symbolic value in participating in what resembles a giant poker game. Along similar lines, Macintosh, Shearer, Thornton & Welker (2000), drawing on Jean Baudrillard's 'orders of simulacrum' and 'phases of the image' schemes, investigate the ontological status of the information in accounting reports, particularly reports of income and capital. They conclude that accounting no longer functions according to the logic of transparent representation, stewardship or information economics, but rather increasingly model only that which it is itself a model circulating in a hyperreal domain of self-referentiality. Macintosh & Baker (2002), taking a literary theory perspective, treat accounting reports as texts to indicate how four literary genres — expressive realism, the new criticism, structuralism and poststructural deconstruction — represent different ways which individuals and various accounting schools of thought try to understand the meanings in accounting reports. They conclude, following the Russian literary theorist Mikhail Bakhtin, that heteroglossic accounting should replace the current practice of producing monologic reports.

Next, two articles adopt an institutional theory perspective to develop new insights into how accounting works in society. First, Oakes *et al.* (1998), drawing on some of Pierre Bordieu's concepts of how society at large works (e.g. cultural capital, fields of relational networks) provide fresh insights into understanding how pedagogical exercises, language and power are central to the way management control structures work to shape values and constitute societal change. They illustrate this in the context of a Canadian provincial government change program, which shifted the meaning of its museum programs from cultural heritage to one of economic value. Then, Covaleski, Dirsmith & Samuel (2003), drawing on early transaction cost economists' work, show how the calculus of accounting can be appropriated for legitimacy seeking purposes in contentious politically fragmented contests such as the deregulation and privatization of public organizations within the context of global institutionalism.

The last two articles expand the domain of accounting thought in two different but complementary directions, one looking back to link premodern era theology to sophisticated accounting, reporting and organization structuring practices not unlike today's, and the other looking forward to challenge the ideology of postmodern economic theory-based globalization underpinning accounting's future. In the first of these, Shearer (2002) observes how we are all caught in the web of a global economic system that we are increasingly unable to control, challenge, confront or change. She then reveals the potential of looking to philosophy as a way of critiquing accounting by demonstrating how Emanuel Levinas's 'ethics-of-being-for-the-other' establishes a broader accountability on the part of economic entities than that in the discourse of economic theory. Shearer concludes that extant accounting theories are inadequate to reflect such accountability, since the discourse they are conceived in and rendered constructs the moral identity of economic entities as answerable only to itself, thus negating any moral accounting to others.

In the final article, Quattrone (2004) documents how the fifteenth century Jesuit Order had developed, refined and instantiated sophisticated organizational reporting and accounting practices including a formal system of 'accountability for the soul' of each member of the Order. These practices constituted a complex system of compromise among theological, religious, political, institutional, economic and social factors reflecting the absolutist ideology of the Roman Catholic doctrine of the Counter Reformation at the time. They rendered visible those aspects of the soul which were vital for 'making the good "soldier", the good "teacher", the good "manager": in short, the good Jesuit' (668). These characterizations seem paradigmatic of the demands put on today's executives and managers.

The articles in Part III, then, indicate how Lukka & Mouritsen's plea for heterogeneity in accounting research can usefully and insightfully expand the boundaries of accounting research well beyond a narrow economics-based hegemony. So it would not be too surprising if some of them prove to be seminal in their own right. Moreover, it is not unlikely that some will act as 'pointer readings' for future generations of accounting scholars and researchers.

Chapter 28

Homogeneity or Heterogeneity of Research in Management Accounting?[1]

Kari Lukka, *Turku School of Economics and Business Administration*

Jan Mouritsen, *Copenhagen Business School*

Viewing Zimmerman (2001) as propagating an economics-based monolithic paradigm for management accounting research, we examine the nature and implications of such Kuhnian 'normal science'. Acknowledging that normal science can produce cumulative knowledge efficiently, we examine its risks as well. Like any normal science, one based on economics inherently offers a narrow window to the world, and creates areas of 'non-discussables'. We illustrate how such a regime would limit our abilities to construct and examine interesting propositions and develop meaningful stories about management accounting in its social, organizational and behavioural contexts. Accepting the rule of a monolithic economics-based paradigm would limit our abilities to develop a critical stance, and threatens the ability of management accounting research community for good scientific conversation and progress. Hence, in contrast to Zimmerman, we argue to remain open for heterogeneity in management accounting research.

Introduction

Is normal science a good model for management accounting research? This question presses itself forward when reading Zimmerman's (2001) concerns about the state of affairs in the area of empirical management accounting research. In a commentary to Ittner & Larcker's (2001) review paper, Zimmerman appears to suggest that the best and probably only way to develop a cumulative body of theoretical knowledge in management accounting is to enter a period of 'normal science' (Kuhn 1970), i.e. to preserve but one research programme, or paradigm, for management

---

[1]Reproduced in full from Kari Lukka and Jan Mouritsen, 'Homogeneity or Heterogeneity of Research in Management Accounting?' *The European Accounting Review*, 2002, 11:4, pp. 805–811 with permission of the EAA (http://www.tandf.co.uk).

Accounting, the Social and the Political
N. Macintosh and T. Hopper (Editors)

accounting research. For Zimmerman, this paradigm should be based on economics. We think this is dangerous, not only because it leaves out important types of findings related to understanding management accounting practice, but also because the price to pay for increased efficiency in the research process will be a decrease in reflexive tinkering with management accounting practice and theory. In addition, accepting the rule of a monolithic economics-based paradigm would threaten the ability of management accounting research community for good scientific conversation and hence progress.

The Aspiration of Management Accounting Research

Zimmerman's concern is legitimate and important: how can we create good management accounting research? His conclusion is worth listening to: we need more rigour, more testing and more theory. This proposition looks appealing, since who could be against it: less rigour, less testing, less theorizing? However, the fundamental question is what these propositions stand for. To us, theorizing can be a liberating effort: an attempt to make sense of our world in a more abstract level than that of merely describing the immediately perceived practice. Testing can be viewed as seeking to find out the connections that hold in the world. Rigour again can be about seriousness in finding this out. These propositions offer one set of qualitative criteria to create knowledge — good knowledge, relevant knowledge, insightful knowledge. However, they also illustrate that the meaning of being rigourous, to test, and to theorize is not a given. Both knowledge and its criteria of goodness are constructed, reproduced and reconstructed (e.g. Latour 1987). Consequently, epistemological notions such as these get their meaning within the framework of assumptions and metaphysics in which they are applied. In the discipline of management accounting, the spread of paradigms in use illustrates researchers' degrees of freedom. The fewer paradigms present at a particular point of time, the narrower will be the available spread of propositions about rigour, testing and theorizing.

Ittner & Larcker (2001) are clear about this in their review and point out explicitly what the domain of their interest is. They are also aware that certain propositions about rigour, testing and theorizing are not present in their sample. Their strategic choice to limit their review 'to organization level studies that use archival and survey data' (ibid: 350) leads them to focus on statistical research, hypothesis testing and cross-sectional research. They place their analysis in the North American mainstream and the economics paradigm. There are yet alternatives to this choice. Economics-based research has its merit, but it is just one voice, and for the academic community to exist and develop a critical stance, the possibility for multiple voices is there (e.g. Mouritsen *et al.* 2002). Though this is no doubt less visible in the North American academia, a global perspective shows that the management accounting research community *in toto* accepts a plethora of different approaches to conducting research. We believe that an attempt to stop this would mean regression, not progress, within the management accounting academia.

Homogeneity versus Heterogeneity

Our concern with Zimmerman's mono-paradigmatic position is that it makes theorizing, testing and rigour mechanisms for confining research rather than liberating it. We get the impression that adopting his suggestion would increase rather than decrease prejudice. As there cannot be a way of definitely privileging any paradigm by empirical or logical arguments, propagating for one is a value judgement, having a political tone. Adoption or sponsoring a paradigm is hardly a scientific act.[2] Even if we agree that economics-based research has a lot to offer, we think that pressing management accounting towards a mono-paradigm status is to silence insights about management accounting. It is to create and protect a set of 'non-discussables' — things that cannot be debated even if we sense they are important.

The key benefit of normal science is to produce cumulative knowledge efficiently. This is since researchers can take certain fundamental assumptions and the appropriate research methodology as granted. These issues are 'black-boxed' in normal science, and researchers are often even unaware about the assumptions they have adopted. Normal science typically leads to concentration on small puzzles and incremental contributions to the extant knowledge by individual studies. The efficiency of normal science may be appealing and comforting, but it is also inherently deceptive and dangerous: it ignores the fact that any empirical observation, even if collected from a specific theoretical perspective, will under-determine its explanation. Observations do not speak for themselves, and they can always be spoken for via different paradigms.

Each paradigm builds boundaries between what is acceptable and what is not. If we were only to adopt an economics-based paradigm, the following propositions in management accounting would not be possible. Miller (1998) suggests that management accounting does not have a stable essence, but that it rather changes all the time both at the margins and sometimes very fundamentally as responses to social situations. Armstrong (1985) proposes to see the techniques of management accounting as an effect of struggles between intra-organizational professions such as accountants and production people for corporate attention. Wallander (1999) proposes that the techniques of management accounting such as budgeting systems never work, are a waste of time and generally lead to conflicts; for instance, about budget targets and playing the numbers game.

Propositions such as these about management accounting would fare with difficulty if a mono-paradigm based on economics were to be installed. They could be stipulated in a formally testable form — as typical of economics-based research — but in such a form these propositions would be interested primarily in 'whether'

---

[2] It is important to notice that Kuhn's (1970) theory of research paradigms and their dynamics is in itself an attempt to describe the way academic disciplines function and develop, and does not include any prescriptive elements. In contrast, propagating for a certain paradigm, as Zimmerman does in his piece, is a highly normative act.

management accounting works, and not so much in 'how' it works. Yet, the 'how' question is much more part of the agenda of Miller, Armstrong and Wallander, and it is this 'how' that allows them to appreciate the historically contingent and situationally specific character of management accounting practices. These issues would be silenced by the economics-based paradigm.[3]

More generally, the 'how' tends to be interested in a proposition, which says that things can only work in a situation, in a particular stream of life, and therefore this stream of life has to be the object of the research question. It focuses the researcher's attention to the way (new) management accounting gets an interest, how management accounting techniques develop, how they are mobilized and used, and how they are disposed off again.

The different pictures of management accounting illustrated by the three examples outlined above allow us to be critical about management accounting in a different way than economics-based reasoning does. They are based on different metaphysics than that behind the economics paradigm. It is the variation of different conceptions of the metaphysics of management accounting that gives us the breadth of possible propositions. And it is, paradoxically, this breadth that can make debates over the empirical observations possible between the economics-based paradigm and other paradigms. In fact, this is the only possible test of the metaphysics behind the paradigms. By just conducting normal science research within one certain paradigm the fundamental assumptions will never be tested.

How Do We Generalize?

Zimmerman wishes management accounting research to produce general knowledge. However, one needs to acknowledge that generalization plays a role both in the economics-based management accounting research and its alternatives, though the nature of generalization differs vastly. The economics-based empirical research applies statistical generalization rhetoric from a random sample to the population. It allows researchers to gain insights into the use of management accounting techniques across contexts, but separates management accounting practice from its production, which becomes 'black-boxed'. Cumulation of knowledge occurs if many researchers add to existing confirmed, or non-falsified, propositions.

Generalization conducted in other kinds of management accounting studies (for example, in field research) builds on a different language game. Empirical propositions are compared with situations described and analyzed in prior studies. The 'contextual generalization rhetoric' these studies tend to apply means that outcomes of individual field studies are generalized by looking at how findings of various studies relate and can be made to talk to each other

---

[3] In management accounting studies of all kinds, responding to the 'why' question is typically appreciated. Since economics-based studies do not notably differ from those representing alternative paradigms in this regard, we omit discussing this question here.

(Lukka & Kasanen 1995). They can be silent on quantities related to the 'whether' question, but they can also be critical of this. Since the quantities that can be learnt about are all produced within a particular culture, discourse or social system, making comparisons between, or drawing conclusions from, findings coming from different social systems need to be made with great care. But when such comparisons are made, disagreements become voiced, even to the point where the original 'paradigmatic' differences get aired.[4]

Is this not to advocate 'mere' folklore or idiosyncrasies? Probably it is to a certain extent, but this kind of 'detour' is often necessary and interesting, because it can help us open the black box regarding how management accounting techniques are related to managerial practices. It shows how things are connected and fabricated in empirical settings. They can add to, qualify, but also question, statistical generalizations, which are seldom very strong. Even if statistically significant, correlations are often meager. In addition, there are many obviously or probably true generalizations, which are either irrelevant or uninteresting. From this viewpoint, it may be that contextual generalizations, being drawn from practical settings situated in specific social, organizational and behavioural contexts, can produce meaningful results compared also with the promises produced by the statistical generalization rhetoric.

Different Research Agendas, Different Stories

Responding to the 'whether' questions, typical of economics-based research, may supply answers that are difficult to understand. Responding to the 'how' ones may make it possible to understand the sequence of elements that have to be in place for a management accounting technique to be organizationally interesting.

To illustrate this, Miller & O'Leary's (1994) study of the introduction of management accounting at Caterpillar could be represented as a causal model: the discourse on US competitiveness leads the firm to adopt management accounting techniques which are more in accordance with a process-based view of the firm than before. But is this an interesting generalization? The story can be told in a completely different way: the problem of competitiveness along with problematizations of the state of US competencies, along with a debate on the failure of the US factory system and the success of a Japanese competitor were seized by Caterpillar management as a window of opportunity to install corporate restructuring. This process involved redefining the customer, changing the factory layout to suit a customer-oriented, process-focused approach. It also involved reorganizing production workers in cells and involved the installation of huge systems of information technology to allow lateral communication to proceed.

---

[4] See, for example, the special issue on the debate between Marxism and Foucauldian analysis in *Critical Perspectives on Accounting*, vol. 5, no. 1, 1994.

In this situation, management accounting was drawn upon to provide a lateral view of the firm rather than a traditional hierarchical one.

The two stories outlined above differ notably even though they deal with the same issues and are based on the same case evidence. They bring out very different lessons. The first storyline suggests that social and economic problems translate easily into corporate restructuring. The latter story (and the even longer and stronger ones provided by Miller & O'Leary in their paper) suggests a series of mechanisms and types of alignments that have to be 'in place' for this transformation to go on. There will be interest in all the people, systems, organizational routines, emerging strategies and sense of identity that can be theorized as part of the uptake of new management accounting methods. The two stories are different theories of management accounting, they are charted very differently, and they pay attention to different things: the first to certain predefined inputs and outputs; the latter to many of the mechanisms that need to be put in place to allow the transformation to go on. But could there not be more mechanisms? Yes, but this is a criticism that can be leveled at economics-based research as well — and at all research paradigms, for that matter.

The point here is that it is possible to wrap an observation in many types of theoretical understandings. If we attempt to police them by projecting normal science within merely one paradigm, such variation would be lost. Sure, by doing that, certain puzzle-solving would be successful, but it would not produce the possibilities to debate the reasonableness of the assumptions of the research. As pointed out above, if an economics-based paradigm were adopted, the economics base would never be tested under such a regime. Hence, even if items of falsification were built up, they would be relegated to another realm of the 'non-discussables', or be reinterpreted as 'anomalies'. Consequently, the possibility for good scientific conversation would get violated and the progress of the discipline would be at risk (Longino 1990; Reiter & Williams 2002).

More reflection is possible, if we could debate the fundamentals of research, even if we know that it is difficult to get agreement on such issues. It would demonstrate that research is open-minded, and in line with the well-established ethical corner-stone of criticalness in scholarly work. To us this is a good value, even if in practice it is difficult to achieve. Undoubtedly, there is a politics of research involving journals' quality criteria and preferred modes of theorizing; Zimmerman himself has been exposed to this (Tinker & Puxty 1994). However, rather than giving up on this, we should attempt to make this politics accessible and analyze it as part of the production of facts about management accounting.

For Heterogeneity

What does the market for research look like? Is it possible to accept heterogeneity rather than homogeneity in the marketplace for research? Paradoxically, it may be that for the scholarly market to work — say, for a journal — it may have to be bounded by institutions such as research paradigms. It is interesting to note that the call for normal science is to wish to establish norms for the functioning of (a section of) the market for research. It may be that the market cannot handle variation and that it presupposes institutions that allow it to function smoothly. This would be a tendency towards homogeneity. However, this is costly since the inducement for change, brought in by allowing heterogeneity, would be lost. The critical value judgement here is whether it is necessary, or good, to keep the door to change open or not. We would prefer to keep the door open towards heterogeneity. It is probably difficult, but also vibrant. And it would make the life of a researcher more interesting.

References

Armstrong, P. (1985). Changing management control systems, the role of competition between accountancy and other organizational professions. *Accounting, Organizations and Society*, *10*(2), 129–148.

Ittner, C.D., & Larcker, D. (2001). Assessing empirical research in managerial accounting: A value-based management perspective. *Journal of Accounting and Economics*, *32*, 349–410.

Kuhn, T.S. (1970). *The structure of scientific revolutions*, 2nd (ed.). Chicago: University of Chicago Press.

Latour, B. (1987). *Science in action: How to follow scientists and engineers through society*. Milton Keynes: Open University Press.

Longino, H. (1990). *Science as social knowledge: Values and subjectivity in scientific inquiry*. Princeton: Princeton University Press.

Lukka, K., & Kasanen, E. (1995). The problem of generalisability: Anecdotes and evidence in accounting research. *Accounting, Auditing and Accountability Journal*, *8*(5), 71–90.

Miller, P. (1998). The margins of accounting. *European Accounting Review*, *7*(4), 605–621.

Miller, P., & O'Leary, T. (1994). Accounting, Economic citizenship and the spatial reordering of manufacture. *Accounting, Organizations and Society*, *19*(1), 15–43.

Mouritsen, J., Thorsgaard Larsen, H., & Hansen, A. (2002), Be Critical! critique and naivete — Californian and French connections in critical Scandinavian accounting research. *Critical Perspectives on Accounting*, *13*, 497–513.

Reiter, S.A., & Williams, P.F. (2002). The structure and progressivity of accounting research: The crisis in the academy revisited. *Accounting, Organizations and Society*, *27*(6), 575–607.

Tinker, T., & Puxty, T. (1994). *Policing accounting knowledge. The market for excuses affair*. London: Paul Chapman.

Wallander, J. (1999). Budgeting. An unnecessary evil. *Scandinavian Journal of Management*, *15*(4), 405–421.

Zimmerman, J.L. (2001). Conjectures regarding empirical managerial accounting research. *Journal of Accounting and Economics*, *32*, 411–427.

Chapter 29

Hyperreal Finance[1]

Elton G. McGoun,   *Bucknell University*

Once upon a time a group of congenial people got together (at a coffeehouse, beside a curb, or under a buttonwood tree in different versions of the story) for a game. They each paid a bit of money for tokens and began to play. The game turned out to be especially interesting and exciting and it attracted passerbys, who asked to join in. They were allowed to do so, but their tokens were a little more expensive than the original tokens because the game had become so desirable. This raised the value of all of the tokens in the game.

There was no guarantee that anyone in the game would be a winner, but with new players steadily boosting the value of tokens, everyone could rationally expect to come out ahead in the long-run. Players could still lose all of their tokens, and if forced out of the game for one reason or another, end up cashing in their tokens for less than they paid for them originally. But as a few new players were always being attracted to the game and as not too many players cashed in tokens to make purchases, the game proceeded happily along, with everyone enjoying the thrill of competition and the prestige of increasingly valuable stacks of tokens.

As it grew, the game attracted journalists and scholars, responding to what had become an insatiable demand by players for more information regarding the game. Government officials also took a keen interest, since such a popular game involving vast sums of tokens had to be regulated for the protection of its participants. Eventually, there were few in society whose lives were not touched by the game in one way or another, and all agreed that the game was indeed a grave matter.

Introduction

The fundamental behavioral assumption of economics (the science of the allocation of *things* — the omnipresent 'goods and services') is utility maximization. The fundamental behavioral assumption of finance (the science of the allocation of money) is wealth maximization. As finance has traditionally been a branch of economics, there ought to be some connection between these assumptions. No one believes that wealth and utility are equivalent, but what makes the replacement acceptable is that money (wealth) *can* often buy happiness (utility). Of course, money

---

[1] Reproduced (in an abridged form) from E.G. McGoun, 'Hyperreal Finance', *Critical Perspectives on Accounting*, 1997, vol. 8, pp. 601–632, with permission of Elsevier.

Accounting, the Social and the Political
N. Macintosh and T. Hopper (Editors)

does not actually buy happiness. Rather, it buys *things*, and in a modern market economy in which more and more *things* have a price, everyone is free to exchange their money for those *things* which give them the most happiness. As long as finance is willing to ignore the happiness that money *can't* buy, then wealth maximization is indeed utility maximization.

Without things, then, money should have nothing to do with happiness. When money itself is obviously a source of happiness or unhappiness for someone, as for the miser or the spendthrift, we regard such behavior as aberrant. In both our scholarship and our society, we are wedded to the notion that the financial economy (of money) exists for, refers to, and is meaningless without the so-called real economy (of things).

But is it? What if 'real' finance (finance which refers to the real economy), is in fact 'hyperreal' finance (finance which refers to nothing but itself)? What if financial transactions are not moves in an economic (real) game concerning things but moves in a non-economic (hyperreal) game having nothing to do with things? What if wealth does not measure the ability to buy things but instead measures both the capacity to play this game (in which no one ever buys things) and the success with which one has played it? What if it is the game money can play that gives someone happiness and not the things money can buy?

At the very least, capital markets research, in which we use the reactions of financial markets to measure the impacts of real events, would be a more questionable undertaking. In a broader sense, however, our entire understanding of finance and our attempts to develop effective public policy regarding financial markets would be transformed. Many phenomena would be less baffling. We observe the seemingly endless proliferation of financial assets and institutions, limitless growth of transactions volumes, boundless volatility of prices, countless mergers, acquisitions, and divestitures of businesses, and relentless pursuit of greater and greater wealth.

There are often no discernible causes for such phenomena, and concepts like market completion, liquidity, information, signaling, agency, utility and market efficiency are then tortured into providing dubious explanations. In the spirit of William of Occam, it may be so much simpler to understand finance as a *thing* itself — as a popular post-modern game, open to all that can afford the price of admission.

The idea here is not to create a 'post-modern finance theory' to supplant so-called 'modern finance theory', for it is a mistake to believe in such grand tales that purport to encompass all human behavior. It is rather to tell a new story that might make more sense of some observations than our old stories.

Value

Intrinsic Value

Finance believes that a financial asset has a 'real' value, the 'real' value being what someone ought to pay for it. This definition assumes that there is a correct value for a financial asset ('ought') and that this value is important in exchange ('to pay').

In standard finance theory, the intrinsic value of a financial asset is the present value of whatever will be received in the future to settle the claim represented by that financial asset. To know the intrinsic value then is to know both the value of the settlement and the correct rate at which to discount that value to the present. As it will occur in the future, the value of the settlement is, of course, uncertain, and this uncertainty should be reflected in the discount rate in the form of a risk premium.

One obvious problem with this theory is that the intrinsic value is still an exchange value; that is, the value at which the financial asset is exchanged for the medium of settlement of the claim. The problem of real value has simply been passed on from the financial asset to the medium of settlement. Stating the value of one form of money in terms of another begs the question of where the value of money ultimately resides.

Another obvious problem is the uncertainty. To know what the value of the settlement *will* be requires one to have perfect foresight. Our inability to see the future with certainty prevents us from knowing what the value of the financial asset *ought to be*. Furthermore, to know the correct discount rate requires us also to know what the value of the settlement *could* be, as uncertainty determines the discount rate. So, even if we could see the future with perfect clarity, we still would not know the intrinsic value because our perfect foresight would necessarily be blind to the uncertainty that determines the discount rate.

That we cannot know the intrinsic value or real value of a financial asset, however, does not mean that it does not have one. Even if we cannot know what the intrinsic value is, we can still ask why there is one. Financial assets are still exchanged and unless we are willing to accept that exchange can occur purely for the sake of exchange, there must indeed be some sort of real value behind it. To get at this value, whatever it may be, let us first consider Marx's well-known concept of 'use' value.

Use and Exchange Value

Marx's distinction between use value and exchange value is very familiar. The use value is a natural property of a thing that satisfies needs or desires. This reference to 'needs' and 'desires' makes use value sound similar to utility, although the utility of a thing is a consequence of not only *its* natural properties, but also the needs and desires of some *one* who may use it. In contrast, Marx implies that use value is an inherent property of a thing itself that comes out of the labor by which it was created and use value does not require that anyone actually use the thing.

As opposed to the qualitative attribute of use value, exchange value is the quantitative attribute by which otherwise incommensurable things can be measured and compared. Marx was concerned about the relation of use value and exchange value, especially its effects on a society increasingly concerned with exchange.

Although exchange value 'ought' to be derived from use value, he was concerned with an eventual separation of the two, such that exchange value would take on a life of its own. We would have exchange for the sake of exchange and not to acquire the use value of commodities we desire.

According to Marx, financial assets, being a form of money, have only exchange value. They have no use value. If use value is the only 'real' value, we must accept that in the case of financial assets, there is indeed exchange for the sake of exchange, which for Marx was a source of concern. If not use value, then, what is the 'alibi' for the exchange value of money? We know that financial assets, as money, can be exchanged for things that do have use value. In effect, money stands for those things it can buy. While it may have no use value of its own, in addition to exchange value, money has 'symbol' value.

Symbol Value

The list of the functions of money, which opened this section, was obviously written to emphasize the dependence of money upon the purchase of things. The list equally emphasizes the dependence of money on the discharge of claims, but the only reason to incur a claim is to purchase a thing. From an economic standpoint, money always exists for things.

In a sense, then, money always refers to, or is a symbol for, things.

As money is a generalized medium, it does not symbolize a specific thing. Rather, it symbolizes the utility obtainable when the money is exchanged for things, and since as far as economics is concerned money can be exchanged by any one for any thing, money is free to symbolize any thing any one happens to desire. This makes it an especially potent symbol; it is 'pure' wealth.

It is an important point that money acquires its exchange value because it is a symbol for the use value of the things it can buy and not because it is a symbol for the use value of some reserve commodity underlying it. Nixon declared that US dollars were no longer redeemable in gold. Indeed, the dollar did lose exchange value against other currencies. But if the exchange value of money were wholly attributable to its value as a symbol for the gold in which it could be redeemed, it would have lost much more of its exchange value. And one must certainly question whether the exchange value of gold is attributable to its own use value or instead more to its own symbolic value as another form of money.

Money, including financial assets and gold, is indeed a symbol for the things it can buy and it is society that is responsible for this symbolic value through its creation of a system to exchange things for money. Money is in effect a social, not a natural or even a purely economic, phenomenon. As such, then, it would not be unexpected to find that the symbolic value of money is not simply a neutral, objective quantity. While money would have no value if it were not a symbol, its value is not only attributable to its being a symbol. Along with its symbolic value, money has what might be called 'sign' value.

Sign Value

The previous section discussed money as a symbol for the things it can buy; in other words, money can stand in place of those things. But money is more than just a symbol, it is a cultural sign; that is, something having qualitative or non-economic meaning within a culture. While the terms 'symbol' and 'sign' are often used interchangeably and can be easily confused, defining a symbol as 'standing in place of something' and a sign as 'having cultural meaning' should sufficiently differentiate the two admittedly somewhat confusing terms.

Sign Value

Perhaps adding to the confusion, the French cultural philosopher, Jean Baudrillard has used both 'symbolic' value and 'sign' value to extend Marx's analysis of 'use' value and 'exchange' value.

Baudrillard uses 'symbolic exchange' value to refer to what is defined in this paper as 'sign' value. Elsewhere in the work cited above, he more explicitly distinguishes between 'symbolic' value and 'sign' value. The former concerns 'a logic of ambivalence or of the gift' and the latter 'a logic of difference or of status or fashion'.

One interpretation of these phrases, consistent with the definitions of 'symbol' and 'sign', is that ambivalence refers to indifference between the symbol and what it stands for and that difference refers to the structuralist notion that what distinguishes a sign is not something inherent in the sign, but its difference from other signs. For example, one is ambivalent regarding the choice between a thing and sufficient money to purchase that thing. On the other hand, the meaning of having money (and even of having different forms of money) is determined by the social and cultural differences between those that have it and those that don't.

Baudrillard distinguishes *economic* exchange value from *symbolic* exchange value, saying that the exchange value can be a consequence of utility/use value or sign value.

According to Marx, we need or desire things because of their use value, and their exchange value ought to be a consequence of this use value. According to Baudrillard, however, it is far more likely that we need or desire things because of their sign value, and their exchange value is then a consequence of this sign value.

Money is a different sort of thing, which according to Marx and others is pure exchange value, symbolic of things in general. In this way of thinking, money has no specific underlying use value, just symbolic value. In the case of financial assets, finance believes in some underlying 'intrinsic value' somehow tied to the real economy, but there is no way to know exactly what this is.

According to Baudrillard's logic, money does not have a privileged position as the 'god among commodities'. It is a thing or object like any other, having its own sign value. Combining these two perspectives, we can say that either use value (in the case of money, symbolic value) or sign value can provide the alibi for exchange value. The price of a financial asset can be a consequence of what it can buy or of what it means.

Thus, it is possible to envision two economies — an economy in which the exchange value of money is largely a function of its symbolic value and an economy in which the exchange value of money is largely a function of its sign value. On the surface, both economies will look the same, because money in one economy is also money in the other. This paper refers to one as the 'real' economy and the other as the 'hyperreal' economy. While the first term is self-explanatory; the second requires explanation and justification.

The Hyperreal Economy

Hyperreality

> This would be the successive phases of the image: — it is the reflection of a basic reality — it masks and perverts a basic reality — it masks the *absence* of a basic reality — it bears no relation to any reality whatever: it is its own pure simulacrum. In the first case, the image is a *good* appearance — the representation is of the order of sacrement. In the second, it is an *evil* appearance — of the order of malefice. In the third, it *plays at being* an appearance — it is of the order of sorcery. In the fourth, it is no longer in the order of appearance at all, but of simulation (Baudrillard 1983: 11).

With regard to money, Baudrillard's first phase is its familiar function as the generalized symbol (or image) of wealth. The second phase is the basis for the concern that Baudrillard shares with Marx that 'political economy is this immense transmutation of all values (labor, knowledge, social relations, culture, nature) into economic exchange value' (Baudrillard 1981: 113). The third phase is exchange for the sake of exchange, but justified by the eventual exchange for the sake of consumption. In the fourth stage, the justification is dropped. In phases one, two and three, the alibi for the exchange value of money is its use value, i.e. the money is still a symbol for the use value of the things it can purchase. In the fourth, the hyperreal stage, the alibi for money is purely its sign value.

These phases might be applied more specifically to financial assets. For stock prices, for example, phase one is a stock price that accurately indicates some intrinsic value of the corporation; phase two, a stock price that because of distortions and noise, is an imperfect indicator of some intrinsic value of the corporation; phase three, a stock price that is the only value one knows for the corporation, as there is no such thing as intrinsic value; and phase four, a stock price that is in a sense a 'pure' value, as the corporation to which it is attached is irrelevant.

'Hyperreality' literally means over, above or more than the real. For Baudrillard, the hyperreal is, in effect, 'more real than real'. How is that possible?

Regarding nuclear deterrence, as a case in point, it is not the real destructive power of nuclear weapons themselves that determines the outcome of conflicts (as their only two uses in open warfare occurred fifty years ago), but the meaning of nuclear weapons possession in geopolitical calculations. Real decisions are made on the basis of what nuclear weapons mean to natures and not on their actual use against nations. It is not the 'real' weapon that shapes 'reality'. The weapon as a sign is hyperreal, more 'real' than the weapon itself.

Capital works similarly when decisions are made for financial reasons and not for economic reasons. Financial markets are the cause of changes in the real economy. Decisions affecting production and employment are made on the basis of stock price and not on the basis of production and employment. It is not the 'real' economy that shapes 'reality', but activity in the financial economy. The financial economy is thereby more 'real' than the real economy itself; it is a hyperreal economy.

Borgmann (1992) has yet another perspective on hyperreality that takes on something of the medical and psychological meanings of the prefix 'hyper'; that is, agitated or even pathological.

> Instrumental hyperreality, to start with, has ingested and digested the realm of abstraction that is the bequest of Cartesian universalism. To organize and control the assault on reality, it had become necessary to step back from the personal and immediate involvement in industry and commerce, to recreate and coordinate on paper and on a grand scale what forever would escape control were it attached with bare hands. The results were the intricate and far-reaching legal and financial machineries that lent the modern economy coherence and resilience ... there is a concern among economists that American instrumental hyperreality will detach itself from its physical under-parts and, like Icarus, take off on an irresponsible and treacherous course (Borgmann 1992: 83).

Although Borgmann's conception of hyperreality appears in this quotation to be very similar to that of this paper, he tends to view the hyperreal economy more as an electronic 'virtual reality' that has the potential for getting out of hand. For our purposes, hyperreal money is exchange value without use value or even symbolic value. It does not stand for any *thing*. It is a pure sign. The hyperreal economy is an economy of signs, detached from real things, but nonetheless having the ability to affect real things. It need not be electronically mediated, although that certainly adds to the effect.

Post-modernity

What is relevant for this paper is Lyotard's (1984) and Jameson's (1984) connection between post-industrial society and post-modern culture. With the transition from industrial to post-industrial society and from modern to post-modern culture comes an increase in abundance that causes a shift in emphasis from production to consumption. In other words, this is a shift in emphasis from use value to sign value.

In the industrial society, financial assets were closely linked to real assets, and problems in financial markets were accompanied by problems in real markets. The stock market crash of 1929 was accompanied by a very serious, and very real, depression. In the post-industrial society, financial assets trade almost wholly independently of real assets, and problems in financial markets have little or no lasting effects on real markets. The stock market 'crash' of 1987 had no discernible causes outside the markets themselves and its aftermath was not a 'depression'.

In the early 1930s, a vast economics literature was generated over the social value of speculation, because speculation was suspected as having been a major cause of the depression. In the late 1980s, an equally vast finance literature was generated over automated trading, not because of any effect it had on real markets, but because of its effect on the financial markets themselves. The 'crash', along with its academic post-mortem, was wholly hyperreal.

The difference between real and hyperreal finance boils down to a difference between money with symbol value and money with sign value, between money that provides utility through the use value and sign value of things and money that provides utility through its own sign value. While some privilege the real over the hyperreal, neither is superior to the other. Both are games played for utility/gratification. The two games have always coexisted, but there is indeed some evidence that the sign game has become relatively more important and the symbol game relatively less.

In Search of Hyperreal Finance

Speculation

The hyperreal economy is *not* a consequence of speculation. In the hyperreal economy, there are no speculators and investors nor are there speculative-grade securities and investment-grade securities. We can no longer say that speculation trades on psychology and noise and that investment trades on fundamentals and real value. There are no fundamentals or real value for the traders; it is all psychology and noise. There is no distinguishable speculation when everyone is a so-called speculator. Lowenstein (1988) calls the stock market a mirror of reality. Perhaps a better metaphor is that of a hall of mirrors, where reflections and images of images constitute the only reality that matters.

What speculation and investment used to have in common was that both were undertaken more for the purpose of earning money, the purpose of which in turn was eventually to purchase things. What speculation and investment now have in common, regardless of how one may choose to differentiate them if they can be differentiated at all, is that they are both undertaken more for their sign value. It is trading for the sake of trading; not trading as a form of gambling, but trading for the sake of what trading means in the culture.

One possible explanation for the timing of the transition in finance is the computerization that not only provided unprecedented amounts of information regarding financial assets and facilitated their trading, but probably changed the very nature of money. Money (currency) is a symbol for the things it can purchase, which symbolic relationship is reinforced whenever a purchase is made. Written numbers (on checks or credit card slips) are in turn symbols for money, which have some reality when written. This symbolic relationship is again reinforced by a checking accounting statement or credit card statement. Electronic displays are symbols for money, which symbolic relationship is never reinforced. The medium itself, let alone the staggering amounts involved, has removed financial transactions so far from reality that they come to be interpreted in a way consistent with personal experiences that seem similar rather than in a way consistent with what they are really meant to be. As it all looks more like a gigantic poker game than like economic transactions, for example, that is the behavior it engenders.

So what we have now is trading for the sake of trading, which is a source of amusement and pleasure. And trading for the sake of trading begets still more trading.

Trading for the Sake of Trading

The closest anyone comes to acknowledging true trading for the sake of trading is a joke recounted by Lowenstein.

There is an old story on Wall Street about the trader who, having watched the market bid up a can of sardines to $100, entered the bidding. Having won the auction and opened the can, only to find ordinary fish, he complained. 'Fool', he was told, 'those were trading sardines, not eating sardines'. (Lowenstein 1988: 20).

The reason true trading for the sake of trading is so obscure is that it can only occur if it appears to be occurring for a 'real' reason. It must look as if, in the long-run, everyone can make money. Every trader and every intermediary must be able to show they *can* earn a return from the activity and in fact *will* if they play at it long enough. In the hyperreal economy, everyone can earn a hyperreal profit. It is a Ponzi scheme, but one which never collapses, because enough of the earnings continue to be funneled back into the game so that everyone thinks that they are continuing to earn. In other words, not too many people open the can and eat the sardines.

Few want to withdraw their earnings, because the hyperreal game *is* the thing. There is no other *thing* that is quite so real. There is not so much a financial economy as a financial culture that has nothing to do with the underlying economy of things. Financial Assets are valued not by what things they can buy, but by the cleverness required to obtain them. They are themselves something to be consumed. Each day the financial press prints an elaborate display of merchandise and financial journalists communicate the message that 'something important is happening every day and...you can't afford to relax, even for a moment' (Lowenstein 1988: 4). In Veblen's time, people had to see you, and you had to have *things* to make you look as if you had money. Within the financial community served by mass communication, people who never see you can know that you have money. *Things* are no longer necessary.

But why should it matter that there is such a hyperreal economy, or at least an economy more hyperreal than it used to be?

To examine the implications, consider the opening story concerning a game (poker, perhaps?), which the preceding sections have hopefully established as aptly analogous to financial markets. What, or more appropriately where, is the value of the tokens in this hypothetical game? Their exchange value is equal to the price at which the newest player bought into the game, and the symbolic value is what the token wealth of any player will buy if it were converted to currency. Their underlying use value, however, is the 'liquidation' value if the game were terminated and all of the money in the bank were distributed to all of the players on the basis of their token holdings. If the game had been going on for some time and had grown large, this use value would be substantially less than the exchange value. The component of exchange value not attributable to use value is the sign value — the value of the popularity of the game derived from the personal and social utility of playing it.

Conclusion

So what, if anything, ought to be done about 'casino capitalism'? If much of it is trading for the sake of trading and trading for the sake of trading does not have any unusual or extraordinary effect on the real economy, then there does not seem to be a problem. As Tobin (1984) lamented, massive resources are devoted to moving money from one place to another that could perhaps be deployed in more 'productive' ways.

But is money spent to facilitate playing with financial futures indices a worse expenditure than money spent on any other diversion or recreation that demands the use of more 'things'? It may even be better, as the environmental impact of S&P Midcap Index Options is probably far less than that of Ferrari Testarossas. This suggests that the appropriate public policy response to hyperreal financial markets ought to be similar to that of the casino industry or professional sports leagues — ensure that they are run honestly and pay their taxes, but allow them to make their own rules.

What is clearly required to make better public policy decisions is a greater understanding of financial markets and their effects. This will never occur, however, until their hyperreal nature is acknowledged and explored. Treating financial markets as 'rational' institutions for the reallocation of resources perpetuates our ignorance — an ignorance reflected in our meaningless metaphorical 'explanations' or daily price changes. No matter what occurs, it is an 'adjustment', if relatively small and a 'correction' if relatively large.

While the notion of a hyperreal economy is quite new, the notion of trading for the sake of trading is not. In an interview in the *Financial Analysts Journal*, Benjamin Graham (1976: 20) said that 'the stock market resembles a huge laundry in which institutions take in large blocks of each other's washing'. Lowenstein (1988) also laments trading for the sake of trading: 'Once the wheels have been lubricated, added grease helps only the merchant of grease' and '(days) when the market trades 100 million shares...are a curse for owners, not a blessing — for they mean that owners are paying twice as much to change chairs as they are on a 50-million share day...These expensive activities may decide who eats the pie, but they don't enlarge it' (Lowenstein 1988: 85 quoting Warren Buffet in the 1983 Berkshire Hathaway annual report).

References

Baudrillard, J. (1981). *For a critique of the political economy of the sign.* Telos Press.

Baudrillard, J. (1983). *Simulations.* New York: Semiotext(e).

Baudrillard, J. (1990). *Cool memories.* New York: Verso.

Borgmann, A. (1992). *Crossing the postmodern divide.* Chicago: The University of Chicago Press.

Graham, B. (1976). A conversation with Benjamin Graham. *Financial Analysts Journal.* September/October: 20–23.

Jameson, F. (1984). Postmodernism, or the cultural logic of late capitalism. *New Left Review, 146,* July/August: 53–92.

Lowenstein, L. (1988). *What's wrong with wall street.* Reading, MA: Addison-Wesley Publishing Company, Inc.

Lyotard, J-F. (1984). *The Post-modern condition: A Report on Knowledge.* Minneapolis, MN: University of Minnesota Press.

Tobin, J. (1984). On the efficiency of the financial system. *Lloyds Bank Review,* July: 1–15.

Chapter 30

Accounting as Simulacrum and Hyperreality: Perspectives on Income and Capital[1]

Norman B. Macintosh, Teri L. Shearer, Daniel B. Thornton and
Michael Welker,   *Queen's University*

Introduction

This paper draws on Baudrillard's orders-of-simulacra theoretic to investigate the ontological status of information in accounting reports. Our major thesis is that many accounting signs no longer refer to real objects and events and accounting no longer functions according to the logic of transparent representation, stewardship or information economics. Instead, accounting increasingly models only that which is itself a model.

Orders of Simulacra

Baudrillard uses his ideas about simulacrum, implosion and hyperreality to propose a radical description of postmodern society. Briefly, *simulacrum* is a sign, image, model, pretence or shadowy likeness of something else. *Implosion* occurs when the boundary between two or more entities, concepts, or realms melts, dissolves or collapses inward and their differences disappear. *Hyperreality* refers to the current condition of postmodernity where simulacra are no longer associated with any real referent and where signs, images and models circulate, detached from any real material objects or romantic ideals. 'We are now in a new era of simulation in which...the organization of society according to simulations, codes and models, replaces production as the organizing principle of society' (Baudrillard 1994: 118).

---

[1] Reproduced (in an abridged form) from N. Macintosh, T. Shearer, D. Thornton and M. Welker, 'Accounting as Simulacrum and Hyperreality: Perspectives on Income and Capital', *Accounting, Organizations and Society*, 2000, vol. 25, no. 1, pp. 13 50 with permission of Elsevier.

Accounting, the Social and the Political
N. Macintosh and T. Hopper (Editors)

Ontology and Epistemology

Ontologically, Baudrillard believes postmodern society to be dominated by the linguistic and textual sphere, which is now more important than the economic (material and production) realm that held sway during the industrial era. In this he follows the 'literary turn' or 'crisis in representation' taken for some time now in many of the social sciences and humanities. *Homo semioticus* looms larger today than *homo economicus*.

Given that language and discourse dominate the nature of being in postmodernity, Baudrillard draws on his radicalization of Saussure's semiotics for his epistemology. Saussure, concerned only with the form of language, identified four elements in his theory of structural semiotics: signifiers (words written or spoken); signifieds (the mind image invoked by each work); signs (one-to-one combinations of unique signifiers with particular signifieds); and referents (the real objects or ideas to which signs refer). Both the sign-to-referent and the signifier-to-signified relationships, Saussure (1959) revealed, are arbitrary, so a sign has no meaning of its own. It has meaning only because it differs from all other signs in its linguistic system.

Eras of the Sign

Baudrillard also pays particular attention to the sign-to-referent relationship but proposes four successive phases or eras of the sign. (He refers to the sign variously as simulacrum, image and model.) In the first phase, the sign is a reflection of a profound reality. It is a *good* appearance in the sense that it is a faithful and transparent representation. In the second phase, the sign masks and denatures a profound reality. It is a *bad* appearance — a distorted or twisted image — which deprives reality of its deep-seated quality. In the third phase, the sign hides the *absence* of any profound reality. Akin to magic, it plays at being an appearance of a reality. Finally, in the fourth phase, the relationship is reversed: the sign *precedes* reality; it has neither rapport with nor resemblance to any reality; it is pure simulacrum.

Baudrillard extends his phases of the image scheme into a grand account of successive historical phases of more recent Western civilization. In a typical postmodernist gesture, he dismisses the modernistic idea that history is a linear progression (albeit with setbacks along the way) towards some utopia. Instead, each new era appears and is only different from, not necessarily better than, its predecessors. These 'orders of simulacra', as he labels them, which followed the Feudal era are: (1) *Counterfeit*, the dominant scheme of the classical period from the Renaissance to the Industrial Revolution; (2) *Production*, the dominant scheme of the Industrial era; and (3) *Simulation*, the reigning scheme of the current phase.

Baudillard's successive phases of the sign provide one framework for interpreting historically documented changes in the meanings of accounting signs.

Prehistoric Accounting — Reflecting a Profound Reality

Mattessich (1987, 1989) argues that the ancient Sumerians had developed a prehistoric form of accounting, complete with debits and credits, to track physical flows of goods and social obligations to pay for them. By 3500 BC, before people knew how to read, write or count, they were making kiln-fired tokens that represented resources such as cows, goats and wheat. Mattessich interpreted each token-shape as an account. Thus, in Sumerian urn-accounting, the tokens as signs referred unambiguously and transparently to real physical resources.

Feudal Era Accounting

As Baudrillard describes the Feudal era, the relationship between signs and their referents was fixed, clear and transparent. Even social position and status were obvious from appearances. The king's crown and castle, like the peasant's cap and hovel, clearly signaled the social position at the top and bottom, respectively, of a many-layered and rigidly enforced social hierarchy.

Medieval accounting also evidenced the influence of the social order. In medieval England, for example, relations of accountability were as indelibly inscribed as those of the social hierarchy. Ownership of assets was concentrated in the hands of the nobility, while those lower in the social order were responsible for maintaining and deploying the assets in accordance with the wishes of a king or lord. The social hierarchy was both comprised of and dependent upon a network of vertical relationships that made *stewardship* and *agency* the overriding accounting issues of the day.

On the agriculturally based and largely self-sufficient manors, the predominant bookkeeping mechanism was the *charge and discharge statement*, a report prepared by manorial stewards to attest to their own integrity and competence in the discharge of their duties.

Much like an ancient Sumerian urn, the charge and discharge account bore a direct and transparent relationship to an underlying physical and social reality occurring contemporaneously in space and time. The physical reality reflected in the statement was the transference of assets to or by the agents of the manor. The social reality was the obligation of stewardship grounded in the social hierarchy of the feudal order. Since the manor was largely self-sufficient, maintaining the distinction between income and capital was neither meaningful nor straightforward.

Thus, accounting in medieval England reflected the agency relationships inscribed in the feudal social order. And charge-and-discharge accounting, like ancient urn-accounting, can be viewed as a prototypical example of the sign/referent relationship that Baudrillard describes as characteristic of feudal or caste societies.

Charge and discharge accounting is not, however, generally viewed as a direct antecedent of today's financial accounting because charge and discharge accounting did not serve a commercial purpose and was not a double-entry system. Rather, the roots of double-entry are generally held to be in the bookkeeping practices of

medieval Italy, where merchants of the city-stages practiced the most sophisticated accounting of the medieval period and accounting procedures evidenced
a direct correspondence with the physical and social activities that constituted trade.

But even among Italian merchants, income and capital were not strictly
demarcated. Indeed, even after double entry had provided the means, interim calculations of income were rarely made. Rather, the referent to which the accounting
income sign pointed was the ex post surplus of liquidation proceeds over original
cost, calculated at the conclusion of a discrete trading endeavor.

In the earliest days of Italian trading, each trader accompanied his own goods
abroad, so most traders did not need accounting records. But with the increase in
trading activity that accompanied the Crusades, the 'commenda' or silent partnership quickly became the norm. The investment of capital by a non-active partner
created a need for agency accounting, similar to the accountability reporting of
feudal England. Significantly, however, these early trading partnerships were
more like a series of discrete joint ventures than a continuing business enterprise,
with profit or loss materializing on the distribution of goods and proceeds at the
conclusion of each venture:

> This was profit in the *true* sense of the word rather than income. It was
> the result of liquidation; it measured the net of a closed venture,
> not a periodic calculation from continuing operations (Littleton
> 1968: 290, emphasis added).

Income, then, was not distinguished from invested capital — except to the extent
that each partner's share of the proceeds differed from his initial cost. Accounting
signs were transparent reflections of the receipt and disposition of goods in agency;
even 'income' was the obligatory reflection of the liquidiation-outcome of a
concluded commercial endeavor.

Counterfeit Order Accounting

As the Feudal era gave way to the Renaissance era, the first order of simulacra — the
counterfeit era made its appearance. In this new era, Baudrillard claims, the sign
became a counterfeit of the referent. The advent of stucco, for example, led to
imitations of nature — artificial signs and images of real referents. Stucco
created simulacra of natural materials in the construction of buildings, churches
and objects of art, making possible the transubstantiation of all nature into one
medium.

Such counterfeit signs not only imitated real objects and ideas but also began
to distort them. A sign 'played' at reflecting the real, pretending to be an original
and imitating nature. Importantly, the sign could pretend to refer to the referent,
since it was now arbitrary and liberated from it. Simulacra, however, were more
than theatrical games played out with images and counterfeits; they also suggested
social position and power arrangements.

The counterfeit order witnessed the appearance and rise of a new social class — the bourgeoisie. The many-tiered feudal order regrouped mainly into three layers: nobility, bourgeoisie and the rest. Situated between the aristocrats and the lowest segments of society, the bourgeoisie claimed that 'natural' rights, embedded in nature's laws, should be the referent for social arrangements instead of the divine rights of monarchs and the Church.

Accounting practices also evolved with medieval Italy's burgeoning trade. By the time Pacioli committed to paper the 'method of Venice', the relationship between the sign 'accounting income' and its underlying referent had already undergone a major transformation. We can depict this as accounting's rebirth into Baudrillard's order of the counterfeit, accompanied by the introduction of periodic income calculations and a concomitant change in the relation of the accounting sign to the real.

Beginning in the thirteenth century, Italian merchants' joint ventures began to take a more permanent form. The significance of this event for accounting is substantial. Double-entry accounting emerged as a systematic integration of real and nominal accounts, the latter being closed into a profit and loss account and then into capital accounts. For the first time, Italian merchants could continuously observe the interaction between capital and income and make interim calculations of income as desired.

It is interesting to speculate on the origin of the words 'real' and 'nominal'. These early merchants probably recognized that any 'income' that accumulated in the nominal accounts would not be 'real' until it was ultimately distributed in goods or money. It was very likely in this era that such a distribution would be possible, since most of the referents of the accounting signs that comprised income were easy to identify. Still, the merchants evidently recognized that this income would not become 'true' capital until it was ultimately distributed; perhaps they labeled the profit and loss accounts as 'nominal' to reflect this fact. It would be some time, however, before income, like stucco, began to assume the quality of a sign that 'played' at reflecting the real, pretending to be an original and imitating nature.

As well, at the end of the feudal period, England had little need to integrate capital and income because commercial ventures had not yet acquired the continuity that double entry is uniquely suited to portray. Production and trade were not continuous undertakings but a series of separate ventures that earned profit or loss. Even in joint stock companies, the proceeds from each completed undertaking were divided and new stock was solicited for subsequent endeavors, so income was not distinguished from invested capital. Rather, each investor inferred his income by deducting initial investment from proceeds. Thus, as in early Italian trading partnerships, income was the transparent and obligatory sign of a realized referent that was co-determinate with the sign itself.

In 1613, the East India Company made an initial (if tentative) move toward replacing terminable with permanent stock. With this decision, the company *had* to distinguish income from capital; Italian double-entry bookkeeping, already well developed and in a sense awaiting its destiny, afforded the organic mechanism for accomplishing this.

The shift to permanent investment, in turn, radically changed the understanding of business activity through time, leading to an appreciation of the business entity as a going concern. Accounting had entered the order of the counterfeit.

Though the accounting sign 'income' lost its correspondence to 'profit' in the sense of liquidation-proceeds, it remained grounded in a conception of income as the realized profits of a liquidated venture. The introduction of accruals, deferrals and other means of apportioning the ongoing activities of a business unit into periodic segments served to recreate in nominal accounts — in counterfeit — the natural conclusion of a completed venture, much as stucco produced counterfeit signs of nature.

The accounting sign of income, therefore, served as an *analogy* of the Feudal era's liquidation-proceeds. But rather than serving as the obligatory and transparent reflection of this profit, as it had in the Feudal order, 'income' had entered the order of imitation. The accounting sign 'income' could henceforth only play at being real as the rationale began to fade for why double-entry accounting had originally relegated the components of income to 'nominal' accounts. This problematic relationship was to change dramatically with the appearance of the industrial era in late eighteenth-century England.

Order of Production Accounting

The Industrial Revolution ushered in Baudrillard's second order of simulacrum, what he called the order of production. Its major defining feature was the appearance of serial, mass production technology. One vital aspect of this was the transmutation of the sign-to-referent relationship. Recall that in Feudal times the sign referred in a direct and transparent manner to its object, while in the counterfeit order the sign 'played' at being the referent and was a distortion of it. In the order of production, however, the sign came to 'absorb' the object.

Serial production made it possible to produce identical objects ad infinitum. These commodities were no longer reflections, counterfeits or analogues of any original goods as in previous eras. Rather, they were simply images of the other objects manufactured by their particular serial production process. As such, they were simultaneously both sign and referent, or what Baudrillard labels 'object-signs'.

Crucially, the social order too came under the sway of technical rationality with its 'rules' of serial manufacturing. Just as material goods were produced ad infinitum, now both workers and bourgeois owners were serially produced, that is to say, commodified. This meant the decline of the natural rights of man and the code of the counterfeit, and the appearance of the new code of political economy whose rules and laws were instantiated in the social realm. In consequence, the individual was no longer in the image of God, nor a counterfeit of the aristocracy, nor a natural sentient being. The individual was merely an image of other workers or bourgeois persons. Serial production simultaneously generated the producing–consuming individual as well as the material commodity.

In general terms, serial production came to dominate the social realm just as it dominated the material, economic domain. The industrial machine now corresponded to the rational, functional, historical consciousness of society. Accounting followed a similar path.

The advent of the Industrial Revolution saw the proliferation of long-lived assets used for the mass production of identical goods. This exacerbated the accounting problem inherited from the classical era: the growth of the corporate form and severance of ownership from control made accounting's traditional proprietorship focus less and less appropriate. Over the next century, accounting would experience another momentous rupture — this time, into Baudrillard's order of serial production.

Accounting's transformation from the order of the counterfeit to the order of serial production entailed a significant transfiguration of the signs of income and capital. Whereas 'income' in the preceding order had served as an analogy for a proprietor's liquidation proceeds or profits, income in the order of production was reconceived as the serialized, periodic return to depersonalized capital. This seemingly subtle distinction masks a profound transformation in the relationship between the sign and the real: capital and income relinquished their grounding in the productive endeavors of an entrepreneur. The logic and code of the market now governed them instead. Comparability and reproducibility became the end and the measure of the system.

As the influences of the Industrial Revolution spread, changes in the nature of production and organizational forms prompted a rethinking of accounting income and capital. This rethinking, in turn, precipitated further slippage between these signs and their original referents.

With the continuity of production, the financial reporting period became increasingly arbitrary and artificial; allocations with little import became crucial for computing income; and the sign of accounting income slipped another notch away from its original referent. Eventually, the income sign came to repudiate its claim to be the analogical equivalent of termination proceeds, and became instead a standardized, serialized production commodity in its own right whose principal value was to facilitate the market exchange of depersonalized capital.

Even more significant than the change in the nature of production was the change in organizational forms. The growth of large corporations effected an abrupt transfiguration of the notion of the firm, especially with respect to its temporal characteristics. The nature of capital had changed. To an increasing extent, it was composed not of tangible goods, but of organizations built in the past and available to function in the future.

This suggests what was, perhaps, the most significant impact of the corporate form on accounting: a transmutation of the *source* of the value of corporate assets. As the import of the corporation's quality as a going concern came to be appreciated, so did the view that 'real' balance sheet values do not depend on cost, liquidation or market values. They depend on the firm's future earning capacity, which is reflected in its current profits. The nominal accounts were seen to be at least as important as, and certainly no less 'real' than, the real accounts.

Several accounting principles and conventions quickly followed the acceptance of this future-oriented view of asset valuation. By the 1940s, income computations relied on a series of interlocking assumptions that included historical cost, continuity, conservatism and periodicity, as well as matching and realization and the income statement deposed the balance sheet as the main focus of accounting.

This shift in the relative importance of the two statements is congruous with the reconceptualization of capital that occurred with the rise of the large corporation. Limited liability and the separation of ownership from control changed the meaning of capital from a personalized, proprietary investment to a depersonalized, aggregated concept, encompassing all of the property used in a business. Profit, the distribution of which remained discretionary, stemmed not from the entrepreneurial efforts of a proprietor but from the deployment of capital. These shifts mark a transition in accounting from the proprietary view toward the entity view of accounting that persists today.

In sum, with the adoption of the entity theory, income measurement assumed a more economic form. Abandoning any pretence of bearing an analogical relationship to liquidation proceeds, the sign of accounting income absorbed the referent (the profit of a specific venture) and the sign itself became an exchangeable commodity, serially produced and used to facilitate the allocation of capital in an exchange market. In this role, its most important attributes became those that guarantee its reproducibility: objectivity, verifiability, reliability, consistency and comparability. The serial production of income fed the market's valuation of capital according to the code of political economy that governed value in the production era. No longer partaking of a 'nostalgia for a natural order', income sought not to imitate the natural conclusion of a business endeavor but to dominate it. The imperatives of market exchange dislodged recourse to nature as the legitimating social principle.

Order of Simulation Accounting

The transmutation of the sign–referent relationship reached its present phase in today's *order of simulation*. The sign no longer refers directly to any referent as it did in the Feudal era. The sign, however, is not just a counterfeit of a referent that observers readily distinguish from it — like nominal and real accounts — as it was in the counterfeit age. The sign, moreover, does not merely absorb the referent and dominate it, blurring the distinction between real and nominal in everyday use as it did in the production era. No longer an abstraction of anything in the simulation era, the sign is now its own pure simulation. The difference between the sign and referent implodes.

Abetted by the explosion of information-technology devices, these non-referential images literally bombard the individual with a surplus of idealized models, images and simulations of all aspects of life — work, exercise, hobbies, sports, sex, diet, even accounting. As distance melts and time is compressed, attachments to place no longer matter. Local values, childhood and schoolmate friendships, sentiments for institutions and aesthetic feelings for things that were important in previous eras are readily discarded.

The future collapses into the present as corporations, individuals and governments use new techniques to parry potential shocks. Many corporations, for example, use financial-engineering technology (implemented with options, futures and other derivative securities) to hedge or sell off uncertainty. Clearinghouses pass on the risk to individuals or to different companies that will buy it — for a price. The buyers then 'reinsure', selling smaller chunks of the risk to additional investors. Other corporations discount the future by securitizing their accountings receivable or other expected future receipts, bundling them together as synthetic securities and selling them to financial institutions without recourse for a negotiated 'present value'. Individuals participate in innovative insurance contracts, welfare programs, marriage contracts, funeral packages, cryogenic preservation and sperm banks to 'presentiate' things once and for all. The future is discounted; it does not count anymore. Past and future implode into the present.

Communication also undergoes a momentous transformation. The order of simulation features the mass consumption of signs and images that contain 'senseless' meaning. Accounting signs follow suit.

If Baudrillard's description of the simulation era holds, one would expect the advent of the order of simulation to have heralded momentous changes in the referential properties of 'income' and 'capital'. Neither mainline accounting texts nor Generally Accepted Accounting Principles (GAAP), however, have instantiated such mutations. Instead, the accepted vocabulary of income and capital remains grounded in beliefs and assumptions that formed during the production era, while accounting practice clings to double-entry techniques that emerged nearly five centuries ago in the counterfeit era.

Transparency Lost

Much of extant accounting theory and practice sees accounting signs as being related to some 'real' economic activity or production process, which occasions costs (efforts) and revenues (accomplishments) and gives meaning to basic notions like 'costs attach' and 'realization'. As some put it, economic activity 'consists of uniting material, labor and various services to form new combinations having new utilities'. So, 'it is a basic concept of accounting that costs can be marshaled into new groups that possess real significance' and the purpose of marshaling costs is 'to trace the efforts made to give materials and other components additional utility' (Ijiri 1980: 13).

Accounting regulators today know they cannot ignore the depiction of the more fundamental things that go into any computation of income and capital. But their approach to addressing the issue — financial statements should *reflect* underlying events and transactions in a *transparent* manner — seems inconsistent with the nature of accounting signs in the order of simulation.

In 1998, for example, the chairman of the Securities and Exchange Commission (SEC) called for 'technical rule changes by the regulators and standard setters to improve the transparency of financial statements' (Levitt 1998) and stated that '[c]orporate management and Wall Street need to undergo a wholesale cultural change, rewarding those who practice greater transparency and punishing those who don't' (Levitt 1998). Previously, a Financial Accounting Standards Board (FASB) exposure draft on accounting for financial instruments and hedging activities identified 'lack of transparency' as a major flaw in accounting for financial instruments that the proposed accounting rules for derivatives would seek to overcome. In fact, the words 'transparent' and 'transparency' appear seven times in that important exposure draft. Thus, contemporary conventional accounting thought still seems implicitly wedded to the proposition that there is an underlying objective reality to which accounting signs should correspond and against which the faithfulness of the sign may be judged.

In their continued quest for transparency, then, the SEC and the FASB divulge their realist ontology and the attendant conviction that accounting signs should correspond to some underlying, objective and independent reality that would be the standard for judging the fidelity of the signs. This realist ontology, as Lukka (1990) argues, still dominates accounting theory and practice and shows little danger of waning. In contrast, Baudrillard's radical semiotic theory suggests that accounting signs such as 'income' and 'capital', like other signs in the simulation era, have already slipped free of their putative referents. They now circulate in the realm of hyperreality where self-referential models engage each other without ground. In the hyperreal economy, 'serial production yields to the generation of models' (Baudrillard 1983: 103). Signs, including accounting signs no longer refer to any referent, nor do they absorb the object — they are their own pure simulacrum.

Earnings Management

Current accounting theory does not explain why people care about formally recognizing the effects of events and transactions like the granting of stock options in the income statement. The information conveyed by data disclosed in financial statement notes, proxy statements or elsewhere, the theory goes, should be the same as that of data reported in the income statement, since readers could readily adjust income to reflect the disclosures if they wanted to. But if, in this hyperreal financial economy, accounting signs have indeed lost their association with 'real' referents, then the informational perspective's presupposition that investors can 'see through' accounting numbers to discern true market value is no longer sustainable. There is nothing to see through to. But, as Kinney (1996: 183) asks, 'Why then do official earnings matter'?

From Baudrillard's perspective 'official earnings' do matter. Fox (1997: 77) captured the idea: '[T]he simplest, most visible, most merciless measure of corporate success in the 1990s has become this one: Did you make your earnings last quarter'? The presence of this yardstick [a simulacrum] demands the practice of 'managing earnings' in order to report official earnings [another simulacrum] that pretty much match analysts' forecasts, presumably in the hopes of simulating value in the eyes of investors and so bolstering the company's stock price along with buyers' hopes for stock market gain.

While the practice of earnings management is certainly not new, the extent and nature of the practice appears to be evolving. As SEC chair, Arthur Levitt recently observed 'this process [earnings management] has evolved into what can best be characterized as a game among market participants' (Levitt 1998). He describes the self-referential process surrounding the production and consumption of earnings numbers as follows:

> This is the pattern earnings management creates: companies try to meet or beat Wall Street earnings projections in order to grow market capitalization and increase the value of stock options. Their ability to do this depends on achieving the earnings expectations of analysts. And analysts seek constant guidance from companies to frame those expectations. Auditors, who want to retain their clients, are under pressure not to stand in the way (Levitt 1998).

General Electric Company (GE) is a striking case in point. Due to its large size, wide spectrum of technologies and its global diversity, GE enjoys 'a very large amount of flexibility to...deliver strong, consistent earnings growth in a myriad of global economic conditions' and is thus recognized as one of the world's leading, 'aggressive practitioners of earnings management' (*Managing Profits* 1994). Indeed, GE often develops a model of how an acquisition, a divestment or the restructuring of a division would affect official earnings before going ahead. So, in effect, unlike the traditional thinking where strategy is implemented and accounting later reports the results, in GE's case the accounting model (the map) precedes the implementation of the strategy (the territory). As Baudrillard describes the hyperreality of the simulation era, 'The territory no longer precedes the map...[rather] the map engenders the territory' (Baudrillard 1983: 167). So instead of accounting reflecting the real outcomes of GE's strategic decisions, the ex-ante accounting model (itself a simulation of analysts' expectations) precedes and engenders the strategy which in turn recirculates into reported earnings. Similarly, motion picture companies like Walt Disney forecast reported earnings when deciding when to release videocassettes of hits like *Snow White*. By carefully timing videocassette releases, they can maintain the smooth trend in earnings that analysts can easily forecast. Analysts' earnings forecasts, in turn, sustain value. Figure 30.1 depicts the potential simultaneity introduced by the earnings management 'game'.

In sum, as Figure 30.1 and the quotes from SEC chair Levitt suggest, analysts look for clues about a company's future earnings in its current financial statements and investment decisions. But management simultaneously takes analysts' earnings forecasts as yearly targets and selects investments and accounting GAAP that are likely to produce reported income equal to or exceeding those forecasts. In turn, the market capitalizes analysts' earnings forecasts into stock prices. The company's investment decision model, the analyst's forecasting model and the investor's valuation model circulate simultaneously. They refer to each other but, for investors,

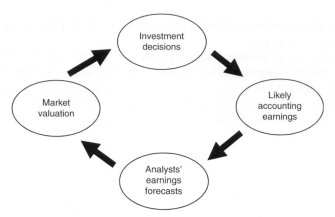

Figure 30.1: Why earnings matter.

they lack any relation to a real referent such as cash flow or 'true' income. Granted, the company's investments would not generate any earnings if they did not also generate cash flows. But neither analysts nor investors know how earnings relate to cash flows and hence to value. Rather, they produce and consume accounting earnings which, when coupled with a 'price/earnings multiple', can be used to simulate value.

So Baudrillard might address Kinney's question, 'Why do official earnings matter'? as follows. Extant accounting theories are poorly equipped to address the question, since they are based on antiquated presuppositions about the relation between accounting signs and underlying referents. In the order of simulation, the surplus of non-referential signs such as earnings has exploded, especially in the financial economy that McGoun (1997) aptly describes as 'hyperreal'. Amid ongoing discussions of 'meltdowns' and 'irrational exuberance' in financial markets, a former SEC chair called accounting 'a reality check — in many cases, the only reality check — before important economic and investment decisions are made' (Levitt 1996). But this is surely not the kind of 'reality' the ancient Sumerians knew. Instead, earnings create a simulated reality of their own because investors' valuation models still treat earnings as if they have the underlying referents of bygone eras.

This decoupling of income from its underlying referents does not, however, suggest a diminished importance for earnings. Indeed, as the financial economy becomes increasingly volatile, it becomes more important to maintain the predictability of the income calculation. Equally important is the appearance that the calculation of income, seen as a crucial 'reality check' in sustaining the financial economy, is exogenous to that economy. Formal earnings matter because to 'recognize' a transaction or event in the income statement is to 'hyperrealize' — providing that transaction or event with an aura of 'reality' in the realm of self-referential models that constitutes the financial economy. Without such earning, even though they are hyperreal, it would become obvious that the stock market itself is ungrounded and free-floating.

Financial Instruments

The debate and controversy surrounding the FASB's financial instruments project provide another striking example of the problematic nature of accounting signs in the simulation era.

The chief issue, which continues to engender debate, is when and how to formally recognize and measure the value of financial instruments in a company's financial statements. Standard setters recently forged a consensus around the 'mark to market' rule, which states that the balance sheet should carry most financial instruments at fair value, normally current market value. 'Fair value is the most relevant measure for financial instruments and the only relevant measure for derivative instruments' (FASB 1998: 1).

Ironically, however, just as accounting standard setters are embracing the use of market values on company balance sheets, analysts and others use financial statement data to gauge whether the market value of the company's stock has strayed from its fundamental or 'intrinsic value'. As Figure 30.2 shows, on one level, derivative instruments are subject to the ultimate market discipline because their values can be unambiguously derived, through 'no-arbitrage arguments', from 'the underlyings' — the prices of assets on which the derivatives have claims. At this level, expectations and probabilities are irrelevant because a hedge portfolio, consisting of fundamental financial instruments, can always be constructed to replicate a derivative's payoffs in every eventuality. It cannot sell for anything but the price an investor would pay for the hedge portfolio.

But what determines the prices of the underlyings? We argued in the previous section that the market uses accounting earnings, along with other information, to value companies' stock and other securities. The prices of these securities then become the underlyings that sustain the derivatives' prices and the self-referential sequence is complete. Companies' earnings determine security prices, which

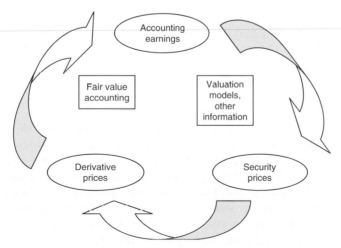

Figure 30.2: Hyperreality in accounting for financial instruments.

determine derivative prices, which determine companies' earnings. So, neither the accounting sign nor the financial market sign appear to be grounded in any external reality. Instead, each model appeals to the other model for the only 'reality check' available. In sum, accounting signs model market signs, which in turn model accounting signs. Thus, in the hyperreal financial economy of simulation, the difference between the sign and the referent implodes. The signs become images of themselves in an imbroglio of ungrounded, self-referential simulation, as shown in Figure 30.2.

Summary

Income and capital signs appear to be paradigmatic examples of Baudrillard's notions of simulacra, hyperreality and implosion. In the order of simulation, the distinction between an accounting sign and some underlying reality has imploded. The accounting sign now precedes (and even creates through its 'sign value') the referent that it once purported to represent. It is no longer an abstraction or an appearance of any 'real' thing. It is its own pure simulation, making circular references to other models which themselves make circular references to accounting signs. Just as postmodern individuals become images of models that precede them and the difference between the real person and the image implodes, the accounting sign becomes an image of a model of the accounting sign itself.

In more general terms, accounting is one among many models that precede and subsequently create a hyperreal financial economy that is characterized by 'fundamental changes in global financial markets', which have 'transformed the financial activities of all entities' (Johnson & Swieringa 1996: 165). These transformations have unmoored the financial economy from the real economy of labor and production so that the former increasingly bears no temporal or spatial relationship to the latter. For example, the so-called stock market crash of October 1987 had few noticeable consequences outside the financial economy. Contemporary accounting and finance seem to circulate on their own place, parallel to, but insulated from the material economy of labor and production.

Conclusions

In the order of simulation, the accounting sign of income has slipped free from any putative referent to circulate simultaneously with other non-referential models of itself. So, a Baudrillardian perspective might lead to the conclusion that accounting today has lost its bet, so to speak, on the reality principle and the rule of transparency on which it has traditionally been grounded. As Baudrillard might put it, the struggles standard setters are having with the above issues look like a hopeless effort '... in order to save at all costs the truth principle and to escape the spectre raised by simulation: namely that truth, reference and objective causes have ceased to exist' (Baudrillard 1988: 168).

References

Baudrillard, J. (1983). *Simulations.* New York: Semiotext(e).

Baudrillard, J. (1988). *Jean Baudrillard: Selected writings.* M. Poster (ed.). Stanford: Stanford University Press.

Baudrillard, J. (1994). *Simulacra and simulation.* Ann Arbour: University of Michigan Press.

Financial Accounting Standards Board (1998). *Accounting for Derivative Instruments and Hedging Activities.* Norwalk: Financial accounting standards board.

Fox, J. (1997). Learn to play the earnings game (And Wall Street will *love* you). *Fortune* (March 31), 76–80.

Ijiri, Y. (1980). An introduction to corporate accounting standards: A review article. *Accounting Review*, 620–630.

Johnson, L., & Swieringa, R. (1996). Anatomy of an agenda decision: Statement No. 115. *Accounting Horizons*, 149–79.

Kinney, W. (1996). What can be learned from FASB's process? *Accounting Horizons*, 180–184.

Levitt, A. (1996). *The accountant's critical eye.* Text of remarks delivered at the 24th Annual Conference on Current SEC developments. AICPA. Washington, DC, 10 December 1996.

Levitt, A. (1998). *The numbers game.* Text of remarks delivered at the NYU Center for Law and Business. New York, 28 September 1998.

Littleton, A. (1968). The antecedents of double-entry bookkeeping in M. Chatfield (ed.). *Contemporary studies in the evolution of accounting thought.* Belmont. Dickenson Publishing Company, 21–29.

Lukka, K. (1990). Ontology and accounting: The concept of profit. *Critical Perspectives on Accounting*, 239–261.

Mattessich, R. (1987). Prehistoric accounting and the problems of representation: An archeological evidence of the Middle East from 8000 B.C. to 3000 B.C. *Accounting Historians Journal*, 71–91.

Mattessich, R. (1989). Accounting and the input-output principle in the prehistoric and ancient world. *Abacus*, 74–84.

McGoun, E. (1997). Hyperreal finance. *Critical Perspectives on Accounting*, 97–122.

Saussure, F. (1959). *Courses in general linguistics.* New York: McGraw Hill.

Chapter 31

A Literary Theory Perspective on Accounting: Towards Heteroglossic Accounting Reports[1]

Norman B. Macintosh,   *Queen's University*

Richard Baker,   *Adelphi University*

This paper adopts a literary theory perspective to depict accounting reports and information as texts rather than as economic commodities and so, available for analysis from the vantage point of semiotic linguistic theory. Thus, it compares and contrasts four dominant genres of literary theory — expressive realism, the new criticism, structuralism, and deconstructionism — to developments in accounting.

Expressive Realism

Expressive realism refers to the common sense view of literature. It takes language to be a transparent medium and assumes that a novel acts like a mirror to reflect reality. Language is seen as a way of naming things and, as with a clear window, gives access to the pre-existing world of objects and ideas. So a good literary work is seen as re-presenting that world in a way that the reader recognizes as commonsensical and true. The canons of literature are those valuable novels which are deemed to tell the truth about human nature, reflect the historical period that produced them, provide deep insights about the world in general and so in a special way are worth reading. These great works capture a literal mirroring of the reality and of our ideals about the world 'out there' which, it is assumed, exist independently of either the author's intentions or consciousness or the novel itself.

Expressive realism assumes that these authors have captured the world more insightfully and imaginatively than have run-of-the-mill writers. Like the oenophile, the literary critic can 'taste and smell' greatness, mediocrity or dross in the product. While it takes an exceptional author to produce a great work, it requires the eye of the sensitive critic to spot it.

Expressive realism, however, brings with it a major conundrum. If the world exists for all to perceive and capture, why do different narratives (even those of gifted

---

[1] Reproduced (in an abridged form) from N. Macintosh and R. Baker, 'A Literary Theory Perspective on Accounting: Towards Heteroglossic Accounting Reports', *Accounting, Auditing & Accountability Journal*, 2002, vol. 15, no. 2 with permission from MCB, UP Limited.

authors) of the same pre-existing, objective reality come into being? Are some true and some false? The expressive realist response, 'That reality can be re-presented in different ways without any of them being simply wrong' seemed to many to be unconvincing, since it leads to an endless trail of different and competing rather than a clear window on reality and truth.

Accounting as Expressive Realism

The conventional or traditional perspective of accounting has some similarities with expressive realism. It takes accounting to be a translucent medium which presents factual data to the world about an enterprise's financial transactions and economic events. A good accounting is deemed to be one that represents the entity in a way that users recognize as commonsensical. Solomons (1991a,b) captures this perspective in describing accounting as being like a telephone — a neutral medium that promotes the exchange of information between the enterprise and the user; and while it is not an actor in the exchange, it is important that accounting measures be representationally faithful.

Perhaps the most prevalent view of accounting information even today sees it as corresponding to some *real* object, activity, or process which leads to *real* efforts [costs] and to *real* accomplishments [revenues] and so, gives meaning to basic accounting notions such as 'costs attach' and 'realization'. This accounting criterion for income recognition holds that revenue should be recognized whenever there is a market transaction — a *real* event — and that receipts have been received or are reasonably assured — another *real* event.

Such a position, it is important to realize, adopts, if only implicitly, the correspondence theory of philosophy. This position argues that the truth of a statement, such as accounting income or capital, exists independently of its capture in linguist [alpha and numeric] or other representational media. The gauge or measure for judging its truthfulness, then, is whether or not it mirrors — that is to say corresponds to — the intrinsic nature of the object 'out-there' or the *thing-in-itself*, as Nietzsche called it. In short, a true representation is deemed to be one that corresponds to reality as it exists in its own right.

This reality-representation distinction is vital to the objectivist accounting position. It holds that a statement is true by being a linguistic 'picture' of a fact in virtue of the way its linguistic elements are arranged. Statements that correspond to facts are deemed to be true. They are assumed to have relationships with something outside of language; something *extra-linguistic*. Something like 'net income' then is assumed to exist before its capture in a financial statement. Yet, it can only be represented linguistically and so, it too is embedded in language.

Correspondence theory, however, can only provide 'reasons' for the belief that a linguistic representation corresponds with some *thing-in-itself*. Since these reasons are also linguistic, they must come between 'it' and its linguistic representation. But these reasons are also beliefs. So the correspondence notion, although still the common sense or taken-for-granted conventional view of accounting, looks more like an infinite regress of subjective linguistic reasons and beliefs about the properties of the *thing-in-itself* than it does about its true nature. So it seems doubtful that such a notion of truth explains anything at all.

New Criticism

The new criticism came on the scene and flourished as an important genre of literary theory in the 1930s through the 1950s. Its central tenet holds that instead of assuming that a novel (text, poem, work of art, etc.) reflects some pre-existing reality or ideal, it could be appreciated for its aesthetic qualities as a genuine work of art. This called for focusing on the *form* of the text and the *artistry* with which it was constructed. A text can be read for its aesthetic qualities in accordance with accepted principles of good taste. Its true meaning, its essential property, is deemed to be its artistic internal organization which was more important than an accurate representation of some external reality or ideal. Thus, the new criticism concentrates on the relationships *within* the text, focusing on those elements which give it its distinctive aesthetic form and character.

This approach required establishing a distinct, unique literary language, a set of codes and some standard criteria of excellence which all competent writers and readers could use. These criteria would make it possible to arrive at a consensus among literary scholars and critics concerning the merits of a novel and so, put an end to the endless stream of subjective reinterpretations of canonical works. The achieved meaning was not necessarily in some outside reality; nor in the author's mind or intentions; nor in the critic's subjective interpretation. It was an aesthetic accomplishment right there on the printed page. Paraphrasable ideas and extractable propositions from a particular novel — its content — were less important than artistic form. It could be read for its beauty in accordance with the principles of good taste.

For new critics, this meant that a novel should be appreciated for the way it uses literary devices such as: harmonized connotations, tones, images, symbols and other semantic devices such as parody, irony and contradiction to create a coherent, balanced, solid and artistic edifice. A great work could be spotted by its subtlety, integrity and mastery of these textual elements which give it a recognizable distinctive character all of its own. It is deemed to be a carefully crafted, orderly object whose aesthetic form can be recognized by an objective, hard-headed, stringent and critical decomposition of the work. Special attention needed to be given, for example, to repetition not only of images and symbols but also of sound effects and poetic rhythms. A trained reader could, by means of a close reading, reveal whether or not a text was a carefully crafted, orderly object containing observable aesthetic formal patterns.

While the new criticism skirts the issue of whether or not a novel or other text corresponds to some thing-in-itself, it too rests on a philosophical foundation — the coherence theory of truth. Coherence theory recognizes that language must always come between us and the true nature of objects 'out there' and so, adopts the position that what is *true* is simply the statement or belief that best *coheres* with the overall network of our experience and beliefs. So, a true principle is one that fits with our other principles; a true argument is one that follows from our other beliefs and conclusions; and a true piece of evidence is one that fits into our hypotheses. Our principles, arguments and hypotheses add up to give a coherent picture.

Coherence theorists, then, judge the truthfulness of a linguistic representation by whether or not the statements about it cohere with all the other statements making up the accepted package of statements. So, a false statement is one that does not cohere with the others. Importantly, coherence theory does not claim that there is no 'brute reality' out there. It only claims that while a *thing-in-itself* may well exist, the truth of it is not out there. So, it is beyond our ability to represent it in some single, absolute final way using language. As such, coherence theory adopts an *intra-linguistic* position in contrast with the *extra-linguistic* position taken by correspondence theory.

One major defect that became apparent, however, lay in the claim that a text's true meaning (even if complex and ambiguous) is its aesthetic value which is permanent, unchanging and timeless. Since language changes over time, as does the social-historical circumstances of readers and interpreters, so must the meaning of a particular text change. For most of the great novels, their own historical, cultural setting was too different from today's setting to allow for valid interpretation in the present.

Another problem concerned the promise that a common language and standardized codes of excellence would reduce and even eliminate subjectivity. Instead, it seemed that subjectivity had merely shifted to competing interpretations of aesthetic tastes and the artistry of the text. And, crucially, literary theory seemed to be out of step with the increasing demand within universities in general for scientific, objective and rational inquiry. In consequence, as we shall see later, a new genre — 'structuralism' — developed in the hopes that literary theory might regain a place of respectability within the academy.

Accounting Similarities

The accounting profession's undertaking more than half a century ago to develop and elaborate *fundamental* accounting standards, postulates, or principles bears some resemblance to the new criticism initiative. By the 1940s, while there continued to be a strong emphasis on the notion of accounting as an accurate, faithful, representation of financial transactions and events, there was also a mounting desire to establish accounting as a deductive process in which fundamental principles could be recognized and from which unchallengeable rules and procedures could be derived. The goal was to reduce the number of alternative ways of producing accounting reports from the same events and transactions. Just as the new criticism sought to develop a methodology for unequivocally determining the aesthetic merit of a work of literature, so too, accounting academics and practitioners sought to develop a uniform set of postulates, principles and standards for indubitably determining the proper way of presenting true and fair accounting information (Paton & Littleton 1940).

This set of principles would, it was hoped, overcome the prevailing subjectivity and variations in reporting for similar transactions and events. Such a common system would result in self-contained, self-referential accounting reports that all could respect and admire as carefully crafted, orderly texts with observable formal patterns that readers would appreciate as solid pieces of professional work. Accounting reports would feature uniformity, precision, feasibility, objectivity, verifiability, freedom from bias, etc.

Accounting's postulates and standards period, however, soon encountered similar problems to those that kept nipping at the heels of the new criticism. For one thing, even though, or if, all accountants agreed to follow them to the best of their ability, quite different renderings of net income and capital were still possible from the same data base of events and transactions, even though the accountants closely followed the prescribed rules of the chosen method since many of the rules and standards could only be stated in general terms. So, the professional accountant still had to exercise considerable subjective judgement in applying them.

Structuralism

Structuralism came into prominence in literary theory in the 1960s. Structuralists contend that the individual elements of any purposive system have no meaning in their own right but only by virtue of their relationship with the other elements in the system. Structuralists are less interested in what a novel has to say on the surface than they are with the structure that allows it to say what it says. The surface imagery (essential for the expressive realist) and the aesthetic aspect (vital for the new critic) are seen as merely variations of some fixed, permanent, organized ordering of the elements below the novel's surface where its true meaning lies waiting to be excavated. Meaning and reference are the effects of deep structures and the organized play of language. The words on the page are a reflection of concealed depths.

Structuralism in Accounting

Structuralism, in the form of neo-classical economic theory, emerged as an important theoretical base for accounting in the 1960s, gained momentum in the 1970s, and in the next two decades came to dominate research and practice, especially in the USA. That economics is a structuralist endeavour has been often overlooked, but as Sturrock (1986) opined: 'Economics, be it noted, is the structural study par excellence...An economy is the ideal example of the functioning whole all of whose parts interact and depend on one another...' while econometrics '...is unadulterated structuralism' (pp. 64–65). Moreover, Saussure (1959) used economics as the model for developing his influential, seminal structuralist semiotic theory of language.

Moreover, economic theory found its way into GAAP and practice. A key aspect of this development was the net present value model. Asset and liability accounts were seen not so much as representative of *past* expenditures, but as repositories of *future* streams of cash flows. Regardless of what was reported on the face of financial statements, the true economic meaning could be revealed by uncovering the below-the-surface structure which followed the rules and logic of the net present value model.

Marxist-based accounting research is also founded on structuralist presuppositions. As with economics-based accounting studies, Marxist accounting researchers sought out the below-the-surface organizing laws which structure accounting practice and reports (Cooper 1980; Tinker 1980).

Conundrums

While the structuralist movement gave literary theory a boost, the subjectivity problem that plagued expressive realism and the new criticism had not, it seemed, gone away but had simply shifted to another ground. In order to deploy structuralism, the literary theorist had to subjectively pre-select the particular theoretical framework which would illuminate the deep, below-the-surface meaning of the object. Different researchers appropriated different structuralist theories (Marxism, Freudian or Lacanian psychology, various branches of philosophy, categories of cultural anthropology, etc.) to analyze a particular work. Each of these interpretations came across as equally forceful, yet yielded quite different meanings for any particular novel.

So, on the one hand, it looked like specific structuralist scholars rigidly and mechanically extracted the same themes and patterns from a variety of works, thus making every novel they analyzed a carrier of the identical meaning. On the other hand, depending on which framework was deployed, a particular novel could mean almost anything. Structuralist analysis seemed to merely corroborate the truth of the particular theory drawn upon rather than unearthing the narrative's achieved meaning.

As with expressive realism and the new criticism, structuralism is underwritten by a specific philosophical theory — positivism. Positivism is firmly grounded on science and scientific description. Science is a hypothetical-deductive process featuring the formulation of laws derived from descriptive generalization and unbiased observation. It holds that 'science provides humanity with the clearest possible ideal of knowledge' (Beck 1979: 28). Phenomena of all kinds — natural and social — can be explained by scientific laws. Any speculation as to ends, final causes or transcendental grounds is ruled out as mere illusion. So, positivists look empirically at social conduct in terms of its concrete workings and observable relations amongst its members.

While positivism is primarily concerned with producing facts, it runs into trouble, ironically, since scientific statements are by their very nature, linguistic descriptions and so, as with correspondence theory, language always comes between both the natural and social world out there and the scientific descriptions of them. Since language is always historically and socially contingent, no such statement can ever be a final permanent thing.

Science came on the scene as a highly successful attempt to replace traditional handed down narrative knowledges contained in and legitimated by myths, legends, superstitions and various religions which had no firm grounding except for belief. Yet Science itself was underpinned and legitimated only by narrative knowledge contained in other metanarratives — Progress, Reason, Truth, History and Identity. Thus, while Science is critical of and wanted to replace narrative knowledge with scientific knowledge, ironically, Science relies on narrative knowledge for legitimation, the very process it originally wanted to eliminate. Science itself was grounded in narrative knowledge.

Deconstruction

Deconstruction emerged in the late 1970s as a way of circumventing the problems with expressive realism, new criticism and structuralism as an *avant garde,* radical genre of literary theory and criticism. Developed by Derrida (1976, 1981) as a poststructuralist strategy for reading important philosophical texts and later for reading a text of any kind, a deconstructive analysis proceeds by unpackaging [or un-constructing] the text in order to reveal how the text came to *construct* some central, coherent meaning and to expose the struggle over centrality of meaning embedded therein. Importantly, however, it does not attempt to destroy or destruct the text. Rather, it aims to open it up in order to reveal the plenitude of meaning therein.

While expressive realism, the new criticism and structuralism attempted to write or interpret a text in such a way as to construct some sovereign meaning, package it neatly and present it to the reader as a tidy bundle with a central, coherent and final substantial essence, a deconstructionist reading, in contrast, reverses this process to show how that meaning came to be constructed. The deconstructor scrutinizes and interrogates the text to ferret out the linguistic moves and literary ploys used to arrive at that meaning. As Derrida (1976: 10) puts it, the goal is neither the destruction nor the demolition 'but the de-semination, the de-construction' of the text.

A deconstructive reader also scrutinizes the particular text in question in an attempt to expose the implicit or explicit metanarratives or logocentric impulses which underpin the achieved meaning. A deconstructionist reading reveals these metanarratives and logocentric moves in order to show how they were defined and legitimated by what they marginalized or excluded. It attempts to disrupt, disturb and de-theologize that meaning.

So, deconstruction involves producing a historical narrative to show how a particular text got constructed in the way that it did. This history is 'genealogical' in the sense of beginning with the achieved, central meaning and going back in time to uncover the rhetorical steps taken to arrive at it.

The first step consists of carefully sifting through the textual material to reveal something already there. In particular, the deconstructor looks for the way that some crucial words (signifiers) got hierarchized by ceding them a place of privilege over their alterities [their self-same, binary opposites such as: good/evil, white/black, man/woman, heaven/hell, young/old, culture/nature] and which comprise its metaphysical hierarchy. The second step involves temporarily reversing the text's metaphysical hierarchy by privileging the opposite side. The third and final step reveals how the struggle for dominance is undecidable.

Deconstruction is philosophical only in the sense that it 'refuses to grant philosophy the kind of privileged status it has always claimed as the sovereign dispenser of reason' (Norris 1982: 18). Deconstruction does not endorse philosophy's quest for some meaning that lies outside of the play of language — a meaning that exists in itself as foundational and unchanging. Since philosophers must use language to construct their texts, they are, in a sense, novelists; conversely novelists rely on philosophical positions and truths to tell their tales. Thus, the difference between philosophy and literature is unstable and shifting.

Although a deconstructivist reading can result in increasing our awareness of what is at stake in constructing and in reading accounting reports, it does not say much about what might be done to improve on accounting practises. For this, the paper now turns to Mikhail Bakhtin's (1895–1995) conception of the heteroglossic novel, to speculate about a different kind of accounting report.

Deconstruction Illustrated

In the biblical story of Adam and Eve, God created the earth and then made man [Adam] in his own image. On second thought, so the narrative goes, believing Adam needed company, god made woman [Eve] out of one of Adam's ribs. Eve, however, urges Adam to disobey god, listen to the snake [Satan] and to partake of the forbidden fruit. So he did, and God banished both from the Garden of Eden. Humans were doomed to an eternity of struggling for a living instead of living in paradise. In the story, the signifiers — man, God, first, good, paradise — get packaged up and elevated [hierarchized] above another bundle of signifiers — woman, Satan, secondary, evil and hell. The hierarchy elevates God above man, and man above woman.

The hierarchy, however, can be readily destabilized. Man, after all, is born out of woman; so without woman there can be no man. She is prior to and more important than man. And, since man made the story about god, man is more important than God. [Over the centuries, man has made many, many gods.] Woman above man and man above God. The hierarchy is now reversed.

But this new gradation is also unstable for it is man that provides the seed from which woman is born. So it is a matter of, 'Which came first, the chicken or the egg?' The matter is permanently undecidable. Moreover, such a reading exposes the politics of the story. Males, over the centuries, have appropriated it in order to legitimate patriarchal societies and to dominate women in the secular life world.

Such a superior position, however, is ungrounded and challenged by a deconstructive reading of the biblical story. Eve, the first woman, is and remains 'that dangerous supplement' to Adam and thus, to man.

Deconstruction can also be employed as a radical way to read accouting reports. Oil and gas accounting can be used as a case in point. The metaphysical hierarchy in the statements privileges the accountant's *historical cost* metanarrative over the economist's *discovery value* grand narrative. Companies normally present the historical cost financial statements as the main narrative, but may also include the discovery value report but label it as 'supplementary' information. [Such a practice was officially required in the early 1980s by the SEC and the FASB.]

The metanarrative underpinning the full cost is the traditional accounting story. It holds that expenditures incurred to discover oil and gas reserves are to be capitalized and written-off as the reserves are produced on a unit-of-production basis. [The expense is the proportion of reserves produced in that period as a percentage of total reserves.] This story holds that original [historical] cost is the primary basis for the measurement of the productive assets and for the incurred laibilities. Historical cost is deemed to be objective when there has been an arm's length transaction between the entity and an outside party and is verifiable when there is factual documentation [invoice, receipts, bank cheques, contracts, production receipts, etc.] of that transaction.

In contrast, the economist's discovery value method is underpinned by the neo-classical economics metanarrative. It holds that what is crucial in terms of information is the marginal [next, incremental, future] cost which should be the basis for the measurement of assets and liabilities. While the economist recognizes that subjective judgments must be made to arrive at and predict these future events and costs, they are nevertheless deemed to be more relevant than past costs which are 'history' and so, 'sunk'.

So the accounting story packages up past, historical, objective, verifiable and factual into a bundle of signifiers which it privileges over the economist's bundle of future, next, subjective, speculative and contingent. This hierarchy, however, can be reversed by pointing out that the past expenditures were incurred to earn those future cash flows so important to the economist. Such a move temporarily privileges the economist's metanarrative.

The final deconstructionist move, however, involves permanently disturbing the oppositional metaphysical hierarchy. While future cash flows may seem more important today than past costs, they would not be forthcoming were it not for the fact that past expenditures had been made. Arguably, future cash flows are very much a function of past expenditures and so, cannot be privileged over past costs. Conversely, past expenditures were made in order to acquire future cash flows and the decision to incur them was based on estimates of future cash flows. So while the future depends on the past — the past depends — anticipates the future. Neither side of the oppositional hierarchy seems able to claim superiority.

The politics of the accounting report is the struggle embedded therein between the historical cost and the discovery value metanarratives. The latter always lurks as 'that dangerous supplement' to the accountant's metanarrative. And, crucially, the different accountings get appropriated by various stakeholders. Governments use them to decide on incentives to discover energy. Taxing authorities use them for tax policy. Corporations use them to influence oil and gas prices and stock market values. And, unions and employee associations use them for negotiating terms of employment.

Heteroglossic Texts

Bakhtin (1963, 1994) identified two major genres of novels — the monologic and the heteroglossic. In the monologic, the author dominates the characters and events. He or she knows everything about them, including things the characters themselves do not know. Bakhtin sees Tolstoy as the master of the monologic novel. In *Three Deaths*, Tolstoy describes and analyzes the lives and deaths of a noblewoman, a coachman and a tree. He knows all about them and gives each, including the tree, a definite and final meaning. He 'finishes' them and 'finalizes' the narrative.

The heteroglossic novel, in contrast, gives equal weight to the characters' and the author's voices. The latter is not the ultimate authority and does not impose any unique, final meaning or ideological view on either the characters or the plot. For Bakhtin, Dostoevsky is the master of the heteroglossic novel. His characters exist as autonomous, self-conscious, unfinished beings who interact dialogically and on an even plane with the other characters, and with Dostoevsky himself. Moreover, the characters' and the author's views are contradictory, developing and unfinished.

The reason for this, Bakhtin contends, lies in the nature of 'utterances', a key concept in Bakhtin's theoretic. Utterance denotes any concrete conversation, discourse, thought, or word as it is uttered in social settings. They are two-sided social acts with a speaker (author, character, etc.) on the one side and a listener (responder, character, etc.) on the other. Words do not arrive with a pre-existing meaning before they are uttered, rather meaning is realized only in the process of active, responsive understanding. Words when uttered are alive.

Utterances, Bakhtin explains, contain two major contradictory forces — centripetal and centrifugal. The centripetal is a centralizing force which tends to drive the novel towards a unified, central, final meaning. Its opposite, the centrifugal force, is a decentralizing power which tends to drive the novel towards contradiction and complexity. These two forces interact to produce 'heteroglossia' — defined as multi-voiced, discursive acts. Heteroglossia ensures that meaning stays alive, in-process, unfinished and engaged in a continuing social dialogue or conversation. Any utterance is a continuation of the dialogue which preceded it as well as the one which will follow. Utterances arrive imprinted with a social history and leave with a social future.

Implications for Accounting

Bakhtin's ideas can be applied to accounting reports. In the first instance, it seems clear that current practice strives to produce monologic accounting statements.

Preparers and auditors strive to tame the centrifugal force embedded therein which wants to keep the meanings of the statements open, alive and unfinished. Just as Tolstoy arrived at a final, single meaning in his novel, the professional accountant arrives at one definite, single, final meaning in the form of 'net income', *the* bottom line. Yet, this can be achieved only by suppressing the other 'voices', in this case the centrifugal force in the annual report.

Following Bakhtin, then, an argument can be made that accounting practice, principles and theory should move towards heteroglossic accounting. This could entail giving the various voices equal expression. For example, a financial report could include three different statements; one based on historical cost, another based on price-level adjusted cost and a third based on economic replacement cost (relying on Black and Scholes modeling). In the use of oil and gas accounting, three different methods — successful efforts, full costing and discovery value — could be used to produce three statements. In fact, it would not be very difficult to prepare financial statements which included each of these narratives along with a succinct explanation of how each was prepared and an outline of the theory behind it. The report could also outline the major points of disagreement and contradiction between various ways of accounting for the same set of events and transactions, with each method having a rejoinder. The result would be an open, dialogic and multiple perspective report.

Heteroglossic accounting would be underwritten by pragmatism, a philosophical position. Pragmatism holds that the processes and materials of knowledge are determined by practical or purposive considerations. So pragmatists argue that the function of philosophy is not to think up timeless laws of life, eternal principles, or natural laws. Rather, they look to concrete cases where ideas and meanings make a difference in achieving a *satisfactory* solution to a *practical* problem. A true belief or hypothesis leads to the successful resolution of a problem. And 'the test of whether a belief is true is whether acting upon it leads to practical consequences which are satisfying'. What is 'true' is what 'works'.

Pragmatism is also vitally concerned with the workings of language and vocabularies and their relation to notions of truth. So, pragmatists are not interested in questions such as, 'Can a linguistic representation correspond to some *thing-in-itself* out there beyond language?' Or, ' Does this linguistic representation cohere with the other linguistic statements in a package of statements about the particular *thing-in-itself?*' Pragmatists instead say that while the world is out there, descriptions of it are not. The truth is deemed to be the property of sentences, which are part of vocabularies, and which are made by humans. For the pragmatist, this means that vocabularies can be changed and truths are historically contingent.

Some pragmatists, especially ironic liberal ones, speak of a 'final vocabulary'. It consists of those words which one uses to describe and justify personal opinions, sentiments, viewpoints and outlooks on the world in general especially the 'big questions' of life. Such words are 'final' in that they are as far as one can go with language to describe and justify personal beliefs.

But the ironic liberal pragmatist is not satisfied with this. He or she believes it is possible to invent a new final vocabulary in the hopes that a change of vocabulary might open spaces for improving the public sphere, especially institutions of liberal democracy, work towards the greatest happiness of the greatest number, promote ideas that might improve the public sphere in the hopes society will become freer, less cruel, more leisured, richer in goods and experiences.

The ironic liberal pragmatist, however, recognizes that in creating a new final vocabulary for the betterment of the public sphere, one must also harbor private doubts about that vocabulary. He or she realizes that the final vocabulary is contingent and fragile and so, while prescribing for the public sphere, in her private sphere is never quite able to take herself seriously. The ironic, liberal pragmatist accountant, then, would realize that the current final vocabulary for any accounting is contingent and fragile and would try to invent a new final vocabulary for public use while realizing that he or she would harbor private doubts about it. Heteroglossic accounting reports would be such a new 'final vocabulary'.

References

Bakhtin, M.M. (1963). *Problems of Dostoevsky's poetics*. Minneapolis. MN: University of Minnesota Press.

Bakhtin, M.M. (1994). *The Bakhtin reader: Selected writings*. London: Edward Arnold.

Beck, R. (1979). *Handbook in social philosophy*. New York: Macmillan.

Cooper, D.J. (1980). Discussion of towards a political economy: Arguments for a political economy of accounting. *Accounting, Organizations and Society,* 161–166.

Derrida, J. (1976). *Of grammatology*. Baltimore, MD: Johns Hopkins University Press.

Derrida, J. (1981). *Positions*. Chicago. IL: The University of Chicago Press.

De Saussure, F. (1959). *Courses in general linguistics*. New York: McGraw-Hill.

Norris, C.M. (1982). *Deconstruction: Theory and practice*. London: Methuen.

Paton, W., & Littleton, C. (1940). *An introduction to corporate accounting standards*. New York: The Macmillan Company.

Solomons, D. (1991a). Accounting and social change: A neutralist view. *Accounting, Organization and Society,* 287–295.

Solomons, D. (1991b). A rejoinder. *Accounting Organizations and Society,* 311–312.

Tinker, T. (1980). Towards a political economy of accounting: An empirical illustration of the Cambridge controversies. *Accounting, Organizations and Society,* 147–160.

Chapter 32

Business Planning as Pedagogy: Language and Control in a Changing Institutional Field[1]

Leslie S. Oakes, *University of New Mexico*

Barbara Townley, *Edinburgh University*

David J. Cooper, *University of Alberta*

Language and power are central to an understanding of control. This paper uses the work of Pierre Bourdieu to argue that an enriched view of power, in the form of symbolic violence, is central. Bourdieu's work stresses what is at stake in control and change. Business planning should be seen as a profound mechanism of control, a pedagogic practice that can fundamentally change organizational identities by changing what is at stake: the capital — in Bourdieu terms — of an organizational and institutional field. Like many other social theorists, Bourdieu sees power as central to understanding how control works in modern society and organizations. Bourdieu's understanding is closer to views of power and control that focus attention on the constitution of interests and the shaping of values. In this version, power can be at its most effective, when there is no visible conflict.

While there is no doubt that control can be directly coercive (for example, by threatening people's jobs) and can be executed through organizational hierarchies, it is also important to understand how control works more subtly through language and the construction and use of knowledge. Regarding planning as coercive and hierarchical is incomplete; it also provides and sanctions legitimate forms of discourse and language and thus serves as a mechanism of knowledge that produces new understandings of the organization. As a form of pedagogy, business planning is not a neutral mechanism of transcription but, rather, has significant implications for the forms and amounts of capital within a field and for organizational identities. Business plans not only announce that change is coming, but it is through the activity of business planning that change actually occurs.

As Mintzberg (1994) suggested, the goals implicit in the use of business planning are forced on an organization that relies on the process. In the Cultural Facilities Historical Resources (CFHR) division, business planning has been premised on cultural and historical sites being, if not businesses, organizations that may be

---

[1]Reproduced (in an abridged form) from Leslie S. Oakes, Barbara Townley and David J. Cooper, 'Business Planning as Pedagogy: Language and Control in a Changing Institutional Field', *Administrative Sciences Quarterly*, 1998, vol. 43, pp. 257–292 with permission from Cornell University.

Accounting, the Social and the Political
N. Macintosh and T. Hopper (Editors)

likened to businesses. Thus, isomorphism is implicit in this initial step. Described as competitors for a fixed amount of tax payers' leisure, time and money, cultural and historical sites were asked to identify other organizations in Alberta that attract visitors and encourage spending. West Edmonton Mall, Canada's largest shopping mall, became a point of comparison. Thus, planning in the CFHR followed the pattern described by DiMaggio's (1991: 287) history of art museums in which 'unreflective allusions to organizational models from other fields . . . was the object of fateful debate'.

Business plans were presented as an integrated hierarchy of ordered and organized actions, a cascade through goals, outcomes, strategies and performance measures. Emphasis was on content, principally increased gate visitation and revenue generation activities and strategies for implementation. Planning thus controlled the premises that underlay the decisions, if not the actual decisions themselves. Most sites were obliged to engage in this process; those that were not obliged worried about the implications of their exclusion. Although sites are front-line organizations with high performance ambiguity and may be assumed to have a decentralized power structure, our view is that the opportunities for loose coupling between actions and talk were minimized and change was real.

The pedagogic effect of planning was that it was appropriate to expand revenue, increase admissions, introduce new products, or improve the coffee shop. Sites were not encouraged to include plans for collections, research or restoration. Such plans, where produced, were rejected as irrelevant. Plans that were long and individualized were rejected in favor of simple and abbreviated plans. Thus, mechanisms of transcription (like business plans) were never neutral but involved strict, although unstated rules about what was appropriate. A second reason why these sites, even though they are front-line organizations, had limited opportunities not to conform to divisional and government pressures was that their plans and performance measures were reported through standardized annual accountability reports.

The business planning process was pedagogical in three ways. First, it required a receptivity to change. By receptivity, Bourdieu (1991) did not mean a welcoming or acceptance, but simply a preparation for change. In this situation, receptivity was invoked by a changing discourse at the provincial level as well as through budget cuts and the rapid pace and unpredictability of change. In a period of destabilization, the very indeterminacy of the business planning exercise was also acutely disorienting.

Second, business planning actively involves organizational actors who appear to be creating the process as they go along. The business planning process was very unstructured, although it is unclear whether the lack of instruction at the governmental level was intentional. Some of those interviewed felt it epitomized the new approach — that the process of developing plans could be quite varied and that all that mattered was results. For others, there was a great deal of tension surrounding getting the business plan and the performance measures 'right'. Frequently, managers remarked on the lack of a blueprint for change and spoke about 'feeling their way', an expression that symbolizes managers' attempts to 'read' the government's actions specifically and the wider Albertan power structure more generally. In this sense, business planning encouraged managers to try to learn a feel for the new situation and to try to absorb some of the cultural capital to be gained by appearing entrepreneurial.

For example, a divisional manager stated: 'We wanted to be entrepreneurial and if we wanted to be players in the private sector we were going to have business plans. We were going to operate our facilities like small businesses. So we got small business planners in and we went through that educational process'. Managers generally began to use the business planning process to gain legitimacy in the larger environment by using 'the language of business'. Business plans were also used to signal to lower-level managers and employees that their organizations were changing.

Third, the planning process involved the pedagogy of learning the new official language and the evolution of organizational language is the most important aspect of isomorphism. As one site manager noted, 'It is very important to us to have these business plans be credible with business people...it has recently become a good public relations tool with us. It has also allowed us to, you know how your Mama always told you, speak to people in a language that they understand? It is wise to have a common language with people in business. It has also taught some of our people to get out of their own professional jargon and into somebody else's'. The meaning of everyday words like 'goals' and 'objectives' became precarious. The difficulty in remembering a new language and all its categories — goals, objectives, measures, etc. — was expressed several times. As one site manager lamented, 'Well, as you are aware, there is a whole field of planning, with all the charts and all the steps. I have tried, I can't even remember them. I can't even classify them and by background I am a classifier. That is what we do. We are interested in Taxonomy and I can't lump these buggers together'. It was a language that was alien to most personnel: 'Out of [planning] comes the goals, strategies, actions — sorry, goals, objectives, strategies and actions. And to those we attach measures' (division manager). Some departments presented their completed business plans to the legislature only to be told that what they described as objectives were really goals and that what they defined as outcomes were really processes or outputs.

A significant part of Bourdieu's general argument is that the dualism between the content and process of business plans is often unhelpful in understanding the production and reproduction of social life. In our study, managers were learning and producing strategy in the process of forming strategies. The content of the strategies not only came out of the process, it informed the continuing process. Pedagogy helps us understand how organizational actors make sense of and construct change through both participation and resistance. Meaningful pedagogical exercises cause the capital and positions within a field to shift. These shifts create points of examination at which members of a field are encouraged to examine their existing activities and identities. At such a point, people name and categorize themselves. This leads some people to try to remake themselves, while others may stop contributing or withdraw completely. Some, particularly those with curatorial backgrounds, felt uncomfortable and tended to become less involved as they no longer understood the rules of the game; others not only embraced the new field but helped give it shape. These processes are both conscious and preconscious, in that they occur as participants recognize in their own language and dispositions that either they fit or do not fit in a field.

Business planning was also an act of symbolic violence. Through a process of naming, categorizing and regularizing, business planning replaced one set of meanings, defined by the producers within the field, with another set that was defined in reference to the external market. By doing so, this change threatened the relative autonomy of the field and its cultural and symbolic capital. In concrete terms, it reduced the control that people in the field had over their own work lives. The appearance of business plans as mere acts of technical transcription concealed the force this process involved. In particular, it directed attention away from the shifting of cultural capital toward economic capital and the diminution of existing identities.

Fields of Large-scale Production

The field that emerged from the business planning process has a number of characteristics that parallel Bourdieu's description of fields of large-scale cultural production and that differ significantly from the characteristics of a field of restricted production, as shown in Table 32.1. The focus is no longer on preserving cultural capital, but on the ability to quickly translate or convert all forms of capital into economic capital. This is because the field can no longer depend on internal rules to define its cultural capital and to defend its boundaries. It must depend on outsiders' evaluations of the economic value of its cultural capital. Accountants and economists move in to place an economic value on artifacts, now conceived as 'assets', and economic balance sheets become more salient as a management tool.

Within this new logic, the currency of its capital is defined by products to be sold to the public without commensurate increases in artifacts to be discovered and preserved. The evaluation of a site is based increasingly on its ability to produce and market successful products to museum 'customers', The success of these products is determined by the public's willingness to attend or consume them and, ultimately, to pay for them. Increasingly, the work at the sites is evaluated by its market value and the acceptability of its message to a large-scale audience. Legitimacy lies in the environment, and the adoption of external assessment criteria and employing external criteria of worth are some of the features of isomorphism, which produces legitimacy.

As a case in point, the business plan encouraged one manager to rethink the original site plan in terms of market shares and competitors: 'It [the business plan] would help us focus... on product development and would give us the guidance in terms where some of our competitors are going to have to go through the process. It would help us formulate any future directions, capital initiatives as we go through looking at who is in the market place, what is happening, what can we realistically afford, and how potential change can be built into, or how we need to modify the

Table 32.1: Comparison of fields of restricted and large-scale cultural production.

	Field of Restricted Production	**Field of Large-scale Production**
Orientation between capital and field		
Dominant capital	Cultural	Economic
Orientation of field	Definition of capital and distribution of positions is based on rules internal to the field	Definition of capital and distribution of positions more dependent on rules external to the field
Function of management	Focused on preservation of cultural capital. Accomplished through facility and exhibition planning based on professional interpretation of the necessities of history and culture	Focused on ease and speed of convertibility of cultural to economic capital. Accomplished through business planning and performance monitoring
Organizational identity	Cultural/historical site capable of preserving and generating cultural capital	Small business capable of generating economic capital
Product	Collection, preservation, study, interpretation and exhibition of artifact	Products for revenue generation
Positions within the field		
Professional identity	Curator, researcher, interpreter, educator, historian accountable to artifact and profession	Entrepreneur, accountable to the bottom line
Orientation	Internal: Based on professional standards. Able to define and educate appropriate consumers	External: Dependent on finding and attracting consumers who are willing to pay
Criteria for evaluation	Aesthetic, historical and representational faithfulness	Visitor counts and admission fees; entertainment value

position statement, or the goals that we have in terms of heritage preservation in terms of issues'.

Organizational purpose, then, had become more focused on revenue generation. Often when interviewed about planning in a generic sense, without reference to business plans or site plans, managers focused on their plans to increase revenue or to introduce new products for 'target markets', rather than the elaborate site plans. Although some managers differentiated between educational and interpretive activities (programs) and T-shirts, gifts and postcards (products), many managers described any identifiable activity that was provided by the site as a product.

Management now centers around a process named 'business planning'. Increasingly, site managers suggested that only by articulating missions, goals, objectives and strategies would their organization stand a chance of success. Further, missions, goals and objectives were not enough. In addition, the organization had to specify beforehand the visible and measurable outcomes it intended to achieve and provide evidence that it had achieved these outcomes. As outcomes were defined by revenue generation, evidence required proof that the sites were producing products that would translate into economic capital, for example, increased admissions and gift shop sales. Evaluation was no longer to be seen as an afterthought of a process, it was considered necessary and integral to the success of the whole planning process. In this sense, accountability becomes defined as representational faithfulness to the business plan and specified outcomes; management, as meeting the pressing needs of the market by successfully carrying out the business plan.

Whereas the primary value of museum work was viewed as intrinsic to the objects or artifacts museums collected, in the field of large-scale production, the value of their work must be imparted to an object through its economic value. Further, evaluation within the field takes the form of relatively continuous self-reporting of formally established outcomes and performance measures: consumer surveys, attendance figures, revenue generation and measures of local economic impact. The ability to generate revenues, no matter how small in proportion to overall funding, has now become a source of symbolic capital. Even these sums provide valuable discretionary or 'soft' money to site managers.

Within this new logic, people in the organizations are encouraged to see themselves, perhaps for the first time, as working in businesses rather than working in museums that are run in a businesslike manner. The desirable positional identity is no longer solely curator, researcher, interpreter or educator. It is also entrepreneur, often described as being 'realistic' and becoming 'change-agents' and 'risk-takers'.

For Bourdieu (1990), 'fields' are networks of social relations, structured systems of social positions within which struggles or maneuvers take place over resources, stakes and access. He described positions within fields as 'positions of possibility', because they are not stable but reflect relations of power. These positions are always in flux. Further, fields are hierarchically distributed, depending on the kinds of capital, the number and types of positions in the field and whether the field can influence issues in other fields. In our study, historical and cultural institutions constitute a field in their own right. Within this field, positions are negotiated and created by the maneuverings of curators, historians, archaeologists, researchers, volunteers and native and immigrant communities. This field is located in a hierarchically structured set of fields, one of which is the dominating field of the provincial government.

In considering how business planning may introduce change into a particular organizational field, we refer to Bourdieu's concept of capital. Fields are defined by different forms of capital at stake, be they cultural, symbolic, social or economic, as exhibited, for example, in cultural goods, intellectual distinction, or social or economic class. Further, fields are characterized by an on-going struggle for capital. Capital is not restricted to financial or monetary assets but can have other tangible and intangible nonmonetary forms. While capital may be economic, it may equally be cultural, as represented, for example, by education and expertise; or symbolic, as, for example, the capacity to define and legitimize cultural values. It may also be social, defined by access to and positioning in important networks. These types of capital have different degrees of liquidity (that is, the speed with which they may be transformed into other forms of capital); convertibility (the extent to which they may be exchanged for other forms of capital); and differing susceptibility to attrition (through loss, flight or inflation). According to Bourdieu (1985: 724), 'Capital... represents a power over the field (at a given moment)... The kinds of capital, like the aces in a game of cards, are powers that define the chances of profit in a particular field (in fact to each field, or sub-field there corresponds a particular kind of capital, which is current, as a power or stake, in that game)'.

For Bourdieu, forms of capital and the structure of a field are interdependent. Actors are positioned in fields according to the overall volume and relative combinations of capital available to them. Capital also structures the possible strategies and actions available to actors. The ability of those within the field to define its boundaries, thereby determining the degree of autonomy of a field, is intimately related to capital. Thus, actors and capital are not pluralistically distributed in a field.

Capital is also central to changes that occur within a field. For example, in the field of historic sites, the distribution of historians, educators, facility managers, publishers, local business people and communities and professional associations will determine the capital. The relations between these actors is always in flux because the capital and positions with a field and between fields, are continually being contested. If historians occupy a dominant position, capital will be cultural, as interpreted through professional values; if business communities dominate the field, economic capital (e.g. tourism or employment) would be more central.

Implications of Capital and Fields

The internally related concepts of field and capital also inform practices of management, evaluation and accountability, organizational positions, responsibilities and functioning. They provide individuals with a vocabulary of motives and a sense of identity and generate values and prevailing concepts of organizational

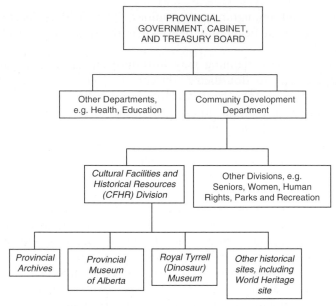

*Names in upper-case letters represent dominating fields. Names in italics represent dominated fields.

Figure 32.1: Position of cultural facilities and historical resources division in
provincial government of Alberta*.

work and worth. Each field has its own logic, as different forms of capital tend to impose their own logic on a field.

Bourdieu's concept of field breaks with understandings of organizational structures and relations based on conventional charts. Thus, in Figure 32.1, we locate the provincial government in a separate, but hierarchically related field to the various sites. While the figure may look like an organizational chart, we stress that the provincial government is a *dominating* field, while the CFHR division and its elements are *dominated* fields.

Bourdieu's notion of capital renders the concept of legitimacy more meaningful by requiring us to examine what is at stake in change and by prompting us to ask what role legitimacy plays in the constitution, preservation and exchange (i.e. the control) of various forms of capital. Institutional theory implies that organizations have a material substance that exists separately from organizational practices. Although organizations may be challenged, they may adopt changes and still continue to exist. Change alters the organization, but the organization could survive. Chameleon-like, an organization could adopt another appearance or structure if necessary. Organizations may incorporate socially legitimated and rationalized elements into their formal structures, but protect a technical core by loosely coupling operating practices from the institutional environment.

For Bourdieu, a practice that is deemed 'technical' is one that has gained the status of being taken for granted. It is technical because it is not challenged. The ability to claim a practice as taken for granted or technical is part of the cultural capital of a field. It is part of what those in the field are able to identify and define as natural and legitimate. For example, the body of knowledge that the curatorial profession recognizes as technical, the taken-for-granted element of being a curator, constitutes the cultural capital of the field. If that profession can no longer hold on to this body of knowledge, that is, if it becomes open to question, then the cultural capital of the field is lost.

If an institution or organization is sufficiently challenged, that is, if the form or amount of capital shifts significantly, the institution would cease to exist in any meaningful sense. Thus, even if a field were primarily identified by its physical capital, its bricks and mortar (e.g. a museum building), if the distribution of positions and capital could no longer be maintained, the bricks and mortar would become like a shell that is no longer occupied by the same entity. In losing symbolic, cultural or economic capital, a field loses legitimacy and its autonomy to define its own criteria for the production and evaluation of its organizational identity, functions of management and product. In losing its capital, a field loses its ability to define and control its own products, consumers and the market in which its capital will be exchanged.

In Bourdieu's conception change is part of the way fields work. Fields are always in flux or open to change because the capital of, and consequently positions in, the field are always being contested. There is continuous competition over the form and type of capital. Bourdieu (1993: 34) suggested that 'the generative unifying principle of the "system" is the struggle, with all the contradictions it engenders'. These struggles and negotiations can occur exclusively within a field, or they may be influenced by changes occurring in another field, especially in a dominant one.

In our research, museums and cultural sites constitute a field in which the positions available, the power between these positions and the distribution of capital result from that field's specific history. At stake is the interpretation of what is 'authentically' historical or cultural and what, therefore, deserves to be preserved, studied and exhibited. For example, at one site there has been an ongoing debate between paving a road for visitors' convenience and improved attendance, and maintaining the authenticity of the site by keeping the dirt road. More generally, what is at stake is the repository of Alberta's collective history, the source of cultural and symbolic capital.

Business Planning as Pedagogy in Action

In its first budget, the provincial treasurer of Alberta discussed the creation of a new 'management control structure for all departments'. 'This fall,... each department, agency and organization receiving government funds will be called upon to develop a three year business plan by January 1994... These plans will include measures of outcome and performance and strategies to reduce costs. Future funding will be tied to the achievement of those results' (Dinning 1993: 14–15). Alberta's 'New Approach to Government' was not just about planning and performance measurement. It was about *business* planning and it is in this undefined term that we see pedagogic processes at work. Business planning, designed to incorporate alleged business values (such as economy, efficiency, output orientation and entrepreneurialism) in a system of accountable planning, is central to this new approach, as is the changing discourse.

For example, the first business plan of the Cultural Facilities Resources Division [CFHR] division stated: '[The division] will focus on the economic contribution of its facilities, programs and services by emphasizing quality, aggressive regional marketing and sound reinvestment in infrastructure. One of the primary goals it to develop regional anchors for national and international tourism, thereby helping to sustain community vitality and prosperity' (Alberta Community Development 1994: 5). Further, services came to be described as 'products', and the aim of the government emphasized 'results, results, results'. As an Albertan commentator noted, 'People all over were reading...economic and management theories from the likes of Peter Drucker, Tom Peters, Kenichi Ohmae, Ted Gaebler and David Osborne and others' (Lisac 1995: 43).

The CFHR division, although at the time a field of restricted production, also existed within the larger political and economic field, one that gave rise to the Klein government. Senior division managers described the changes in philosophy and practices emanating from the Klein government as fundamental changes — changes in fact, not in rhetoric. At times they even anticipated (and helped constitute) the changes. And, as Meyer & Rowan (1991: 53) noted, in 'institutionally elaborated environments, sagacious conformity is required: Leadership (in a university, hospital, business) requires an understanding of changing fashions and govern-mental programs'. We observed this throughout 1994 as all levels of government struggled to come to terms with the changes that were occurring.

During this period, divisional representatives met frequently to attempt to learn how the department was interpreting the actions of the provincial treasurer and to attempt to determine what constituted a successful business plan. Pedagogy worked here as a form of learning through discovery and self-reflection. The CFHR believed that it would have to change the way the managers and people working in these sites viewed themselves, their activities and the management of the sites to survive this government retrenchment. As one senior divisional manager observed: 'We know what we are trying to do. We know what we are trying to accomplish as an organization. We think we know what the government wants us to do. And that is what drives us. We think we know what the government wants us to do. As civil servants...we see that as our job. How we get there varies enormously'.

The division thus began its own, somewhat independent business planning process for the historical sites and, in late 1993, hired consultants from Alberta's Department of Economic Development and Tourism to conduct a series of five day-long workshops on business plans and to visit the sites to provide specific advice. Business planning in the CFHR division followed the SWOT design school model, in which organizations conceptualize their environment in terms of opportunities and threats and their own capabilities in terms of strengths and weaknesses (Mintzberg 1994). Business plans in Bourdieu's 1977 terms, are 'culturally arbitrary'. There is no reason why a business plan should contain certain things and not others. The SWOT model, however, was presented as a legitimated vocabulary, a technical procedure, the way things should be done if business planning was to be done properly. Fiol & Huff (1992: 282) emphasized that 'the categories "threat" and "opportunity" are important mapping devices influencing the way managers act on issues'. For example, other historic sites were now labeled as competitors and threats. Charging entrance fees was seen as an opportunity to create discretionary funds. Symbolic power operates through a process of naming and categorization.

Conclusion

Management practices are regarded as common across organizations. We live in the age of the generalist manager, skilled in the ways of the economic market. Economists, accountants and marketing people seem likely to take over from curators, archeologists and scientists in the management of cultural facilities and historical sites. Homogenization also means that the sites and those who work in them are increasingly unprotected from market pressures in the larger economy. It is therefore perhaps unsurprising that an emphasis on business planning, marketing and revenue generation is associated with increased prominence given to local business groups in the management of the sites we studied. Thus, 'friends' organizations have taken on a new significance, raising funds and collecting entrance fees, with millions of dollars now moving through these groups, outside the formal control of the Provincial Treasury or even the site manager. The friends organizations now have considerable influence in determining how the money they raise will be spent.

It is important to emphasize, however, that we are not advocating nostalgia for a golden age of museums untarnished by commercialism. There are aspects of a field of restricted production that may be elitist and exclusionary. There may be a need for public involvement in the use of public money for public facilities. And, some of the changes have drawn groups to museums who might not otherwise have come. Nor were managers opposed to the money this introduced, if it meant increased spending on sites and better exhibits. Some managers feel that their status as entrepreneurs (not civil servants) has increased, as has their autonomy. When changes affect the capital of a field, they redefine the field, and this has significant implications for the work lives of those employed in these facilities and for what will count as valued history in the future.

Finally, there are unanswered questions about the degree of permanence of the shift from restricted to large-scale production and whether it is possible to make any statements regarding possible global shifts in this direction. There may be shifts toward and away from the field of large-scale production, but what seems certain is that the symbolic violence of the business planning process permanently changes the identity of producers and the capital of the field. The power of pedagogy lies in actors' complicity in their own control, not only changing themselves but also what is valued in the field in which they operate.

References

Alberta Community Development (1994). Business Plan: 1994–1995 to 1996–1997. Edmonton. Alberta Community Development, February.

Bourdieu, P. (1985). The social space and the genesis of groups, *Theory and Society*, *14*, 723–744.

Bourdieu, P. (1990). *The logic of practice*. Cambridge: Harvard University Press.

Bourdieu, P. (1991). *Language and symbolic power*. Cambridge: Harvard University Press.

Bourdieu, P. (1993). *The field of cultural production*. New York: Columbia University Press.

DiMaggio, P. (1991). Constructing an organizational field as a professional project: U.S. art museums, 1920–1940, in W.W. Powell & P.J. DiMaggio (eds). *The new institutionalism in organizational analysis*. Chicago: University of Chicago Press, 267–292.

Dinning, J. (1993). A financial plan for Alberta: Budget '93. Edmonton. Alberta Treasury, May 6.

Fiol, M., & Huff, A.S. (1992). Maps for managers: Where are we? Where do we go from here? *Journal of Management Studies*, *29*, 267–285.

Lisac, Mark (1995). *The Klein Revolution*. Edmonton: NeWest.

Meyer, J.W., & Rowan, B. (1991). Institutionalized organizations: Formal structures as myth and ceremony, in W.W. Powell & P. J. DiMaggio (eds). *The new institutionalism in organizational analysis*. Chicago: University of Chicago Press, 41–62.

Mintzberg, H. (1994). *The rise and fall of strategic planning*. New York: Free Press.

Chapter 33

Changes in the Institutional Environment and the Institutions of Governance: Extending the Contributions of Transaction Cost Economics within the Management Control Literature[1]

Mark A. Covaleski, *University of Wisconsin, Madison*

Mark W. Dirsmith, *Pennsylvania State University*

Sajay Samuel, *Independent Scholar*

Introduction

Transaction cost economics (TCE) has been proposed as a useful approach for examining management control (MC) issues. The purpose of this paper is to explore the articulation of TCE and MC through the use of work of early institutional economist John R. Commons. In keeping with Commons' work, we incorporate institutional change as important to considerations of the viability of alternative forms of governance including various management control practices. Also consistent with Commons' work, our paper elaborates upon the significance of the concepts of 'asset specificity' and 'opportunism' through an illustrative analysis of contemporary efforts to de-regulate the utilities industry in the State of California, and the related role of Enron Corporation in those de-regulatory efforts. This context provides a rich backdrop to highlight the joint articulation of TCE and MC issues.

Governor Pete Wilson signed a law in September 1996 that reconstructed California's electricity market, declaring: 'We've pulled the plug on another outdated monopoly, and replaced it with the promise of a new era of competition' (*Los Angeles Times* 2000: A1). In his January 2001 State of the State address, Governor

[1]Reproduced (in an abridged form) from Mark A. Covaleski, Mark W. Dirsmith and Sajay Samuel, 'Changes in the Institutional Environment and the Institutions of Governance: Extending the Contributions of Transaction Cost Economics Within the Management Control Literature', *Accounting, Organizations and Society*, 2003, vol. 28, pp. 417–441 with permission of Elsevier.

Accounting, the Social and the Political
N. Macintosh and T. Hopper (Editors)

Gray Davis called California's electricity deregulation a 'colossal and dangerous failure' (*Reuters Newswire* 2001). According to the popular press, California is 'totally at the market's mercy. And markets have no mercy' (*Newsweek* 2001: 23).

The debate, the forces and the tension inherent in these conflicting views about the 'waste and inefficiencies' in a regulated environment versus the 'opportunism' in a deregulated environment, offer a fruitful setting within which to consider and extend the TCE perspective as it applies to MC. This setting presents an opportunity for re-examining Baiman's (1990: 346) contention in the accounting literature that although TCE has been applied in the managerial accounting and control literature for quite some time it 'has not, as yet, had a significant effect on the direction of managerial accounting research'.

Williamson (1991) recognized that there are two major forces influencing the TCE research agenda — the institutional environment *and* the institutions of governance. According to Williamson (1993: 11), the institutional environment includes the broad, sweeping 'set of fundamental political, social and legal ground rules that establish the basis for production and distribution'. In contrast, the institutions of governance construct is more micro-analytical and focuses on the comparative efficacy with which alternative generic forms of governance economize on transaction costs. Williamson (1991) argued that *both* parts of the TCE research agenda — the institutional environment (the primary focus of institutional sociology) and the institutions of governance (the primary focus of institutional economics) should be explicitly conjoined for a complete depiction where the institutional environment serves as a set of parameters whose modification generates changes in the comparative costs between the different institutions of governance. Thus, interpreted according to Williamson, the scope of TCE must include an appreciation of political forces shaping the transactional milieu.

The purpose of our paper is to contribute to and extend Baiman's (1990) thesis on how the insights of TCE can be applied to management control issues. More specifically, our contribution relies on using the work of early institutional economist John R. Commons (1893, 1924, 1934, 1965) to provide a more fine-grained depiction of how such regulated organizations as electric utilities work in their social/institutional setting. In keeping with Commons' work, we will seek to focus on institutional change.

The Significance of Recognizing the Sociological Dimensions in TCE

The fundamental question addressed by TCE is why certain types of transactions are consummated within particular organizations forms, while other transaction types are consummated by systematically different organizational forms (Williamson 1985).

For Williamson (1985: xiii), contracting between parties is inherently fuzzy on account of two 'concessions to human nature' — 'bounded rationality' and 'opportunism'. Whereas, bounded rationality refers to cognitive limitations that prevent complete foreknowledge of every future exigency potentially affecting the contract, opportunism — the focus of our analysis — is defined as 'self-interest seeking with guile' (Williamson 1985: 47) according to which people seek to serve their own ends, often strategically. Transactions, in turn, exhibit a variety of characteristics that contribute to contracting problems, among which is 'asset specificity'. Asset specificity concerns the ability of assets involved in a transaction to be put to alternative uses, should the contract be prematurely terminated: the greater the asset specificity, the less able is the contracting party to put it to alternative uses and the greater the risk of 'hold-up', or the opportunistic expropriation of asset value. Importantly for TCE, 'asset specificity in conjunction with opportunism explain when and why achievement of successful adaptation [to a changing institutional environment] cannot be taken for granted' (Spekle 2001: 421).

Williamson (1996) theorized that arms-length market contracting may be expected to be effective when asset specificity and the risk of hold-up are low, but that other governance structures (i.e. management control devices that serve as alternatives to market-based contracts) are needed where asset specificity and the risk of opportunism are high. There tends to remain, however, an emphasis on efficiency within the TCE perspective.

TCE theory has accordingly been criticized as offering an under-socialized account of organizational design issues and for failure to explain why certain efficient designs are not adopted, as well as why certain inefficient designs endure. Williamson (1987: 176) recognized the limitations inhering in TCE, concluding that 'few economists would insist on an unrelieved efficiency theory of economic organization', and called for an enlarged perspective to fully grasp organizational design issues.

The framework that Commons developed essentially identified the transaction as the focal point to define economic activity and related issues of social and managerial control. Organizations actively participate in constructing meaning around these transactions, and this construction process generates ideologies of rationality, which legitimate and reinforce particular forms of organizing and governing economic activities. That organizations are both responding to and constructing these transactions, renders particular organizing and governance of economic activities 'endogenous': the content and meaning of these transactions are determined within the social field that it is designed to govern.

Contemporary sociological institutional theorists have taken the notion of the transaction as a critical focal point in understanding organizational design and control by recognizing that certain transactions between the institutional environment and the organization are particularly significant and pervasive. These 'strategic transactions' exert the tangible forces in an organization's environment that either directly or indirectly divert organizational design selection away from adopting *efficiency-optimizing* designs and toward adopting designs that enhance *legitimacy*. Thus, there are transactions that cause actors to knowingly adopt certain organizational designs to achieve ends other than economic efficiency. Organizational agency and institutional process coexist through operations of a local rationality within the context of global institutionalism: organizations seek to act rationally to adopt *efficiency-optimizing* designs, but the definition of rationality is constructed and evolves at the environmental level, driven by institutionalized stories about the value and *legitimacy* of particular organizational structures and strategic transactions.

Commons' work also offered a dialectical and pragmatic view of institutional change. Changes to the working rules come from customs and laws that evolve historically in a society, which, in turn, are produced and reproduced by an accretion of numerous common practices, and by the decisions of common law courts in resolving disputes. Commons viewed institutional change affected through strategic transactions as being a process of cumulative modification of the collective working rules for solving new problems and conflicts among willful and powerful individuals. Commons approached questions of efficiency within a broader context that emphasized power relationships and the need for a 'reasonable' framework of institutional rules. Although courts consider efficiency to be important to society, ethical criteria of justice and equity appear to be at least as important to its functioning. Therefore, institutional assessments of transactions are not simply based on reducing transaction costs and optimizing efficiency.

Essentially, Commons offered a volitional theory, which located the source of institutional change in conflicts among purposeful individuals within collective action. Commons' replacement of natural selection with artificial, purposeful selection to achieve strategic ends places human willfulness, values and vested interests at center stage inside (not outside) of the conceptual framework. The construction of such collective action is invariably contested. The more ambiguous and politically contested the collective action, the more open it is to social construction, thus raising the issue as to who is being constrained or influenced, as well as how this influence is being exerted.

Because of opportunism, contracting problems arise and impact the transaction in question. Moreover, asset specificity, in conjunction with opportunism, explains when and why successful adaptation of governance structures to the institutional environment cannot be taken for granted.

Asset specificity refers to the degree to which an asset can be redeployed to alternative uses and by alternative users without loss of its productive value (Williamson 1991: 281). The value of these losses is — in absence of sufficiently powerful safeguards — in turn, exposed to the risk of opportunistic expropriation. TCE's basic proposition is that transactions are aligned between the institutional environment and the governance structures in a discriminating, economizing way. Market control is exerted for transactions that score low on asset specificity. Rising asset specificity, however, impedes the smooth functioning of the market and alternative governance devices, such as hierarchies and accounting-based monitoring mechanisms, are needed to protect the transaction against opportunistic behavior.

The fundamental issue of opportunism in the contracting problem is inherent in Commons' work that essentially defines institutional change (thus impacting the governance of economic activity) as emerging from resolutions to strategic problems in social relationships among willful and conflicting individuals.

Commons' volitional institutional economics located the source of institutional change in conflicts among purposeful individuals within collective action. Moreover, this strand of volitional behavior within the TCE relationships is inherent in Commons' replacement of natural selection with artificial, purposeful selection to achieve strategic ends.

Opportunism and Asset Specificity: Regulation of the Utilities Industry

Recent problems in the California utilities industry has had the press longing for a regulated environment: 'In the old days, when utilities were regulated, there was often waste and inefficiency, but power was reliable and utilities cared desperately about keeping the lights on' (*Newsweek* 2001: 23).

Simply put, there were three major actors impacting the delivery of electricity for over 100 years (*Los Angeles Times* 2000: A1). First, there were the *utility companies* which produced the electricity, put it on their distribution systems and shipped it to their customers. Second, there were the *consumers* who used electricity and sent checks to utility companies for electricity. And third, there was the *Public Utilities Commission* which regulated and set a 'fair rate of return' on assets owned by utility companies. Such a model was seen, however, as generating electricity in an inefficient manner, necessitating a change in the institutional environment.

Within this effort of 'cutting through 100 years of sedimentary layers', the major quandary essentially became: perpetuating inefficiencies in a regulated sector versus dealing directly with the issue of opportunism and asset specificity. As expressed in the earlier quote, there is a certain sense of moral obligation to re-pay the utility companies/shareholders for their investment in assets (i.e. for the state to not opportunistically exploit the asset specificity that the utility companies have committed themselves to by requiring their abandonment).

Much of this regulatory regime, and also current efforts to de-regulate the electric utility industry, can be traced to the work of John R. Commons, whose work 100 years ago provides a rich illustration of the impact that institutional constraints have upon the institutions of governance (i.e. standards of organizational practice). For example, concerning politics and society, Commons contrasted the rampage of 'public passions' (often expressed in terms vested interests) against the 'rule of law and reason'. Social order is sought via institutions that quell and channel the destructive spirit of vested interests and contain the disordering implications of democracy. In turn, these demarcations were based on a singular preoccupation: the divergence between private and public interests, or the tension between the individual and society. Accordingly, the problem for Commons emerged from recognizing that a transformation in relations between companies and government, such as in modifying the regulation of utility monopolies, threatened to be at odds with, if not subvert, public interests. Societal rules such as the regulation of utility monopolies enter organizational life not only as adjustments to the costs and benefits of specific instrumental behaviors, but also as pervasive normative and cognitive frameworks for the social construction of reality. Commons recognized that the relationship between organizations and their regulatory environment is highly endogenous and reciprocal.

Commons sought to lend more formality to the social construction of 'reasonable value' in the form of collected opinions expressed in courts of law. Harter (1962) suggested that in order to learn the meaning of the concept of 'reasonable value', Commons turned to the study of common law, which the institutional economist maintained was the central means by which many societal habits and customs become encoded in governance structures. In an evolving socio-economic political system, new forms of social behavior emerge in response to new needs or opportunities, and these new forms give rise to conflicts which must be resolved by the courts. Those forms that are 'reasonable' or good in the eyes of the court are accepted, while those that are 'unreasonable' or bad are suppressed. 'Reasonable value' represents some notion of objective worth, as being 'good' or 'viable' in the eyes of competing parties in a court of law.

Commons drew his calculus of economic efficiency from a broader context that emphasized societal needs, conflicts of interest, power relationships and the need for a 'reasonable' framework of institutional rules of the game which necessarily incorporated the institutional environment. Commons apparently recognized that 'facts', 'objectivity', 'rationality' and 'reasonable value', upon which the *Public Utilities Law* was ostensibly built, were quite 'elastic' in their interpretation, and that power relations drove this elasticity. Commons' reliance on socio-political processes rendering the objective calculations elastic and manipulable did not go unnoticed by critics of the era, who challenged the discretionary nature of physical valuation in utility regulation.

Consistent with other institutional economists of the era and the Progressive political movement of the period, Commons' 'pecuniary calculus of accounting' was deployed in support of government intervention vis-à-vis regulation. Here, economic calculation performed two roles in augmenting long-term, incomplete contracts that required special adaptive mechanisms to effect realignment and restore efficiency when beset by unanticipated disturbances. First, the calculus of efficiency was deployed in the hope of making the private public by rendering the inner workings of such monopolies as utilities and railroads transparent to State regulatory commissions. And second, this calculus transformed conflicts of interest into discursive affairs, as compared to physical conflict in the form of boycotts, picket lines and armed Pinkerton agents typical of the era. This latter role of the calculus of efficiency aided in bringing confrontations from street level violence to the negotiating table, thus making unnecessary the overt exercise of power. The consequences of opportunism and asset specificity were expected to be more socially damaging than the embedded inefficiencies of regulated rates based on a cost-plus rate of return on investment pricing regime.

The design of such a mechanism for pricing implied that the rate of return, traditionally considered an MC device, simultaneously serves as a transaction cost reducing mechanism. The regulated electric utility is an organizational form perhaps best characterized as an 'administered market'. Neither wholly a hierarchy, where executive directives replace prices, nor wholly a market, where the interaction of pure demand and supply determines prices, the 'administered market' is an organizational form that prevents market failure. Commons was well aware that markets might fail due to either low levels of ex-ante investment due to fear of ex-post hold-up, or the potential for price gouging by monopolistic suppliers. The regulated environment for electric utilities offered the producer a guaranteed return of investment, while also giving the consumer protection from price gouging. By promoting and generalizing the use of a cost-plus rate of return as a pricing formula, Commons' and other progressives cut the Gordian knot of their time: the accounting-based mechanism permitted public utilities to be privately owned, thus avoiding the charge of socialism, while nevertheless preventing transactions from 'fracturing under hammer of unassisted market forces'. It was not efficiency that was sought in devising and establishing the mechanism for regulating utilities, rather Commons sought to find a way to make markets work for the public interest without being directly owned and controlled by the State. In this sense, the cost-plus mechanism is not merely a tool to aid in making resource allocation decisions and affecting managerial control, but also crucially, a means for legitimizing the market economy.

Commons, however, saw effective rate setting to be as much about preventing governments from reducing the rates of utility companies to the point where the government actually ran the utility, or de facto confiscated its property or allowed others to do, as it was about protecting society from exploitive monopolies. For Commons, the relevant comparative costs would have been the costs of publicly owned and managed utilities as against the costs of administered or regulated markets. Despite the apparent motive to accommodate business interests, one can argue that Commons' motive was more to strike a balance between the powers of government *and* business. This motive becomes more prominent in light of the financial failures of some of the major utility companies in California and the resultant new role of the State as the financial guarantor of providing electricity to its citizenship.

In short, organizations and social actors of Commons' era were not only *efficiency seeking*, but rather were also *legitimacy seeking* — a duality that continues to this day. In this regard, the accounting information provided legitimacy to deal with opportunism *and also* served as a solution to the problem of asset specificity — a solution which is being demanded by social actors in the contemporary, deregulated environment. Documents showing that Enron manipulated California's power market have been described by politicians, lawyers and consumer groups as the 'smoking gun' they needed to help recover billions of dollars they allege the customers were overcharged by Enron and other companies for electricity in 2000 and 2001.

Opportunism and Asset Specificity in the De-regulation of the Utilities Industry

Recent events in California have threatened the very legitimacy of de-regulation that has transformed public policy over the last two decades. The notion of deregulation condenses a large number of innovations in organizational forms, management control devices, institutional relations between the state and private corporations and investors, that have changed the economic landscape in a variety of industries from telecommunications to the airlines. The deregulation of the electric utility industry has shattered the 'monopolistic market structure' that was established and consolidated over the past century (Hirsh 1997: 36). The vertically integrated utility was supposed to give way to a 'virtual utility — one in which partnerships and joint ventures flourish to add value to the customers' use of electricity' (Hirsh 1997: 36). This effort is now open to an intense questioning and doubt.

In the wake of the rolling blackout, the impending bankruptcy of the principal electric utilities and the mounting bill to the California State Government, the *California Manifesto* identified a number of causes of this debacle and offered remedies. For example, the authors pointed to the need to raise consumer prices, to devise better long-term contracts between generators and distributors, to promote retail competition and pricing flexibility while leaving the deregulation template in place. On the other hand, Federal legislators increasingly criticized the deregulated market solution and urged a return to the previous cost-based regulatory regime.

Harmonious relations for much of the century degenerated with the 1973 oil crisis as pressure groups challenged state-level regulatory/monopoly regimes. Corresponding US Congressional mandates in 1977, generally favoring deregulation, encouraged 'time of use' pricing rather than the traditional sliding scale, volume discounts for electric power. Importantly, these mandates also called for utility companies to inter-connect their power grids as well as buy power from small power generating companies. This latter mandate was created by the Federal level Public Utilities Regulatory Policies Act of 1978 (PURPA) which served as a foundation for the independent power production industry that, in turn, served a pivotal role in California. Among its provisions, PURPA mandated that utilities buy power from small co-generators or 'qualifying facilities' (QFs) that were at the time largely industrial and fuel extraction plants which produced electricity as a by-product of their operations. PURPA not only 'deregulated the generating sector of the utility industry' but also gave a fillip to the development of small scale and renewable technologies, both of which challenged the vertically integrated electric utility.

Nowhere was this challenge to the utilities more pronounced than in California, where 'under the leadership of Governor Jerry Brown, . . . the state's Public Utility Commission encouraged windpower development' to such an extent that 'the state became host to 85% of the world's wind powered capacity by the end of the 1980s' (Hirsh 1997: 32; Joskow 1997).

Pricing, as in Commons' era, remained contentious under PURPA, this time with respect to prices charged by QFs. The Federal Energy Regulatory Commission (FERC) charged state regulatory commissions with the tasks of setting rates (specifically based on the costs avoided by the utility in buying from the QF) as had traditionally been done, though with a different cast of actors. One critical issue was that if a clear rate development methodology was not developed, the QFs faced a highly uncertain contractual contingency. According to Russo (2001: 60), despite the hope that avoided costs would mirror objective marginal costs: 'Due to the accounting vagaries of regulated firms, however, setting actual avoided costs required both interpretation and judgment. This gave great latitude to State Commissions as they fashioned policies for QF's power'. More specifically, problems arose because accounting focuses on aggregate, not marginal costs, thus necessitating development of a strict definition of 'avoided costs'. With the independent power producers having become institutionalized within US Law, energy developers observed in 1983 that: '. . . there is an implicit compact between utilities and regulatory agencies to allow them to *sell power at cost plus a reasonable rate of return . . . .* A regulatory commission could not simply declare that a utility's power could not be sold at all, or had to be sold below costs . . .', (Floyd & Marcus 1983: 11).

Under California's 'simple' approach to deregulation, there were no longer simply two players (*utilities companies* and *consumers*) and a referee (the *Public Utilities Commission*). First, there are now *energy companies* that produce electricity, often at power plants purchased from California utilities. Second, there still exist the *utilities companies*, that no longer produce electricity, but simply distribute it; the *utilities companies* now acquire electricity from the *energy companies*, but not directly from them. A third party has been introduced to the system: the *Independent System Operations* (*ISO*) that is the conduit between the producers of electricity (the *energy companies*) and the distributors of electricity (the *utilities companies*). The *ISO*'s run most of the state's long distance transport grid and makes sure that power gets to the utility distribution systems. The *ISO* buys extra power when it is needed to keep electricity supplied. As such, with a mission of keeping the electricity flowing, the *ISO* is often caught purchasing much of its electricity from the *energy companies* (who might sell it elsewhere in the nation, or withhold it) at almost always spot market, premium prices and then bill the utilities companies for it. This trend has been welcomed by some favoring continued deregulation as a way to get generating assets into the hands of the best operators. Others decry the concentration of ownership as an invitation to market manipulation.

The consequences of opportunism and asset specificity around long-term transactions in the California utilities industry are playing out in the manner in which John Commons would have feared. For example, Governor Davis vowed to save the state's two biggest utilities from bankruptcy, proposed a new California power authority and promised a crackdown on price gougers (*Los Angeles Times* 2000). But the Governor was not able to keep his vow: Pacific Gas and Electric Company, the utility unit of PG&E Corporation, filed for reorganization under

Chapter 11 of the US Bankruptcy Code in San Francisco bankruptcy court in 2001 (*Yahoo Finance* 2001a,b). And with the biggest utilities no longer economically viable, it has forced the State of California to come in and 'lay out an estimated $50 million each day to buy power for the cash strapped PG&E, Southern California Edison, and San Diego Gas & Electric' (*Los Angeles Times* 2001: December 8).

As the State of California has become the only significant, economically viable entity engaged in transactions pertaining to the acquisition of utilities, it brings an appreciation of Commons' defense of his accounting calculus notion of 'fair rate of return', as he was being charged by *US Senate Hearings on the Physical Valuation of Property of Common Carriers* with using his accounting to serve as a 'private nurse' for the corporate world. The financial failure of PG&E, the California utility companies, and the resulting increased role of the State of California in the electricity business, raises a haunting concern for Commons' obscure comment in the *Milwaukee Journal* (28 July 1918), where he forewarned that one possible set of consequences inherent in opportunism and asset specificity would be the transfer of power from private organizations to the state:

> We have learned in all democratic countries of the world one important lesson from the way which Germany's power has been built up and used. The democratic nations have learned to dread Socialism. And government ownership of railways in Germany is probably the main instrument by which the power of autocracy has been built up in that country. Other nations dread government railroads when controlled by autocracy and military power, for it means that the railroad system can be used to dominate the business people, and to bring submission on the part of labor. [Ibid.]

The contemporary version of Commons' insight may be seen in the financial demise of the three major utility companies in California and the resultant increased role of the State in providing electric services (*Wall Street Journal* 2001b: A1; emphasis ours):

> Gov. Davis has put California on the road to creating what amounts to a mammoth stated owned electric utility, answerable largely to the governor... His actions in some ways hark back to the system of central control that preceded the disastrous 1996 foray into utility deregulation. *But they aren't simply a return to the days of monopoly utilities strictly regulated by the state's Public Utilities Commission. What is emerging now is a California power colossus that operates in important ways beyond the reach of regulators or the public...* Mr. Davis says his actions will ensure that Californians have a secure supply of reasonably priced electricity. 'This is not a power grab', the Democratic governor says in an interview.

Yet in the past six months, pushed by what he calls the 'colossal failure' of a deregulation plan, the governor has put the state deep into the power business....
The governor has in effect seized control of the state's electricity-grid operator, installing his hand picked team as board members...Mr. Davis also is pushing to have the state buy huge chunks of the transmission system that are owned by the financially beleaguered utilities. He recently signed into law a bill that creates a state power authority, whose director will be appointed by the governor.

> Having healthy utilities is extremely important, says the governor. He adds that he has been working hard to revive the state's two biggest utilities. *But as the state's role in the electricity business has grown, the utilities don't seem as essential as they once did.*

The State's foray into the electricity business, meanwhile, was not costless to the State, as a *Wall Street Journal* article (2001a; see also *Wall Street Journal* 2001b: C1) recently stated:

> As if California didn't have enough headaches, the State's growing financial problems mean it will pay a steep price to sell a record bond issue that is designed to help deal with the State's energy crisis. The recent downgrading of California's debt ratings have added to investors' concerns that likely will cost an extra $55 million or so annually in interest expenses on a planned $13.4 billion bond offering that will be issued by a department of the State of California. California is facing a cash crunch because it has spent more than $6 billion this year buying electricity on behalf of financially troubled utilities to limit blackouts that have threatened the State's economic well-being. That money has come out of the State's general fund, which is being depleted. Money from the bond sale would replenish that fund, with the aim of having enough money left over to pay for additional electricity purchases by the state in the summer and fall.

Thus, Commons' instincts as to the inability of contracts to contain the natural opportunism inherent where there is a high degree of asset specificity appears well founded, as such consequences transcend three major utility companies to now impact the State of California and its population.

Implications for Accounting and Managerial Control

The common focus of the TCE tradition and the management control literature is on informing control structure choice that serves purposive control in organizations. Control structure choice, and the manner in which purposive control is carried out, however, is more nuanced than merely involving an instrumental focus on efficiency. *The construction of collective action is invariably contested.*

The more ambiguous and politically contested the set of collective actions possible, the more open it is to social construction and influence (Russo 2001). As Commons and other institutional economists of his day astutely recognized, the meaning of such control structures as accounting becomes transformed as a function of shifts in politics and power, vacillating from serving instrumental *efficiency seeking* efforts as to control structure choice, to facilitating the *legitimacy seeking* efforts of powerful social actors. Our basic message is that researchers should attend to both the efficiency seeking and legitimacy seeking facets of management control systems in examining the control structure choice problematic. These two facets of management control systems are inexorably inter-twined and cannot be easily separated from one another.

When one considers the richness of the expanded TCE framework in terms of the merging of the economic and sociological dimensions, as proposed by John Commons, issues of 'control structure choice', 'purposive control' and 'efficiency' take on a much more variegated existence. Societal rules enter organizational life not merely as adjustments to the costs and benefits of specific instrumental behaviors, but also as pervasive normative and cognitive frameworks implicated in the social construction of reality. The relationship between organizations and their regulated environment is a highly endogenous and reciprocal one.

More specifically, we conclude that the concept of 'efficiency', as developed within the institutional economics framework of John Commons, and widely applied to utilities regulation since the turn of the twentieth century, was not merely instrumental in character. It also fundamentally represented a form of political exchange, symbolic display and means of social discourse for engendering societal stability or instability as the case might be. And the dark side of the instability is readily apparent in the case of Enron that joined with three other California utility companies in declaring bankruptcy.

Organizations actively participate in constructing meaning around such strategic transactions as selling and acquiring electricity generating facilities and this construction process itself generates ideologies of rationality, which legitimate and reinforce particular organizing and structures for governing economic activities. That organizations are both responding to and constructing these strategic transactions, renders particular organizing and governance structures 'endogenous' in that the content and meaning of these transactions are determined *within* the social field that they are designed to govern. Therefore, organizations and social actors involved with utility regulation should not solely be considered as *efficiency seeking*, but rather were also *legitimacy seeking*. Institutional economists such as John Commons recognized that the 'pecuniary calculus of accounting' provided economic generalizations that served as systems of rationalization for the on-going system of economic power embedded in the oligopolistic markets of the time (Merino 1993) — markets that are rising with renewed vigor in a de-regulated, and indeed, what amounts to be a post-deregulated environment.

The question arises, however, as to the efficiencies of accounting information serving *efficiency seeking* versus *legitimacy seeking* purposes in contentious, politically fragmented contexts. As asset specificity increases and the possibility of opportunism in strategic transactions becomes heightened — thus exacerbating an already contentious context — the instrumental, efficiency-seeking role of accounting takes on less significance. Commons recognized that his 'pecuniary calculus of accounting' did not provide optimal, instrumentally efficient solutions but perhaps put government in the role of playing a 'private nurse' for corporate agents. But his 'pecuniary calculus of accounting' did, as Merino (1993) observed, serve as a system of rationalization for the ongoing system of economic power embedded in the oligopolistic markets of his and indeed our time. The desire to avoid the more extreme consequences of high asset specificity in utility contracts, such as the divestiture of electric utilities and consequential dramatically increased state involvement in the industry, provided an arena within which accounting could play a much more variegated role than merely generating instrumental efficiency solutions to technical problems. Organizational agency and institutional process coexist through a process of local rationality within the context of global institutionalism. Indeed, accounting plays an even more effective role in facilitating efforts to legitimize the shifts in power needed to contain the opportunism (i.e. serve in the minimization of contracting costs) inherent in relationships among a fluid number of actors and a newly emerging and rapidly institutionalized range of actors involved with these transactions.

Ironically, as accounting serves an increasingly important role in supporting control structure choice, thereby legitimating shifts in power, it perhaps serves a more fundamental role in affecting purposive control than it would in any effort to serve in a solely instrumental efficiency-seeking capacity. Simply put, minimization of transaction costs fostered by accounting's role in legitimacy-seeking behavior perhaps more than offsets the resultant 'inefficiencies' embedded in the system of rationalization in that it provides for the ongoing system of economic power to regulate the oligopolistic markets. As evidenced in California, since the 'pecuniary calculus of accounting' and the previous regulatory milieu have been removed ('*We've pulled the plug on another outdated monopoly, and replaced it with the promise of a new era of competition*'), we have seen transaction costs increased dramatically ('*a $30 billion extortion*'), as three major provider utility companies, as well as the major power broker Enron, have gone bankrupt and the State of California has become the utility provider of last resort. In contrast, we have yet to see any fruits of efficiency-seeking efforts realized ('*Someday, markets may give us total reliability at a cheaper price than regulation would. But in the meantime, get used to . . . opportunism*'). As succinctly summarized in the *Wall Street Journal* (2001c: A1, A8):

> It was one of the great fantasies of American business: a deregulated power market that would send cheaper and more reliable supplies of electricity coursing into homes and offices across the nation.
>
> But look what's happened instead. Enron Corp., the vast energy trader at the center of the new freewheeling US Power markets, now faces collapse amid a blizzard of questionable financial deals. And California, the first big state to deregulate its electricity market, has watched its experiment turn into a debacle, with intermittent blackouts

and retail power rates as much as 40% higher than they were a year ago. Now, with the power industry hovering uneasily between regulation and deregulation, it faces a prospect of a market that combines the worst features of both: a return to government restrictions, mixed with volatility and price spikes as companies struggle to meet the nation's energy needs.

References

Baiman, S. (1990). Agency research in managerial accounting: A second look. *Accounting, Organizations and Society*, *15*, 341–371.

Commons, J.R. (1893). *The distribution of wealth*. New York: Macmillan.

Commons, J.R. (1924). *Legal foundations of capitalism*. Madison. WI: University of Wisconsin Press.

Commons, J.R. (1934). *Institutional economics. It's place in political economy*. New York: Macmillan.

Commons, J.R. (1965). *A sociological view of sovereignty*. New York: Kelly.

Floyd, N., & Marcus, W.B. (1983). *The regulatory factors in wind power contract development*. Paper presented at the American society of mechanical engineers. Second wind energy symposium. Houston TX.

Harter, L.G. (1962). *John Commons: His assault on Laissez-faire*. Corvallis. OR: Oregon State University.

Hirsh, R. (1997). Consensus, confrontation and control in the American electric utility system: An interpretative framework for the virtual utility conference, in S. Awerbuch & A. Preston (eds). *The virtual utility: Accounting, technology and competitive aspects of the emerging industry*. 19–41. Boston: Kluwer Academic Publishing.

Joskow, P.L. (1997). Restructuring, competition and regulatory reform in the U.S. electricity sector. *Journal of Economic Perspectives*, *11*, 119–138.

Los Angeles Times (2000). How state's consumers lost with electricity deregulation. (December 9), A1.

Los Angeles Times (2001). The power game is a contest involving many risks. (January 29), B1.

Merino, B. (1993). An analysis of the development of accounting knowledge: A pragmatic approach. *Accounting, Organizations and Society*, *18*, 163–186.

Newsweek (2001). Profiting from the darkness, (May 14), *23*.

Reuters Newswire (2001). California power crisis, (February 8).

Russo, M.V. (2001). Institutions, exchange relations, and the emergence of new fields: Regulatory policies and independent power production in America, 1978–1992. *Administrative Science Quarterly*, *46*, 57–86.

Spekle, R.F. (2001). Explaining management control structure variety: A transaction cost economics perspective. *Accounting, Organizations and Society*, *26*, 419–441.

Wall Street Journal (2001a). California will pay a steep price for energy bond issue, (July 17), A1, A6.

Wall Street Journal (2001b). Hurt by deregulation of utilities, California gives itself lead role, (May 17), C1, C19.

Wall Street Journal (2001c). Enron's swoon leaves a grand experiment in a state of disarray, (November 30), A1, A8.

Williamson, O. (1985). *The economic institutions of capitalism.* New York: The Free Press.

Williamson, O. (1987). Economics and sociology: Promoting a dialogue, in G. Farkas & P. England (eds). *Industries, firms and jobs.* 159–185. New York: Plenum Press.

Williamson, O. (1991). Comparative economic organization: The analysis of discrete structural alternatives. *Administrative Science Quarterly, 36,* 269–299.

Williamson, O. (1993). Transaction cost economics and organization theory. *Industrial and Corporate Change, 2,* 107–156.

Williamson, O. (1996). Economic organization: The case for candor. *Academy of Management Review, 21,* 48–57.

Yahoo Finance (2001a). Pacific gas and electric company files for Chapter 11 reorganization.

Yahoo Finance (2001b). Bankruptcy filing depends California crisis.

Chapter 34

Ethics and Accountability: From the For-Itself to the For-the-Other[1]

Teri L. Shearer, *Queen's University*

Introduction

The rapid acceleration of the global market economy has spawned increasing concern over the past decade with related social issues, including environmental stewardship and a concern for justice in economic life. As world trade and free markets continue to expand, the influence of economic activity on the wealth and sovereignty of nation-states, the financial and social well-being of individuals, and the fortunes of corporate entities and the people they employ becomes more pervasive. But at the same time that market forces exert a greater discipline over our individual and collective lives, we find ourselves increasingly unable to control, direct, confront, or challenge the system that supports them. We are all, it seems, caught in the web of a global economic system that we feel increasingly powerless to change.

To be sure, the global economic web has produced significant benefits in the form of cheaper consumer goods, rising standards of living (for many) and higher per capita incomes. But the unparalleled scope of the global market system also means that individuals and their governments must secure those benefits, not by making the system work for them, but by making themselves work within the system. The price of success can be dear. Regional labour forces increasingly sacrifice wage and benefit provisions, work-place safety regulations, job security and maximum work-week provisions, or the right to collective representation in order to make their employment competitively attractive to transnational corporations. Similarly, nation-states may sacrifice tax revenues, the environmental resources of their countries, state control of essential services and the social and economic well-being of significant segments of their populations in order to attract new investment or secure economic aid. Even the largest transnational corporations, whose activities

---

[1] Reproduced (in an abridged form) from Teri Shearer, 'Ethics and Accountability: From the For-Itself to the For-the-Other', *Accounting, Organizations and Society*, 2002, vol. 27, no. 6, pp. 541–573 with permission of Elsevier.

Accounting, the Social and the Political
N. Macintosh and T. Hopper (Editors)

and interests largely drive the global market, find themselves simultaneously enslaved by it. Firms which fail to earn 'competitive' rates of return on invested capital find themselves subject to the swift and often severe discipline of the market. As the global economic system continues to expand, it is difficult to determine who, if anyone, is in control.

In short, the triumph of free market capitalism on a global basis has elevated the need for economic accountability to a pressing social concern. The stakes, as Schweiker (1993) appreciates, are high: 'If it is impossible to render economic forces morally accountable, then human beings have become slaves to their own financial and corporate creations, and the world is subjected to unending exploitation under the aegis of "efficiency"' (231). It is for this reason that we urgently need to reconsider the moral dimensions of economic life, to explore anew the adequacy of economic accountability in an increasingly market-driven world.

This essay is an effort to address the ethical considerations on which theories and practices of economic accountability must rest. Such consideration is critical, for any theory of moral responsibility must ultimately rest on ethical considerations regarding the nature of the economic entity, including its relationship to the human community within which it operates. Moreover, it is this notion of moral responsibility that grounds the *accountability* of the entity with respect to this community, and hence the accounting practices that are undertaken to discharge this accountability. In short, the very possibility of an enhanced 'social accounting' presupposes fundamental challenges to our received notions of accountability, and consequently to the moral status of economic entities as well as the ethical presuppositions from which moral status derives.

As I will subsequently argue, economic theory presupposes a specific conception of the human subject, and a determinate social order in which these subjects interact. These presuppositions on which economic theory rests create a specific conception of the common good, and serve to ground theoretically the moral identity — and hence the accountability — of the economic subject. To apprehend this identity, and to evaluate the adequacy of the accountability inscribed within it to the broader realm of human purposes and pursuits, it is necessary to look closely at the way that economic discourse constructs subjectivity and intersubjectivity.

Constructing the Economic Subject

Neoclassical economics is characterized by an overriding concern with the individual, conceived in isolation from the social, political and economic institutions in which she exists. The focus of the theory is on explaining and predicting the behavior of this isolated individual; explanations and predictions of social phenomena are presumed to follow from the laws of individual behavior. Indeed, neoclassical economics attributes the very existence of market economies to man's 'natural propensity to truck, barter, and exchange' (Smith 1937: 13). Hence, not only is the economic subject presumed antecedent to the institutional features of social life, but it is the very nature of this subject that is presumed to determine the form that these institutions assume. In its focus on the individual, neoclassical economics is synonymous with the theory of economic man.

Although neoclassical economics is ostensibly concerned only with individual choice behaviour, the construction of the economic subject as (broadly) self-interested also, and unavoidably, defines the nature of this subject's relationships with others and hence also the social arrangements that govern commerce among them. For this reason, economic theory is as much a discourse of *intersubjectivity* as it is of *subjectivity*. To evaluate the economic subject's relationship to others, and thereby to evaluate the adequacy of economic discourse to discharge moral accountability, it is necessary to examine the model of intersubjectivity that is implied and instantiated by economic theory.

Neoclassical economics presumes that the individual begins with a desire (a 'preference'), the origin of which is exogenous to the theory. The self-interested drive to fulfill this desire leads to economizing behavior on the part of the individual which, when aggregated with the self-interested actions of other individuals, determines the 'value' of the desired object (the 'good'). In the neoclassical model, therefore, desire serves as an exogenous variable that creates the impetus for economic activity; value is the endogenously determined outcome of this activity. The economic relationship between desire and value is thus characterized by a *temporal* and *causal* precedence of desire over value; value, both in use and exchange, is granted only on condition that the object remain the target of a desire that originates from outside of itself.

When desire and value assume the temporal and causal relationship specified by the economic model, desire becomes an unavoidably appropriative act, one that grants value to the desired object only insofar as the object stands in instrumental relation to the desiring subject. Moreover, the desire that in this way gives rise to value is always and unavoidably a self-interested desire, inasmuch as the desire signifies a lack on the part of the desiring subject, in relation to which the valued object stands as the means to its fulfillment (Xenos 1989: 4). At first glance, this observation would seem to mark the limits of the theory's ability to describe and prescribe human behavior. But on closer inspection, it becomes apparent that, even though economic theory cannot accommodate non-appropriative desires, such desires do not serve effectively to create a sphere of human action and interaction with respect to which the theory has no descriptive or prescriptive force. This is because the theory imposes its normative force in all circumstances in which a choice appears freely to have been made; if the desire that compels the voluntary allocation of 'resources' is in fact inappropriate to the logic of the theory, this fact will be obscured as the theory reinscribes the desire in the language of self interest and appropriation for which the economic model is appropriate.

An Ethics of the Other

The conclusion that can be drawn from the above analysis is that if one seeks to hold economic actors accountable for purposes beyond their own interests, then one cannot do so solely on the basis of the moral identity that is enacted when these parties render accounts of themselves. Economic theory constructs moral identity such that the obligation to account *to* a community of others always already reduces to the obligation to account *for* the economic agent's self-interested endeavours. Within economic discourse, in other words, the distinction between private interests and the wider good is obscured as the obligation to account *to* the other is deemed to be adequately discharged by the accounting-for-itself of the self-interested economic agent.

If we are to succeed in holding economic entities accountable to 'wider human and environmental purposes', then, we must have some way of marking these purposes as *distinct from* the self-interests of the economic entity. This, in turn, requires an ethical imperative that can radicalize accountability such that it is irreducible to the self-interested accountability of the economic subject. I submit that the French philosopher and ethicist, Emmanuel Levinas, has radicalized the intersubjective relation of accountability in just this way. For this reason, Levinas' work both demonstrates the ethical inadequacy of the economic conception of accountability and provides the ethical foundation for a greater moral responsibility on the part of economic agents and entities.

Levinas' project seeks to challenge transcendental philosophy with an ethics that grounds subjectivity in the asymmetric encounter with the radically other. For Levinas, the primacy accorded to ontology in the tradition of Western philosophy has, by privileging the intentionality of Being, effectively suppressed alterity and transmuted what is Other into the Same. Klemm (1989) poses succinctly the question that motivates Levinas' project: 'How can the transcendental subject constitute the being of the Other except as alien 'I'? Is not transcendental philosophy thereby committed to viewing the other as a modification of the same, thus violating the other's autonomy and rendering itself ethically suspect?' (403).

In contrast to the tradition of transcendental philosophy, Levinas accords primacy to the ethical relation, as revealed in the face of the radically other. In the encounter with the Other, the self is confronted with an obligation that ante-cedes the Being of the self, a responsibility that subordinates the freedom of the self to the edict that issues from the face of the Other: you shall not kill. Thus, Levinas (1986) argues that ethics precedes ontology, that 'it is my inescapable and incontrovertible answerability to the other that makes me an individual "I"' (27).

In the relationship of the face-to-face, the intentionality of the subject is subordinated to the command of the Other. Thus, for Levinas (1985), the intersubjective relationship is irreducibly asymmetrical; 'I am responsible for the other without waiting for his reciprocity' (98). In insisting on the asymmetry of the ethical relation, Levinas is rejecting Martin Buber's description of the self–other relationship as a 'symmetrical copresence' (Levinas 1986: 31) of two subjectivities. In Levinas' view, intersubjective reciprocity both destroys alterity and occludes the responsibility that I have for the other. This responsibility, Levinas insists, is not generalizable to other 'I's'; rather, that my responsibility exceeds that of all others is the basis of the asymmetry on which the ethical relation is founded.

In the asymmetry of the face-to-face, therefore, Levinas found an obligation of accountability to the other that exceeds the 'accounting for itself' of the equal and sovereign subject. Moreover, this obligation precedes the very constitution of the subject *as a subject*; it is not a voluntary election, but rather imposes itself on the subject by virtue of the superior alterity of the Other. As Levinas (1986) explains, 'even if I deny my primordial responsibility to the other by affirming my own freedom as primary, I can never escape the fact that the Other had demanded a response from me *before* I affirm my freedom not to respond to his demand' (27). In his introduction to Levinas' (1987) text, *Time and the Other*, Richard Cohen describes this obligation as the 'reorientation despite-itself of the for-itself to the for-the-other' (17), a description that captures well the radical relation of accountability that Levinas' ethical project instates for the self with respect to the Other.

Even though this 'radicalized accountability' necessarily follows from the greater responsibility of the 'I' to the 'Other', it in no way *negates* the more traditional relation of accountability that exists between reciprocal 'I's'. Rather, Levinas argues, it *founds* the reciprocity from which the latter emanates. For Levinas (1969), equality is deduced from the originary inequality of the face-to-face relation (214). This occurs when the immediacy of the face-to-face, in which the essential asymmetry is experienced, is viewed in the abstract, as by a third-party observer (213). For Levinas, the inequality of the face-to-face remains the originary relation from which this equality follows, because it is only in the obligation to the other that the 'I' assumes an identity at all. As soon as the intersubjective relationship is viewed from the outside as 'two subjects facing one another', however, those subjects assume a symmetry with respect to one another that renders them equals.

This, Levinas (1969) argues, is the transformation that takes place when one moves from the domain of ethics to a concern for justice and the rules of moral life. Moreover, this transformation also characterizes the intersubjective relations of citizens in commerce with one another: 'I and the Other become interchangeable in commerce... [T]he particular man, an individuation of the genus man, appearing in history, is substituted for the I and for the other' (226). In this substitution, the ethical relationship is lost: '[The] social relationship becomes total reciprocity. These beings are not interchangeable but reciprocal, or rather they are interchangeable because they are reciprocal. And then the relationship with the other becomes impossible' (Levinas 1987: 82).

The point that I want to make is that Levinas' ethics suggests a radical accountability to the Other that neither reduces to nor negates the 'accounting for' of reciprocal and autonomous individuals, but indeed *founds* it. This project, I suggest, has profound implications for the way that we understand economic accountability. Specifically, Levinas' grounding of ethics in the asymmetry of the face-to-face points to the fundamental ethical inadequacy of the self-interest motive — no matter how broadly construed and no matter how congruous with the collective good of a moral community. This is so because in the self-interested discourse of economic accountability, any account of human action proceeds only from the sovereignty of the acting subject, from his essential equality with the subjectivity of the other. In this irreducible equality, the ethical encounter with the face of the other is denied, a denial that serves to eradicate the originary asymmetry from which equality derives.

My claim, then, is that economic accountability cannot be adequately conceived in terms that are exclusively self-interested, since the quality that such accountability both demands and instates is itself grounded in an *inequality* to which self-interest can never be accountable. That self-interest cannot account to the alterity of the other is an inescapable consequence of its location in a discourse that always already objectifies the other in instrumental relation to the needs of the self. By contrast, an accounting *to* the other necessitates a reconceptualization of self in which one's subjectivity is subordinated to the demands of the radically other. Self-interest is thus inadequate to account for this self-subordination that founds the ethical relation; self-interest as a measure of accountability is therefore also inadequate to the ethical needs of a moral community.

Corporate Accountability

The problems of economic accountability at the corporate or business level seem at first glance to be far removed from the discursive construction of economic subjectivity and intersubjectivity that has been the focus of this essay. Yet policies and practices at the societal level are a product of cultural presuppositions about relations of subjectivity and intersubjectivity at the personal level and shared conceptions of the individual's relationship to the wider social order. The economic conception of the private intersubjective relationship legitimates the pursuit of private interests and specifies that all transactions into which two or more individuals enter are mutually advantageous and hence facilitative of the collective good.

This translates into an ethical order in which economic agents are properly held accountable only for the advancement of their private economic goals, the well-being of the collective and of the individuals whose lives are affected by these pursuits being presumed to be congruous with the attainment of these goals. As a result, the economic depiction of society as an aggregation of interest-seeking, sovereign and reciprocal subjects serves to legitimate at a theoretical level the restriction of economic accountability to the pursuit of economic goals.

The influence of economic precepts on notions of accountability at the business entity level is nowhere more evident than in Benston's (1982) influential essay on accounting and corporate accountability. Both the shape of Benston's analysis and the conclusions that he draws from it, are premised on the unarticulated presupposition that the collective good is defined and achieved by the pursuit of private interest. This conviction is underpinned by an economic conception of the private, intersubjective relationship, wherein each individual is conceived as an autonomous, reciprocally situated subjectivity, to whom the Other appears only as an object that may or may not facilitate the subject's interests. These unarticulated presumptions guarantee the logical integrity of the analysis and hence legitimate the conclusions that Benston draws from it.

Benston makes evident in the opening pages of the essay his presupposition that the collective good can be none other than the outcome of the [legal and assuming for the moment perfect ownership rights and markets] pursuit of shareholders' interests. He does so by claiming that proponents of theories of corporate accountability implicitly or explicitly assume that managers have the discretion to use shareholders' resources in ways that do not benefit the shareholders. This claim, which provides the starting point for his analysis, clearly reveals that Benston takes '*corporate* accountability' to mean '*management* accountability'; from this point of view, if management does not have the discretion to use shareholders' resources to serve parties other than shareholders, then 'corporate' accountability is not a meaningful issue.

Benston's conclusion with respect to the accountability proper to the economic entity draws its legitimation from the economic construal of the intersubjective relationship. It can readily be seen that the contracting parties are presumed to be sovereign, reciprocally situated subjectivities who are engaged in pursuing their own private interests. Since each party enters the contract of its own volition, each party is presumed thereby to maximize its own utility. If there are no other parties impacted by the transaction (i.e. if there are no externalities) then the contract thus enacted will also serve the collective good, inasmuch as it will be deemed to benefit all participants and to hurt no one.

But Benston's conclusion, standard in economic theory, that any voluntary exchange between two parties promotes the collective good, is a far cry from the conclusion, implicit but unacknowledged in Benston's analysis, that the collective good is *only* that which is attainable through self-interested and free exchange. Benston's tacit assumption can be understood as a simple consequence of economic conceptions of the intersubjective obligation. As previously noted, Benston's depiction of human agents as sovereign, reciprocally situated subjectivities leads him to conclude that any contractual exchange between agents fully incorporates all responsibility that either has for the interests of the other, and hence advances the collective good. But to conclude from this, as Benston does, that there can be no obligation of accountability — even at the societal level — that would not, under the proper market conditions, be discharged by the shareholders' pursuit of their own interests, requires the further presupposition that there exists in society no Other whose interests override the interests of the shareholders. And this is a presupposition that follows easily from the fact that the discourse of economics negates alterity, transforming the world of others into a world of objects with which the economic subject interacts.

The consequences of such a monologic approach to accountability can be tragic. The lives of people, the existence of non-human life forms, the integrity of ecosystems and the sovereignty of nations all are made subservient to the instrumental pursuit of profit or productive growth. For example, Buarque (1993) and Waring (1988) both speak from experience of the unacknowledged (i.e. unmeasured and unaccounted for) human and environmental costs that accrue when developing nations uncritically adopt agendas of economic 'development' conceived in and appropriate to the 'developed' world. These agendas, Buarque notes, are frequently 'poorly suited to [a developing country's] cultural and natural environment and ill matched to the needs of the local population' (46). As a result, the adoption of development programs often results in the destruction of the adopting country's natural resources, its increasing economic dependence on foreign capital, and the uncompensated destabilization of traditional ways of life or means of subsistence.

The impact of our collective failure to hold economic agents accountable to purposes other than their own interests has made itself felt on the environment, as well. Pollution, the depletion of natural resources and the destruction or diminution of air, water and ecosystems all are becoming increasingly pressing social problems. Moreover, the growing impetus towards removing barriers to global free trade increasingly puts these problems beyond the reach of citizen groups and makes it difficult to tighten environmental standards, even locally. Again, our systems of accountability overwhelmingly fail to reflect responsibility to these environmental concerns. Whether at the national or the corporate level, the need to hold economic actors accountable to purposes beyond their personal interests would seem to be clear.

On the basis of the foregoing analysis, I suggest that what is needed is an infusion into our structures of accountability of a counterbalancing ethic that takes seriously the obligation to the other, and that possesses the potential to inscribe a 'radical accountability' that is irreducible to those purposes that are the economic agent's own. My claim is that an ethics such as Levinas offers, in which being itself is subordinated to the ethical obligation to the other, offers some hope of achieving this broader accountability. This is because the ethical encounter preempts the economic agent's subjectivity; the other demands a response *before* the economic agent even assumes a subjectivity. My response to this demand therefore precedes my constitution as an economic agent; it is prior to and distinct from the economic choice behaviors that constitute me as an economic subject. In other words, the egoism that defines the very being of the economic subject is suspended or held at bay by this primordial responsibility to the other.

Implications for 'Social Accounting'

The reluctance of accountants to question the adequacy of economic theory to accounting practice is of concern in light of the observation that it is the practice of accounting, manifest in the activity of rendering accounts, that enacts economic identity as intersubjectively constituted and morally obligated. The concern arises because economic theory radically restricts the potential for intersubjective relations, thereby also imposing radical restrictions on the exercise of accountability. In particular, any system of accountability that is restricted to a purely economic rationale is inadequate to discharge the obligation to the Other because, within economics, the very existence of the Other is subordinated to the instrumental purposes of the egoist self. This means that the accountability enacted in economic accounts reduces to an accounting-for-itself that is inadequate to the ethical requirement of accountability *to the Other*.

I suggest that an ethically adequate accountability on the part of economic entities demands an answerability *to the Other* that cannot be accommodated in the objectifying and other-denying discourse of neoclassical economics. This is so because the discourse itself transmutes all relations of intersubjectivity into relationships of symmetry in which moral obligation reduces to accounting for oneself. Extant accounting practices are therefore inadequate to reflect account-ability *to the Other* because, the discourse in which they are conceived and rendered constructs the moral identity of the economic entity as answerable only to itself.

Conclusion

The discourse of economics legitimates the discharge of accountability by exclusive reference to the interests of the economic agent. At all levels of economic life, the absence of accountability *to the Other* permits the unrestrained pursuit of economic goals and threatens, as Schweiker (1993) notes, to make human beings 'slaves to [our] own corporate and economic creations' (231). Indeed, it is this concern that suggests that economics is in need of a regulatory ethic that restricts its application in situations where significant and harmful side effects are likely to occur. Such an ethic would impose a corresponding accountability on the economic agent to the community of others, with whom the agent is intersubjectively situated.

To achieve a wider obligation to accountability on the part of economic agents, what is needed is an ethic that is incapable of assimilation to the logic of economics. However, if such an ethic is successfully to compete with economic discourse, it cannot be *merely* regulatory or prohibitive in its aim, but must rather comprise a discourse of human identity that is irreducibly distinct from economic man and it must be capable of infusing our self-understanding as economic subjects with a moral obligation that exceeds our own self-interest. Levinas' project seems to me to provide a point of resistance to the imperialism of economic discourse. It grounds ethics in the encounter with the Other and is resistant to the imperialism of economic theory for two reasons. In Levinas' metaphysics, the Other confronts the self as a non-reciprocal subjectivity whose very being forbids the commodification and objectification of the economic relationship. This non-reciprocity instates an asymmetry in the self–other relationship that subordinates the self to the Other and hence permits the Other to make claims on the self. This latter consequence is crucial because it disrupts the self-interested intentionality that defines the very being of the economic subject, and supplants it with a compulsion or imperative that is irreducible to the instrumental motives of economic man.

References

Benston, G.J. (1982). Accounting and corporate accountability. *Accounting, Organizations and Society*, 7(2), 87–105.

Buarque, C. (1993). *The end of economics? Ethics and the disorder of progress.* London: Zed Books.

Klemm, D. (1989). Levinas's phenomenology of the other and language as the other of phenomenology. *Man and World*, *22*, 403–426.

Levinas, E. (1969). *Totality and infinity.* Pittsburg: Duquesne University Press (A. Linguis, Trans.).

Levinas, E. (1985). *Ethics and infinity.* Pittsburg: Duquesne University Press (R. Cohen, Trans.).

Levinas, E. (1986). Interview with Richard Kearney, in R. Cohen (ed.). *Face to face with Levinas.* 13–33. Albany: SUNY.

Levinas, E. (1987). *Time and the other.* Pittsburg: Duquesne University Press (R. Cohen, Trans.).

Schweiker, W. (1993). Accounting for ourselves: Accounting practice and the discourse of ethics. *Accounting, Organizations and Society*, *18*(2/3), 231–252.

Smith, A. (1937). *The wealth of nations.* New York: Random House. (Original work published 1776.)

Waring, M. (1988). *If women counted: A new feminist economics.* London: Macmillan.

Xenos, N. (1989). *Scarcity and modernity.* New York: Routledge.

Chapter 35

Accounting for God: Accounting and Accountability Practices in the Society of Jesus (Italy, XVI–XVII Centuries)[1]

Paolo Quattrone, *Saïd Business School, University of Oxford*

> Indeed the name hierarchy means, first of all, a jurisdiction overall, a thing which is to be considered proved for jurisdiction in this meaning finds its sound basis.
>
> > (Diego Laynez, *De Hierarchia*, on the Divine Origin of Hierarchy. Laynez was the General of the Society of Jesus from 1558 to 1565.)

It is argued in this paper that the development of accounting and accountability practices within the Society of Jesus from the sixteenth to the seventeenth centuries cannot be reduced to an economic explanation that views them merely as tools for measuring and allocating economic resources thereby explaining the formation of hierarchies. Rather, their development and refinement were tightly linked to the absolutist ideology of the Roman Catholic doctrine of the Counter-Reformation, conceived of here as a complex work of compromise among theological, religious, political, institutional and social instances, of which the hierarchical structure of the Order and its accounting records were only the visible traces.

Introduction

In an article exploring the attention paid to organizational issues by the founders of the Society of Jesus, Höpfl (2000) observed:

> Both the provenance and the connotational range of hierarchy in its current usage are [...] unclear [...]. The provenance may be military, given the partiality of organizational discourse to military metaphors

---

[1]Reproduced (in an abridged form) from Paolo Quattrone, 'Accounting for God: Accounting and Accountability Practices in the Society of Jesus (Italy, XVI–XVII Centuries)', *Accounting, Organizations and Society*, 2004, vol. 29, no. 7, pp. 647–683 with permission of Elsevier.

(strategy, objectives, leadership, chains of command, campaign, communication and so forth). But a less banal provenance, namely a religious one, is supported by the no doubt forgotten etymology of 'hierarchy': hiereus, priest, and hieros, what is holy, and arkhe, rule (hence sacred or priestly rule).

Despite this insightful etymology, in discussion of early fundamental theorists of hierarchies and organizations this is often forgotten.

Drawing on archival evidence, the present research interprets the conditions that led the Society of Jesus to develop and refine its system of accounting and accountability, from its founding in 1540 and its extension in late sixteenth and seventeenth centuries in Italy. So powerful was the role played by this system, that it allowed the Society to exert strict hierarchical control and to act at a distance. Whether or not the development and refinement of this system can be viewed as the result of an economic rationale is the theoretical issue which pervades this paper. The Jesuit accounting and accountability system permitted the coordination of the Jesuit Houses through a unitary and hierarchical structuring of the Order. This was not the result of a search for efficiency, reflecting an economic rationale. It is argued that this coordination was instead the result of the enactment of the absolutist ideology that inspired the Roman Catholic doctrine and policy during the sixteenth century.

This paper summarizes the debate on the nature of religious reforms in Modern Catholicism, in an attempt to facilitate an understanding of the heterogeneous historic milieu which surrounded the foundation of the Society of Jesus. This approach allows the reader to conceptualize the absolutism of the Roman Catholic Church during the sixteenth century as emergent from religious, theological, institutional, political and social pressures. The focus of the paper then shifts to the Society of Jesus and its ordering which is illustrated through the methodological apparatus devised by Saint Ignatius, the founder of the Order. This apparatus facilitated the emergence of the specific systems of accounting and accountability, which framed the hierarchical organization of the Society and are referred to here as 'accounting for sins' (Holistic individualism and the (self) definition of the self'), 'accounting for the College' ('Analytical (de-)differentiation and the definition of a spatio-temporal dimension'), and 'accounting for the soul' ('Double reductionism and the definition of the visible'). The paper focuses on questions about the economic nature of accounting and accountability systems and their relation to the hierarchical forms of organizing.

The Jesuit Order and the Ordering of the Jesuits

The Society was founded by Saint Ignatius of Loyola (1491–1556) in 1539 and received the formal approval of Pope Paul III through the Papal Bull *Regimini militantis Ecclesiae* on the 27 September 1540, taking the Italian name of *Compagnia di Gesù*. The Papal Bull closely resembled the *Formula Instituti* which Ignatius and his companions followed since 1537. Originally, the project of Ignatius and his companions was to go to Venice, from where they were to embark on a 'pilgrimage to Jerusalem in order to engage the ministry there'. Only because they did not find a passage to the Holy Land did they go to Rome and offered their services to the Pope.

The *General Constitutions* of the Society outlined the principles on how to structure the Order. The Society was organized in Assistances (e.g. Italy) and Provinces (e.g. Sicily), to which the Jesuit Colleges belonged. Assistants, Provincials and Rectors were appointed directly by the General of the Society, who was elected by a General Congregation and placed at the top of this hierarchy. The General, the Provincial and the Rector were assisted by a Procurator, who was in charge of administrative and accounting issues. The Rector was also supported by a Prefect who dealt with pedagogical issues.

Despite the supposed rigidity implied by the hierarchical structure (see Figure 35.1), the Order was characterized by great flexibility and a capacity for adaptation to the most disparate lands and situations in which they operated (for instance, the Jesuits successfully reached India and Japan before the end of

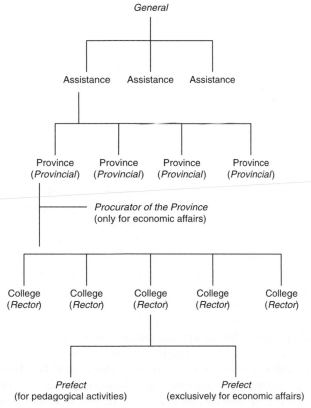

Figure 35.1: The hierarchical organization of the Society of Jesus.

the sixteenth century). This approach was enabled by a system of self-discipline, outlined in the *Spiritual Exercises* and inserted in the grand design of the *Constitutions*. Central to these Exercises was the individual and his self-control.

The character of the Society, as defined by Saint Ignatius in the *Spiritual Exercises* and in the *Constitutions*, was quite different from that of the medieval religious Orders. First and foremost, the Jesuits were animated by an activism previously unknown in the Catholic Church, where monastic organizations were devoted to contemplation and isolation. The Jesuits' aim was to take them outside the cloister for 'the salvation of souls', requiring them to engage in numerous activities: notably, missionary, educational and economic enterprises and also theatre and dance. Unlike members of other Catholic Orders, the Jesuits could take a fourth vow (unconditional and prompt obedience to the Pope) *sine ulla tergiversione aut excusatione*, in addition to the three vows of chastity, poverty and obedience normally assumed by members of other religious orders. This fourth vow, along with the words of Saint Ignatius, who described the Order as the Militia of Christ, the harsh discipline imposed on its members, and its hierarchical structure, resulted in a Society that was often compared to an army in service to God.

The Jesuit ideal, *ad maiorem Dei gloriam*, implied a reductionism for which the multiplicity of actions, beliefs and interests needed to be reduced to the glory of God (*reductio ad unum*). 'Accounting for the soul', along with the 'accounting for sins' of the Spiritual Exercises and the 'accounting for the College' of Ludovico Flori, allowed the General to supervise (*episcopio*) his Order through the accurate and recursive process of accumulation of information on the Jesuit members, Colleges and Provinces, the General could now *see* them, at leisure in his own office in Rome without any pressing need for visiting them. He was able to act at a distance through the accounting devices which were developed in the various geographical and virtual spaces that the Order created and occupied. The General was thereby empowered, an attribute reflected in his nickname, the 'Black Pope', given the colour of his garments.

However, this is merely one of the directions in which reductionism based on accounting inscriptions works from the top descending to the bottom of the Jesuit hierarchy. The Jesuit members did not perform the directives of the General because they were requested to do so in the Jesuit attempt to reduce them to God. Rather they did so because (for example, through the Spiritual Exercises), the search for God was a search for their self; and the choice of a Standard (God or Lucifer) was the enactment of their ideals, which were fused with the glory of God. Along with the *reduction ad unum*, which worked from the top to the bottom of the hierarchy, there was also a *reduction ad* simple (another unity, but constituted this time by each individual Jesuit), which worked ascending from the bottom to the top.

The role played in this double reductionism by the accounting devices in use in the Society was crucial because the normative power of a 'bottom line' in the three systems of accountability allowed one to believe that a base had been achieved — a base, from which action was prompted. The bottom line is the ultimate point of reduction — a point that was as precarious as the self that was constructed in the Spiritual Exercises. In this sense, the Jesuit Order was the continuous and incomplete

Jesuit attempt at ordering. What is left of this attempt is nothing but a visible trace —
an ordered hierarchy — the Jesuit Order. This clear trace is what makes one think
that hierarchies and accounting systems worked in practice for a 'Kantian' pure
reason (e.g. an economical reason, in a Chandlerian argument), creating a
totalitarian space and time. Rather, hierarchies as well as accounting systems are
incomplete attempts to reduce the irreducible complexity of human beings and
relations to a trace of ink on a sheet of white paper. A reduction which may seem to
be underpinned by a homogeneous rationale (e.g. economics, pedagogy, politics or
faith) as the prompting (and necessary) condition for both its existence and its
interpretation and that instead is always destined to remain as partial as its
underpinnings.

So the development of accounting and accountability practices in the Society of
Jesus in the sixteenth and seventeenth centuries, it seems, cannot be reduced to an
economic argument, as suggested by mainstream interpretations that view these
practices merely as tools for measuring and allocating economic resources that
facilitate the formation of hierarchies. Rather, these practices were developed and
refined on the basis of an absolutist ideology of the Roman Catholic doctrine during
the Counter-Reformation, conceived of here as the result of a complex political work
of compromise among various forces (theological, religious, political, institutional
and social) which characterized the early modern era. This complexity was reflected
in the birth and development of the Society of Jesus and its accounting and
accountability practices. The three systems of accountability of the Order (accounting for sins, accounting for the College and accounting for the soul) have been
conceptualized as the homogeneous result of the heterogeneous interests mediated by
the absolutist project of the Roman Catholic Church. Accounting and accountability
in the Jesuit case emerged because of the enactment and the coagulation of
multifaceted interests around the ideal of God, of which the hierarchical structure of
the Order is only a visible trace. A strictly economic analysis of the nature and role of
accounting as an instrument for allocating, monitoring and administering resources
within the hierarchical structure of the Society of Jesus would leave undiscovered
important aspects of the practices deployed by the Order to manage, organize and
account for its multifaceted activities. The system of accountability devised in what
has here been called 'accounting for sins' and 'accounting for the soul' would be left
at the margin of the accounting history of the Jesuits. This history would therefore
be limited to the technical aspects of the accounting systems devised to manage the
Jesuit Colleges, but would not offer insights for theorizing on the emergence of
accounting as an organizational and social practice in the Society of Jesus.

Correspondence

Correspondence among Rome, the Provinces and the Colleges played a crucial role
as an instrument of government in the Order. All correspondence received by the
General was kept at the *Archivum Romanum Socistatis Iesu* which was created as an
organ of governance. The flow of this correspondence was intense. An example of

this correspondence was constituted by the *Catalogi* — a set of detailed reports sent to Rome periodically by each Province. The *Catalogi triennales*, sent every three years, comprised three parts. The first, the *Catalogous primus* gave personal details about the members. The second, the *Catalogous secundus*, gave personal details about the character and attitudes of each member. The *Catalogous tertius* gave details about economic activities, reproducing the balance sheet of each college: information which was then 'consolidated' in the *Stato temporale dei Collegi d'Italia*, a book which summarized all the balance sheets of the Italian Colleges.

The *Catalogus Secundus* represented what could be here defined as 'accountability for the soul'. The dimensions chosen in the heading of each column (ingeniousness, intellect, prudence, experience, ability to profit from studies, character and talents) do not seem to be random. Choosing these dimensions was a way of providing visibility to those aspects of the soul which were important in making the good 'soldier', the good teacher, the good 'manager': in short, the good Jesuit. Through a methodical assessment of each Jesuit by grading and ranking the above-mentioned qualities in a 4-point scale from *malus* to *optimum*. The grade and the ranking of each member of the Society constituted for each of the eight dimensions a device (a bottom line) for rendering the members accountable.

Conclusions and Implications

The arguments in this paper may be of interest for several reasons, to which further lines of investigation may correspond. First, on a general level, the paper has provided arguments to reflect on the emergence of capitalism and its links to religious and spiritual matters. This issue has often been treated in paradigmatic ways, with (Weber 1991) stressing its links to the Protestant Ethic and with (Novak 1993) connecting it to Catholicism. The arguments of the paper, in contrast, recall recent historical debates, which see Protestant Reform and Catholic Counter-Reform as part of the same process of mutation, and may provide stimuli for seeing managerial practices as underpinned by multiple spiritual and religious instances. The importance of the individual (a Protestant invention) as well as the unity of the church (a Catholic tradition) coexists in the Jesuit accountability system. This perspective is even more relevant if one examines those studies (notably, Chatellier 1987) which have observed that the Jesuit disciplining principles were exported from the Order and disseminated on a European scale though the Marian Congregations.

Second, the paper has offered material for speculating on the role which accounting and accountability systems have played in the birth of modern and capitalist enterprises. In addition to being a complement to Chandlerian arguments, it is a source of arguments for debating the disciplinary nature of accounting (see the Foucaldian perspective), stressing the multifaceted nature of this practice, yet maintaining its Panoptic nature.

Third, the paper has largely drawn upon studies, which, in various disciplines, have questioned the paradigmatic distinction between premodern, modern and postmodern eras. The Jesuit case adds to that literature which increasingly questions the assumption that the conditions creating the emergence of accounting and accountability should be sought in the modern era and that categories of modern thought can profitably be used in this search.

Finally, the paper has argued that accounting and accountability emerged in the Jesuit case for the convergence (in some respect, fortuitous) of multiple interests around the absolutist project of the Catholic Church, individually enacted in the ideal of God. This enactment reached a compromise which satisfied (and modified or 'translated') this multiplicity. Therefore, accounting and accountability cannot be conceived exclusively as expressing a unitary rationale (be it economic, pedagogical, religious or of whatever nature). The issue for the accounting scholar, however, seems to be one of providing a framework which contributes to making sense of the different and varied accounts that accounting can provide without imposing another theory to the exclusion of others. The combination of 'holistic individualism', '(de-) differentiation' and 'double reductionism' tried in this paper, at least in the intentions of the author, is an attempt to do so. To do differently would entail the boxing of various existing accounting perspectives into a series of modernist categories such as *right* and *wrong*, *after* and *before*, *here* and *there* — trying without success to silence the participants to the debate rather than allowing them to speak, if they wished to do so.

References

Chatellier, L. (1987). The Europe of the devote. *The Catholic Reformation and the Formation of a New Society*. Cambridge: Cambridge University Press.

Höpfl, H.M. (2000). Ordered passions: Commitment and hierarchy in the organizational ideas of the Jesuit founders. *Management Learning*, *31*(3), 313–350.

Novak, M. (1993). *The Catholic ethics and the spirit of Capitalism*. New York: The Free Press.

Weber, M. (1991). *L'etica protestante e lo spirito del capitalismo* Milan: Rizzoli (A. Marietti, Italian Transl.).

Part IV

Prospects for Future Research

Whomsoever thinks he knows the future — doesn't.

[Anon.]

Reviewers of an earlier draft of this book suggested that we speculate about the directions for future research in accounting, the social and the political. So it is at their urging, and with the above epigraph in mind, that we offer the following hunches. Before launching into this treacherous task, however, it might be helpful to define the social and the political. As we use the term, the social refers to the relationships of individuals to their communities and to society at large. So sociologists and political scientists attempt to understand how social systems such as organizations, institutions, professions, families function and change, particularly why and how individuals accept [or resist] social controls and their power effects. The interest for us, then, is in understanding the role of accounting as one of the many important bonding agents that hold social systems together, as well as acting as the catalyst for conflict and resistance to social controls and their power effects.

Anthony Hopwood said it well in his inaugural editorial to the first edition of *Accounting, Organizations and Society* [Vol. 1, No. 1, 1976]. 'Accounting has played a vital role in the development of modern society. To this day it remains the most important formal means of analyzing and communicating information on the financial activities and performance of all forms of organization...but there is a need to consider and study the relationships that have existed between accounting and organizational power' [pp. 1–2]. At the time he predicted that there would be increasing attention paid to the wider accountability of organizations to social and political concerns concluding presciently that, 'The debate on accountability is only one of the many issues which is focusing attention on the assumptions which accounting makes of the social institutions, power structures and values' [p. 1]. A quarter of a century later, *The Financial Times* added *Accounting, Organizations and Society* to their list of the top 40 management and business journals in the world as one of the top four accounting journals. Thus, it can be said that accounting, the social and the political has been 'officially' promoted to world-class ranking. And today, many other excellent journals around the world also publish such research.

Returning to the task at hand, we suspect that Lukka and Mouritsen's call in Part III for heterogeneity in accounting research will prevail, at least for a while. Such eclecticism is the hallmark today of many disciplines as witnessed recently in the field of organizational analysis and behavior where a wide variety of theoretical genres and research methodologies have become 'acceptable' scholarly endeavors such as 'neo-institutional theory' and 'discourse analysis'. So, it will be no great surprise if we see a variety of research genres being brought into play, perhaps with greater emphasis on combining the empirical and the theoretical into single accounting studies.

That having been said, our next conjecture is that we will see a lot more research investigating accounting as an important cultural discourse. Culture, as the term has been used traditionally, signals to 'a whole way of life' of a particular people or peoples living in a particular place where the habitants have a cultural identity. In this sense culture is what people live *in*, what they live *for* and what they live *by*. In today's rapidly shrinking world, however, culture as the bedrock of various distinctive communities of like-minded peoples seems to be giving way to a universal mass culture, energized by the commercialization of goods, services and images, which today flood the world, bringing with it the universalization of a narrow set of Western core values.

Accounting today is a vital strand in the whole cloth of this mass culture that commodifies facets of life, previously governed by local social mores, under the embrace of the impersonal market place. So how accounting comes to be enculturated, what it means to people around the globe and how it gets mobilized, as a vital discourse in the inevitable struggles over power and wealth would seem to be pressing issues. Such investigations would not simply identify how managers, in say Taiwan, respond differently to accounting information and official accounting principles than do managers in Scotland or California. Rather, some researchers will focus on the way accounting brings with it a set of core values and discourses which it articulates as not only inherently true, but also necessary.

This globalizing phenomenon raises issues related to our next prediction. In less than half a century, transnational capitalism has been transformed from Keynesian combined market and social welfare economies focusing on mass production and consumption inside individual nation states, into what David Harvey in his seminal book, *The Condition of Postmodernity*, calls post-Fordism and flexible capital accumulation, featuring giant global multinational firms that operate pretty much beyond the control of individual nation states. This is a unique moment in the history of humankind as capitalism expands its reach into the most remote regions of the planet.

In this regard, some see the globalization of market and financial capitalism as a panacea for the world's troubles, which they admit are vast, but nonetheless they eulogize free trade and the forces of capitalism. Others, in contrast, see globalization as a nostrum promulgated by the have nations to continue their colonization of three quarters of the world ignoring the riots and protests against the actions and policies of the undemocratic institutions of globalization. Accounting's role in this has recently emerged as a new topic and research along these lines will very likely increase and become part and parcel of the current debates regarding globalization, not least as the effects of global environmental degradation continues to mount alarmingly. As part of this, we foresee more research appearing by accounting scholars in the poor, developing nations focusing on indigeneous problems rather than imitating the dominant accounting research paradigms of the rich nations.

A closely related and astounding development at the center of the globalization phenomenon, bolstered by the onslaught of information and communication technologies, has been the appearance of what has been labeled 'entrepreneurial paper capitalism'. It exists, not so much on paper any more, but more so in computerized data form which makes possible the global integration of capital markets, stock exchanges, merchant banks, offshore tax havens, to say nothing of the harmonization of accounting standards world-wide. The result has been the transformation of the global financial system and the vastly enhanced power and possibilities of financial maneuvers and manipulation. Armed with 'digital capital' of immense sums, transnational corporations can 'take-over' and colonize large areas of the world by means of financially based electronic communication and paper documents without their top executives physically setting foot on these territories. The role of accounting in all of this will likely motivate much scholarly research. After all, most of the data and discourse for financial capitalism comes in accounting language.

This development leads to a 'wild card' hunch. We are guessing that more accounting research will take 'the linguistic turn' adopted by most of the social sciences and humanities in recent decades. This means adopting ontological, epistemological and philosophical positions that differ in crucial ways from those of either the conventional capital markets and informational perspective or the critical theories used in the past. It means treating the accounting reports as texts or narratives with qualitative meanings that can be studied relying on methodologies from semiology, linguistics and literary theory. This approach would be under-written by the 'late' Wittgenstein's insight that language is not merely a neutral window on reality, but rather plays an active role in the realms of meaning and knowledge.

More specifically, in *Tractatus Logico-Philosophical*, Wittgenstein following the logical positivist line of thought, argued that language is a picture of reality that depicts the logical structure of facts, that the structure of reality determines the structure of the language and that a proposition would have the same logical form as the fact it depicts. But later in *Philosophical Investigations*, he repudiated this position and came to believe that while words could be used to name things, they could also be used, like tools in a toolbox, in a variety of ways. So they mean different things in different contexts which he called 'language games'. Investigating the various accounting language games played today by participants in organizations and society, in both the private and the public sectors, seems a promising new direction for researching accounting, the social and the political. Language, however, is closely tied to philosophy and this brings us to our last speculation.

We think that a lot more research will get under way investigating the philosophical and related ethical side of accounting. This research, importantly, will involve ethics, but not in the mold of, say, those studies asking undergraduate students in business or employees in professional accounting firms whether or not they would follow accounting principles and rules in various scenarios involving pressure from higher ups or clients. Instead, they will be concerned with ethics in the philosophical sense. Paul Ricoeur, hailed as one of the twentieth century's most important thinkers, articulates it well.

Ethics and morality, he explains, should not be confused even though they are related. Term ethics should be reserved 'for the a*im* of an accomplished life and the term "morality" for the articulation of this aim in *norms* characterized at once by the claim to universality and by an effect of constraint'.[1] Ethics, then, gets place of privilege over morality where the latter is the obligation to respect and honor the socially constructed *mores* [norms] of one's community. Moral obligations come from outside oneself while ethics is internal and concerns the intention of aiming for what many traditional philosophers refer to as an accomplished *life* '*aiming at the good life with and for others in just institutions*'.[2] This means living well for oneself *and* for the other. So, crucially, it is not enough to intellectually understand and theorize that one should aim for an accomplished life, rather one seeks it in Praxis. On the moral plane, we follow the customs and norms of the community — but on the ethical plane, as Emanuel Levinas proclaims, it is our obligations to the other person that makes us human.

On this view, it would seem that the professionally certified accountant has a moral obligation to accept and to follow the generally accepted accounting principles [GAAPs] of her particular professional body when 'doing' accounting. But the teleological aim of achieving an accomplished life, takes precedent over such a rule following social obligation. We expect more serious research will ensue along philosophical ethics lines. It is, for many, the most vital long run issue facing accounting today.

On a final note, and it may seem a trivial thing to say, but we will say it anyhow, the traditional way of thinking about accounting, the social and the political — as a neutral and objective window on reality — must surely be treated as fatuously naïve. Until we sort out its social, political and philosophical role in society, the general public and no doubt our students as well, will remain, as in Plato's cave, only able to see dim shadows on the wall about accounting's actual role in the order of things. We hope the works of the authors included in this book will help bring this role into the light of day.

---

[1] Ricoeur, P. (1992). *Oneself as Another*, University of Chicago Press, p. 170.

[2] Ibid., p.180 [italics in the original].